Praise for *Business Research* 4th edition:

One of the best Research Methods texts available. It is well structured and takes students through the 'maze' of research methods, making what is often a new and challenging subject highly accessible. This fourth edition will be a valuable resource to all research students at whatever level. Its strong student focus makes it stand out, and the end of chapter activities and online resources provide a wealth of support for students embarking on research. A pleasure to review and read.

Jan Rae, London South Bank University, UK

Since the first edition became available I have recommended Collis and Hussey's *Business Research* to colleagues and students alike. Undertaking research is always a challenge but Collis and Hussey lead us through the research maze in an uncomplicated manner. The textbook is easy to follow and provides a clear and logical exposition of complex theoretical and practical research-related concepts; it also stimulates interest in business research by encouraging further reading. I applaud the inclusion of research ethics, the distinction between mixed methods and multiple methods, given its emerging relevance in contemporary research. The chapter on analysing qualitative data further enhances the standing of this edition. Particularly useful to students are the guidelines on preparing a research proposal and the advice provided on troubleshooting.

Lynette Louw, Rhodes University, South Africa

I am impressed by both the range of subjects the book covers and the simple clarity of the explanations it provides. It is never easy introducing students to more abstract ideas of how science relates to the practical world of business, and this book will be an excellent aid in helping students move from descriptive to analytical writing.

John McCormack, University of Bristol, UK

This new edition is nicely laid out and an easy text for both students and researchers to follow. The detailed chapters on both qualitative data analysis and basic statistical analysis mean this text has strengths over other research methods texts on the market which often focus on one or the other, making this text good value for money.

Kristel Miller, Queen's University Management School, UK

An appealing cohesiveness between practical advice on how to select specific research activities (and how to find solutions) while also indicating how to reflect on these choices and their consequences on the outcome of a research project.

Bartjan Pennink, University of Groningen, the Netherlands

Student opinions on previous editions of *Business Research:*

Comprehensive, clarifying, convincing … from front to back this book offers everything that the research student requires. Practical help is accompanied by a clear analysis of theoretical concepts. If you have struggled with research in the past, this book will be a good companion for your research projects in the future.

Elizabeth Mantzari, PhD student, University of Essex, UK

Business Research by Collis and Hussey offers a coherent, extremely well thought out and stimulating book on research in business. Activities and progress tests allow the text to be used in class, and can also be used to refine one's 'knowledge' individually. Having recently joined a university at postgraduate level, I think the majority of my recent troubles and woes would have been made less dramatic had I read it before I arrived. I have already recommended the book to many of my colleagues teaching both undergraduate and postgraduate students. An excellent book, which can be used as a checklist for experienced researchers, or treated as a 'sacred text' by students new to research.

Simon Parker, Postgraduate Assistant Researcher, Lincoln Business School, UK

I purchased your book some time ago and am now in the throes of a dissertation at Sheffield University. I just wanted to say thank you for writing such a wonderful book that explains everything really logically and is also inspiring and interesting! Yes, I never thought I would say that about research methods! It's worth every penny!

Donna O'Brien, nearly-finished dissertation student, Sheffield University, UK

a practical guide for undergraduate & postgraduate students

jill collis & roger hussey

fourth edition

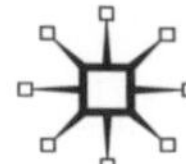

First edition 1997
Reprinted nine times
Second edition 2003
Reprinted ten times
Third edition 2009
Reprinted eight times

This edition first published 2014 by
PALGRAVE MACMILLAN HIGHER EDUCATION

Palgrave Macmillan in the UK is an imprint of Macmillan Publishers Limited, registered in England, company number 785998, of Houndmills, Basingstoke, Hampshire RG21 6XS.

Palgrave Macmillan in the US is a division of St Martin's Press LLC, 175 Fifth Avenue, New York, NY 10010.

Palgrave Macmillan is the global academic imprint of the above companies and has companies and representatives throughout the world.

Palgrave® and Macmillan® are registered trademarks in the United States, the United Kingdom, Europe and other countries.

ISBN: 978–0–230–30183–2

This book is printed on paper suitable for recycling and made from fully managed and sustained forest sources. Logging, pulping and manufacturing processes are expected to conform to the environmental regulations of the country of origin.

A catalogue record for this book is available from the British Library.

A catalog record for this book is available from the Library of Congress.

Typeset by Aardvark Editorial Limited, Metfield, Suffolk

Printed and bound in Great Britain by TJ International Ltd, Padstow, Cornwall

brief contents

contents

list of figures

list of tables

list of boxes

about the authors

Jill Collis is a Reader in accounting and Director of the Accounting and Auditing Research Centre at Brunel University, London. Her writing reflects her experience as a mature student, which has given her considerable insight into the needs of students and their lecturers. Jill's research focuses on the impact of changes in the regulation of accounting and auditing for micro- and small companies in Europe. She has conducted research for government departments (DTI and BERR), the Professional Oversight Board and the accountancy bodies (ACCA, ICAEW and ICAS).

Roger Hussey is a Fellow of both the Association of Chartered Certified Accountants and the Association of International Accountants. He holds an MSc in Industrial Relations and a PhD in Accounting from Bath University, UK. After several years in industry he was appointed Director of Research into Employee Communications at the Industrial Relations Unit of St Edmund Hall, Oxford. After six years at Oxford, he moved to the University of the West of England. In the year 2000, Roger became the Dean of the Odette School of Business in Windsor, Canada. He subsequently became Dean of Guangzhou International Business School, China. He is now Emeritus Professor at the University of the West of England and the University of Windsor, Canada.

preface to the fourth edition

Aim of the book

The success of the previous editions of *Business Research* has led to the development of this fully revised and expanded fourth edition. It is intended to provide practical guidance to students and early career researchers who are conducting research in business and management disciplines. The successful format of the earlier editions has been retained, but the design has been improved to better meet the needs of students and those responsible for teaching research methods.

Each chapter is clearly structured around a particular topic and the different aspects are simply described and explained. As many first-time researchers find the language of research off-putting, we introduce terms gradually and provide key definitions in the margin. For ease of reference, the key terms are listed in the glossary at the end of the book. There is further reading at the end of each chapter, together with practical activities that encourage discussion and reflection. The companion website contains progress tests and detailed *Microsoft PowerPoint* slides for each chapter that cover the main learning outcomes, as well as other teaching and learning materials.

Students on taught courses often need to complete their research within a relatively short period of time. Consequently, they have to balance the conceptual demands of the subject with pressing practical considerations. In contrast, doctoral students generally have more time, but need to develop greater knowledge of the conceptual aspects of research. The main problem for all students is how to find the most efficient and effective way of collecting, analysing and presenting their data while maintaining academic rigour. Therefore, we cite a range of studies that illustrate the methods covered in this book. These were chosen for their richness, clarity and variety of approach rather than because they are classic studies.

Changes in the fourth edition

Existing users will find the fourth edition retains the familiarity of the original and will notice the expansion of some chapters and the insertion of new chapters. The success of the book in different countries has led to a more international perspective. The main changes are:

- We have moved old Chapter 2 *Making academic decisions* to the website, but we have retained the section on supervision by incorporating it in Chapter 1.
- We have extended the section on research ethics in new Chapter 2 *Dealing with practical issues.*
- We have substantially revised and restructured the two chapters on collecting and analysing qualitative data in the third edition and now provide three chapters in the new edition: Chapter 7 *Collecting qualitative data*; Chapter 8 *Analysing qualitative data*; and Chapter 9 *Integrated collection and analysis methods.*

- Our new *vox pop* feature adds the voice of students to the chapters. Not only does this illustrate their experience at a particular stage in their research, but it provides insights into the topics that different undergraduate, postgraduate and doctoral students have chosen to study.
- We have moved the end-of-chapter progress tests to the companion website where they will be available in *Microsoft Word* and as an online test.

Structure of the book

Business Research offers a succinct and accessible guide to research methods, which makes it an ideal core text. Students and lecturers will find that the chapters follow the typical pattern of the research process, from the design of the project to the writing-up stage. The practical activities and references to further reading can be used for independent study or as basis for group work. At any time, students can refer to the 'Troubleshooting' chapter for advice. Indeed, despite the new materials included in this edition, the book is still small enough to carry around as a constant source of reference.

Suggested lecture programmes

Undergraduate students on a 10-week course

Week of course	Suggested chapter(s)	Notes
1	1 Understanding research	
2	2 Dealing with practical issues	
3	3 Identifying your paradigm (overview) and 4 Designing the research	
4	5 Searching and reviewing the literature	supported by training on using e-resources and software for managing references
5	6 Writing your research proposal	
6	7 Collecting qualitative data	
7	8 Analysing qualitative data	
8	10 Collecting data for statistical analysis	
9	11 Analysing data using descriptive statistics	supported by training on statistical software
10	13 Writing up the research	

Postgraduate and doctoral students

It is suggested that these students work through the book sequentially. For the chapters indicated below, further training would be useful to support the chapter content.

Chapters	Notes
1 Understanding research	
2 Dealing with practical issues	
3 Identifying your paradigm	
4 Designing the research	
5 Searching and reviewing the literature	supported by training on using e-resources and software for managing references
6 Writing your research proposal	
7 Collecting qualitative data	
8 Analysing qualitative data	
9 Integrated qualitative data methods	
10 Collecting data for statistical analysis	
11 Analysing data using descriptive statistics	supported by training on statistical software
12 Analysing data using inferential statistics	supported by training on statistical software
13 Writing up the research	

acknowledgements

We are grateful to our colleagues around the world and the many cohorts of students who have kindly commented on previous editions of this book.

We are grateful to the following people who acted as external reviewers and made many useful comments and suggestions for this edition.

Barbara Allan, Westminster University, UK
Graham Eysselein, University of Johannesburg, South Africa
Graham Heaslip, National University of Ireland Maynooth, Ireland
John McCormack, University of Bristol, UK
Kristel Miller, Queen's University Belfast, UK
Bartjan Pennink, University of Groningen, the Netherlands
Jan Rae, London South Bank University, UK

We are indebted to our publisher, Martin Drewe, and the team: Helen Bugler, Nikini Jayatunga, Linda Norris, Bryony Allen, Julie Lankester and Jo Booley for their forbearance and support. Finally, we are deeply indebted to Sir Timothy John Berners-Lee for the gift of the World Wide Web, which allows this transatlantic duo to continue writing together and communicate with their publishers without leaving their desks!

Jill Collis, *Brunel University, London, UK*
Roger Hussey, *University of Windsor, Canada*

The authors and publishers are grateful to the following for permission to reproduce figures, tables, extracts of text and screenshots:

Academy of Management for our Table 3.3 Typology of assumptions on a continuum of paradigms based on Morgan, G. and Smircich, L. (1980) 'The case of qualitative research', *Academy of Management Review*, 5, pp. 491–500.

Ackermann, F., Eden, C. and Cropper, S. for our Box 9.5 Procedure for cognitive mapping from (1990) 'Cognitive Mapping: A User Guide', Working Paper No. 2. Glasgow: Strathclyde University, Department of Management Science.

Ashgate for our Table 13.6 Indicative assessment criteria for a dissertation or thesis from Howard, K. and Sharp, J. A. (1994) *The Management of a Student Research Project*. Aldershot: Gower.

Elsevier for our Table 8.1 Files documenting the study from Jinkerson, D. L., Cummings, O. W., Neisendorf, B. J. and Schwandt, T. A. (1992) 'A case study of methodological issues in cross-cultural evaluation', *Evaluation and Program Planning*, 15, p. 278; our Box 9.2 Example of coding from hazardous waste study from Pidgeon, N. F., Turner, B. A. and Blockley, D. I. (1991) 'The use of grounded theory for conceptual analysis in knowledge elicitation', *International Journal of Man–Machine Studies*, 35, p. 160; our Box 10.3

Checklist for reducing interviewer bias from Brenner, M. (1985) 'Survey Interviewing' in Brenner, M., Brown, J. and Canter, D. (eds) *The Research Interview: Uses and Approaches*. New York: Academic Press, pp. 9–36.

Human Kinetics for our Figure 9.3 Theoretical model of academic corruption from Kihl, L. A., Richardson, T. and Campisi, C. (2008, p. 284) Fig 1, 'Towards a Grounded Theory of Student-Athlete suffering and Dealing with Academic Corruption', *Journal of Sport Management*, 22(3), pp. 273–302.

International Business Machines Corporation for permission to use screenshots of their IBM® SPSS® Statistics software (SPSS) for our Figures 11.1, 11.2, 11.3, 11.4, 11.5, 11.6, 11.7, 11.11, 11.12, 11.13, 11.18, 12.1, 12.2, 12.7, 12.8 and 12.9; and for our Table 12.3 (© International Business Machines Corporation).

John Wakeford and the Missenden Centre for permission to reprint the Missenden Code (our Box 2.1) from Daly, R. (2002) *The Missenden Code of Practice for Ethics and Accountability – The Commercialisation of Research in Universities: An Ethical Intervention*. Great Missenden: The Missenden Centre for the Development of Higher Education.

John Wiley & Sons for our Box 6.7 Ten ways to get your proposal turned down from Robson, C. (2011), *Real World Research*, 3rd edn. Chichester: John Wiley & Sons.

M. E. Sharpe Inc. for our Figure 9.5 Sample individual causal cognitive map from Boujena, O., Johnston, W. J. and Merunka, D. A. (2009) 'The benefits of sales force automation: A customer's perspective', *Journal of Personal Sales and Sales Management*, XXIX(2), pp. 137–50.

Microsoft for use of a screenshot from *Microsoft Excel* in Figure 10.3.

ProQuest for our Table 5.1 and use of screenshots for Figure 5.1 and Figure 5.2.

SAGE Publications for our Figure 8.2 Events flow network: A student's learning and work experience and Box 8.3 Effects matrix: Organization changes after implementation of the ECRI Program from Miles, M. B. and Huberman, A. M. (1994) *Qualitative Data Analysis*. Thousand Oaks, CA: Sage, pp. 114 and 138; our Box 9.4 Sample individual repertory grid based on Dunn, W. and Ginsberg, A. (1986) 'A sociocognitive network approach to organisational analysis', *Human Relations*, 39(11), p. 964; for our Figure 9.4 Example of a cognitive map from Cropper, S., Eden, C. and Ackermann, F. (1990) 'Keeping sense of accounts using computer-based cognitive maps', *Social Science Computer Review*, 8(3), p. 350; our Table 10.1 Determining sample size from a given population from Krejcie, R. V. and Morgan, D. W. (1970) 'Determining sample size for research activities', *Educational and Psychological Measurement*, 30(3).

The Society for Research into Higher Education and the author Pat Cryer for our Box 1.2 from Cryer, P. (1997) 'Handling common dilemmas in supervision', *Issues in Postgraduate Supervision, Teaching and Management No.2*, November. London: Society for Research into Higher Education and the Times Higher Education Supplement, p. 10.

Taylor & Francis Ltd for our Box 6.2 Example of a purpose statement in a positivist study from Collis, J. (2012) 'Determinants of voluntary audit and voluntary full accounts in micro- and non-micro small companies in the UK', *Accounting and Business Research*, 42(4), pp. 1–28; for our Figure 9.1 Developing grounded theory from Hutchinson, A. J., Johnston, L. H. and Breckon, J. D. (2010) 'Using QSR-NVivo to facilitate the development of a grounded theory project: An account of a worked example', *International Journal of Social Research Methodology*, 13(4), p. 286; for our Table 13.1 Planning and writing strategies adopted by students from Torrance, M., Thomas, G. V. and Robinson, E. J. (1992) 'The writing experiences of social science research students', *Studies in Higher Education*, 17(2).

tour of the book

Learning objectives
What you will learn. Helps organize your study and track your progress.

learning objectives

When you have studied this chapter, you should be able to:

- identify potential sources of secondary data
- search the literature
- use the Harvard system of referencing
- review the literature

Key definitions
Key terms appear in bold and are defined in the page margin for quick reference. A full glossary, also featuring other useful terms (in blue in the text), can be found at the back of the book and online.

4.3.1 **Experimental studies**

An **experimental study** is a methodology used to investigate the relationship between variables, where the independent variable is deliberately manipulated to observe the effect on the dependent variable.

An **experimental study** is a methodology used to inves ship between variables, where the independent var noise levels) is deliberately manipulated to observ dependent variable (for example the productivity o Experimental studies permit causal relationships to experiment is conducted in a systematic way in natural setting.

One of the advantages of conducting experiments in an artificial researcher is better able to eliminate certain variables or keep some This is necessary because one of the main challenges is to control

Vox pops
Students share their experiences. Bringing theory to life, they help you relate to key challenges that others have overcome.

Vox pop What has been the highpoint of your research so far?

Pippa, final year PhD student investigating how a small town is affected by increased tourism

The experiences of towing a campervan to remote places for my fieldwork and meeting a lot of wonderful people who gave me a lot of time.

Nesrine, fourth year PhD student investigating supply chain agility

Solvi collecti I'd started primary data interviews] in E 'Arab Spring' happ safe to go there. I tho mean that I had t again in anothe at last, afte was able again

Tables, figures, flowcharts and boxes
Summarizing important information, illustrating key concepts visually, and offering checklists.

Table 5.3 Data required for referencing

Books	Journal articles
Name(s) of author(s) or editor(s)	Name(s) of author(s)
Year of publication	Year of publication
Title of book	Title of article
Edition (if not the first)	Title of journal
Place of publication	Volume number and issue
Name of publisher	Page numbers

Identify a sample or case(s)

↓

Choose data collection metho

↓

Determine what data will be coll and design any questions

↓

Conduct pilot study and mod methods as necessary

↓

Collect the research data

Figure 7.1 Overview of data collection interpretivist study

Conclusions
Check your understanding of the chapter material.

5.6 Conclusions

Searching and reviewing the literature is a major part of your research
intensive phase at the start of the project, will continue on a smalle
submit your dissertation or thesis. Therefore, it is essential to start as
This will be when you have chosen a general topic that is relevant to yo
not matter that you have not yet identified a particular research pro
investigate, because you will identify this from studying the literature an
need for your study. Most students will be required to incorporate a p

References
Full details are provided of important texts that are cited within the chapters. These references help identify key publications for further research.

Activities
Consolidate your learning with these reflective and practical exercises.

Troubleshooting
Resolve problems quickly, by examining common challenges that can arise during the main stages of the research process. Guidance is offered on how to resolve these issues, with cross-references to specific chapters in the book for further information.

References

Arksey, H. and Knight, P. (1999) *Interviewing*
Scientists. London: SAGE.
Bolton, R. N. (1991) 'An exploratory investig
questionnaire pretesting with verbal pro
analysis', *Advances in Consumer Resea*
pp. 558–65.
Boddy, J. and Smith, M. (2008) 'Asking the e
Developing and validating parental diar
children's minor injuries', *International J*
Social Research Methodology, 11(1), pp.
Bowen, D. (2008) 'Consumer thoughts, actio
feelings from within the service experie
Service Industries Journal, 28(10), pp. 15
Brockman, B. K., Rawlston, M. E., Jones, M.
and Halstead, D. (2010) 'An exploratory

Activities

1 Select three different academic jour
publish research in your field of stud
case, read the abstracts and list the
types of methodology used. Decide w
the editor of each journal favours pos
interpretivist approaches.
2 The manager of a large business in y
neighbourhood believes that the mor
of employees is low. Select one posit
methodology and one interpretivist m
that you could use to investigate the
List the advantages and disadvantag
3 Imagine you are a member of a resea
committee about to interview studen
their proposed research. One propos
triangulation. Prepare five questions
ask to ensure that the student is awa

14.2 Getting st

Problem
You are una
about and w

Before you ca
what business

1 Start with t
the definitio
2 The next st
– Identify a
– Identify a

Companion website
www.palgrave.com/business/collis/br4

Visit the companion website for interactive progress tests, an online glossary, *Microsoft PowerPoint* slides for lecturers, and other useful resources to help support teaching and learning.

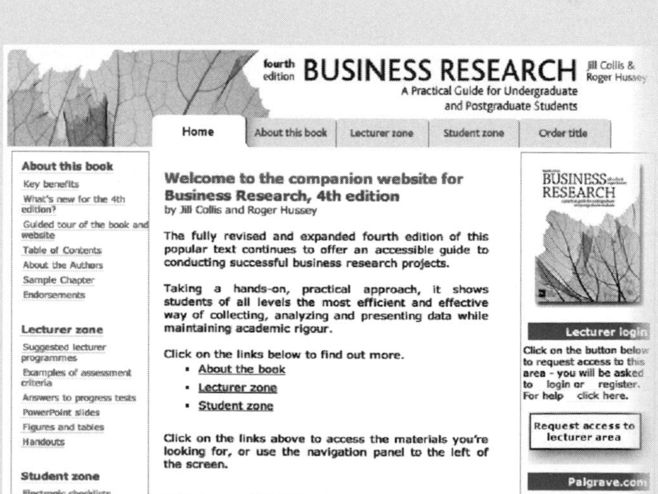

1

understanding research

learning objectives

When you have studied this chapter, you should be able to:

- explain the nature and purpose of research
- classify different types of research
- identify the main stages in the research process
- understand the role of supervision
- develop a plan for managing the project.

1.1 Introduction

The aim of this chapter is to explain the concept of business research in academic context. Whether you are an undergraduate student conducting your first research project or a postgraduate student conducting research at Master's or doctoral level, the explanations in this chapter will help you develop a firm understanding. We start by examining the nature and purpose of research that focuses on business issues and the different ways in which studies can be categorized. We then examine the general differences between undergraduate, postgraduate and doctoral research projects. Finally, we explain the main stages in the research process before going on to discuss what makes a good project.

1.2 Nature and purpose of business research

Although **research** is central to both business and academic activities, there is no consensus in the literature on how it should be defined. One reason for this is that research means different things to different people. However, from the many definitions offered, there is general agreement that research is:

- a process of inquiry and investigation
- systematic and methodical, and
- increases knowledge.

As far as the nature of research is concerned, the above definition tells us that researchers need to use appropriate methods for collecting and analysing research data, and that they need to apply them rigorously. The general purpose of academic research is to investigate a **research question** with a view to generating knowledge. A research question is the specific question that the research is designed to investigate. It provides a focus for your research. Do not confuse it with the questions that you might ask participants in the research, which are detailed questions designed to collect research data. Your research question will relate to a particular problem or issue that you have identified. We will look at what this entails later on in this chapter.

Research is a systematic and methodical process of inquiry and investigation with a view to increasing knowledge.

A **research question** is the specific question that the research is designed to investigate.

A research project offers both undergraduate and postgraduate students an opportunity to identify and select a research problem and investigate it independently under the guidance of a supervisor. It allows you to apply theory to or otherwise analyse a real business problem or to explore and analyse more general issues. It also enables you to apply techniques and procedures to illuminate the problem and contribute to our greater understanding of it or to generate solutions. In the process of doing your research, you will develop skills that will enhance your employability. The typical objectives of research can be summarized as follows:

- to review and synthesize existing knowledge
- to investigate some existing situation or problem
- to provide solutions to a problem
- to explore and analyse more general issues
- to construct or create a new procedure or system
- to explain a new phenomenon
- to generate new knowledge
- a combination of any of the above.

A **dissertation** or **thesis** is a detailed discourse that is written as part of an academic degree.

A **discourse** is a lengthy treatment of a theme that involves a formal discussion of a topic.

From this you can see that research is purposeful and is conducted with a view to achieving an outcome. The research report may be called a **dissertation** or a **thesis**. A dissertation or thesis is a detailed **discourse** involving research that is written as part of an academic degree and a discourse is a lengthy treatment of a theme that involves a formal discussion of a topic (Waite and Hawker, 2009). Academic research can also be conducted for the purpose of publishing the study as a book or an article in an academic journal or for consultancy purposes. This book focuses primarily on the needs of students carrying out some form of business research for a qualification and those pursuing academic careers.

Types of enterprise to research include small and medium-sized enterprises (SMEs), businesses with limited liability (such as companies), and organizations in the not-for-profit or public sectors. The focus in the media is mainly on big business, yet 99% of businesses are SMEs and you may find yourself employed by one or even starting one. Whatever type of entity you choose as the focus of your research, you will find a wide range of issues to investigate.

The typical users of business research are:

- the government – for developing/monitoring policies, regulations, and so on
- owners, managers and business advisers – for keeping up to date with new ideas and specific developments in business
- management – for developing internal policies and strategies (for example comparing research results relating to their own business with those with previous periods, their competitors and/or industry benchmarks)
- academics – for further research and educational purposes.

1.3 Classifying research

Studying the characteristics of the different types of research helps us to examine the similarities and differences. Research can be classified according to the:

- *purpose* of the research – the reason why it was conducted
- *process* of the research – the way in which the data were collected and analysed
- *logic* of the research – whether the research logic moves from the general to the specific or vice versa
- *outcome* of the research – whether the expected outcome is the solution to a particular problem or a more general contribution to knowledge.

For example, the aim of your research project might be to describe a particular business activity (purpose) by collecting qualitative data that are quantified and analysed statistically (process), which will be used to solve a business problem (outcome). Table 1.1 shows the classification of the main types of research according to the above criteria.

Table 1.1 Classification of main types of research

Type of research	Basis of classification
Exploratory, descriptive, analytical or predictive research	Purpose of the research
Quantitative or qualitative research	Process of the research
Applied or basic research	Outcome of the research
Deductive or inductive research	Logic of the research

1.3.1 Exploratory, descriptive, analytical and predictive research

If we are classifying research according to its *purpose*, we can describe it as being exploratory, descriptive, analytical or predictive. At the undergraduate level, research is usually exploratory and/or descriptive. At postgraduate or doctoral level it is much more likely to be analytical or predictive. Table 1.2 shows this classification in increasing order of sophistication and gives examples. One drawback of increasing the level of sophistication in research is that the level of complexity and detail also increases.

Table 1.2 Examples of research classified by purpose

Type of research	Example
Exploratory	An interview survey among clerical staff in a particular office, department, company, group of companies, industry, region, and so on, to find out what motivates them to increase their productivity (that is, to see if a research problem can be formulated).
Descriptive	A description of how the selected clerical staff are rewarded and what measures are used to record their productivity levels.
Analytical	An analysis of any relationships between the rewards given to the clerical staff and their productivity levels.
Predictive	A forecast of which variable(s) should be changed in order to bring about a change in the productivity levels of clerical staff.

Exploratory research is conducted into a research problem or issue when there are very few or no earlier studies to which we can refer for information about the issue or problem. The aim of this type of study is to look for patterns and ideas and develop rather than test a hypothesis. A **hypothesis** is a proposition that can be tested for association or causality against empirical evidence. **Empirical evidence** is data based on observation or experience, and **data**[1] are known facts or things used as a basis for inference or reckoning. In exploratory research, the focus is on gaining insights and familiarity with the subject area for more rigorous investigation at a later stage.

A **hypothesis** is a proposition that can be tested for association or causality against empirical evidence.

Empirical evidence is data based on observation or experience.

Data are known facts or things used as a basis for inference or reckoning.

Typical techniques used in exploratory research include case studies, observation and historical analysis, which can provide both quantitative and qualitative data. Such techniques are very flexible as there are few constraints on the nature of activities employed or on the type of data collected. The research will assess which existing theories and concepts can be applied to the problem or whether new ones should be developed. The approach to the research is usually very open and concentrates on gathering a wide range of data and impressions. As such, exploratory research rarely provides conclusive answers to problems or issues, but gives guidance on what future research, if any, should be conducted.

Descriptive research is conducted to describe phenomena as they exist. It is used to identify and obtain information on the characteristics of a particular problem or issue. Descriptive research goes further in examining a problem than exploratory research, as it is undertaken to ascertain and describe the characteristics of the pertinent issues. The following are examples of research questions in a descriptive research study:

- What is the absentee rate in particular offices?
- What are the feelings of workers faced with redundancy?
- What are the qualifications of different groups of employees?
- What type of packaging for a box of chocolates do consumers prefer?

1 This term is a Latin plural noun, the singular of which is 'datum'.

- What information do consumers want shown on food labels?
- Which car advertisements on television do men and women of different ages prefer?
- How many students study accounting in China compared with students in Australia?
- How do commuters travel to work in capital cities?

You will notice that many of these questions start with 'what' or 'how' because the aim is to describe something. However, further clarification would be required before the study could begin. For example, we cannot ask everyone in the world about which car advertisements or chocolate box packaging they prefer. Even a study that compared the number of students studying accounting in China and Australia requires clarification of the types of students (for example age, sex and nationality) and what is studied (for example level/stage in the course, main subjects covered and qualification). Therefore, even in a descriptive study, you must spend time refining your research questions and being specific about the phenomena you are studying. We will explain how this can be achieved in subsequent chapters.

Analytical or explanatory research is a continuation of descriptive research. The researcher goes beyond merely describing the characteristics, to analysing and explaining why or how the phenomenon being studied is happening. Thus, analytical research aims to understand phenomena by discovering and measuring causal relations among them. For example, information may be collected on the size of companies and the levels of labour turnover. A statistical analysis of the data may show that the larger the company the higher the level of turnover, although as we will see later, research is rarely that simple. An important element of explanatory research is identifying and, possibly, controlling the *variables* in the research activities, as this permits the critical variables or the causal links between the characteristics to be better explained. A **variable** is a characteristic of a phenomenon that can be observed or measured.

A **variable** is a characteristic of a phenomenon that can be observed or measured.

Predictive research goes even further than explanatory research. The latter establishes an explanation for what is happening in a particular situation, whereas the former forecasts the likelihood of a similar situation occurring elsewhere. Predictive research aims to generalize from the analysis by predicting certain phenomena on the basis of hypothesized, general relationships. Thus, the solution to a problem in a particular study will be applicable to similar problems elsewhere, if the predictive research can provide a valid, robust solution based on a clear understanding of the relevant causes. Predictive research provides 'how', 'why' and 'where' answers to current events and also to similar events in the future. It is also helpful in situations where 'what if' questions are being asked. The following are examples of research questions in a predictive research study:

- In which city would it be most profitable to open a new retail outlet?
- Will the introduction of an employee bonus scheme lead to higher levels of productivity?
- What type of packaging will improve the sales of our products?
- How would an increase in interest rates affect our profit margins?
- Which stock market investments will be the most profitable over the next three months?
- What will happen to sales of our products if there is an economic downturn?

1.3.2 Quantitative and qualitative research

Looking at the approach adopted by the researcher can also differentiate research. Some people prefer to take a quantitative approach to addressing their research question(s) and therefore design studies that involve collecting quantitative data (and/or qualitative data that can be quantified), and analyse it using statistical methods. In some cases, they do not collect new data but use statistics to analyse existing data from an archive, database or other published source. Other researchers prefer to take a qualitative approach to addressing their research question(s) and therefore design studies that involve collecting qualitative data and analysing that new data using interpretative methods. As you will see in later chapters, a large study might incorporate elements of both as their merits are often considered to be complementary in gaining an understanding in the social sciences.

Referring to a research approach as quantitative or qualitative can be misleading, as a researcher can design a study with a view to collecting qualitative data (for example published text or transcripts of interviews) and then quantifying the research data by counting the frequency of occurrence of particular key words or themes. This allows the researcher to use statistical methods to analyse the data. On the other hand, a researcher can collect qualitative data with the intention of using non-numerical methods to analysing the research data, or collect data that are already in numerical form and use statistical methods to analyse the research data. In this chapter, we will continue to refer to quantitative and qualitative approaches, but we will discuss alternative terms you may wish to use later in the book.

Some students avoid taking a quantitative approach because they are not confident with statistics and think a qualitative approach will be easier. Many students find that it is harder to start and decide an overall design for a quantitative study, but it is easier to conduct the analysis and write up the research because it is highly structured. Qualitative research is normally easier to start, but students often find it more difficult to analyse the data and write up their final report. For example, if you were conducting a study into stress caused by working night shifts, you might want to collect quantitative data such as absenteeism rates or productivity levels, and analyse the data statistically. Alternatively, you might want to investigate the same question by collecting qualitative data about how stress is experienced by night workers in terms of their perceptions, health, social problems, and so on.

There are many arguments in the literature regarding the merits of qualitative versus quantitative approaches, which we will examine later on in the book. At this stage, you simply need to be aware that your choice will be influenced by the nature of your research project as well as your own philosophical preferences. Moreover, you may find that the access you have been able to negotiate, the type of data available and the research problem persuade you to put your philosophical preferences to one side.

1.3.3 Applied and basic research

A standard classification of research divides projects into **applied research** and **basic research**. Applied research is a study that has been designed to apply its findings to solving a specific, existing problem. It is the application of existing knowledge to improve management practices and policies. The research project is likely to be short term (often less than six months) and the immediacy of the problem will be more important than academic theorizing. For example, you might be investigating the reorganization of an office layout, the improvement of safety in the workplace or the reduction of wastage of raw materials or energy in a factory process. The output from this type of research is likely to be a consultant's report, articles in professional or trade magazines and presentations to practitioners.

Applied research describes a study that is designed to apply its findings to solving a specific, existing problem.

Basic (or pure) research describes a study that is designed to make a contribution to general knowledge and theoretical understanding, rather than solve a specific problem.

When the research problem is of a less specific nature and the research is being conducted primarily to improve our understanding of general issues without emphasis on its immediate application, it is classified as basic or pure research. For example, you might be interested in whether personal characteristics influence people's career choices. Basic research is regarded as the most academic form of research, as the principal aim is to make a contribution to knowledge, usually for the general good, rather than to solve a specific problem for one organization.

Another example of applied research that is conducted in academic institutions often goes under the general title of *educational scholarship* (or *instructional research* or *pedagogic research*). This type of study is concerned with improving the educational activities within the institution and the output is likely to be case studies, instructional software or textbooks.

The primary objective of basic research (also called *fundamental* or *pure* research) is the advancement of knowledge and theory through the understanding of relationships between variables (see Chapter 10, section 10.3). It is exploratory and is often driven by the researcher's curiosity and intuition. Although it is conducted without a practical end in mind, it can have unexpected results that point to practical applications. The term 'basic' is used because through theory generation it provides the foundation for further (often applied) research. Since there is no guarantee of any short-term practical gain, it can be difficult to obtain funding for basic research.

From this you can see that basic research may focus on problem solving, but the problem is likely to be theoretical rather than practical and the typical outcome is knowledge. Basic research may not resolve an immediate problem, but will contribute to our knowledge in a way that may assist in the solution of future problems. The emphasis, therefore, is on academic rigour and the strength of the research design. The output from basic research is likely to be papers presented at academic conferences and the articles published in academic journals.

There are many instances when the distinction between applied and basic research is not clear. It can be argued that the difference between basic and applied research lies in the time span between the research and reasonably foreseeable practical applications. Research in the field of genetics is a good example. Increasing our understanding of the chromosomes that carry genetic information for the sake of knowledge alone would be basic research, but subsequently using that knowledge to develop genetically engineered crops to improve yields would be classified as applied research.

1.3.4 Deductive and inductive research

Deductive research is a study in which a conceptual and theoretical structure is developed and then tested by empirical observation; thus, particular instances are deduced from general inferences. For this reason, the deductive method is referred to as moving from the general to the particular. For example, you may have read about theories of motivation and wish to test them in your own workplace. This will involve collecting specific data of the variables that the theories have identified as being important.

Inductive research is a study in which theory is developed from the observation of empirical reality; thus, general inferences are induced from particular instances, which is the reverse of the deductive method. Since it involves moving from individual observation to statements of general patterns or laws, it is referred to as moving from the specific to the general. For example, you may have observed from factory records in your company that production levels go down after two hours of the shift and you conclude that production levels vary with length of time worked.

Deductive research describes a study in which a conceptual and theoretical structure is developed which is then tested by empirical observation; thus particular instances are deduced from general inferences.

Inductive research describes a study in which theory is developed from the observation of empirical reality; thus general inferences are induced from particular instances.

All the different types of research we have discussed can be helpful in allowing you to understand your research and the best way to conduct it, but do not feel too constrained. It is important to recognize that one particular project may be described in a number of ways, as it will have purpose, process, logic and outcome. For example, you may conduct an applied, analytical study using a quantitative approach. In a long-term project, you may wish to use qualitative and quantitative approaches, deductive and inductive methods, and you will move from exploratory and descriptive research to analytical and predictive research. The key classifications we have examined can be applied to previous studies that you will review as part of your research and you can use these typologies to describe your own study in your proposal and later on in your dissertation or thesis.

1.4 Academic levels of research

The academic level of your research in terms of the sophistication of the research design and duration of the project will depend on your reasons for undertaking it. The requirements for undergraduates are very different from those for postgraduate students and doctoral students. However, the basic principles, issues and practicalities are the same.

1.4.1 Undergraduate level

If you are an undergraduate student, you may be required to undertake a research project as part of a course or it may even be a complete course. You are normally expected to be familiar with the main concepts and terms as explained in this book and undertake one or more of the following activities:

- Design a research project – On some courses you will be expected to design a research project and then write a report that explains the rationale for your chosen design and describes its strengths and weaknesses.
- Write a research proposal – A research proposal requires you to design a project as above, but also to include a preliminary review of the literature.
- Conduct a research project – In many cases you will be required not only to design a project and write a proposal, but also to do some actual research. This would entail writing a review of the literature and also collecting and analysing existing data or new data (for example from interviews or from a questionnaire survey). In some cases, you may be allowed to base your entire project on a critical literature review, where you will analyse the literature on a chosen topic and draw conclusions. In all cases, you will be required to write a research report (with a typical size constraint of 10,000–15,000 words), which may be called a dissertation or thesis.

1.4.2 Postgraduate and doctoral students

If you are on a taught Master's programme, such as an MBA or a specialized Master's programme, it is likely that you will be required to design a research project, write a proposal, conduct the study and write a report (with a typical size constraint of 20,000 words), which may be called a dissertation or thesis. In some cases, you may find that you are allowed to conduct a critical literature review only, where you will be expected to analyse and synthesize the literature on a chosen topic and draw conclusions. The processes are very similar to undergraduate research, but a more comprehensive approach is needed and a higher quality of work will be required.

If you are doing a Master's degree by research or you are a doctoral student (DBA or PhD), the intensity of the research will be much greater. The typical length of a Master's degree by research is 40,000 words, 50,000 words for a taught doctorate and 80,000 words for a doctorate by research. You will need to study this book carefully and the recommended reading that is relevant to your subject. It is important to remember that the expectations of your institution will have a significant influence on the process and outcome of your research.

1.4.3 Academic researchers

If you are looking for an academic post or already working in academia and looking for promotion, this book will reinforce your knowledge or give you a new perspective on a particular issue you have not considered previously, and help you to write conference papers and journal articles.

1.5 Overview of the research process

Whatever type of research or approach is adopted, there are several fundamental stages in the research process that are common to all scientifically based investigations. The simplified diagram shown in Figure 1.1 illustrates a traditional and highly structured view of the research process. This model presents research as a neat, orderly process, with one stage leading logically on to the next stage. However, in practice, research is rarely like that. For example, failure at one stage means returning to an earlier stage and many stages overlap. Thus, if you were unable to collect the research data, it may be necessary to revise your definition of the research problem or amend the way you conduct the research. This is often a good reason for conducting some exploratory research before commencing a full project.

To give you an overview of the nature of research, we will now look briefly at each stage in the research process. You will find greater detail in subsequent chapters.

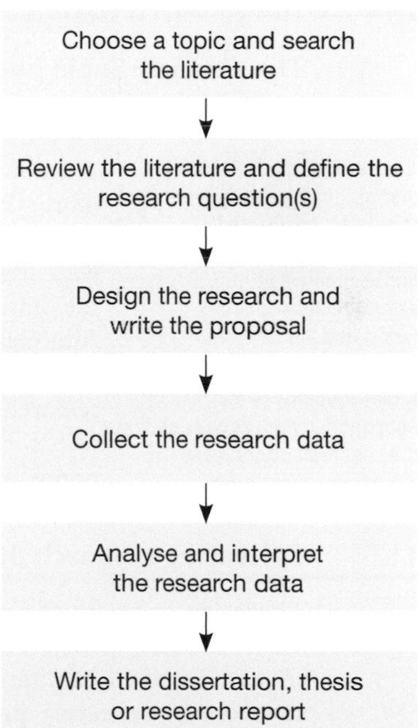

Figure 1.1 Overview of the research process

1.5.1 The research topic

The starting point is to choose a research topic, which is a general subject area that is related to your degree if you are a student or your discipline if you are an academic. You may find a research topic suggests itself as a result of your coursework, job, interests or general experience. For example, you may be interested in the employment problems of minority groups in society, the difficulties of funding small businesses, what makes managers successful, or the commercial sponsorship of sport.

1.5.2 The literature

Once you have chosen a general topic, you need to search the **literature** for previous studies and other relevant information on that subject and read it. By exploring the existing body of knowledge, you should be able to see how your topic is divided into a number of different areas that will help you focus your ideas on a particular research problem.

The **literature** is all sources of published data on a particular topic.

1.5.3 The research problem

All students experience some difficulty in narrowing down their general interest in a research topic to focus on a particular research problem or issue that is small enough to be investigated. This is often referred to as defining the research problem and leads on to setting the research question(s). In academic research, the classic way to identify a research problem is to consider the literature and identify any gaps, as these indicate original areas to research. You will also find that many academic articles incorporate suggestions for further research in their conclusions. If you have conducted an undergraduate dissertation already, that subject area may lead you to your Master's or doctoral research questions. If you are an academic, you may also have conducted previous academic or consultancy research that suggests research questions for your present study. You will need to focus your ideas, decide the scope of your research and set parameters. For example, perhaps your study will investigate a broad financial issue, but focus on a particular group of stakeholders, size of business, industry, geographical area, or period of time.

1.5.4 The research design

The starting point in research design is to determine your research **paradigm**. A research paradigm is a framework that guides how research should be conducted; it is based on people's philosophies and assumptions about the world and the nature of knowledge. Some researchers advocate the use of methods from more than one paradigm and we discuss the issues this raises in Chapter 3. We recommend that you find out at an early stage whether your supervisor favours a particular paradigm. Your overall approach to the entire process of the research is known as your **methodology**. Although, in part, this is determined by the research problem, the assumptions you use in your research and the way you define your research problem will influence the way you conduct the study. In other words, the way in which you choose to investigate your research question will be driven by your research paradigm.

A **paradigm** is a framework that guides how research should be conducted, based on people's philosophies and their assumptions about the world and the nature of knowledge.

A **methodology** is an approach to the process of the research encompassing a body of methods.

1.5.5 Collecting research data

There are a variety of ways in which you can collect research data and we look at the main methods of data collection in Chapters 7, 9 and 10. Because of the many differences between quantitative and qualitative methods, these are explained in separate chapters. If you have a quantitative methodology, you will be attempting to measure variables or count occurrences of a phenomenon. On the other hand, if you have a qualitative methodology, you will emphasize the themes and patterns of meanings and experiences related to the phenomena.

1.5.6 Analysing and interpreting research data

A major part of your research project will be spent analysing and interpreting research data. The main methods of data analysis used will depend on your research paradigm and whether you have collected quantitative or qualitative data. We will be looking at this in more detail in Chapters 8, 9, 11 and 12. It is important to realize, however, that although data collection and data analysis are discussed separately in this book, the stages are sometimes simultaneous. You should not make decisions about your data collection methods without also deciding which analytical methods you will use.

1.5.7 Writing the dissertation or thesis

It is at the writing-up stage that many students experience problems, usually because they have left it until the very last minute! It is important to start writing up your research in draft as soon as you start the early stages of the project, and continue to do so until it is completed. To a large extent, the stages outlined above will be captured in the structure of your dissertation or thesis. It is valuable at the outset to consider a possible structure, as it will give you an idea of what you are aiming for and Table 1.3 shows a typical structure. The title should be descriptive but not lengthy. Remember that any planned structure will have the disadvantage of making the research process look much more orderly than it really is. Although all research reports differ in structure according to the problem being investigated and the methodology employed, there are some common features.

Table 1.3 Indicative structure of a dissertation or thesis

	% of report
1. Introduction – The research problem or issue and the purpose of the study – Background to the study and why it is important or of interest – Structure of the remainder of the report	10
2. Review of the literature – Evaluation of the existing body of knowledge on the topic – Theoretical framework (if applicable) – Where your research fits in and the research question(s) and propositions or hypotheses (if applicable)	30
3. Methodology – Identification of paradigm (doctoral students will need to discuss) – Justification for choice of methodology and methods – Limitations of the research design	20
4. Findings/Results *(more than one chapter if appropriate)* – Presentation and discussion of the analysis of your research data/statistical tests and their results	30
5. Conclusions – Summary of what you found out in relation to each research question you investigated – Your contribution knowledge – Limitations of your research and suggestions for future research – Implications of your research for practice or policy (if appropriate)	10
	100
References *(do not number this section)* – A detailed, alphabetical (numerical, if appropriate) list of all the sources cited in the text	
Appendices – Detailed data referred to in the text, but not shown elsewhere	

Your dissertation or thesis is likely to be the largest project you have undertaken to date and, therefore, it presents quite a challenge. However, having a good understanding of the nature and purpose of research, the main stages in the research process, and the basic structure of the research report you will be writing will help you develop a sense of direction.

Vox pop What has been the biggest challenge in your research so far?

Lee, first year PhD student investigating foreign direct investment in international business

Not knowing where to start with my PhD. It's not like being on a Master's degree where there's a structured environment and there doesn't seem to be a single 'right' way. I tried talking to other students but their advice wasn't always relevant. It seems you've got to find your own path and, like Lewis Carroll said in Alice in Wonderland, *'begin at the beginning and go on till you come to the end; then stop.'*

1.6 Supervision

Supervision plays a vital role in both undergraduate and postgraduate degrees and is a formal requirement. A **supervisor** is the person responsible for overseeing and guiding a student's research. In the UK, undergraduates and students on taught Master's degrees typically have one supervisor, whereas MPhil and doctoral students have two. In the latter cases, the supervisors will have specialist knowledge of the topic and at least one of them will have experience of successful supervision at that level.

A **supervisor** is the person responsible for overseeing and guiding a student's research.

1.6.1 Choosing a supervisor

If you are an undergraduate or Master's student, you may find that you have no choice but are allocated a supervisor. You will find it useful to discuss with your supervisor how he or she wishes to supervise you. It is important that you understand what is expected of you and when. It is to your advantage to find out as much as you can about your supervisor to help you develop a good relationship, such as:

- what their teaching and research interests are
- what they have published (for example books or articles in academic journals, magazines or newspapers)
- whether they favour a particular paradigm and/or methodology.

Some Master's and most doctoral students are likely to have some influence over the appointment of their supervisor. Phillips and Pugh (2010) suggest that you obtain as much information as possible before choosing a supervisor by visiting prospective universities or colleges. Although this advice was aimed at PhD students, it is equally applicable to MPhil and other postgraduate students. This will allow you to meet potential supervisors, assess the quality of facilities and resources, and evaluate the relative importance of research in that institution. When talking to potential supervisors, you need to bear in mind that most academic staff are involved in five main activities:

- teaching
- writing assessments, teaching materials and/or textbooks
- managing research centres, departments, programmes or subject fields
- conducting research, and
- writing research papers, articles and reports.

If possible, talk to current research students or those who have been supervised in the past by the academic you have in mind. Box 1.1 provides a checklist for choosing a supervisor.

Box 1.1 Checklist for choosing a supervisor

- Does the supervisor have knowledge and interest in your research topic?
- Is the supervisor sympathetic to your proposed methodology?
- Is the supervisor an experienced researcher?
- Has the supervisor got a record of successful supervisions?
- Has the supervisor got a good publication record?
- Has the supervisor got enough time to take on your supervision as well as managing his/her other work?

You need to bear in mind that selection is a two-way process in which the potential supervisor will also be assessing you and your research proposal. A supervisor may decline to take you on if your research topic holds no interest for him or her; if your research proposal is considered to have serious flaws or you do not appear to have a number of other characteristics that are likely to contribute to the successful completion of your research. The latter are particularly important if you are applying for an MPhil or doctorate, where you need to engage with your research at a deeper level and/or maintain your momentum over a period of three or more years. Cryer (1997) aptly describes these attributes as the non-paper entry qualifications for research students and her checklist is shown in Box 1.2.

Box 1.2 Attributes supervisors look for in research students

- Ability to grasp concepts and reason analytically
- Motivation and perseverance in achieving objectives
- Capacity for independent thought
- Organizational skills
- Independence as a learner
- Self-confidence
- Enthusiasm for the research programme
- Nature and extent of any relevant work and life experience
- Nature and extent of any previously undertaken training in research
- Likelihood of establishing good working relationship
- Language skills, particularly for overseas candidates

Source: Cryer (1997, p. 10). Published by kind permission of the Society for Research into Higher Education and the author Pat Cryer.

It is usually the responsibility of the head of the department or director of research to exercise as much care as possible in matching students to supervisors. He or she will take into account such factors as the research topic, the number of students already being supervised by that member of staff, and the student's academic ability and personality. Sometimes the student is accepted on condition that he or she undertakes to do a project in one of the ongoing areas of research in the department. Students who have only a general idea about their research topic may develop their ideas after discussions with their supervisors. However, a final decision should be made as soon as possible.

1.6.2 Supervisor/supervisee relationship

Once you have agreed who your supervisor(s) will be, it is important to realize that the supervisor/supervisee relationship is a two-way relationship in which you play an active part. Howard and Sharp (1994) recommend that the student should:

- at the outset, attempt to find out the supervisor's views of the supervisor/student relationship; for example, on impromptu versus formal meetings and punctuality
- agree with the supervisor the routine aspects of the relationship and take responsibility for their implementation; for example, agree the maximum interval between meetings and ensure it is not breached
- produce written lists of queries prior to meetings with the supervisor in order to define the agenda and structure the meeting

Vox pop What has been the biggest challenge of your research so far?

Lee, first year PhD student investigating foreign direct investment in international business

Well, it's a real rollercoaster doing a PhD – sometimes you're up and sometimes you're down. You need to be committed and stubborn!

Pippa, final year PhD student investigating how a small town is affected by increased tourism

That initial transition to self-guided learning and the lack of direction provided in studying for a PhD, and then sustaining motivation and focus. A bit later my main concern was choosing a methodological approach that would best answer my research question.

Kevin, third year PhD student investigating the personalization of products and services

Keeping myself motivated. There's a point at which your enthusiasm for the subject wanes – you stop thinking this is novel, new and a challenge. It gets a bit solitary and you need some positive reinforcement. It's difficult to get from the other PhD students because we're all studying different topics and there's so little time to meet. Then I discovered meetup.com and found a group of people who design their own products and talking to them really brought back the feeling that what I'm doing is worthwhile.

- keep written notes of meetings with the supervisor (even if the supervisor also does so) and submit copies to him/her
- agree with the supervisor the nature and timing of written material, such as progress reports and drafts chapters, to be submitted to him/her.

Although your supervisor will play a very important role in guiding your research, 'it is the responsibility of the researcher to identify a [research] question' (Creedy, 2001, p. 116). Therefore, even if supervisors are willing to offer suggestions based on their research interests, you must take ownership of your research project and identify the specific research problem or issue and the research question(s) yourself.

Research into the supervision of postgraduate students (Phillips, 1984) shows that supervisory style is important. Phillips found that the more supervisors left their students to get on with their work, intervening only when specifically asked for help, the shorter the length of time before the students became independent researchers. She argues that too much contact and cosseting delays the necessary weaning process.

From this, you can see that the ideal relationship is one where the researcher is initially tutored by the supervisor and eventually becomes a respected colleague. Thus, they start as master and pupil, and end up as equals. Therefore, it is important that you and your supervisor are well matched. This is not so difficult if you know the academic staff at the institution already. If you have chosen to continue your studies at the same university or college, you may have been stimulated by a particular subject and a particular lecturer, and wish to approach that person to be your supervisor. If you are registering for a degree at an institution that is new to you and you do not know the staff, you may have only a few days in which to talk to potential supervisors and other students.

The longer the period of research, the more important it is that the relationship between the supervisor and the supervisee is resilient enough to cope with every stage in the research process. Drawing on Phillips (1984), Figure 1.2 summarizes this process. The emotional commitment involved in conducting research should not be underestimated. Research involving independent inquiry requires considerable intellectual activity and, often, considerable stress. This is especially true of doctorates, where a major piece of research is conducted over several years. Your initial enthusiasm and interest may turn into frustration, boredom or writer's block, and you may begin seriously to question your ability to continue. However, with the help of your supervisor, you can minimize the likelihood of serious stress through careful planning and time management, and eventually reach the final phase when your main concern is to get the research finished.

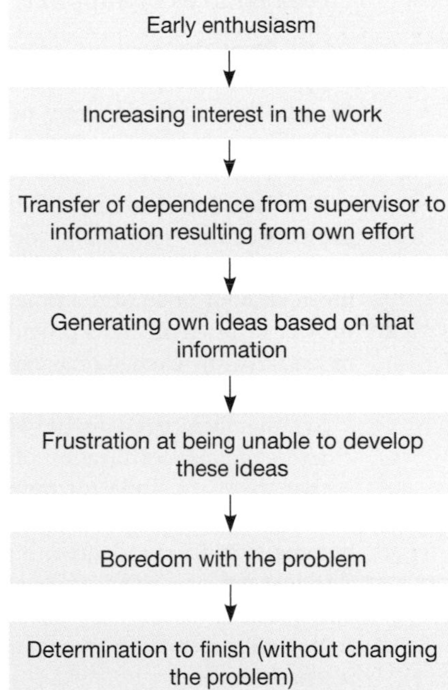

Figure 1.2 Changing attitudes shown by students during their research
Source: Adapted from Phillips (1984, p. 16).

1.6.3 Supervision models

There are a number of different supervision models and it would be a mistake to think exclusively in terms of one supervisor for each researcher. Although one supervisor per student is typically the model at the undergraduate level and on taught Master's courses, it is usual to have at least two supervisors for MPhil and doctoral research. At some institutions, there may be a committee. You may find that the administrative, pastoral and academic roles of supervision are delegated to different individuals, which reduces the risk of failure by allowing the student's progress to be monitored closely.

An alternative approach is *de facto supervision*. This model encourages the researcher to develop a number of different surrogate supervisors, possibly in other establishments, who can offer skills lacked by the main supervisor. This is particularly useful where company-based projects are concerned, where both academic and consultancy skills are required.

In the natural sciences, group and team projects are a widely used approach. Research students are often clustered round a major research issue and each student is part of the team. This allows specific areas of work within the same problem area to be the responsibility of individual researchers. Such approaches are research-skills based. On the other hand, business and management research in the social sciences is more likely to involve solitary, knowledge-based activities and include a relationship with one or more supervisors.

1.6.4 Other sources of support

Apart from the support provided by your supervisor(s), other potential sources of support include *peer support* (fellow students), mentors, work colleagues, family and friends. You can find sources of peer support outside your institution by networking with other researchers at academic conferences and events for doctoral students. You should also attend any taught sessions offered, such as methodology courses.

The isolation that can sometimes be felt by students while conducting their research projects can be reduced by developing *support sets*. A set comprises approximately five students and a tutor and meets for a full day every one or two months. Each person is given an hour or so of the time available, during which the group focuses on a particular project or problem. This provides an opportunity to use the group as a sounding board, in addition to exchanging experiences and ideas. It also enables group members to support and encourage one another.

Set members need to be working in loosely related areas, in order to increase the chances of cross-fertilization of ideas without undue competition. The main requirement is that there are sufficient numbers of students attached to a department or faculty to produce viable group sizes. They may be supplemented by company managers who are not registered for a degree, but who wish to conduct their own in-company research. Support sets can be a feature of more traditional research activities in the social sciences and need not be founded exclusively on process. They should be seen as being additional to normal supervision arrangements and are particularly valuable in the early stages of a research project.

1.7 Managing the project

Research is a time-consuming and expensive activity and therefore you will need to develop your project management skills to ensure you meet your aims and objectives.

Although a few lucky individuals are in a position to conduct studies purely out of personal interest, most research requires specific outcomes. This may be a dissertation or thesis that gets you a good grade as a student, transferable skills that improve your employability or a journal publication that will help you further your academic career. The main steps are:

- Getting organized
- Identifying your desired outcome(s)
- Choosing a research topic
- Determining the research problem/question(s)
- Drawing up a detailed table of contents
- Establishing a timetable or schedule
- Being serious about writing.

These aspects will be discussed in depth throughout this book, but so that you can start developing your research strategy straightaway, we give some helpful pointers now.

1.7.1 Getting organized

You will not be successful in doing research if you are not organized. We can all think of exceptions of brilliant researchers who ignore this rule but, for most of us, success depends on being administratively competent. This entails having a good filing system, dating and recording all your research activities and committing everything to paper or computer. At this stage, you need to work out how much time you have, what financial resources you need and what physical resources you have in terms of computer hardware and software and any other technology. You will also need to draw up a list of contacts, groups and institutions that may be helpful. They may be able to help by offering advice and guidance, allowing you access to facilities such as a library or to collect data, or by assisting you in some way to achieve your desired outcomes.

1.7.2 Identifying the contribution and outcome(s)

You need to be specific when identifying the outcome(s) of your research. It is not sufficient to say that you want a high grade for your research project or to publish in one of the top academic journals. If you want to get the top grades for your dissertation or thesis, you need to understand the requirements you have to satisfy, and these are discussed in Chapter 2. If you want your work to be published, you need to read articles in the journal you have chosen and understand the editorial policy. We offer advice on this in Chapter 13.

1.7.3 Choosing a research topic

There is often a conflict between what you would like to do and what is feasible. The level of research and the outcome you desire will frequently determine the research you will conduct. You may be very interested in the history of sea bathing, but this may not be suitable if the particular aspect of sea bathing you choose is not relevant to your degree programme. If you are pursuing an academic career, you will need to think whether the topic you choose will provide you with a research niche upon which to build an impressive reputation. At the other end of the scale, the time constraints you face on a Bachelor's or Master's programme make it unlikely that you will be able to conduct a large survey of the opinions of directors of the world's top companies. Even a seasoned researcher with an enviable reputation would find such a project a challenge. Your research must be feasible and lead to your expected outcome(s).

1.7.4 Determining the research problem/question(s)

Do not focus solely on the immediate outcome(s) of your research, but think about how you might be able to develop your work. For example, if you are a student, you might want to examine an issue in a particular industry where you hope to find employment when you graduate. For those pursuing research to further their careers, there is a good argument for choosing an issue that will help you to build a reputation and become one of the experts in a particular field.

1.7.5 Being serious about writing

You will be judged by your ability to communicate, particularly your written output; a poorly crafted dissertation, thesis, conference paper or article can destroy what may have been a well-designed and carefully executed study. We give considerable guidance on writing in the later chapters but the immediate advice is to start writing notes and drafts now and to continue to write, review and revise your work so that your final draft will represent the highest quality in terms of substance, structure, grammar and spelling.

1.7.6 Characteristics of good research

Methodological rigour refers to the appropriateness and intellectual soundness of the research design and the systematic application of the research methods.

Many of the characteristics of good research can be developed by adopting a methodical approach. **Methodological rigour** is very important and this term refers to the appropriateness and intellectual soundness of the research design and the systematic application of the methods used. Therefore, it requires a careful, detailed, exacting approach to conducting the research. Litman (2012) suggests that a good research project will include the following:

- a well-defined question
- a description of the context and existing information about the issue
- consideration of various perspectives
- presentation of evidence, with data and analysis in a format that can be replicated by others
- discussion of critical assumptions, contrary findings, and alternative interpretations
- cautious conclusions and discussion of their implications
- adequate references, including original sources, alternative perspectives, and criticism.

The characteristics of a good research project vary according to the philosophical assumptions that underpin your research. These assumptions are discussed in Chapter 3 and are very important at all academic levels. A soundly based research design should allow a degree of flexibility to enable you to pursue new developments in the topic if they are relevant to the study and you have sufficient time. In subsequent chapters, we will explain how this can be achieved. At this stage, it is useful to have an overview of what makes a good research project. Therefore, in Table 1.4 we compare the main characteristics of good and poor projects.

Table 1.4 Characteristics of good and poor research projects

Criteria	Good project	Poor project
Research problem and scope	Sharply focused Related to academic debate	Unclear and unfocused
Literature review	Critical evaluation of relevant, up-to-date literature Linked to focused, feasible research questions	A list of items Relevance unclear Little or no evaluation Research questions missing, impractical or unfocused
Methodology	Cohesive design Excellent review of research design options Linked to the literature	Little appreciation of research design No justification of choice Not linked to the literature
Analysis and discussion	Clear findings discussed in an analytical manner that generates new knowledge and insight Linked to the literature	Unclear findings, unrelated to research questions Little or no attempt to discuss in relation to literature review
Conclusions	Conclusions clearly linked to research questions Attention given to implications and limitations	Some conclusions but not linked to research questions Implications and limitations of results not addressed
Referencing	All sources cited in the text and full bibliographic details listed at the end	Plagiarism through omission or inadequate referencing
Communication	Clear flow of ideas Appropriate spelling and grammar	Difficult to follow Many spelling and grammar mistakes

1.8 Conclusions

This chapter has examined the purpose and nature of research, and the ways in which it can be classified. We have given an overview of the different types of research and the factors that need to be considered at various levels. A research project offers an opportunity to identify and select a research problem to investigate independently under the guidance of a supervisor. It gives you the opportunity to apply theory or otherwise analyse a real business problem or issue. Your research needs to be systematic and methodical and your study will illuminate the problem or issue and contribute towards our greater understanding of it. To ensure you are satisfied with your research and achieve the outcomes you desire, you must develop a research strategy. The most important part of that strategy from the outset is to start writing. You should make sure that you keep careful records to ensure that other people's contribution to knowledge is not confused with yours.

References

Creedy, J. (2001) 'Starting research', *The Australian Economic Review*, 34(1), p. 116.

Cryer, P. (1997) 'Handling common dilemmas in supervision', *Issues in Postgraduate Supervision, Teaching and Management No. 2*, London: Society for Research into Higher Education and the Times Higher Education Supplement.

Howard, K. and Sharp, J. A. (1994) *The Management of a Student Research Project.* Aldershot: Gower.

Litman, T. (2012) *Evaluating Research Quality: Guidelines for Scholarship*, Victoria Transport Policy Institute. Available at: http://www.vtpi.org/resqual.pdf

Phillips, E. M. (1984) 'Learning to do research', *Graduate Management Research*, Autumn, pp. 6–18.

Phillips, E. M. and Pugh, D. S. (2010) *How to Get a Ph.D.* Buckingham: Open University Press.

Waite, M. and Hawker, S. (eds) (2009) *Oxford Paperback Dictionary and Thesaurus.* Oxford: Oxford University Press.

Activities

1 Select two academic journals from your discipline in the library and construct a table that classifies articles according to whether the research is exploratory, descriptive, analytical or predictive.
2 Construct a second table that classifies the same articles according to whether the research is quantitative or qualitative.
3 Now construct a third table that classifies the same articles according to whether the research is applied or basic.
4 Finally, construct a table that classifies the same articles according to whether the research is deductive or inductive.
5 Reflect on the results shown in your four tables and write notes on similarities and differences in these classifications. Summarize your notes in the form of a diagram.

Go online to try a progress test for this chapter and for access to the searchable glossary at www.palgrave.com/business/collis/br4/

Have a look at the Troubleshooting chapter and sections 14.2, 14.3, 14.4, 14.16 in particular, which relate specifically to this chapter.

2

dealing with practical issues

learning objectives

When you have studied this chapter, you should be able to:

- determine the knowledge, skills and personal qualities researchers need
- use techniques for generating research topics
- negotiate access to data and consider ethical issues
- plan the management of the research process
- identify any funding constraints.

2.1 Introduction

A successful researcher establishes a firm base on which to develop his or her research study. Projects fail, not because the researcher was lazy, incompetent or unmotivated, but because he or she did not recognize the importance of project management. You need to make certain that you have a clear idea of what you are going to investigate, access to the relevant data, a realistic timetable, an efficient system for managing the research and sufficient funds. You also need to take account of any ethical guidelines or regulations when conducting your research. Time management is crucial, which means using what time you have productively. It is a combination of your practical and intellectual skills that will determine the quality of your research. This chapter examines the main practical issues you should take into account when planning your research.

2.2 Knowledge, skills and personal qualities

Conducting research in business and management requires certain knowledge, skills and personal qualities and different attributes are needed at different stages in the research. Kervin (1992) summarizes the main stages in the research process as:

- research problem stages
- research design stages
- data gathering stages
- data analysis and interpretation stages.

The research problem stages include gathering preliminary data from the literature and may also incorporate exploratory research (Kervin, 1992; Sekaran, 2003). This leads to the identification of the research problem and the development of the specific research questions to be addressed by the study. Before the main data gathering and analysis stages can commence, some studies require time for negotiating access and addressing ethical issues (Saunders, Lewis and Thornhill, 2009). Figure 2.1 shows a more detailed model of the stages in the research process than the one shown in Chapter 1.

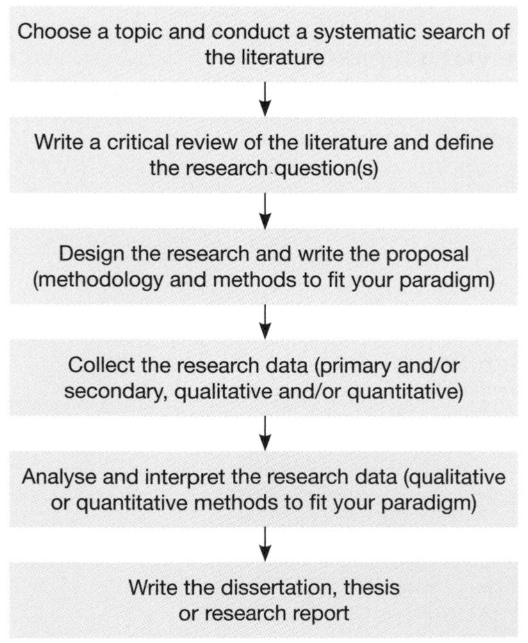

Figure 2.1 Stages in the research process

Little has been written on the issues arising at each stage in the research process. Howard and Sharp (1994) identify 20 factors that have a beneficial, neutral or adverse effect on research projects, while Easterby-Smith, Thorpe and Jackson (2012) classify the qualities required of researchers under the headings of knowledge/awareness, skills and abilities, and personal qualities. A study of eight successful researchers (Hussey, 2007) brought these factors together by examining the process of the research and the skills, knowledge and personal qualities needed at each stage. The main findings were as follows:

- Knowledge – Knowledge of research was particularly beneficial during the literature search, research design and writing stages. Business knowledge provided a context for negotiating access and enriched the analysis of data and illuminated the conclusions.
- Skills – Good administrative skills were particularly needed during the literature searching stage. Communication skills were most important when negotiating access and collecting data. Negotiating access and dealing with ethical issues tended to be regarded as challenges to be overcome and had little effect on the process of the research. Not surprisingly, communication skills were also of great benefit at the writing stage and when presenting conference papers. Researchers near the beginning of their careers regarded conferences as opportunities for networking, obtaining feedback and getting papers published in conference proceedings, while established academics tended to focus on writing articles for publication in academic journals rather than attending conferences. IT skills were beneficial during the data collection and data analysis stages.
- Personal qualities – Creativity was most important when identifying the research problem and research questions. Motivation was rated highly during the literature search, data analysis and writing stages. Perseverance was most needed at the data collection and writing stages. Participants referred to the discipline required in conducting interviews, administering questionnaires and maintaining a consistently rigorous approach to every aspect of data collection. Time management was influential throughout the research, with every stage adversely affected by lack of time, particularly the writing stage.

It would appear that appropriate knowledge, time management and the ability to remain motivated and persevere are key features of successful research. Figure 2.2 develops our simple model of the stages in the research process to incorporate the above findings.

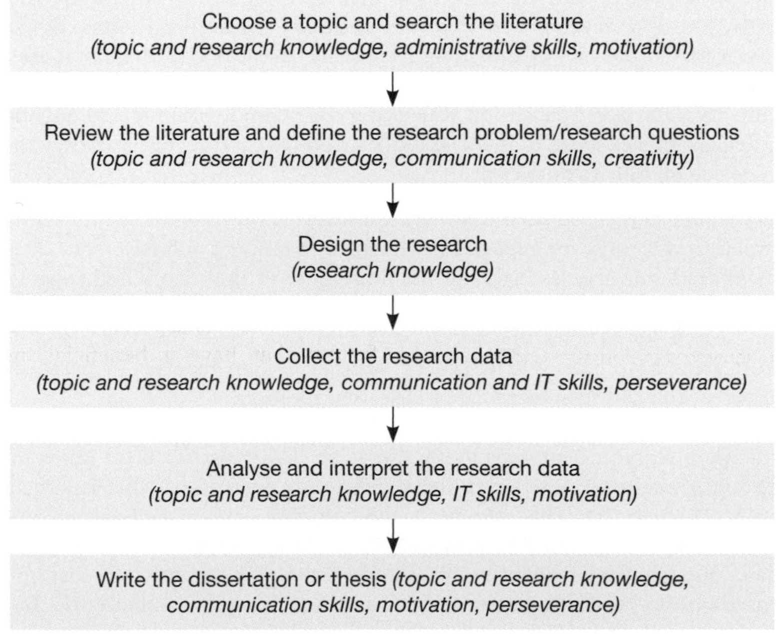

Figure 2.2 Attributes needed during the main stages in the research process

Vox pop

	What has been the biggest challenge in your research so far?	What has been the highpoint of your research so far?
Gurdeep, first year PhD student investigating the strategic significance of brand love in branded entertainment	*Having no lectures and seminars means I have to decide what to read and how to use my time – it's a big jump into independence.*	*Well, it's the other side of the coin – not having lectures and seminars means I have freedom over my time.*

A critical and early stage of your research is deciding on an appropriate topic, reading the literature on that topic and identifying a research question. The main steps are:

1 Select a topic that interests you and/or of which you have some knowledge. Then identify a business problem related to that topic by reading previous studies and reflecting on current issues being discussed in media, on campus or at work. Check with your supervisor whether you can choose a topic that is not directly related to your degree programme. You may think of some very interesting topics but they need to be feasible. If you are an undergraduate or taught Master's student, you will want to design a research project that will help you achieve a high grade.
2 Ensure that you have the resources to conduct the research and that you have access to the research data you will analyse. This will mean considering the methods you will use to collect and analyse your research data. Subsequent chapters of this book cover a range of methods.
3 Generate an overarching research question that the study will investigate. Subsequently, you may develop one or more subsidiary research questions. Even doctoral students should be wary of designing impressive research questions that are too wide-ranging or too difficult to be investigated in depth.
4 Finally, try your question out on your supervisor, family, friends and anyone else you can. See if it makes sense to them. If it does, you have a research question and you can then decide on how to answer it.

A very common method used to generate a research question in business and management research is to look for gaps in the literature (Sandberg and Alvesson, 2011a). Most authors of academic articles highlight the limitations of their work and suggest areas for further research. For example, if your chosen research topic is international marketing, you can search for articles on that subject and skim read them to see whether any particular areas have been overlooked or whether certain theories or perspectives have been ignored. You can then formulate a research question.

Problematization is an approach that may be of interest to postgraduate and doctoral students when searching for gaps in the literature. The objective is 'to know how and to what extent it might be possible to think differently, instead of what is already known' (Foucault, 1985, p. 9). This can be a difficult task and a well-argued approach is described by Sandberg and Alvesson (2011b, p. 267), the aim of which is 'to identify, articulate, and challenge different types of assumptions underlying existing literature and, based on that, to formulate research questions that may facilitate the development of more interesting and influential theories'.

Table 2.1 shows two examples that illustrate the relationship between the research topic, the research problem and the research question.

Table 2.1 Examples of topics, research problems and related research questions

	Example 1	**Example 2**
Topic	Employee retention	Finance
Research problem	Effect of new career-break scheme in Firm A on the recruitment and retention of skilled staff	Access to finance for small firms
Research questions	How has the new career-break scheme contributed to employment in Firm A?	How do small firms meet their needs for finance (in a particular industry, geographical location, time period, etc.)?

2.3 Generating a research topic

You may have already found a research topic because you have a particular interest in one of the subjects you have studied, or perhaps a topic has been allocated to you. However, some students delay starting their research because they have difficulty in generating a topic. If this applies to you, the best advice is to start by thinking of a general subject area that is relevant to your programme. Naturally, you are more likely to have a successful and enjoyable experience if you find this general subject area interesting! Then you could use a very simple technique known as brainstorming. You need at least one other interested person with whom to generate spontaneous ideas. Jot down a list of all the ideas that come up and then review them by deciding what you mean by each idea. For example, if you were interested in financial reporting, you could review the idea by asking yourself the following questions:

- What is financial reporting?
- Do I mean internal or external financial reporting?
- Which organizations produce financial reports?
- Is there a particular aspect of financial reporting I am interested in?
- Am I interested in the regulation of financial reporting?
- Am I interested in voluntary disclosure?
- Am I interested in the communication aspects?

Once you have begun to focus your ideas about financial reporting, you could turn your attention to such questions as:

- What is reported?
- When is it reported?
- To whom is it reported?
- What is the purpose of reporting?
- Are there any ethical issues?

Another way of approaching the problem might be to examine the various ways in which research can be designed or conducted. If you are still unable to generate a research topic, the following techniques may be of help.

2.3.1 Analogy

Analogy is a means of designing a study in one subject by importing ideas and procedures from another area where there are similarities.

Analogy involves designing a research project in one subject by importing ideas and procedures from another area where you consider there are similarities. Thus, you use the research developments in one area to illuminate how you could conduct your own study. It is also possible to develop a research topic if you are aware of methods of analysis that have been used in one study and that can be applied in your own work. The use of existing analytical techniques in a completely new and different area can result in a very interesting study that makes a contribution to our knowledge of the subject.

2.3.2 Morphological analysis

Morphological analysis is a technique for generating research topics whereby the subject is analysed into its key attributes and a 'mix and match' approach is adopted.

Morphology is concerned with the study of form and **morphological analysis** involves drawing up a table and using it to analyse the general subject area that interests you. First, you define the key factors or dimensions of the subject, which you set out as the column headings. Then you list the various attributes of the factor or the ways in which it can occur under the headings. Finally, you define all feasible combinations of the attributes to generate a number of potential research projects. Obviously, your choice is influenced by your research paradigm.

In the example in Table 2.2, we have used the general subject area of research. We have defined our key dimensions as the type of research, the methodology and the unit of analysis.

Table 2.2 Morphological analysis for the topic: research

Types of research	Methodologies	Units of analysis
Exploratory	Cross-sectional study	An individual
Descriptive	Experimental study	An event
Analytical	Longitudinal study	An object
Predictive	Survey	A body of individuals
Quantitative	Action research	A relationship
Qualitative	Case study	An aggregate
Deductive	Collaborative research	
Inductive	Ethnography	
Applied	Grounded theory	
Basic		

The result of your analysis might indicate a descriptive research project that uses a survey for its methodology and focuses on a body of individuals as its unit of analysis; for example professional associations of accountants or lawyers. Another analysis might suggest an exploratory research project that uses a case study approach and is conducted in one division of a particular company. A third analysis might generate a predictive research project that uses experiments with individuals; perhaps a project where you test how alcohol abuse affects individual students' examination performance.

You should restrict yourself to defining only the key dimensions of your chosen subject, as you can see that morphological analysis can generate a huge number of potential projects!

2.3.3 Mind maps

A **mind map** is an informal diagram of a person's idea of the key elements of a subject that shows connections and relationships.

Another way of generating a research topic is to use diagrams. There are a number of ways of constructing diagrams, depending on the purpose you have in mind. While diagrams show how things depend on one another, maps show relationships in space or time. A **mind map** is a highly creative and personal form of diagram. The process is not particularly systematic and focuses on key aspects, rather than detail. These key aspects are jotted down haphazardly, without any particular thought as to their position and are usually joined by lines to indicate connections and relationships.

Figure 2.3 shows an example of a mind map that focuses on the general subject of research. We started the map by writing the word 'research' and then as associated terms came to mind, we wrote them nearby and drew lines connecting them to the word 'research'. We then thought of additional terms and connected them, gradually working outwards. We only stopped because space was limited, but you can see that this process can be continued until you have identified the general subject for your project. Of course, this sort of activity does mean you need some prior knowledge of the topic.

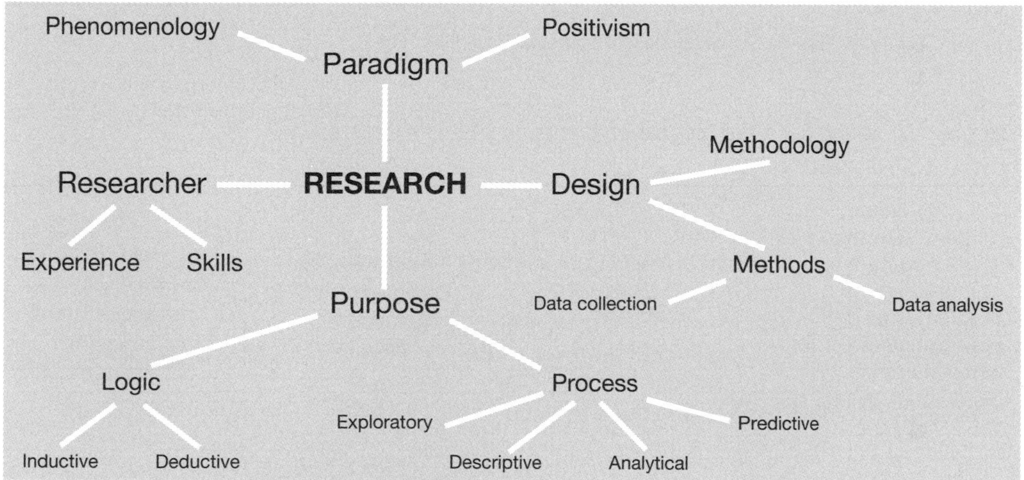

Figure 2.3 Mind map for the topic: academic research

2.3.4 Relevance trees

A **relevance tree** is a diagram that can be used as a device for generating research topics and develops clusters of ideas from a fairly broad starting concept.

Another type of diagram that can be used as a device for generating a research topic is a **relevance tree**. The idea is to develop clusters of related ideas from a starting concept. To be most effective, the starting concept should be fairly broad. Figure 2.4 shows an example of a relevance tree that stems from the starting concept of 'communication'. Using our relevance tree, we identified a number of potential research topics; for example use of body language in formal meetings or, at a more general level, the different forms of two-way communication used in the workplace.

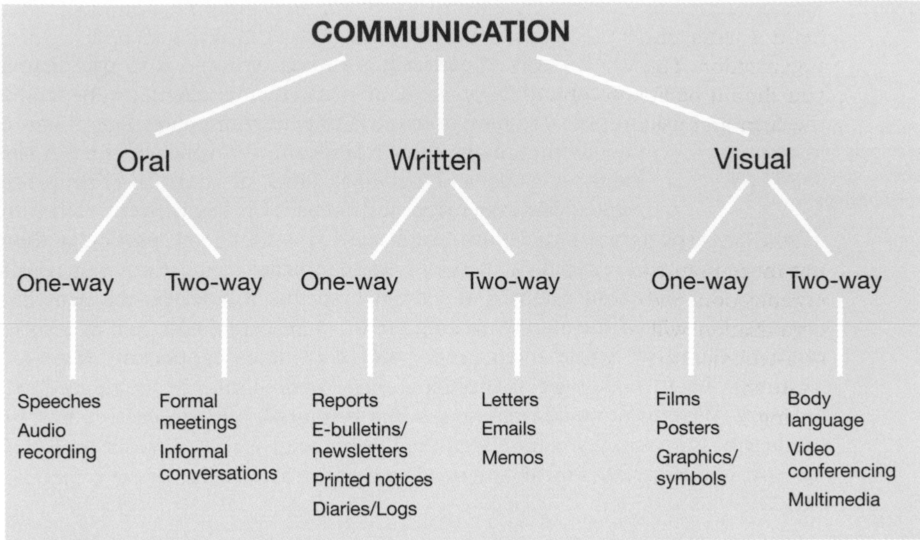

Figure 2.4 Relevance tree for the topic: business communication

Vox pop What has been the biggest challenge in your research so far?

Naim, undergraduate student investigating problems faced by entrepreneurs when starting a business

Choosing a topic was hard – I don't mean the subject itself but the specific issue – and then realizing that I needed to do some work straightaway and not leave it until the week before like other coursework.

Adel, recently completed PhD in management accounting

My main challenge was identifying a relevant research topic and valid research question at the start.

If you are having a problem identifying a research topic and/or a specific problem or issue to investigate, have a look at the advice in Chapter 14 (section 14.4).

2.4 Negotiating access

If you are a part-time student or doing a placement project as part of a degree, your job may give you access to sources that will provide you with research data. Other students need to find their own sources and negotiate access to them. For example, if you have decided to collect your research data by designing a questionnaire and posting or emailing it to potential respondents, you will need to determine what types of people to send it to and obtain their names and contact details.

You may want to conduct a study that requires access to one or more organizations. The first step is to make use of any contacts you may already have. For example, your family and friends may be able to introduce you to an organization that might be interested in your research. Remember that they will only be able to supply an introduction and it will be up to you to negotiate the terms of access.

If the above fails, you may have to approach organizations without an introduction. Send a letter enclosing an outline of your research proposal, suitably modified for the organization. The letter must be addressed to an appropriate named person whose name you should be able to obtain from the firm's printed literature, its website or by ringing the firm and asking the switchboard operator. A well-composed letter addressed to the key person explaining why your project will be of interest to them is likely to be far more successful than 'cold-calling'. It is advisable to follow up with a telephone call to that person if you do not receive a reply to your letter within 10 days.

Your letter should present your project in the form of a brief research proposal, usually not more than two pages of A4. Your proposal should set out clearly the benefits to the organization and what access and information you will require. Remember that the organization will not want an academic document with citations, but a clear, concise, non-technical explanation of what the project is about in report form. If you can demonstrate that your research may provide answers to problems their managers may be experiencing, you are more likely to be successful. Remember, the company will believe that it is doing you a favour, not vice versa, so be very sensitive in the requests you make. Once again, do your preliminary research so that you can focus your proposals on what is likely to be of interest to the company.

Vox pop What has been the biggest challenge in your research so far?

Chris, undergraduate student investigating environmental implications of logistics in the grocery market

Thinking of topics that interested me wasn't a problem, but I had to think of the practical implications. I had access to the company where my dad works, so that helped me make up my mind.

Talha, undergraduate student investigating customer satisfaction with banking services

Choosing a topic was hard. I did it backwards by starting from where I had access to data and then deciding on the topic. I didn't do an internship so I didn't have any outside contacts. So I decided to do a survey of students and then decided on a topic that was relevant to them.

2.4.1 Agreeing terms

If the firm is interested, the manager or director you contact is likely to suggest an informal discussion. This will allow him or her to assess you and your project in greater depth than can be gleaned from your proposal. You may find that certain restrictions are placed on your research, such as how long you can spend in the organization, the documents you can see, the methods you can use, the personnel you can interview and the questions you can ask.

It is important to be sympathetic to the norms and procedures of the firm you approach. Some organizations may be willing to make verbal agreements on the telephone or at an informal meeting, while others require all the issues to be agreed in writing with formal terms of reference. Even if a verbal agreement is made, we recommend that you write a letter confirming exactly what has been agreed, with copies to the relevant members of staff in the organization.

Obtaining permission to publish from your research is not usually an issue at the undergraduate level as it is unlikely that you intend to publish your results externally. However, it is essential that research results are published if you are a postgraduate student wanting to pursue an academic career. You will need to explain that the research report will be used for your degree. If you wish to publish from the research at a later date, it is normal practice to seek prior permission from the organization. It is important to clarify who owns the data you have collected. At the end of your research you should provide the organization with a copy of your report, but beware of offering them a special or interim report, as this can be very time-consuming and expensive. However, if you have agreed to supply a report in exchange for access, you may have to write a special version, as your academic report is unlikely to be sufficiently user-friendly.

2.4.2 Personal safety

It is important to consider your personal safety when conducting research. You will be exposing yourself to new situations and meeting people of whom you have no previous knowledge. Fortunately, few problems arise, but it is important that you are aware of potential dangers and take the necessary steps to minimize them.

If you are negotiating access with a well-known organization, your safety is reasonably well assured, but with small, unknown organizations or individual interviews 'on site', caution is required. You should ensure that you have the full name, title and contact address of anyone you intend to visit. Attempt to establish their credibility beforehand by finding out if they are known to any of your colleagues and checking with your original source for the contact. If you have any doubts, ask your supervisor or a colleague to accompany you.

2.4.3 Courtesy

It is essential that you thank individuals and organizations for their assistance with your research, verbally at the time and afterwards by letter. If you have promised to provide copies of transcripts of interviews or a summary of your final report to participants, make sure that you do so promptly. If your work is published, you should send a copy to those in the participating organization(s) who have helped you and to individual participants where this is practical.

2.5 Research ethics

The term ethics refers to the moral values or principles that form the basis of a code of conduct. In this section we focus on research ethics, which is concerned with the manner in which research is conducted and how the results or findings are reported. Do not confuse it with business ethics, which is a separate field of study that grew out of religion's interest in ethics in business, and management education's concern with social issues (De George, 1987). The history of research into business ethics is well documented by Ma (2009) and Calabretta, Durisin and Ogliengo (2011). If you are considering business ethics as a potential research topic, these articles are a good place to start as they explain the development of business ethics, the issues that have been explored and directions for future research.

Research funding bodies, such as the Economic and Social Research Council (ESRC) and the European Union (EU) have contributed to awareness of research ethics by providing guidelines, and those funded are required to demonstrate how they have met those guidelines. In addition, *The Missenden Code* (Daly, 2002) provides a code of practice for ethics and accountability in the context of the commercialization of research in institutions of higher education in the UK (Box 2.1).

Box 2.1 The Missenden code of practice for ethics and accountability

1 All universities should have an institutional Ethics and Accountability Panel or Committee.
2 Staff, students and the local community should have representation on the Committee.
3 The Committee should take advice from those with a professional expertise in ethics.
4 The Committee should vet all substantial donations, sponsorship and funding that the University applies for or is offered.
5 The Committee should *inter alia* ensure that all sources of funding for any research carried out in the University's name are acknowledged in all publications.
6 Where the Committee accepts a case for limitation on the freedom to publish it should attach an explanatory note to this effect.
7 The brief of the person within the University with responsibility for attracting external 'third mission' funding should have a strong ethical element.
8 The University's policy on Intellectual Property Rights should be disseminated as widely as possible by case studies and be made an integral part of job induction and training programmes.
9 Sponsored research should bear a full share of the institution's infrastructure costs.
10 The right of academic staff to publish research findings should be the primary consideration of any contract between industry and academia. Commercial considerations should never be allowed to prevent the publication of findings that are in the public interest or which add significantly to the body of knowledge in a field.
11 The University should retain the rights of staff to publish without hindrance except where a specific written provision has been made with the agreement of all parties – to include all research students, research assistants and assistant staff involved. This should be explicitly mentioned in all staff contracts.
12 Those obtaining sponsorship for research should not be given undue favour in promotion decisions.
13 Universities should declare details of all investments.
14 Universities should consider the creation of a register of interests for all members of the university.

Source: Daly (2002, p. 35). Reproduced with permission.

Several professional bodies have published ethical guidelines for researchers, from which Bell and Bryman (2007) have compiled the following list of principles:

- Harm to participants – the need to avoid potential harm through the research process and the need to ensure physical and psychological wellbeing of research participants, the researcher and others
- Dignity – the requirement to respect the dignity of research participants, researchers or others and avoid causing discomfort or anxiety
- Informed consent – the need to ensure the fully informed consent of research participants
- Privacy – the need to protect privacy of research subjects or avoid invasions of privacy
- Confidentiality – the requirement to ensure confidentiality of research data whether relating to individuals, groups or organizations
- Anonymity – the protection of anonymity of individuals or organizations

- Deception – the potential for deception during the research process, either through lies or through behaviour that is misleading
- Affiliation – the need to declare any professional or personal affiliations that may have influenced the research, including conflicts of interest and sponsorship, and information about the source of the research funding
- Honesty and transparency – the need for openness and honesty in communicating information about the research to all interested parties, including the need for trust
- Reciprocity – the research should be of mutual benefit to researcher and participants or some form of collaboration or active participation should be involved
- Misrepresentation – the need to avoid misleading, misunderstanding, misrepresenting or falsely reporting the research findings.

Many universities have their own research ethics policies, but in the absence of formal guidance, you should discuss and clarify the main issues with your supervisor at an early stage. Some of the critical issues to discuss are:

- The research must not cause direct or indirect harm to the participant or the researcher. This includes physical harm, harm to self-development, self-esteem, career or employment prospects. In addition, participants must not be encouraged to perform immoral, illegal or other reprehensible acts.
- Participants must be informed of the purpose of the research, voluntary participation, the opportunity to withdraw at any time, the right to confidentiality and anonymity. In addition, researchers should be aware that they do not have the right to invade a person's privacy or to abandon respect for the values of others.

We will discuss the practical issues raised by these points next.

2.5.1 Voluntary participation

One of the most important ethical principles is that coercion should not be used to force people into taking part in the research. In academic research, it is also advisable to avoid offering financial or other material rewards to induce people to take part, as this will lead to biased results. People should be given information about what is required if they agree to take part and how much time it will take. Sometimes, consent is delayed because the potential participants have to ask permission from their line manager or your request has to be approved by a committee. This may take time and, if you are not successful, you will need sufficient time to identify others.

If the research has an experimental design, a balance must be struck between giving sufficient information to permit informed consent and avoiding jeopardizing the purpose of the research. Although it is not likely that participants in business and management research will be exposed to physical risks, it is important to avoid causing distress, stress or other psychological harm. Avoiding causing harm to participants is important for ethical reasons, but also because you could be sued if you harm someone. You must obtain permission if you are planning an internal or external email survey as it is unethical to send unsolicited mass emails.

2.5.2 Anonymity and confidentiality

In principle, you should offer **anonymity** and **confidentiality** to all the participants in your research. Giving participants the opportunity to remain anonymous means assuring them that they will not be identified with any of the opinions they express. In questionnaire surveys, this may contribute to a higher response rate and increased honesty; in

Anonymity is the assurance given to participants and organizations that they will not be named in the research.

Confidentiality is the assurance given to participants and organizations that the information provided will not be traceable to the individual or organization providing it.

interviews, it encourages greater freedom of expression and more open responses. However, in some studies it may be very important to state the name or position of participants because their opinions can only be appreciated in the context of their role. In such circumstances, it is imperative that the participant gives his or her consent. Another example of where permission must be sought is where you wish to name the author of an internal document.

Sometimes it is possible to resolve problems of anonymity by agreeing on confidentiality, which we discuss next, which focuses on the data collected rather than the identity of the participant. If confidentiality is a condition of giving you access to information, you will need to assure participants that the data you collect will be used in such a way that the information is not traceable to any particular individual. For example, your dissertation or thesis need not name the company or companies where you have negotiated access to data; it is sufficient to refer to the organization as an engineering company, a food retailer and so on (or company A, B, C and so on). Similarly, with individuals, they can simply be identified by their position (or interviewee A, B, C and so on), as they cannot be identified if the name of the company is not disclosed.

When writing to potential participants or at the top of any questionnaire you plan to distribute, you should include a sentence such as:

> Neither your name nor the name of your company will be associated with your responses. Unless you have given permission otherwise, your contact details and all data you provide will be treated in the strictest confidence.

You should discuss the issues of anonymity and confidentiality with your supervisors and the organization(s) where you intend to collect your data as soon as possible to clarify these issues. If strict confidentiality is one of the conditions of access, you may be able to agree with the individuals and organization concerned that no one but your supervisor(s) and examiners will have access to your research and it will not be placed in the library or published in any way. Obviously, this would prevent you from writing or presenting any academic papers or articles on your research.

Figure 2.5 shows an example of how some of the key ethical principles were applied in an accompanying letter for an online survey.

2.5.3 Ethical dilemmas

You may have spent some time negotiating access to an organization in order to conduct your research. Naturally, you will be grateful to them for their help and will spend some time developing a good relationship, but what would you do if during the course of your research you found out that the company was doing something illegal? For example, imagine you are conducting research in a small factory that employs a hundred people in an economically depressed area. During your research you observe that proper safety guards are not fitted to the machines, but you know that fitting them would bankrupt the company and put people out of work. What action should you take?

- *Anonymity* and *confidentiality* – Although it is normal to offer anonymity and confidentiality to participants, you might receive information that you think should be passed on to someone else. For example, perhaps you are conducting research into the reasons for high wastage levels of materials in a production process and, while interviewing employees, you discover that part of the wastage is due to one of them stealing goods.

- *Informed consent* – Although it is ethical to inform potential participants of the purpose of the research before they agree to participate, this could present problems in gaining access and obtaining valid responses. For example, if you were to inform participants you were intending to observe that you are studying their working patterns, they might change their behaviour and this would distort your findings.
- *Dignity* – It would not be ethical to embarrass or ridicule participants, but unfortunately, this is easily done. The relationship between the researcher and the phenomenon under study is often complex and it is important to remember that participants may see you as someone with knowledge that they do not have or someone in authority. For this reason, it is important to be courteous and make sure they know they have a choice and will not be coerced into answering sensitive questions.
- *Publications* – The career of an academic is developed through publications and the success of a research student is achieved through the acceptance of their thesis or dissertation. History shows that there are some who are willing to invent data, falsify their results or plagiarize to get published, which is highly unethical. However, it is also unethical to exaggerate or omit results in order to present a more favourable picture. A more complex situation arises when your publication casts a bad light on an individual, group or organization. This can arise if you are conducting a comparative study, when you must discuss your results with great sensitivity.

As you can imagine, there are no easy answers to ethical dilemmas. Some commentators believe that ethical codes should be established for business research; others believe

Survey on the (expected) value of university–industry relationship

Dear participant,

First of all, many thanks for taking the time to support this crucial part of my PhD research.

The study has **ethical approval** from [name of university]. **Participation in the study is entirely voluntary**; you can withdraw from the survey at any point of time without giving reason and without implications for you. Please be assured that the **information you provide will remain strictly confidential and anonymous**. Answers will only be reported in aggregate so that no individual or organisation will be identifiable from any publication presenting the results of the survey. By responding to the questionnaire, your consent to take part in the study is assumed. If you would like to have further information about the project, please contact me via email [email address of researcher] or telephone [telephone number of researcher].

It is very important that you answer all questions, even if some appear similar, to ensure reliable and valid measurement.

Thank you very much again for your time and your valuable contribution to my PhD research.

Yours sincerely,

[Signature]
[Name]
PhD student at [Name of university]

[Photograph]

This study aims to better understand...

1. How academics perceive the (expected) value of relationships with businesses and how the benefits of other stakeholders influence this perception
2. How relationship characteristics such as shared expectations, trust and commitment influence the perceived value
3. How the perceived value influences the academics' satisfaction, future expectations and intentions

Figure 2.5 Example of a participant information letter

Source: Reproduced with kind permission from Thorsten Kliewe.

that rules are too rigid and leave loopholes for the unscrupulous; therefore, it is better to follow ethical principles. It has been argued that it is sometimes necessary to be vague about the purpose of the research, and even covert in collecting data, in order to achieve findings of value. You need to resolve these issues with your supervisor before you embark on your research. Remember, it is your responsibility as a researcher to:

- conform to generally accepted scientific principles
- protect the life, health, privacy and dignity of participants in your study
- assess the risk to participants
- take precautions to ensure your own safety
- obtain permission before sending mass emails.

The checklist in Box 2.2 offers a useful starting point. Some of these questions expose a number of dilemmas that we explore when we look at the design of a research project and the methods for collecting data.

Box 2.2 Checklist for ethical research

- Have you obtained explicit or implicit consent from participants?
- Have you used coercion to persuade people to participate?
- Will the research process or the findings harm participants, those about whom information is gathered or others not involved in the research?
- Have you stored personal/confidential data about participants (people and organizations) securely?
- Have you ensured that participants (people and organizations) are anonymous?
- Are you following accepted research practice in your conduct of the research, analysis and when drawing conclusions?
- Are you adhering to community standards of conduct?
- Have you obtained permission before sending mass emails?

2.6 Planning and project management

There is no doubt that time is a major enemy of all researchers and if you do not make realistic plans, you will run the risk of missing your deadlines. To plan your time you need to know how long your institution allows for the submission of your dissertation or thesis. You also need to know how to allocate your time across the different activities you will undertake.

2.6.1 Setting a timetable

You need to agree a timetable with your supervisor and any individuals or organizations participating in your study. You may find that you need to negotiate access with more than one person in the organization and you should therefore plan to allow plenty of time for this stage. It is likely that the individuals concerned will be helping you with your research in addition to doing their normal jobs. Therefore, the time they are able to allocate to your research interests will be limited and must be arranged at their convenience.

A Bachelor's or taught Master's dissertation is normally completed within one academic year. Table 2.3 shows the approximate length of the registration period for postgraduate research degrees, but you should check the regulations in your institution, as times vary.

Table 2.3 Approximate length of research degrees

	Minimum	Maximum
MPhil thesis		
Full time	18 months	36 months
Part time	30 months	48 months
PhD thesis (transfer)		
Full time	33 months	60 months
Part time	45 months	72 months
PhD thesis (direct)		
Full time	24 months	60 months
Part time	36 months	72 months

Research is a time-consuming activity and the secret of completing on time is to draw up a timetable as soon as possible. You may find Table 2.4 is a useful guide when apportioning your time to fit your deadline. Remember that the amount of time for completing your research depends on the qualification you are working towards and the regulations in your institution. Of course, these figures are only indicative and you will need to adjust this basic timetable to reflect your research design and allow additional time for resolving any problems. A major weakness of Table 2.4 is that it implies that research takes place in orderly, discrete and sequential stages. Throughout this book you will find reminders that this is definitely not the case! Although we encourage you to be methodical in your approach, you will find that all research contains stages that overlap. For example, you may need to go on collecting information about current research in your chosen field right up to the final draft, in order to be sure that you present an up-to-date picture. In addition, we must emphasize that although the writing-up stage is shown as a distinct activity at the end of the research process, you must get into the good habit of writing up your notes straightaway. This means that you will start to write up your research, albeit in draft form, as soon as you start your project. When you have decided on the structure for your dissertation or thesis, you can amend and refine your notes, and place them in the appropriate chapters. It is important not to underestimate how long the writing-up stage takes, even when you have good notes and references on which to base your research report.

Table 2.4 Approximate time for main stages of research

Stage	%
Choose a topic and search the literature	10
Review the literature and define the research problem/research questions	20
Design the research and write the proposal	10
Collect the research data	20
Analyse and interpret the research data	20
Complete the writing of the dissertation or thesis	20
	100

If you are having difficulty starting your research because you are confused about what you are expected to do or you are worried about how to manage your research, have a look at Chapter 14 (sections 14.2–5).

You may find it useful to look at some of the reasons for long completion times or, in the worst scenario, failure to complete. For a start, if you are inexperienced, you will find that everything takes longer than you expect. Therefore, it is important to plan your time carefully, with advice from your supervisor. If you are an undergraduate student, you will only have a matter of months in which to complete your dissertation. You may have to balance your research activities against the demands of an industrial placement and/or your final year studies. If you are a graduate student without funding, you may have to juggle the demands of paid work with your research; indeed, you may be lecturing to students yourself. If you are a mature student, you may have both paid work and family life to fit in.

Many undergraduate students go on to study for a graduate degree straight after their finals. Because they know that they have several years in which to complete their research, they often overlook the importance of planning. The result is a slow start and this is a very common reason for late completion. A second common reason is perfectionism. Some students find it difficult to bring things to a conclusion. They are never satisfied with their results and are always thinking of ways in which to improve them, even before they have written them up. Thus, the writing-up stage is always postponed. Such students find it hard to see whether improvement really is necessary and whether it is desirable to spend so much time on that stage of the research to the detriment of later stages.

A third reason for late completion is that some students are distracted from the main research problem. Some students find the software programs for searching the literature, saving references, extracting data from databases, analysing qualitative or quantitative data, and designing tables, graphs and reports so absorbing that they do not give sufficient attention to the substance of the research. Other problems can occur if the student is not sufficiently focused and collects too much literature or too much research data and does not allow enough time for analysis. Sometimes there has been insufficient collation and analysis of the data and the student does not realize this deficiency until he or she begins to write up and has to break off to complete this earlier stage, often resulting in a delay of months rather than weeks.

An experienced supervisor will be aware of these and other problems. The best way to overcome them is to draw up a realistic timetable with your supervisor that shows the dates on which the various stages in the research process should be completed. It is important to do this at the earliest possible stage. Many students find it extremely helpful to know that they are expected to reach certain stages at certain times, as this removes some of the pressure of managing their time and organizing their research.

2.6.2 Organizing materials

It will not take you too long to realize that a large part of research is concerned with organizing materials, such as articles copied from journals, questionnaires returned, newspaper cuttings, transcripts of interviews and notes you have made. Everyone devises their own system, but we find it useful to sort the materials into their different types and file them according to this classification.

Copies of articles and conference papers can be kept in a file alphabetically under the name of the author. There are several excellent software packages that allow you to collect your references and often be able to download references and abstracts from libraries. For a PhD, you may have several hundred articles; for an undergraduate project, only a dozen or so. No matter how many you collect, it is important that they are stored systematically so that you can easily find them. Materials, such as questionnaires and transcripts of interviews, should be numbered, dated and filed in numerical order. You may find it useful to draw up an index for each set of files. In Chapter 8 we discuss the analysis of qualitative data and you will see that, to a large extent, the success of this rests on the efficient storing and referencing of primary materials. We give some examples in that chapter on how this can be achieved.

During your research you will probably collect a certain amount of miscellaneous materials, such as odd notes, quotations or cuttings, which may be important when you are writing your dissertation or thesis. Once you have decided on a draft structure, which you should do as early as possible, you can set up a file with dividers to separate each anticipated chapter and place these miscellaneous materials in the most appropriate chapter.

Keeping records is a very important component in the management of your research. In Chapter 5 we discuss an important aspect of your research known as the literature review and how to reference articles, books and other hard or soft copy publications properly. It is essential that you keep a full bibliographic record of every item you read which might be useful in your own research. You can keep your bibliography in a simple *Microsoft Word* document in alphabetical order by author's name. We explain this in more detail in Chapter 5.

You will need to set up a filing system for your correspondence so that you can find emails and letters when you wish to refer to them. It is also important to maintain a record of contacts' names, addresses, telephone numbers and other details in a secure place. A computerized record system is particularly useful if you are planning to send out a number of standard letters as the names and addresses can be merged with the standard letter at the time of printing (mail merge). Finally, one further folder you may wish to keep is one in which you can store instructions for using the library catalogue, e-resources and software packages. This is also a good place to keep information on library opening times, health and safety requirements in laboratories and maps of locations you may have to visit.

2.6.3 Networking

In this context, networking simply means setting up and maintaining links with individuals in business and academic life during the course of your research. We have already discussed the importance of negotiating access and the courtesies required. Remember that all the contacts you make may be useful at some future date. Research is not a simple linear process of moving from one stage to the next, but often involves retracing your steps. The contacts you have made and maintained will assist you to do this.

There is nothing worse when you are writing up your research to find that you have not collected an essential statistic from a company or one of your interviews is incomplete. If you wrote to the individuals who have helped you along the way, thanking them for their assistance, it is easier to go back to them for the missing data. Similarly, if you have sent them any reports or articles resulting from your research, you are more likely to be successful if you approach them at a later date with a request to conduct further research.

It is also important to establish and maintain links with academic colleagues in your own and other institutions. These may be people interested in the same or a similar area of research, you meet on campus, on courses or at conferences with whom you can exchange articles and talk about your ideas and problems. You may also be able to exchange early drafts of your dissertation or thesis for mutual comment and criticism.

2.7 Funding the research

Research is not a cost-free activity and it is important to consider the funding implications when planning your research. Even if you were to conduct all your research in your college or university library, you would incur minor expenses such as photocopying and printing. If you visit other libraries and institutions, you will incur more travelling costs. If you are conducting interviews as part of your research, you will need to cover the cost of travel and subsistence. If you are using a postal questionnaire, you may need to pay for paper, printing and postage. Of course, this does not take account of your time, which in most cases is non-chargeable. Unfortunately, research funds are difficult to obtain and you need to have a contingency plan if funding is essential to your project. There is a wide range of potential sources of funding and you should allow plenty of time for writing funding proposals: deadlines for applications are often tight and there is considerable competition for funds. You may wish to consider some of the sources we discuss next.

2.7.1 University funding

Some universities offer bursaries and grants to students from which you can fund any expenses you incur while conducting your research. Alternatively, you may be able to help on an existing large research project and in return receive a salary and/or have your expenses for your own project reimbursed. You may be able to use the part of the project you are working on as the basis for your dissertation or thesis. However, there are some drawbacks to this sort of arrangement, as you will have to demonstrate that the research you submit for your degree is your own work and not that of the group. In addition, you may find the demands of the work you are doing for the group supplant your own needs to complete your dissertation or thesis. Sometimes the arrangement also includes some teaching, but if you can agree suitable terms, you not only benefit from the financial rewards and access to data, but also from working with more experienced researchers.

Your university or college should also be able to direct you to potential sources of funding from national governments and the EU. However, you should bear in mind that obtaining them is very competitive. Moreover, writing a successful proposal is difficult for an inexperienced researcher and you will need help from your supervisor(s).

Vox pop What has been the highpoint in your research so far?

Lee, first year PhD student investigating foreign direct investment in international business

The best moment was after I was interviewed for a graduate teaching position and knew I'd got the funding for my PhD. Before the interview I was thinking they'd never accept me, but I really enjoyed the interview. We [the applicants] had to give a presentation on why we deserved to be funded and I decided not to mention money at all. Instead I told them about what I did for my Master's dissertation and my ambition to be an academic. I feel I've really got a vocation to teach.

2.7.2 Commercial sources of funding

If you have a job or your degree programme includes an industrial placement, you have the opportunity to design a work-based study and your employer may be willing to reimburse any expenses you incur. Even at doctoral level, it may be possible to persuade a present or potential employer to cover your costs if you can demonstrate that your research will be useful to the business as well as contributing to your degree. Receiving funding from commercial sources has a number of disadvantages. Sponsors are more interested in solving their own problems than the academic requirements of your programme and you may find you are expected to conduct two parallel studies with a business report for your employer or commercial sponsor in addition to your dissertation or thesis. Therefore, you should weigh up very carefully the benefits of covering your research costs against the additional pressure this extra work will give you.

If you do not have the benefit of an interested employer, you may be able to find a business sponsor to help fund your research. You may be lucky to have contact with an individual who wants the research done because he or she is particularly interested in the topic (for example a relation or a family friend) or because he or she is conducting a larger project and is willing to meet the costs of your research if it feeds into the larger study (for example your supervisor). If you obtain funding from such a source, you must check the ownership of the data you generate and your independence.

2.7.3 Funding from professional bodies

Many of the professional bodies associated with business and management (for example the professional institutions that represent accountancy, banking, human resource management, marketing and purchasing) offer funding for research. Competition is keen and your proposed research needs to be carefully designed and relevant to the current research interests of the professional body to which you are applying. You may find it useful to include the name(s) of your supervisor(s) in the proposal, especially if that person is a member of the potential sponsoring body.

2.7.4 Funding from the charity sector

Substantial funding is available from some charities and associations, although strict criteria often have to be met. Modest amounts to cover limited expenses such as travelling, postage and printing are less difficult to obtain.

2.8 Conclusions

This chapter has been about preparing yourself to do research. We have given advice on critical issues, such as sources of finance, and also explained more academic issues such as generating a research topic and the skills and experiences you require at different stages of a project. It is important you appreciate that research is more than an investigation; it is also an activity that calls for efficient project management if it is to be successful.

We have also emphasized the importance of setting a timetable. Once you commence your investigations you do not want to be slowed down because you have not been able to organize yourself properly. Efficient organization also means that you are more likely to stick to the schedule you have set. In research you are frequently working to deadlines. If you miss the critical deadlines you may not get a second chance.

Unfortunately, many students ignore questions of ethics, anonymity and confidentiality until they are confronted with them. These considerations are becoming increasingly important and you may find that your research proposal has to be approved by a university ethics committee before you can proceed. The success of the project will be determined by how well you establish the foundations that we have described in this chapter.

References

Bell, E. and Bryman, A. (2007) 'The ethics of management research: An exploratory content analysis', *British Journal of Management,* 18(1), pp. 63–77.

Calabretta, G. Durisin, B. and Ogliengo, M. (2011) 'Uncovering the intellectual structure of research in business ethics: A journey through the history, the classics, and the pillars of Journal of Business Ethics', *Journal of Business Ethics,* 104(4), pp. 499–524.

Daly, R. (2002) *The Missenden Code of Practice for Ethics and Accountability – The Commercialisation of Research in Universities: An Ethical Intervention.* Great Missenden: The Missenden Centre for the Development of Higher Education.

De George, R. T. (1987) 'The status of business ethics: Past and future', *Business and Society,* 38(3), pp. 268–96.

Easterby-Smith, M., Thorpe, R. and Jackson, P. (2012) *Management Research*, 4th edn. London: SAGE.
Foucault, M. (1985) *The Use of Pleasure: History of Sexuality*, Vol. 2. New York: Vintage Books.
Howard, K. and Sharp, J. A. (1994) *The Management of a Student Research Project*. Aldershot: Gower.
Hussey, R. (2007) 'The application of personal construct theory in international accounting research,' *Journal of Theoretical Accounting Research*, 2(2), pp. 34–51.
Kervin, J. B. (1992) *Methods for Business Research*. New York: HarperCollins.
Ma, Z. (2009) 'The status of contemporary business ethics research: Present and future', *Journal of Business Ethics*, 90, pp. 255–65.
Sandberg, J. and Alvesson, M. (2011a) 'Generating research questions through problematization', *Academy of Management Review*, 36(2) pp. 247–71.
Sandberg, J. and Alvesson, M. (2011b) 'Ways of constructing research questions: Gap-spotting or problematization?' *Organization*, 18(23–4), pp. 1–22.
Saunders, M., Lewis, P. and Thornhill, A. (2009) *Research Methods for Business Students*, 5th edn. Harlow: Pearson Education.
Sekaran, U. (2003) *Research Methods for Business*, 4th edn. New York: John Wiley.

Activities

1. Generate a mind map that explores the funding implications of your research and how you can overcome any problems. Discuss your mind map with other students, your lecturers or potential supervisor to evaluate how realistic your assumptions are and to share solutions.
2. Use any two of the techniques described in this chapter to generate a research topic. Discuss the nature of the topic you have generated with other students and whether it would make a feasible research project.
3. In pairs, act out a situation where one of you takes the role of someone seeking access to an organization to conduct research and the other is the senior manager who has the power to grant your request. If possible, record or video the interview and analyse the process.
4. You are conducting research in a charity that saves the lives of many children. The organization has an excellent reputation and receives substantial government funding. During the course of your research you discover that irregular payments have been made to people outside the organization. The financial controller explains that if the charity did not make these payments, their workers would not get access to certain parts of the world where law and order has broken down. Moreover, if the charity workers did not get this access, children would die. How do you deal with this ethical problem?
5. Draft a section for your CV that describes the ways in which your research will provide transferrable skills and knowledge that will enhance your employability.

Now try the progress test for this chapter at www.palgrave.com/business/collis/br4/

Have a look at the **Troubleshooting** chapter and sections 14.2, 14.3, 14.4, 14.7 in particular, which relate specifically to this chapter.

3

identifying your paradigm

learning objectives

When you have studied this chapter, you should be able to:

- describe the main features of positivism
- describe the main features of interpretivism
- compare the assumptions of these two main paradigms
- discuss the strengths and weaknesses of pragmatism
- identify your research paradigm.

3.1 Introduction

Now you have begun to understand the nature of research and we have dealt with some of the practical issues, it is time to look at the philosophical issues that underpin research. This chapter introduces a number of new terms that will help you to extend your knowledge of how research is conducted. We introduce the ideas in a way that allows you to develop your knowledge incrementally and you will soon be using your extended vocabulary with confidence. Your new understanding will provide a valuable framework for expressing your ideas about your proposed research when you talk to your supervisor and other researchers, and will also help you absorb information from any preliminary reading you are doing.

If you are an undergraduate or on a taught Master's programme, you will probably face two major constraints when doing your research. The first is the relatively short period of time you have in which to conduct your research and the second is the size constraint (typically around 10,000 words on an undergraduate programme and 15,000 words on a taught Master's programme). Therefore, you may not need to explore the philosophical issues in this chapter in any great depth. Nevertheless, it is important that you are aware of the assumptions you are making when conducting your research.

If you are doing a Master's degree by research or you are a doctoral student, you need greater understanding of research philosophies and should use the references in this chapter as a guide to further reading. Indeed, at the doctoral level, you may find that a significant part of your thesis is concerned in establishing the appropriateness and credibility of the assumptions you have made.

3.2 The two main paradigms

A research **paradigm** is a philosophical framework that guides how scientific research should be conducted. Philosophy is 'a set or system of beliefs [stemming from] the study of the fundamental nature of knowledge, reality, and existence' (Waite and Hawker, 2009, p. 685). Ideas about reality and the nature of knowledge have changed over time (for example, people used to believe that the world is flat and that the sun goes around the earth). Therefore, it is not surprising that over time new research paradigms have emerged in response to the perceived inadequacies of earlier paradigms. This is captured in Kuhn's definition: 'Paradigms are universally recognized scientific achievements that for a time provide model problems and solutions to a community of practitioners' (Kuhn, 1962, p. viii).

For many hundreds of years there was only one research paradigm because the 'scientific achievements' referred to by Kuhn (1962) stemmed from one source. Today we refer to that source as the *natural sciences* to distinguish them from the *social sciences*. The emergence of the social sciences led to the development of a second research paradigm.

According to Smith (1983), until the late 19th century, research had focused on inanimate objects in the physical world, such as physics, which focuses on the properties of matter and energy and the interaction between them. The systematic methods used by these scientists, involved observation and experiment, and they applied inductive logic to discover explanatory theories that could be used for prediction. Their beliefs about the world and the nature of knowledge were based on **positivism**, which has its roots in the philosophy known as realism. Posi-

A research **paradigm** is a framework that guides how research should be conducted, based on people's philosophies and their assumptions about the world and the nature of knowledge.

Positivism is a paradigm that originated in the natural sciences. It rests on the assumption that social reality is singular and objective, and is not affected by the act of investigating it. The research involves a deductive process with a view to providing explanatory theories to understand social phenomena.

Interpretivism is a paradigm that emerged in response to criticisms of positivism. It rests on the assumption that social reality is in our minds, and is subjective and multiple. Therefore, social reality is affected by the act of investigating it. The research involves an inductive process with a view to providing interpretive understanding of social phenomena within a particular context.

tivism was developed by theorists such as Comte (1798–1857), Mill (1806–1873) and Durkheim (1859–1917).

With the advent of industrialization and capitalism, researchers began to turn their attention to social phenomena. A phenomenon (plural phenomena) is an observed or apparent object, fact or occurrence. Initially, the new social scientists used the methods established by the natural scientists, but the suitability of the traditional scientific methods was challenged by a number of theorists, which led to a debate that lasted many decades (Smith, 1983). The alternative to positivism can be loosely labelled as **interpretivism**,[1] which is based on the principles of idealism, a philosophy associated with Kant (1724–1804) and subsequently developed by Dilthey (1833–1911), Rickert (1863–1936) and Weber (1864–1920).

3.2.1 Positivism

As you can see from the historical developments outlined above, positivism provided the framework for the way research was conducted in the natural sciences and the scientific methods are still widely used in social science research today. Positivism is underpinned by the belief that reality is independent of us and the goal is the discovery of theories, based on empirical research (observation and experiment). Knowledge is derived from 'positive information' because it can be scientifically verified. In other words, it is possible to provide logical or mathematical proof for every rationally justifiable assertion (Walliman, 2011). Today, researchers conducting business research under a paradigm that stems from positivism still focus on theories to explain and/or predict social phenomena. They still apply logical reasoning so that precision, objectivity and rigour underpin their approach, rather than subjectivity and intuitive interpretation. Because positivists believe reality is independent of us, they assume the act of investigating social reality has no effect on that reality (Creswell, 2014).

Under positivism, theories provide the basis of explanation, permit the anticipation of phenomena, predict their occurrence and therefore allow them to be controlled. Explanation consists of establishing causal relationships between the variables by establishing causal laws and linking them to a deductive or integrated theory. Thus, social and natural worlds are both regarded as being bound by certain fixed laws in a sequence of cause and effect. You will remember from Chapter 1 that a variable is an attribute of a phenomenon that can change and take different values, which are capable of being observed and/or measured; and a theory is a set of interrelated variables, definitions and propositions that specifies relationships among the variables. Since it is assumed that social phenomena can be measured, positivism is associated with quantitative methods of analysis based on the statistical analysis of **quantitative research data**.

Quantitative data are data in a numerical form.

3.2.2 Interpretivism

Since interpretivism developed as a result of the perceived inadequacy of positivism to meet the needs of social scientists, it is important to understand the main criticisms of positivism. Box 3.1 sets out the main arguments.

1 Some authors refer to phenomenology (as we did in earlier editions of this book), but we have decided to use interpretivism as it suggests a broader philosophical perspective.

Box 3.1 Main criticisms of positivism

- It is impossible to separate people from the social contexts in which they exist.
- People cannot be understood without examining the perceptions they have of their own activities.
- A highly structured research design imposes constraints on the results and may ignore other relevant findings.
- Researchers are not objective, but part of what they observe. They bring their own interests and values to the research.
- Capturing complex phenomena in a single measure is misleading (for example, it is not possible to capture a person's intelligence by assigning numerical values).

Interpretivism is underpinned by the belief that social reality is not objective but highly subjective because it is shaped by our perceptions. The researcher interacts with that being researched because it is impossible to separate what exists in the social world from what is in the researcher's mind (Smith, 1983; Creswell, 2014). Therefore, the act of investigating social reality has an effect on it. Whereas positivism focuses on measuring social phenomena, interpretivism focuses on exploring the complexity of social phenomena with a view to gaining interpretive understanding. Therefore, rather than adopt the quantitative methods used by positivists, interpretivists adopt a range of methods that 'seek to describe, translate and otherwise come to terms with the meaning, not the frequency of certain more or less naturally occurring phenomena in the social world' (Van Maanen, 1983, p. 9). These important differences lead to a very broad conclusion that interpretive research is any type of research where the findings are not derived from the statistical analysis of quantitative data (Corbin and Strauss, 2008). Instead, the findings are derived from qualitative methods of analysis, which are based on the interpretation of **qualitative research data**.

Qualitative data are data in a nominal (named) form.

3.2.3 Approaches within the two main paradigms

Just as realism gave way to positivism and idealism gave way to what we are loosely referring to as interpretivism, many new paradigms have emerged over the years and few researchers now adopt the pure forms of the main paradigms. New paradigms are distinguished by differences in the philosophical assumptions on which they rest. You may find it helpful to think of positivism and interpretivism as the extremities of a continuous line of paradigms that can exist simultaneously, as illustrated in Figure 3.1. As you move along the continuum, the features and assumptions of one paradigm are gradually relaxed and replaced by those of the next (Morgan and Smircich, 1980).

Figure 3.1 A continuum of paradigms

In addition to reading about different paradigms that were developed towards the end of the 19th century and beyond (for example hermeneutics, phenomenology, existentialism, critical rationalism, linguistics, conventionalism), you may also come across a number of terms that describe different approaches with the main paradigms. You will find the term 'paradigm' is used somewhat inconsistently in the literature because it has different meanings for different people in different disciplines, in different parts of the world and over different periods of time. For example, Mingers (2001) points out that the version of paradigms described by Kuhn (1970) is less restrictive than that described by Burrell and Morgan (1979). To help clarify the uncertainties, Morgan (1979) suggests paradigm can be used at three different levels:

- at the philosophical level, where the term is used to reflect basic beliefs about the world
- at the social level, where the term is used to provide guidelines about how the researcher should conduct his or her endeavours
- at the technical level, where the term is used to specify the methods and techniques that ideally should be adopted when conducting research.

Table 3.1 shows some of the more common terms used to describe approaches within the two main paradigms. You should be aware that the terms under a particular category are not necessarily interchangeable, as they were coined by researchers wishing to distinguish their approach from others. In some cases, the term is being used at the social level (for example a subjectivist approach) or at the technical level where it refers to a particular method for collecting and/or analysing data (for example a qualitative approach). At the undergraduate level, these nuances may not be important, but a postgraduate researcher may be required to argue the appropriateness of the paradigm and the terms he or she is using.

Table 3.1 Approaches within the two main paradigms

Positivism	Interpretivism
Quantitative	Qualitative
Objective	Subjective
Scientific	Humanist
Traditionalist	Phenomenological

3.3 Assumptions of positivism and interpretivism

Before you can design your research project, you must consider the philosophical assumptions that underpin positivism and interpretivism so that you can determine whether your orientation at this stage is broadly positivist or broadly interpretivist. This may change as you progress with your studies. Drawing on Creswell (1994) and other authors, we provide a summary of the assumptions of the two main paradigms in Table 3.2. Remember, we are describing the assumptions that underpin the pure forms of the main paradigms.

Table 3.2 Assumptions of the two main paradigms

Philosophical assumption	Positivism	Interpretivism
Ontological assumption (the nature of reality)	Social reality is objective and external to the researcher.	Social reality is subjective and socially constructed.
	There is only one reality.	There are multiple realities.
Epistemological assumption (what constitutes valid knowledge)	Knowledge comes from objective evidence about observable and measurable phenomena.	Knowledge comes from subjective evidence from participants.
	The researcher is distant from phenomena under study.	The researcher interacts with phenomena under study.

Philosophical assumption	Positivism	Interpretivism
Axiological assumption (the role of values)	The researcher is independent from phenomena under study.	The researcher acknowledges that the research is subjective.
	The results are unbiased and value-free.	The findings are biased and value-laden.
Rhetorical assumption (the language of research)	The researcher uses the passive voice, accepted quantitative words and set definitions.	The researcher uses the personal voice, accepted qualitative terms and limited a priori definitions.
Methodological assumption (the process of research)	The researcher takes a deductive approach.	The researcher takes an inductive approach.
	The researcher studies cause and effect, and uses a static design where categories are identified in advance.	The researcher studies the topic within its context and uses an emerging design where categories are identified during the process.
	Generalizations lead to prediction, explanation and understanding.	Patterns and/or theories are developed for understanding.
	Results are accurate and reliable through validity and reliability.	Findings are accurate and reliable through verification.

If you are still developing your understanding of research, you will probably find this quite difficult. To help you with your analysis, we will provide some explanations of the terms used in the table. The first three assumptions are interrelated and if you accept one of them within a particular paradigm, you will find the other two assumptions for that paradigm are complementary.

3.3.1 Ontological assumption

The ontological assumption is concerned with the nature of reality:

- Positivists believe social reality is objective and external to the researcher. Therefore, there is only one reality and everyone has the same sense of reality.
- Interpretivists believe that social reality is subjective because it is socially constructed. Therefore, each person has his or her own sense of reality and there are multiple realities. This notion of reality as a projection of our imagination is captured by Mercier (2009, p. 214): 'Life is not what we live; it is what we imagine we are living.'

3.3.2 Epistemological assumption

The epistemological assumption is concerned with what we accept as valid knowledge. This involves an examination of the relationship between the researcher and that which is researched:

- Positivists believe that only phenomena that are observable and measurable can be validly regarded as knowledge. They try to maintain an independent and objective stance.
- On the other hand, interpretivists attempt to minimize the distance between the researcher and that which is researched. They may be involved in different forms of participative inquiry. This polarity between the two approaches has been captured by Smith (1983, pp. 10–11), who argues that 'in quantitative research facts act to constrain our beliefs; while in interpretivist research beliefs determine what should count as facts'.

3.3.3 Axiological assumption

The axiological assumption is concerned with the role of values:

- Positivists believe that the process of research is value-free. Therefore, positivists consider that they are detached and independent from what they are researching and regard the phenomena under investigation as objects. Positivists are interested in the interrelationship of the objects they are studying and believe that these objects were present before they took an interest in them. Furthermore, positivists believe that the objects they are studying are unaffected by their research activities and will still be present after the study has been completed. These assumptions are commonly found in research studies in the natural sciences, but they are less convincing in the social sciences, which are concerned with the activities and behaviour of people. Various studies have shown that the process of inquiry can influence both researchers and those participating in the research.
- In contrast, interpretivists consider that researchers have values, even if they have not been made explicit. These values help to determine what are recognized as facts and the interpretations drawn from them. Most interpretivists believe that the researcher is involved with that which is being researched.

3.3.4 Rhetorical assumption

We now move on to the rhetorical assumption, which is concerned with the language of research. This is particularly important when you write your research proposal and your final dissertation or thesis. These documents should be complementary to your paradigm, but they must also be written in a style that is acceptable to your supervisors and examiners.

- In a positivist study, it is usual to write in a formal style using the passive voice. For example, instead of writing, 'As part of my research, I observed a group of employees …' in your dissertation or thesis you will write, 'As part of the research, observations were made of a group of employees …' This is because you should try to convey the impression that your research was objective, that you followed rigorous procedures and any personal opinions and values you possess were not allowed to distort the results. You will use the future tense in your proposal. For example, 'Observations of a group of employees will be made'. There are some cultural differences and you will find that the passive voice has been the more traditional style of writing in the UK, whereas positivist researchers in Europe and North America tend to favour the personal voice.
- The position is less clear in an interpretivist study. In many disciplines, the preferred style reflects the immediacy of the research and the researcher's involvement. If that is the case in your discipline, you would write in the first person. We advise that you review the literature in your discipline and then find out what is acceptable to your supervisor. Irrespective of your paradigm, remember to use the future tense in your project proposal and the present or past tense in your dissertation or thesis.

3.3.5 Methodological assumption

The methodological assumption is concerned with the process of the research:

- If you are a positivist, you are likely to be concerned with ensuring that any concepts you use can be operationalized; that is, described in such a way that they can be measured. Perhaps you are investigating a topic that includes the concept of intelligence, and you want to find a way of measuring a particular aspect of intelligence. You will probably use a large sample (see section 3.4.1) and reduce the phenomena you examine to their simplest parts. You will focus on what you regard are objective facts and formulate hypotheses. Your analysis will look for association between variables and/or causality (one variable affecting another).

- If you are an interpretivist, you will be examining a small sample, possibly over a period of time. You will use a number of research methods to obtain different perceptions of the phenomena and in your analysis you will be seeking to understand what is happening in a situation and looking for patterns which may be repeated in other similar situations.

3.3.6 A continuum of paradigms

Morgan and Smircich (1980, p. 492) offer 'a rough typology for thinking about the various views that different social scientists hold'. Table 3.3 illustrates two of the core assumptions and the associated research methods for the six categories they identify.

Table 3.3 Typology of assumptions on a continuum of paradigms

	Positivism ◄					► Interpretivism
Ontological assumption	Reality as a concrete structure	Reality as a concrete process	Reality as a contextual field of information	Reality as a realm of symbolic discourse	Reality as a social construction	Reality as a projection of human imagination
Epistemological stance	To construct a positivist science	To construct systems, process, change	To map contexts	To understand patterns of symbolic discourse	To understand how social reality is created	To obtain phenomeno-logical insight, revelation
Research methods	Experiments, surveys	Historical analysis	Interpretive contextual analysis	Symbolic analysis	Hermeneutics	Exploration of pure subjectivity

Source: Based on Morgan and Smircich (1980, p. 492).

Starting at the extreme positivist end of the continuum (which Morgan and Smircich refer to as the objectivist end), there are those who assume that the social world is the same as the physical world. Their ontological assumption is that reality is an external, concrete structure which affects everyone. As the social world is external and real, the researcher can attempt to measure and analyse it using research methods such as laboratory experiments and surveys.

At the second stage of the continuum, reality is regarded as a concrete process where 'the world is in part what one makes of it' (Morgan and Smircich, 1980, p. 492). The third stage is where reality is derived from the transmission of information that leads to an ever-changing form and activity. At the fourth stage, 'the social world is a pattern of symbolic relationships and meanings sustained through a process of human action and interaction' (Morgan and Smircich, 1980, p. 494). At the fifth stage, individuals through language, actions and routines create the social world. At the sixth, and extreme interpretivist end of the continuum (which Morgan and Smircich refer to as the subjectivist end), reality is seen as a projection of human imagination. Under this assumption, there may be no social world apart from that which is inside the individual's mind.

Vox pop

What has been the biggest challenge in your research so far?

What has been the highpoint of your research so far?

Raymond, second year PhD student investigating organizational change from a discursive perspective

My relationship with my supervisor. His view is that there's only one way to do research and even my postmodernist approach has to follow what seems to me to be his positivist formula. My formula is to build theory, and it's very hard working in isolation, completely on my own.

Giving a seminar on the ideas behind my research to other PhD students and getting a lot of support.

3.4 Comparing positivism and interpretivism

So far we have tended to focus on the differences between the two main paradigms, but some argue that this is a false dichotomy. 'Even though there is a substantial rift between the two paradigms, there are many more similarities than there are differences' (Onwuegbuzie and Leech, 2005, p. 271). For example, both paradigms:

- use research questions to drive the research
- use various methods to collect quantitative and/or qualitative research data
- use various methods to summarize or otherwise reduce the research data
- apply techniques to analyse the data
- discuss the results or findings
- draw conclusions.

The particular paradigm you adopt for your research will be partly determined by your assumptions, but it will be influenced by the dominant paradigm in your research area and the nature of the research problem you are investigating. It is important to remember that one paradigm is not 'right' and the other 'wrong', but you may find that a particular paradigm is more acceptable to your supervisors, examiners or the editors of journals in which you wish to publish your research. It may not be clear as to why they favour a particular paradigm, as in some cases they are merely following a tradition in the discipline.

To help you discuss your decision with your supervisor, Table 3.4 compares the main features of the two paradigms, which we have polarized in order to contrast them.

Table 3.4 Features of the two main paradigms

Positivism tends to:	Interpretivism tends to:
• Use large samples	• Use small samples
• Have an artificial location	• Have a natural location
• Be concerned with hypothesis testing	• Be concerned with generating theories
• Produce precise, objective, quantitative data	• Produce 'rich', subjective, qualitative data
• Produce results with high reliability but low validity	• Produce findings with low reliability but high validity
• Allow results to be generalized from the sample to the population	• Allow findings to be generalized from one setting to another similar setting

As we have already suggested, it is helpful to think of the two main paradigms as being at opposite ends of a continuum. Regardless of which paradigm you employ, it is important to pay attention to all its features and ensure there are no contradictions or deficiencies in the way you design your research. The table introduces some new terms and concepts, which we will now discuss.

3.4.1 Sample size

A **sample** is a subset of a population.

A **random sample** is an unbiased subset of the population that is representative of the population because every member had an equal chance of being selected.

A **population** is a precisely defined body of people or objects under consideration for statistical purposes.

A **sample** is a subset of a population. In a positivist study, the sample is chosen to be representative of the population from which it is drawn. Therefore, care is taken to ensure that the sample is unbiased in the way it represents the phenomena under study (a **random sample**, for instance). A **population** is any precisely defined body of people or objects under consideration for statistical purposes. Examples of a set of people in a business research project might be the working population of a particular country; all skilled people in a particular industry; all workers of a certain grade in a particular business, or all trainees in a particular department of that business. A collection of items might be all green saloon cars registered in a particular year in a particular region, or one day's production of medium-sliced wholemeal bread at a particular factory.

Sample size is related to the size of the population under consideration. There is no need to select a sample if it is feasible to study the entire population. In Chapter 10, we describe the methods for selecting a representative sample and the minimum size that allows positivist researchers to generalize the results from the sample to the population. This is not an issue for interpretivists because their goal is to gain rich and detailed insights of the complexity of social phenomena. Therefore, they can conduct their research with a sample of one.

3.4.2 Location

Location refers to the setting in which the research is conducted. For example, a positivist might design an experiment in a laboratory where it is possible to isolate and control the variables being investigated. It would be important to investigate the research problems in an artificial setting if you were investigating the effect of lack of sleep on drivers or the effect of alcohol on drivers or shift workers, as it would not be safe to do it in the workplace. However, most positivist research in the social sciences today is based on secondary data (published data) or in natural locations (for example the workplace). Some researchers refer to this as *field research*, a term that illustrates the longevity of the link with the methods of the natural scientists. An example of field research is a study that evaluates the impact of a new training scheme on the productivity levels in a factory. One of the challenges of conducting research in a natural setting is deciding how to control for the influence of other variables, such as noise and temperature levels or the activities of other employees.

3.4.3 Theories and hypotheses

A **theory** is a set of interrelated variables, definitions and propositions that specifies relationships among the variables.

A **variable** is a characteristic of a phenomenon that can be observed or measured.

The normal process under a positivist paradigm is to study the literature to identify an appropriate **theory** (sometimes referred to as a theoretical model) and then construct a **hypothesis**. A hypothesis is an idea or proposition that is developed from the theory, which you can test for against **empirical evidence** using statistics. For example, contingency theory (Fiedler, 1964) contends that that there is no 'best' way to manage an organization because effective management is contingent on the fit between the organization and its environment, and the fit between the organization's subsystems. It is also contingent on the appropriateness of

A **hypothesis** is a proposition that can be tested for association or causality against empirical evidence.

Empirical evidence is data based on observation or experience.

the management style to the nature of the work group and their tasks. Just taking one of these factors, you might decide to test the hypothesis that there is a relationship between effective management (the dependent variable) and the amount of information the manager has about the tasks undertaken by subordinates (the independent variable). You would have to decide how to measure the two variables first and then collect the data and use a statistical test for association.

Under an interpretivist paradigm, you may not wish to be restricted by existing theories or there may be no existing theory. Therefore, you may carry out your investigation to describe different patterns that you perceive in the data or to construct a new theory to explain the phenomenon. If the research was an exploratory study, the findings could be used to develop hypotheses that are tested in a subsequent main study.

3.4.4 Quantitative and qualitative data

In contrast to a number of researchers, we prefer to reserve the use of the terms *quantitative* and *qualitative* to describe data rather than paradigms. This is because the data collected in a positivist study can be quantitative (that is, data in a numerical form) and/or qualitative (that is, data in a nominal form such as words, images and so on).

In a positivist study, it is likely that the purpose of collecting qualitative data is to ensure that all key variables have been identified or to collect information that will be quantified prior to statistical analysis. This contrasts with a study designed under an interpretivist paradigm, where there is no intention of analysing data statistically and therefore no desire to quantify qualitative research data. Some researchers blend the qualitative and quantitative data to such an extent that it is difficult to determine which paradigm is being used. We advise students to be wary of doing this, as it may not be acceptable to your supervisors and examiners.

If you adopt a positivist paradigm, it is essential that your research data are highly specific and precise. Because measurement is an essential element of the research process under this paradigm, you must apply considerable rigour to ensure the accuracy of the measurement. Under an interpretivist paradigm, the emphasis is on the quality and depth of the data collected about a phenomenon. Therefore, the qualitative data collected by interpretivists tend to be rich in detail and nuance (that is, levels of meaning).

Bonoma (1985) argues that all researchers desire high levels of data integrity and results currency. Data integrity describes characteristics of research that affect error and bias in the results, while results currency refers to the generalizability of results. Bonoma claims that positivist methods, such as laboratory experiments, are higher in data integrity than the methods used by interpretivists. However, methodologies used by interpretivists, such as case studies, tend to be high in results currency because they have contextual relevance across measures, methods, paradigms, settings and time. In any research project, there is likely to be a trade-off between data integrity and results currency. In other words, data integrity can only be achieved by sacrificing results currency.

3.4.5 Reliability

Reliability refers to the accuracy and precision of the measurement and absence of differences in the results if the research were repeated.

Reliability refers to the accuracy and precision of the measurement and the absence of differences if the research were repeated. Therefore it is one aspect of the credibility of the findings; the other is validity. You need to ask yourself whether the evidence and your conclusions will stand up to close scrutiny (Raimond, 1993, p. 55). For a research result to be reliable, a repeat study should produce the same result. For example, if you found that a group of workers who had attended a training course doubled their previous productivity levels, your result would be reliable if another researcher replicated your study and obtained the same results. Replication is very important in positivist studies.

Whereas reliability tends to be high in positivist studies, under an interpretivist paradigm, reliability is often of little importance or may be interpreted in a different way. The qualitative measures do not need to be reliable in the positivist sense. However, importance is placed on whether observations and interpretations made on different occasions and/or by different observers can be explained and understood. As interpretivists believe that the activities of the researcher influence the research, replication, in the positivist sense, would be difficult to achieve. Therefore, the emphasis is on establishing protocols and procedures that establish the authenticity of the findings.

It is often possible to design a research study where reliability is high, but validity, which we discuss in the next section, is low. For example, perhaps you are attempting to establish the criteria on which bank managers decide to grant overdrafts to customers. There are some very rational criteria, such as income levels, security of employment, past evidence of repayment and home ownership, and it is possible that repeated questionnaire surveys of bank managers would demonstrate that these are the important criteria. However, observation or in-depth interviews might establish other criteria that are equally important. These could be apparently less rational criteria, such as the bank manager not liking the look of the applicant or how he or she speaks.

3.4.6 Validity

Validity is the extent to which a test measures what the researcher wants it to measure and the results reflect the phenomena under study.

Validity refers to the extent to which a test measures what the researcher wants it to measure and the results reflect the phenomena under study. Research errors, such as faulty procedures, poor samples and inaccurate or misleading measurement, can undermine validity. For example, you may be interested in whether employees in a particular company understand their company's pension scheme. Therefore, you ask them to calculate their pension entitlements. However, you do not know whether their answers reflect their understanding of the scheme, whether they have read the scheme, how good they are at remembering the details of the scheme, or their ability to make calculations.

There are a number of different ways in which the validity of research can be assessed. The most common is *face validity*, which simply involves ensuring that the tests or measures used by the researcher do actually measure or represent what they are supposed to measure or represent. Another form of validity that is important in business research is *construct validity*. This relates to the problem that there are a number of phenomena that are not directly observable, such as motivation, satisfaction, ambition and anxiety. These are known as hypothetical constructs, which are assumed to exist as factors that explain observable phenomena. For example, you may be able to observe someone shaking and sweating before an interview. However, you are not actually observing anxiety, but a manifestation of anxiety.

With hypothetical constructs, you must be able to demonstrate that your observations and research findings can be explained by the construct. It would be easy to fall into the trap of claiming that employees achieve high levels of productivity because they love their work, when in fact they are working hard because they are anxious about the security of their jobs during a period of economic recession. We discuss the question of reliability and validity again in Chapter 10.

3.4.7 Generalizability

Generalizability is the extent to which the research findings (often based on a sample) can be extended to other cases (often a population) or to other settings.

Generalizability is the extent to which the research findings (often based on a sample) can be extended to other cases (often a population) or to other settings (Vogt and Burke Johnson, 2011). If you are following a positivist paradigm, you will have selected a sample and you will be interested in determining how confident you are in stating that the characteristics found in the sample will be present in the population from which you have drawn your sample (see Chapter 10).

However, Gummesson (2000) argues that using statistics to generalize from a sample to a population is just one type of generalization; interpretivists may be able to generalize their findings from one setting to a similar setting. He supports the view of Normann (1970) who contends that it is possible to generalize from a very few cases, or even a single case, if your analysis has captured the interactions and characteristics of the phenomena you are studying. Thus, you will be concerned with whether the patterns, concepts and theories that have been generated in a particular environment can be applied in other environments. To do this, you must have a comprehensive and deep understanding of the activities and behaviour you have been studying.

3.5 Pragmatism

We have emphasized that the two main paradigms represent the two extremes of what can be described as a continuum of paradigms and that paradigms are based on mutually exclusive philosophical assumptions about the world and the nature of knowledge. Most students will find their paradigm falls broadly within one of the two main paradigms. This is also true for experienced researchers, who may modify their philosophical assumptions over time and move to a new position on the continuum. Thus, the assumptions of the researcher's paradigm provide the philosophical framework that underpins the choice of methodology and methods in the majority of business and management research.

Pragmatism contends that the research question should determine the research philosophy and that methods from more than one paradigm can be used in the same study.

However, some argue that three research paradigms prevail in the social sciences: quantitative, qualitative and **pragmatism** (Onwuegbuzie and Leech, 2005, p. 270) and 'an effective researcher should be flexible enough to be able to work within the most appropriate paradigm given the nature of the research problem under investigation' (McKerchar, 2009, p. 6). Rather than be 'constrained' by a single paradigm, pragmatists advocate that researchers should be 'free' to mix methods from different paradigms, choosing them on the basis of usefulness for answering the research question(s). They suggest that by ignoring the philosophical debate about reality and the nature of knowledge, the weaknesses of one paradigm can be offset with the strengths of the other. This pluralist approach is an attempt to 'cross the divide between the quantitative and the qualitative and the positivist and the non-positivist' (Curran and Blackburn, 2001, p. 123).

Drawing on his interpretation of other writers, Creswell (2014) sets out seven strictures of pragmatism and compares them with his views of mixed methods research. We discuss three of the knowledge claims he extracts below.

- Pragmatism is not committed to any one system of philosophy and reality. This is certainly one of the main claims by pragmatists, but your supervisor and examiners may not be sympathetic to this view if they believe that without a commitment to one paradigm, there is no theoretical framework to support your methodology. Our advice is to consider the views of your supervisor (and your eventual examiners) very carefully before declaring yourself a pragmatist in your proposal. You may find that what you are trying to do is to mix methods from the same paradigm, rather than abandon your assumptions completely. This is known as triangulation and is discussed in Chapter 4.

- Individual researchers have freedom of choice. Although one is always sympathetic to claims of academic freedom, having a choice should not lead to an absence of rationality in your choice of research design and rigour in the application of your methods. If you are seeking a higher qualification or research publications, you will find that those who will evaluate your research may have strong opinions on what is good research. Certainly, you have a choice but you should know why you make a particular choice.
- Pragmatists believe we need to stop asking questions about reality and the laws of nature. A quick search of the literature will produce numerous articles that ask questions about reality, but few of them come up with satisfactory answers. Most students will need to demonstrate their understanding of the debate and be able to defend the position they adopt.

If you are thinking of adopting a pragmatic approach, we advise you to discuss it with your supervisor as soon as possible. You must be able to justify your stance if you are seeking a higher degree or considering publishing an article based on your research in an academic journal. At the undergraduate level, it is unlikely that you will be required to discuss your paradigm, as most supervisors will be focusing on your methodology and your ability to apply your methods and draw conclusions. They may expect you to analyse both qualitative and quantitative data; not because you have adopted any particular paradigm, but because they want to be certain you know how to handle both.

A **method** is a technique for collecting and/or analysing data.
A **methodology** is an approach to the process of the research, encompassing a body of methods.

In several parts of this chapter, we have used the terms **method** and **methodology** and this is a good point at which to distinguish between them. A method is a technique for collecting and/or analysing data. As a general term, methodology refers to the study of methods (for example, a student on a taught course might study research methodology). However, in the context of a specific study, it refers to the approach to the process of the research, encompassing a body of methods (for example the methodology chapter in a proposal, dissertation or thesis that describes and justifies the overall research strategy and methods). In some cases, a research strategy embodying a particular set of methods has become established through widespread use in particular disciplines (for example grounded theory, which we discuss in Chapter 9.)

3.6 Conclusions

We have introduced a number of concepts in this chapter that may be new to you. It is essential for you to understand your research paradigm, as this provides a framework for designing your study. The two main paradigms are positivism and what can be loosely referred to as interpretivism. In this chapter, we have examined how the core ontological, epistemological, axiological, rhetorical and methodological assumptions of the two main paradigms differ. Positivism and interpretivism lie at opposite ends of a continuum of paradigms with a range of other paradigms between them. Two key features that characterize research findings are reliability and validity. Reliability refers to being able to obtain the same results if the study were replicated. Reliability is likely to be higher in a positivist study than in a study designed under an interpretivist paradigm. Validity refers to the research findings accurately representing what is happening in the situation. Validity is likely to be higher in an interpretivist study than a positivist study.

If you are doing research at Master's or doctoral level, you will need to explain your paradigm and justify your methodology and methods. Methodological triangulation is where the research design includes complementary methods from within the same paradigm. It is essential that triangulation is an integral part of the design and not an attempt to rectify a poorly designed study and you are not advised to mix methods from opposing paradigms.

Once you have identified your paradigm, you can determine which methodology and methods will be appropriate. This will mean you have reached the research design stage and you will be in a position to develop your research proposal. If you are doing research at the undergraduate level, it is likely that you will not have to concern yourself too much with paradigms and will concentrate instead on managing the research process, collecting the data and analysing them. This is covered in subsequent chapters.

References

Bonoma, T. V. (1985) 'Case research in marketing: Opportunities, problems, and a process', *Journal of Marketing Research*, XXII, May, pp. 199–208.

Burrell, G. and Morgan, G. (1979) *Sociological Paradigms and Organisational Analysis*. London: Heinemann.

Corbin, J. and Strauss, A. (2008) *Basics of Qualitative Research: Techniques and procedures for developing grounded theory*, 3rd edn. Thousand Oaks, CA: SAGE.

Creswell, J. W. (1994) *Research Design: Qualitative and Quantitative Approaches*. Thousand Oaks, CA: SAGE.

Creswell, J. W. (2014) *Research Design*, 4th edn. Thousand Oaks, CA: SAGE.

Curran, J. and Blackburn, R. A. (2001) *Researching the Small Enterprise*. London: SAGE.

Fiedler, F. E. (1964) 'A contingency model of leadership effectiveness', *Advances in Experimental Social Psychology*, 1, pp. 149–90.

Gummesson, E. (2000) *Qualitative Methods in Management Research*, 2nd edn. Thousand Oaks, CA: SAGE.

Kuhn, T. S. (1962) *The Structure of Scientific Revolutions*. Chicago, IL: University of Chicago Press.

Kuhn, T. S. (1970) *The Structure of Scientific Revolutions*. Chicago, IL: Chicago University Press.

McKerchar, M. (2009) 'Philosophical Paradigms, Inquiry Strategies and Knowledge Claims: Applying the Principles of Research Design and Conduct to Taxation', *University of New South Wales Faculty of Law Research Series No. 31.*

Mercier, P. (2009) *Night Train to Lisbon*. London: Atlantic Books.

Mingers, J. (2001) 'Combining IS research methods: Towards a pluralist methodology', *Information Systems Research*, 12(3) pp. 240–59.

Morgan, G. (1979) 'Response to Mintzberg', *Administrative Science Quarterly*, 24(1), pp. 137–9.

Morgan, G. and Smircich, L. (1980) 'The case of qualitative research', *Academy of Management Review*, 5, pp. 491–500.

Normann, R. (1970) *A Personal Quest for Methodology*. Stockholm: Scandinavian Institute for Administrative Research.

Onwuegbuzie, A. J. and Leech, N. L. (2005) 'Taking the "Q" out of research: Teaching research methodology courses without the divide between quantitative and qualitative paradigms', *Quality and Quantity: International Journal of Methodology*, 39(3), 267–96.

Raimond, P. (1993) *Management Projects: Design, Research and Presentation*. London: Chapman & Hall.

Smith, J. K. (1983) 'Quantitative v qualitative research: An attempt to classify the issue', *Educational Research*, March, pp. 6–13.

Van Maanen, J. (1983) *Qualitative Methodology*. London: SAGE.

Vogt, W. P. and Burke Johnson, R. (2011) *Dictionary of Statistics & Methodology – A Nontechnical Guide for the Social Sciences*, 4th edn. Newbury Park, CA: SAGE.

Waite, M. and Hawker, S. (eds) (2009) *Oxford Paperback Dictionary and Thesaurus*. Oxford: Oxford University Press.

Walliman, N. (2011) *Your Research Project – Designing and Planning Your Work*, 3rd edn. London: SAGE.

Activities

1 You have a set of weighing scales that always register 5 kilos above your actual weight. Your friend has a set of scales that measures her weight accurately, but sometimes shows it as 7 kilos above or below her true weight. Explain how these occurrences can be regarded as issues of reliability and/or validity.

2 You are planning a research study that will investigate the feelings of the devoted fans of a local sports team in situations when it wins and when it loses. Compare the advantages and disadvantages of the two main paradigms for this purpose and decide which approach would give you the best understanding.

3 The marketing director of a company promoting health clubs asks you to assess the effectiveness of a recent advertising campaign they ran in a magazine. Compare the advantages and disadvantages of the two main paradigms for this purpose. Then decide whether the marketing director will expect a qualitative or quantitative analysis and which would be the easiest paradigm for you to adopt.

4 Thousands of years ago a Buddhist monk called Chuang Tzu wrote: 'I dreamt I was a butterfly, flitting around in the sky; then I awoke. Now I wonder, am I a man who dreamt he was a butterfly, or am I a butterfly dreaming I am a man?' Decide which of the five core assumptions associated with the main paradigm this addresses and how you would you answer Chuang Tzu's dilemma.

5 Paradigm quiz
Indicate whether you agree (tick the box) or disagree (put a cross in the box) with the following statements. There are no right or wrong answers and the exercise should not be taken too seriously!

a) Quantitative data are more scientific than qualitative data. ☐
b) It is important to state your hypotheses before collecting data. ☐
c) Surveys are probably the best way to investigate business issues. ☐
d) A phenomenon can be measured reliably unless it cannot be investigated. ☐
e) A good knowledge of statistics is essential for all approaches to business research. ☐
f) Case studies should only be used for exploratory research. ☐
g) Using participant observation to collect data is of little value in business research. ☐
h) Laboratory experiments should be used more widely in business research. ☐
i) It is impossible to generate theories from research into business issues. ☐
j) Researchers must remain objective and independent from the phenomena they study. ☐

Interpretation:
More ticks than crosses = positivist
More crosses than ticks = interpretivist
Equal number of each = undecided

Once you have finished, critically reflect on why this quiz might not be very effective in diagnosing your paradigm.

Check your understanding by completing the progress test online at www.palgrave.com/business/collis/br4/

Have a look at the Troubleshooting chapter and sections 14.2, 14.8, 14.10, 14.11, 14.12 in particular, which relate specifically to this chapter.

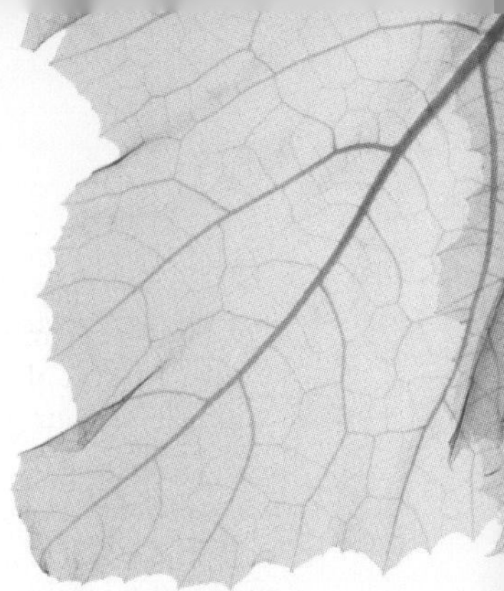

4

designing the research

learning objectives

When you have studied this chapter, you should be able to:

- describe the main methodologies associated with positivism
- describe the main methodologies associated with interpretivism
- compare the strengths and weaknesses of methodologies
- discuss the strengths and weaknesses of triangulation
- choose a methodology that reflects your paradigm.

4.1 Introduction

You will remember from Chapter 3 that a paradigm is more than just a philosophical framework; it also guides how research should be conducted. Therefore, once you have identified your research paradigm, you can take the first step in designing your research, which is to choose a methodology that reflects the philosophical assumptions of your paradigm.

This chapter offers a guide to some of the most widely used methodologies and the connection with the paradigm. We discuss the methodologies under the two main paradigms, positivism and interpretivism, but you should remember that some can be adapted for use under either paradigm. We start with an overview and then describe the methodologies traditionally associated with positivism. These have been developed to support a deductive process, where generalizations lead to prediction, explanation and understanding. We then examine the methodologies associated with interpretivism, which support an inductive process, where patterns and/or theories are developed to understand phenomena. In some studies, there may be scope to employ multiple methods and, therefore, we also discuss the advantages and disadvantages of triangulation.

4.2 Link between paradigm and methodology

A **methodology** is an approach to the process of the research, encompassing a body of methods.

A **method** is a technique for collecting and/or analysing data.

Primary data are data generated from an original source, such as your own experiments, surveys, interviews or focus groups.

Secondary data are data collected from an existing source, such as publications, databases and internal records.

You will remember from previous chapters that your research paradigm is a philosophical framework that guides how your research should be conducted. Therefore, your paradigm is closely linked to your research design, which refers to the choices you will make in terms of the **methodology** and methods that you will use to address your research question(s). There are a number of methodologies and a wide range of **methods** for collecting and analysing primary or secondary data and you need to adopt a cohesive approach to ensure that your research design meets the philosophical assumptions of your paradigm. **Primary data** are research data generated from an original source, such as your own experiments, questionnaire survey, interviews or focus groups, whereas **secondary data** are research data collected from an existing source, such as publications, databases or internal records, and may be available in hard copy form or on the Internet.

If you are designing a study under a positivist paradigm, you may not have to expend much energy in justifying your methodology and methods. This is because positivism still tends to dominate in many areas of business research, although the number of studies designed under an interpretivist paradigm is increasing. If you are designing a study under an interpretivist paradigm, you may find it necessary to provide a stronger rationale for your methodology and give a more detailed explanation of your methods to convince your supervisor and/or research committee that your study will be rigorous and methodical.

It is important to remember that the two main paradigms represent the two extremities on the continuum of paradigms (Morgan and Smircich, 1980) and that your paradigm and associated methodology and methods may represent a blending of some of the philosophical assumptions. Nevertheless, a coherent research strategy will ensure that the choices broadly reflect the core assumptions of one of the two main paradigms. If you are having trouble identifying your paradigm, you can take comfort from Creswell (2014), who suggests that the knowledge claims, strategies and methods used by the researcher determine the tendency of the research approach. He suggests:

- The issue or concern to be addressed needs to be considered fully and the research needs to be designed that best matches the problem.
- The researcher needs to consider his or her skills and experience, and assess which approach best complements these.
- The researcher needs to consider the audience to whom the findings from the research will be addressed.

Table 4.1 lists some of the main methodologies used in the social sciences, some of which are adaptable for use under either paradigm. This is not an exhaustive list and we advise you to examine others you come across when studying previous research on your chosen topic.

Table 4.1 Methodologies associated with the main paradigms

Positivism ◄	► Interpretivism
Experimental studies	Hermeneutics
Surveys (using primary or secondary data)	Ethnography
Cross-sectional studies	Participative inquiry
Longitudinal studies	Action research
	Case studies
	Grounded theory
	Feminist, gender and ethnicity studies

4.3 Methodologies associated with positivism

4.3.1 Experimental studies

An **experimental study** is a methodology used to investigate the relationship between variables, where the independent variable is deliberately manipulated to observe the effect on the dependent variable.

An **experimental study** is a methodology used to investigate the relationship between variables, where the independent variable (for example noise levels) is deliberately manipulated to observe the effect on the dependent variable (for example the productivity of factory workers). Experimental studies permit causal relationships to be identified. The experiment is conducted in a systematic way in a laboratory or a natural setting.

One of the advantages of conducting experiments in an artificial setting is that the researcher is better able to eliminate certain variables or keep some variables constant. This is necessary because one of the main challenges is to control confounding variables. These are variables that obscure the effect of another variable. For example, a subject's behaviour may alter merely as a result of being watched or because he or she is in an unfamiliar environment. Field experiments are conducted in a natural setting (for example a factory or an office). Although field experiments offer the advantage of that natural setting, you may not have such strong control over confounding and extraneous variables. For example, if your study involves an investigation of the relationship between productivity and motivation, you may find it difficult to exclude the effect on productivity of other factors such as a heatwave, a work-to-rule, a takeover or problems the worker may be experiencing at home.

If you choose to conduct an experimental study, the nature of the research problem and the access you have managed to negotiate are likely to play a significant role in determining the specific design. The main choices are as follows:

- In a *repeated-measures design*, the experiment is repeated under different conditions. For example, perhaps you are interested in assessing employees' performance in operating complicated machinery under noisy conditions. You could ask the employees (the subjects of the experiment) to operate the machinery when it was noisy and measure the time taken to perform a particular task and the number of errors. You might ask the same employees to conduct the same task under quiet conditions. If the results are not the same, and all other variables have been controlled, it would be reasonable to assume that the change in performance is due to the level of noise. One problem with this approach is that an employee's performance may be better on the second occasion because they have rehearsed the task by doing it the first time. On the other hand, they may perform less well the second time because they have become bored. These are examples of the *order effect* and the easiest of several solutions to this problem is to ensure there is sufficient time between experiments to remove any ordering effects.
- In an *independent-samples design*, two groups are selected. For example, one group of employees operates the machinery under noisy conditions and the other operates the same machinery under quiet conditions. This provides data from two independent samples, which can be compared. The major problem with this approach is that there may be other differences between the two samples, such as the age, experience and training of the employees. To avoid such inequalities, the employees can be allocated randomly to each group.
- A *matched-pairs design* is a more rigorous approach, which attempts to eliminate other differences between the two groups, by matching pairs of employees and allocating one to each group. Of course, there may be some difficulty in identifying which characteristics should be matched and ensuring that there are enough employees to obtain a sufficient number of matched pairs.
- A *single-subject design* is useful when only a few subjects are available, but this makes it difficult to make generalizations. However, despite this drawback, findings from such a study can be useful in providing knowledge about the phenomena under study in that particular context.

To select the most appropriate design, Kervin (1992) suggests you need to consider three main factors:

- Number of groups – You will compare two or more groups of cases, or look for variations within one group.
- Nature of the groups – It will be important to know how the group is formed, for example by using random allocation or matched cases.
- Timing of the experiments – In our earlier example of a repeated-measures design to measure the effect of noise levels on performance, the experiment was conducted twice only, but it could have been repeated several times on different occasions. However, this is not always possible and you may be limited to collecting evidence from the same groups at one point in time only.

Once you have decided on the type of experimental design, you need to determine the size of your sample. One criterion to use is what you intend to do with the data. Coolican (2009) argues that when the experimental independent variable can be assumed to have a similar effect on most people, the optimum sample size is about 25 to 30. Experimental studies in a laboratory or in a natural setting (field experiments) present specific challenges to the researcher. If you choose to conduct an experimental study, you will need to recognize the limitations of the methodology.

You need to bear in mind that it can be very difficult to arrange experiments in business research due to the difficulty in finding suitable subjects with the time to participate. Many laboratory experiments have been criticized because they use students as surrogates in an attempt to overcome this problem. Experiments also suffer from the criticism that they focus very narrowly on particular variables and are conducted in an artificial setting, thus failing on both counts to reflect the real world. Despite these drawbacks, Dobbins, Lane and Steiner (1988) argue that laboratory experiments are valuable and that even studies using students as subjects have validity. They recommend that the choice of research method should be based on the purpose of the research and the researcher's paradigm. In their view, laboratory experiments are useful for examining work behaviour at the individual level. It is also evident that some activities are best controlled in a laboratory (for example, it would not be a good idea to test the influence of alcohol by asking participants to drive on a public highway).

Others, such as Blumer (1980), argue that laboratory procedures are artificial and inconsistent with the epistemology implied by the interaction theory. Nevertheless, they can be used in an interpretivist study, but the relationship between the researcher and the participants will have a certain level of authoritarianism and the experiments do not give a faithful representation of social action in everyday life. Couch (1987) rejects many of these criticisms and claims that laboratory experiments can be used fruitfully in an interpretivist study, but that care must be taken with the research design. He recommends that the situation should be structured so that participants pay only minimal attention to the researcher. If possible, a mini-social world of short duration, but with a high level of authenticity, should be created in the laboratory. This may require an elaborate layout and the researcher to be involved in a particular role within the phenomenon being studied. The analysis of the data will be based on video recordings and transcriptions. 'The use of the laboratory and recording devices ... [does not] require acceptance of the ontology' (Couch, 1987, p. 166). The results of the field studies can then be compared with the results of laboratory studies so that 'grounded theories of social construct that have universal application can be constructed' (Couch, 1987, p. 175).

4.3.2 Surveys

A **survey** is a methodology designed to collect primary or secondary data from a sample, with a view to generalizing the results to a population.

A **sample** is a subset of a population.

A **population** is a precisely defined body of people or objects under consideration for statistical purposes.

An **archival study** is an empirical study using publicly available data.

In a positivist study, a **survey** methodology is used to collect primary or secondary data from a **sample**, with a view to analysing the data statistically and generalizing the results to a population. A **population** is a precisely defined body of people or objects under consideration for statistical purposes. If the population is large, it may be impractical or too expensive to collect information about every member. Therefore, a random sample is chosen to provide an unbiased subset of the population and statistical methods are used to test the likelihood that the characteristics of the sample are also found in the population. We will be looking at the various sampling methods in Chapter 10. If the population is small, it is possible to collect data about every member of the population and it is not necessary to select a sample. If you are planning to analyse secondary research data, we suggest you avoid using the term 'secondary research', as it is the data you are distinguishing as secondary while your analysis will produce original findings. Instead, it may be more appropriate to describe your methodology as an **archival study**, which is an empirical study using publicly available data.

Surveys can be divided into two types, according to their purpose:

- The purpose of a *descriptive survey* is to provide an accurate representation of phenomena at one point in time or at various times (for example a consumer survey to investigate customers' views on new products or services being developed by the business; an attitude survey to investigate the views of employees on a new productivity scheme).
- An *analytical survey* is conducted to determine whether there is a relationship between pairs of variables or multiple variables. If you wish to carry out this type of survey, you will need to develop a theoretical framework from the literature so that you can identify the dependent and independent variables in the relationship. This may sound a bit technical now, but we will be explaining this in subsequent chapters.

Traditionally, surveys are associated with a positivist methodology, but they can also be used under an interpretivist paradigm (for example in-depth interviews with women holding positions in senior management to investigate their views on gender equality in the workplace). If you are an interpretivist, selecting a sufficiently large and unbiased sample for the survey is not crucial, because the aim of the research is to gain insights from the cases in the sample rather than generalize from the sample to the population. Therefore, you could ask for volunteers to participate in the research, which would not be appropriate under a positivist paradigm.

There are several methods for collecting survey data for a positivist study, including postal and Internet self-completion questionnaires, and telephone and face-to-face interviews. A structured questionnaire will be used so that all participants are asked the same questions in the same order. We will compare these methods in Chapter 10.

4.3.3 Cross-sectional studies

A **cross-sectional study** is a methodology used to investigate variables or a group of subjects in different contexts over the same period of time.

Cross-sectional studies are designed to obtain research data in different contexts, but over the same period of time. They are often used to investigate economic characteristics in surveys of large numbers of organizations or people. Typically, the organizations would represent a range of industries, and the research would look for similarities and differences between industries. In studies focusing on people, employees working in different parts of an organization might be selected to ascertain similarities and differences between groups. For example, if you are investigating the association between labour turnover and productivity, you could select a sample of work groups where you know that labour turnover or productivity differ. You could then collect data relating to a group of workers from factory A and a group of workers doing the same jobs in factory B and conduct statistical tests to test for significant differences between the two groups.

Cross-sectional studies are conducted when there are time constraints or limited resources. The data are collected once, over a short period of time, before they are analysed and reported. Thus, cross-sectional studies provide a snapshot of research phenomena. One of the problems with this research strategy is how to select a sample that is large enough to be representative of the population. A second problem is how to isolate the phenomena under study from all the other factors that could influence the correlation. Finally, cross-sectional studies do not explain why a correlation exists; only that it does or does not exist. On the other hand, cross-sectional studies are inexpensive and are conducted simultaneously, so that there is no problem of change taking place due to the passage of time.

4.3.4 Longitudinal studies

A **longitudinal study** is a methodology used to investigate variables or a group of subjects over a long period of time.

A **longitudinal study** is often associated with a positivist methodology, but can also be used under an interpretivist paradigm. It is the study of variables or a group of subjects over a long period of time. The aim is to examine the dynamics of a research problem by investigating the same variables or group of people several times (or continuously) over the period in which the problem runs its course. This can be a period of several years. Repeated observations are taken with a view to revealing the relative stability of the phenomena under study; some will have changed considerably, others will show little sign of change. Such studies allow the researcher to examine change processes within a social, economic and political context. Therefore, it should be possible to suggest likely explanations from an examination of the process of change and the patterns that emerge from the data. Adams and Schvaneveldt (1991) suggest that by observing people or events over time, the researcher has the opportunity to exercise some control over the variables being studied.

Because of the smaller sample size, it is easier to negotiate access and produce significant results for a longitudinal study of an organization than for a cross-sectional study. However, once started, the study must be continued and there is the problem of losing subjects during the course of the study. Moreover, this methodology is very time-consuming and expensive to conduct. It is unlikely to be appropriate for research students on taught courses as it requires the researcher to be involved for a number of years for the advantages to be enjoyed. However, it may be possible to conduct a longitudinal study using secondary data. The government and other bodies publish a considerable amount of data on various social and economic factors, such as employment, home ownership, household expenditure and income. By concentrating on a specific area, you could investigate whether there have been significant changes over a period of time and how these changes might be explained. In Chapter 12, we explain a technique known as time series analysis, which is a useful method for analysing quantitative data from a longitudinal study.

A longitudinal study under an interpretivist paradigm would focus on qualitative data. Stebbins (1992) describes a chain of studies and what he refers to as concatenated exploration. Each link in the chain is an examination or re-examination of a related group or social process, or an aspect of a broader category of groups or social processes. The early studies in the chain are mainly exploratory, but as the chain of studies progresses, grounded theory is generated (discussed later in this chapter). He argues that the chain of qualitative case studies improves the applicability and validity of the findings. In addition, the researcher gains in knowledge and understanding of the subject as the research develops, and can take account of social processes instead of concentrating only on individuals.

4.4 Methodologies associated with interpretivism

4.4.1 Hermeneutics

Hermeneutics is a methodology that focuses on the interpretation and understanding of text in the context of the underlying historical and social forces.

Hermeneutics is a methodology that focuses on the interpretation and understanding of text in the context of the underlying historical and social forces. It assumes that a relationship exists between the direct conscious description of experience and the underlying dynamics or structures. Hermeneutics was originally concerned with interpreting ancient scriptures, but the approach was formalized and its scope broadened by Dilthey (1976) and others. Although it is still associated with the interpretation of historical texts, hermeneutics has been applied to research in law, where the reasons behind judgments or statutes are sought. According to Lindlof (1995, p. 31), 'The method can be applied to any situation in which one wants to "recover" historical meaning' and the process involves continual reference to the context (Ricoeur, 1977) when interpreting the meaning of contemporary or historic text.

Taylor (1990) links hermeneutics with repertory grid technique, which is a method used to provide mathematical representation of the perceptions and constructs an individual uses to understand and manage his or her world. We discuss this method in more detail in Chapter 9. Taylor's rationale is that the five criteria for text established by Ricoeur (1981) can be rewritten for the data generated by repertory grid technique:

- Words and numbers convey meaning.
- Numbers are chosen according to a structured rationale.
- There is a relationship between this structured rationale and the intended meaning.
- The work of this intended meaning is a projection of a world.
- The uncovering of this meaning is through the mediation of self-understanding.

Taylor stresses the importance of the researcher as an interpreter and a reiterative process of relabelling and reanalysing the data in a hermeneutic circle, since the meaning of any part of the text cannot be understood without reference to other parts, the complete text and the historical and social context. Although hermeneutics is not a widely used methodology in business research, Taylor's unusual approach illustrates the importance of being flexible in classifying methodologies and methods and the value of creativity.

4.4.2 Ethnography

Ethnography is a methodology in which the researcher uses socially acquired and shared knowledge to understand the observed patterns of human activity.

Ethnography is a methodology derived from anthropology (the study of people, their societies and their customs) in which the researcher uses socially acquired and shared knowledge to understand the observed patterns of human activity. Ethnography[1] 'provides insights about a group of people and offers us an opportunity to see and understand their world' (Boyle, 1994, p. 183). Werner and Schoepfle (1987) claim that ethnography is any full or partial description of a group.

The aim of ethnography is to interpret the social world in the same way as the members of that particular world do. The main method of data collection is participant observation, where the researcher becomes a full member of the group being studied. The research normally takes place over a long period of time (often many months), which makes it difficult for students on taught courses. The research takes place in a clearly defined natural setting, such as a factory, and involves direct participation in the activities taking place.

Bogdan and Taylor (1975) and Patton (1990) offer a number of suggestions for researchers conducting ethnographic studies, which can be summarized into the following stages:

- Build trust as early as possible.
- Become as involved as you can with the phenomena, but maintain an analytical perspective.
- Develop strong contacts with a few key informants.
- Gather data from as many different sources as possible, using multiple methods.

1 *Ethno-* means folk and *-graphy* means description.

- Capture participants' views of their experiences in their own words, but remember the limitations of their perspectives.
- Write up field notes as soon as possible after leaving the setting and do not talk to anyone until you have done so.
- Be descriptive when taking your field notes and draw diagrams of physical layouts.
- Include your own experiences, thoughts and feelings as part of your field notes.
- As fieldwork draws to a close, concentrate on making a synthesis of your notes.

A considerable number of disciplines have used ethnography, and business is no exception. Some of them are reviewed by Gill and Johnson (2010). However, there are a great many schisms and Denzin and Lincoln (2011) consider that ethnography is one of the most hotly debated approaches in qualitative research today. These divisions have led to a number of different styles of ethnography, which depend on the skills and training of the researcher, and the nature of the group with which the ethnographer is working.

Students conducting ethnographical studies face a number of problems. First, you have to select an organization in which your particular research interests are present and negotiate access. Second, you have to develop a high degree of trust in those you work with to ensure that you collect the data. Third, if you are using full participation to do your research, you must cope with being a full-time member of a work group as well as doing the research. Finally, there is the issue of whether the particular setting or group best reflects the research interests and whether it will be possible to generalize from the findings. Despite these difficulties, there are a number of advantages. You obtain first-hand experience of the context being studied. Direct observation aids your understanding and interpretation of the phenomena under study, and participation in events may lead those being observed to reveal matters to you or in front of you that might not be known otherwise. When writing up your research, it is important to capture the experiences that the group has gone through by quoting the participants' own words and describing the context in which they were uttered.

4.4.3 Participative inquiry

Participative inquiry is a methodology that involves the participants as fully as possible in the study, which is conducted in their own group or organization.

Participative inquiry is a methodology that involves the participants as fully as possible in the study, which is conducted in their own group or organization. The research may even be initiated by a member of the group and the participants are involved in the data collection and analysis. The participants also determine the progress and direction of the research, thus enabling the researcher to develop questions and answers as a shared experience with a group as co-researchers (Traylen, 1994). Therefore, this type of methodology is 'about research with people rather than research on people' (Reason, 1994a, p. 1).

Concerns about the traditional model of research, which implies an authority imbalance in the relationship between the researcher and the researched, and the associated ethical issues, have led to the development of a strategy that increases the involvement of participants. The objective is to produce higher quality data, but also to address the philosophical arguments and the democratic right of individuals to participate in a study. As one commentator puts it, 'I believe and hope that there is an emerging world view, more holistic, pluralist and egalitarian, that is essentially participative' (Reason, 1994b, p. 324). De Venney-Tiernan *et al.* (1994) contend that the methodology can be employed successfully by novices and those who do not consider themselves to be academics.

Reason (1994b) identifies three types of approach:

- In a study based on *cooperative inquiry*, all those involved in the research are co-researchers, whose thinking and decision-making contribute to generating ideas, designing and managing the project, and drawing conclusions from the experience; they are also co-subjects who participate in the activity being researched.
- In *participatory action research,* the aim is to challenge the power relationship in society. Such studies are often concerned with capturing the knowledge and experiences of oppressed groups.
- The third approach is *action research* (or *action science*), which we describe next.

The basis for all these approaches is that the researcher sees human beings as co-creators of reality through participation, experience and action (Denzin and Lincoln, 2011).

4.4.4 Action research

Action research is a methodology used in applied research to find an effective way of bringing about a conscious change in a partly controlled environment.

Action research is a methodology used in applied research to find an effective way of bringing about a conscious change in a partly controlled environment. Thus, the main aim of action research is to enter into a situation, attempt to bring about change and to monitor the results. For example, you might use it in a study aimed at improving communications between management and staff in a particular organization. The philosophical assumptions underpinning action research are that the social world is constantly changing, and the researcher and the research are part of this change. The term was coined by Lewin (1946) who saw the process of inquiry as forming a cycle of planning, acting, observing and reflecting.

It is usual to conduct action research within a single organization and in some respects it is similar to a case study (we discuss case studies in section 4.4.5). The planning stage is concerned with identifying the objective it is intended to achieve, and how this may be done. The first phase of action is implemented and its effects observed and reflected on before modifying the overall plan, if appropriate. The close collaboration that is required between the researcher and the client organization poses a number of problems. Some action research may not be far removed from a problem-solving, consultancy project. From the beginning, the researcher and the client must be agreed on the aims of the study. There will be mutual control of the research and analysis of the results. The final action plan to be implemented is usually the client's responsibility, supported by the researcher. The research report is often published jointly.

There is considerable debate among academics as to the nature of this methodology, although the notions of involvement of the researcher and improvement in a practice, improvement in the practitioners' understanding of that practice and improvement of the situation in which the practice takes place are central (Robson, 2011). However, it is argued that these features alone do not make for good research and some projects labelled action research are closer to consultancy or journalism (Gummesson, 2000). To avoid such criticisms, some researchers prefer the term *action science*, the main characteristics of which are described by Gummesson as follows:

- Action science always involves two goals: solve a problem for the client and contribute to science.
- The researcher and the client should learn from each other and develop their competencies.
- The researcher must investigate the whole, complex problem, but make it simple enough to be understood by everyone.

- There must be cooperation between the researcher and the client, feedback to the parties involved and continuous adjustment to new information and new events.
- Action science is primarily applicable to the understanding and planning of change in social systems and thus is a suitable research and consulting strategy for business organizations.
- The corporate environment and the conditions of business must be understood before the research starts.
- The methodology should not be judged solely by the criteria used for the paradigm, but by criteria more appropriate for this particular methodology.

4.4.5 Case studies

A **case study** is methodology that is used to explore a single phenomenon (the case) in a natural setting using a variety of methods to obtain in-depth knowledge.

A **case study** is a methodology that is used to explore a single phenomenon (the case) in a natural setting using a variety of methods to obtain in-depth knowledge. The importance of the context is essential. Eisenhardt (1989, p. 534) refers to the focus on 'understanding the dynamics present within a single setting', while Bonoma (1985, p. 204) notes that it must be 'constructed to be sensitive to the context in which management behaviour takes place'. The case may be a particular business, group of workers, event, process, person, or other phenomenon. Detailed information is collected about the chosen case, often over a very long period of time. One or more cases can be selected.

Yin (2009, p. 18) defines a case study as an empirical inquiry that:

- investigates a contemporary phenomenon in depth and within its real-life context, especially when the boundaries between phenomenon and context are not clearly evident
- copes with the technical distinctive situation in which there will be many more variables of interest than data points
- relies on multiple sources of evidence, with data needing to converge in a triangulating fashion (we discuss triangulation in section 4.5)
- benefits from the prior development of theoretical propositions to guide data collection and analysis.

Although we have categorized case studies as a methodology used by interpretivists, you can see from this that they can also be used by positivists, depending on the choice of methods used and the extent of prior theory.

Case study research can be based on a single case. For example, an *exploratory case study* might be conducted where there are few theories or a deficient body of knowledge. Another example is an *opportunist case study* where the opportunity to examine a phenomenon arises because the researcher has access to a particular business, person or other case (Otley and Berry, 1994). Although such a study may be limited to just a few aspects of organizational life, the results can be extremely stimulating and original and this type of case study is popular with undergraduates and students on taught Master's programmes. A research design based on multiple case studies is sometimes referred to as *comparative case studies*. Ryan, Scapens and Theobald (2002) identify four other types of case study:

- *descriptive case studies*, where the objective is restricted to describing current practice
- *illustrative case studies*, where the research attempts to illustrate new and possibly innovative practices adopted by particular companies
- *experimental case studies*, where the research examines the difficulties in implementing new procedures and techniques in an organization and evaluating the benefits

- *explanatory case studies*, where existing theory is used to understand and explain what is happening.

The main stages in a case study are as follows:

1 Selecting the case – It is not usually necessary to find a representative case or set of cases because you will not be attempting statistical generalizations to show that you can generalize from your sample to a larger population. However, you may be attempting theoretical generalizations where you propose that the theory applied in one set of circumstances can be generalized to another. You may wish to select a critical case that encompasses the issues in which you are most interested. You may also decide that you require more than one case. Similar cases will help to show whether your theory can be generalized and dissimilar cases will help to extend or modify any theory. In a multiple case design, 'the cases should serve in a manner similar to multiple experiments, with similar results (a literal replication) or contrasting results (a theoretical replication) predicted explicitly at the outset of the investigation' (Yin, 2009, p. 60).
2 Preliminary investigations – Bonoma (1985) refers to this as drift and it is the process of becoming familiar with the context in which you are going to conduct your research. Some researchers believe that it is best to keep your mind free of any prior beliefs and to learn from the naturalistic evidence at this stage. Others disagree with this approach and consider that the researcher approaches the project with either explicit or implicit theories. To determine your approach, it may be helpful to reflect on your paradigm and also to consider the purpose you attribute to your research.
3 Data collection – You will need to determine how, where and when to collect data. The methods used to collect data in a case study include documentary analysis, interviews and observation. Eisenhardt (1989, p. 534) advises that it is usually best to 'combine data collection methods such as archive searching, interviews, questionnaires and observations. The evidence may be qualitative (e.g. words), quantitative (e.g. numbers) or both'.
4 Data analysis – You have a choice of within-case analysis or cross-case analysis. If you use the former, it is essential that you become totally familiar with the material. This should enable you to build up separate descriptions of events, opinions and phenomena, which can be used to identify patterns. If you use cross-case analysis, you may choose to draw out any similarities and differences to help you identify common patterns.
5 Writing the report – Writing up case study material can be challenging in terms of determining an appropriate structure and demonstrating that your analysis and conclusions can be linked to the masses of data you will have collected. Students often find a chronological structure is the easiest to adopt, as this means they can relate the unfolding of events as they occur. In an interpretivist study, it is essential that you quote extensively from the data you have collected. Diagrams are often helpful for explaining the patterns you see emerging.

Although a case study methodology has many advantages, access to a suitable case can be difficult to negotiate and the research is very time-consuming. It can also be difficult to decide on the scope of the study. Although you may be focusing on a particular organization or group of individuals, they do not exist in a vacuum, but interact with the rest of society. Moreover, your case will have a history and a future, and you will find it difficult to understand the events in a particular period of time without knowledge of what went before and what may follow.

4.4.6 Grounded theory

Grounded theory is a framework in which there is joint collection, coding and analysis of data using a systematic set of procedures to develop an inductively derived theory.

Grounded theory is a framework in which there is joint collection, coding and analysis of data using a systematic set of procedures to develop an inductively derived theory about phenomena. It was conceived by Glaser and Strauss (1967) in reaction to positivist studies that start with a theoretical framework, establish hypotheses and collect data that are used to test the hypotheses. Glaser and Strauss considered that such an approach could lead to early closure where the researchers only collect data relevant to their theories and ignore data that could be useful for explaining what is happening. Grounded theory does not depend on a priori theories, but uses the data generated by the phenomena being studied to generate a theory.

According to Silverman (2013) the key stages in grounded theory are:

- an attempt to develop initial categories that illuminate the data
- the use of theoretical sampling to confirm these initial theoretical categories by including many different social settings in an attempt to 'saturate' the categories with many appropriate cases in order to demonstrate the importance of the categories
- constant comparison as new data are used to modify the categories and develop them into a general analytic framework with relevance outside the research setting.

Originally developed for behavioural research in nursing, grounded theory is a methodology that has since been developed and used in many other disciplines. We look at the procedures in more detail in Chapter 9.

4.4.7 Feminist, gender and ethnicity studies

Feminist studies are a methodology used to investigate and seek understanding of phenomena from a feminist perspective.

There are a number of different perspectives on social stratification. **Feminist studies** are used to investigate and seek understanding of phenomena from the perspective of the role of women in society vis-à-vis men, while *gender studies* are concerned with the experiences of both men and women. On the other hand, *ethnicity studies* focus on the experiences of different ethnic groups in society (often on particular ethnic minority groups). Some studies examine both sexual and racial equality.

At a methodological level, a feminist study is concerned with challenging the traditional research paradigm from the perspective of the politics and ideology of the women's movement (Coolican, 2009). Thus, it challenges the traditional methods by which knowledge is generated and the source of the views of the world such knowledge reflects. Advocating a feminist methodology does not mean that the full range of methodologies is not open and useful to everyone. It is also possible to combine a feminist perspective with another methodology, such as Treleaven's (1994) use of both collaborative action research and feminist discourse analysis to study power and gender in the professional development of women in a particular university in Australia. The aim of the study was to identify better explanations for the marginal position of women working in higher education.

Hyde (1994) captures her initial understanding of using a feminist perspective in the following three principles:

- knowledge is grounded in the experiences of women
- the research benefits women
- the researcher immerses herself or himself in or exhibits empathy for the world being studied.

Adopting a feminist methodology can present both theoretical and practical problems. Gregg (1994) describes difficulties when she interviewed women who held contrasting opinions to her own. Sometimes there was 'a tension between accepting what the women said ... and wanting to hold onto a particular feminist view, a vision of a feminist future as part of a commitment to social change' (Gregg, 1994, p. 53). It has been argued that the language of research can be a barrier. 'It is quite difficult for women to be speaking subjects – harder than for men – and that is true both for women as our research subjects and for us as researchers when we write and talk about our research' (DeVault, 1990, p. 112). Despite these difficulties, feminism brings a new perspective to research and offers insights and understanding of problems that might otherwise be unavailable.

Vox pop What has been the biggest challenge in your research so far?

Nesrine, fourth year PhD student investigating supply chain agility

Discovering that my original plan to design a quantitative study, which is the norm in my topic area, wasn't possible because there wasn't enough literature to support one of my main hypotheses. I then had to switch paradigms and design a qualitative study that would develop theory.

4.5 Triangulation and mixed methods

Triangulation is the use of multiple sources of data, different research methods and/or more than one researcher to investigate the same phenomenon in a study.

Triangulation is the use of multiple sources of data, different research methods and/or more than one researcher to investigate the same phenomenon in a study.[2] This can reduce bias in data sources, methods and investigators (Jick, 1979). In addition, the use of different methods by a number of researchers studying the same phenomenon should lead to greater validity and reliability than a single method approach, providing they all reach the same conclusions (Denzin, 1978).

A simple example of using multiple sources of data might be to ask a number of people to describe a red rose being grown for the Valentine's Day market. You could get a perfectly adequate description by asking one person to describe the colour of the flower, but you would get a much broader picture if you asked a several people to consider a different aspect of the rose, such as the fragrance, the shape of the flower, the texture of the petals, the glossiness of the leaves, the characteristics of the stem, and so on. By collating all these separate impressions, you could get a much richer picture of the way the participants experience the physical aspects of the rose.

Easterby-Smith, Thorpe and Jackson (2012) analyse the potential elements of triangulation in research studies into four main types:

- Triangulation of theories – A theory is taken from one discipline (for example psychology) and used to explain a phenomenon in another discipline (for example accounting).
- Data triangulation – Data are collected at different times or from different sources in the study of a phenomenon.
- Investigator triangulation – Different researchers independently collect data on the same phenomenon and compare the results.

2 The term 'triangulation' is used in surveying and navigation, where an area is divided into triangles and each triangle provides three reference points. This allows an object within a particular triangle to be located.

- Methodological triangulation – More than one method is used to collect and/or analyse the data, but it is important to choose them from the same paradigm (for example exploratory interviews to identify key issues and provide insights into the issues before conducting a questionnaire survey).

A distinction needs to be drawn between the use of multiple methods and mixed methods in the context of methodological triangulation. We advise using the term *mixed methods* when you want to refer to the use of methods drawn from different paradigms. There is much debate over the use of mixed methods. However, there is some evidence of their acceptance in business research. For example, Davis, Golicic and Boerstler (2011) conducted an analysis of five leading marketing journals and concluded that 'multiple methods research offers a promising avenue for advancing the marketing discipline by providing robust findings that overcome the considerable risk of method bias' (p. 473). Nevertheless, they found that less than 4% of articles published in the marketing journals over the past two decades had used multiple methods. In the field of organizational research, Bryman (2009) found that 12–17% of articles at the time of the study were based on a mixed method approach.

Most students can consider using triangulation, but unless you are part of a research team, it is unlikely you will be able to use investigator triangulation. Some of the limitations of methodological triangulation are that replication is more difficult (particularly if qualitative data are generated) and data collection and analysis become more time-consuming and expensive.

If you are uncertain about which methodology to use, have a look at the advice in Chapter 14 (section 14.8).

4.6 Conclusions

This chapter and the last should have given you a valuable framework for your study. Clarity about your paradigm is essential for the progress of your research as it determines your research design and choice of methodology. This, in turn, will lead you to a range of associated methods for collecting and analysing your research data. Therefore, we advise you to discuss the paradigm you will adopt and your choice of methodology with your supervisor at an early stage.

It is not uncommon in business research to use triangulation, particularly in terms of data triangulation and methodological triangulation. This allows you to take a broader, complementary view of the research problem or issue. However, triangulation must be an integral part of your research strategy; it cannot be used to rectify a poorly designed study. Before you can progress to this important milestone, you need to choose a research topic and start reading the literature so that you review the existing body of knowledge and find out how previous research was conducted. We explain this stage in Chapter 5.

References

Adams, G. and Schvaneveldt, J. (1991) *Understanding Research Methods*, 2nd edn. New York: Longman.

Blumer, H. (1980) 'Social behaviourism and symbolic interactionism', *American Sociological Review*, 45, pp. 405–19.

Bogdan, R. and Taylor, S. (1975) *Introduction to Qualitative Research Methods*. New York: John Wiley.

Bonoma, T. V. (1985) 'Case research in marketing: Opportunities, problems, and a process', *Journal of Marketing Research*, XXII, May, pp. 199–208.

Boyle, J. S. (1994) 'Styles of Ethnography' in Morse, J. M. (ed.) *Critical Issues on Qualitative Methods*. Thousand Oaks, CA: SAGE, pp. 159–85.

Bryman, A. (2009) 'Mixed Methods is Organizational

Research' in Buchanan, D. A. and Bryman, A. (eds), *SAGE Handbook of Organizational Research Methods*. London: SAGE.

Coolican, H. (2009) *Research Methods and Statistics in Psychology*, 5th edn. London: Hodder Arnold.

Couch, C. J. (1987) *Researching Social Processes in the Laboratory*. Greenwich, CT: JAI Press.

Creswell, J. W. (2014) *Research Design*, 4th edn. Thousand Oaks, CA: SAGE.

De Venney-Tiernan, M., Goldband, A., Rackham, L. and Reilly, N. (1994) 'Creating Collaborative Relationships in a Co-operative Inquiry Group' in Reason, P. (ed.) *Participation in Human Inquiry*. London: SAGE, pp. 120–37.

Davis, D. F., Golicic, S. L. and Boerstler, C. N. (2011) Benefits and challenges of conducting multiple methods research in marketing', *Journal of the Academy of Marketing Science*, 39(3), pp. 467–79.

Denzin, N. K. (1978) *The Research Act: A Theoretical Introduction to Sociological Methods*, 2nd edn. New York: McGraw-Hill.

Denzin, N. K. and Lincoln, Y. S. (2011) *The SAGE Handbook of Qualitative Research*, 4th edn. Thousand Oaks, CA: SAGE.

DeVault, M. L. (1990) 'Talking and listening from women's standpoint: Feminist strategies for interviewing and analysis', *Social Problems*, 31(1), pp. 96–116.

Dilthey, W. (1976) *Selected Writings* (ed. and trans. H. P. Rickman). Cambridge: Cambridge University Press.

Dobbins, G. H., Lane, I. M. and Steiner, D. D. (1988) 'A note on the role of laboratory methodologies in applied behavioural research: Don't throw out the baby with the bath water', *Journal of Organizational Behavior*, 9(3), pp. 281–6.

Easterby-Smith, M., Thorpe, R. and Jackson, P. (2012) *Management Research*, 4th edn. London: SAGE.

Eisenhardt, K. M. (1989) 'Building theories from case study research' *Academy of Management Review*, 14(4), pp. 532–50.

Gill, J. and Johnson, P. (2010) *Research Methods for Managers*, 4th edn. London: Paul Chapman.

Glaser, B. and Strauss, A. (1967) *The Discovery of Grounded Theory*. Chicago, IL: Aldine.

Gregg, R. (1994) 'Explorations of Pregnancy and Choice in a High-Tech Age', in Riessman, C. K. (ed.) *Qualitative Studies in Social Work Research*. Thousand Oaks, CA: SAGE, pp. 49–66.

Gummesson, E. (2000) *Qualitative Methods in Management Research*, 2nd edn. Thousand Oaks, CA: SAGE.

Hyde, C. (1994) 'Reflections on a Journey: A Research Story', in Riessman, C. K. (ed.) *Qualitative Studies in Social Work Research*. Thousand Oaks, CA: SAGE, pp. 169–89.

Jick, T. D. (1979) 'Mixing qualitative and quantitative methods: Triangulation in action', *Administrative Science Quarterly*, December, 24, pp. 602–11.

Kervin, J. B. (1992) *Methods for Business Research*. New York: HarperCollins.

Lewin, K. (1946) 'Action research and minority problems', *Journal of Social Issues*, 2, pp. 34–6.

Lindlof, T. R. (1995) *Qualitative Communication Research Methods*. Thousand Oaks, CA: SAGE.

Morgan, G. and Smircich, L. (1980) 'The case of qualitative research', *Academy of Management Review*, 5, pp. 491–500.

Otley, D. and Berry, A. (1994) 'Case study research in management accounting and control', *Management Accounting Research*, 5, pp. 45–65.

Patton, M. (1990) *Qualitative Evaluation and Research Methods*. Newbury Park, CA: SAGE.

Reason, P. (1994a) (ed.) *Participation in Human Inquiry*. London: SAGE.

Reason, P. (1994b) 'Three Approaches to Participative Inquiry', in Denzin, N. K. and Lincoln, Y. S. (eds) *Handbook of Qualitative Research*. Thousand Oaks, CA: SAGE, pp. 324–39.

Ricoeur, P. (1977) 'The Model of the Text: Meaningful Action Considered as a Text', in Dallmayr, F. R. and McCarthy, T. A. (eds) *Understanding and Social Inquiry*. Notre Dame, IN: University of Notre Dame Press, pp. 316–34.

Ricoeur, P. (1981) *Hermeneutics and the Human Sciences* (trans. J. B. Thompson). Cambridge: Cambridge University Press.

Robson, C. (2011) *Real World Research*. Chichester: Wiley.

Ryan, B., Scapens, R. W. and Theobald, M. (2002) *Research Method and Methodology in Finance and Accounting*, 2nd edn. London: Thomson.

Silverman, D. (2013 *Doing Qualitative Research*, 4th edn. London: SAGE.

Stebbins, R. A. (1992) 'Concatenated exploration: Notes on a neglected type of longitudinal research', *Quality and Quantity*, 26, pp. 435–42.

Taylor, D. S. (1990) 'Making the most of your matrices: Hermeneutics, statistics and the repertory grid', *International Journal of Personal Construct Psychology*, 3, pp. 105–19.

Traylen, H. (1994) 'Confronting hidden agendas: Co-operative inquiry with health visitors', in Reason, P. (ed.) *Participation in Human Inquiry*. London: SAGE, pp. 59–81.

Treleaven, L. (1994) 'Making a space: A collaborative inquiry with women as staff development', in Reason, P. (ed.) *Participation in Human Inquiry*. London: SAGE, pp. 138–62.

Werner, O. and Schoepfle, G. (1987) *Systematic Fieldwork: Foundations of Ethnography and Interviewing*. Newbury Park, CA: SAGE.

Yin, R. K. (2009) *Case Study Research – Design and Methods*, 4th edn. Thousand Oaks, CA: SAGE.

Activities

1 Select three different academic journals that publish research in your field of study. In each case, read the abstracts and list the different types of methodology used. Decide whether the editor of each journal favours positivist or interpretivist approaches.

2 The manager of a large business in your neighbourhood believes that the morale of employees is low. Select one positivist methodology and one interpretivist methodology that you could use to investigate the problem. List the advantages and disadvantages of each.

3 Imagine you are a member of a research committee about to interview students about their proposed research. One proposal uses triangulation. Prepare five questions you would ask to ensure that the student is aware of some of the dangers of this approach and the advantages.

4 You want to find out what brand of toothpaste people normally buy and why they use that brand. You have just conducted your first interview as part of an interpretivist study. List the information you can extract from the following transcript.

Interviewer: Why did you buy the brand of toothpaste you are using at present?

Respondent: Well, my wife and I usually get the one that's on special offer. It's not that money is tight – that's what she chooses to do. So we tend to get the one where there's money off, 25% extra free, two for the price of one, and so on. But last week the brand on special offer was a new one – we hadn't seen it before. It's really good because it has a strong minty taste. I don't like the ones with fancy fruit flavours. This new one's good – I like it a lot. [Pause] What's it called, now? I can't remember the name of it at the moment. [Pause] That's funny because I clean my teeth at least twice a day, so I see the tube often enough! Anyway, my wife likes it too and I think we'll buy it again, even if it's not discounted when we need to buy the next tube. When you get to my age it is important to look after your teeth, you know!

5 Now consider a positivist approach to the same issue. You have decided to use a self-completion questionnaire to survey households in your area. Design a one-page questionnaire to find out what brand of toothpaste people normally buy and their reasons. Your first question will list various brands of toothpaste and ask the respondent to indicate the one he or she normally uses. You should base your subsequent questions on the information you can extract from the above interview transcript. Then compare the advantages and disadvantages of the two approaches you have taken in questions 4 and 5.

See online for a progress test for this chapter at www.palgrave.com/business/collis/br4/

Have a look at the Troubleshooting chapter and sections 14.2, 14.8, 14.10, 14.11, 14.12 in particular, which relate specifically to this chapter.

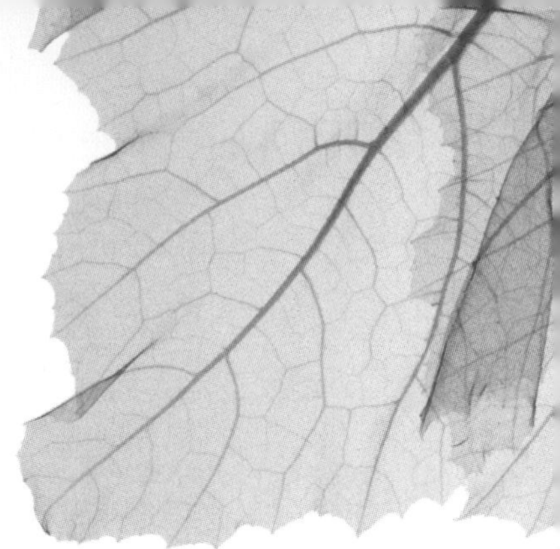

5

searching and reviewing the literature

learning objectives

When you have studied this chapter, you should be able to:

- identify potential sources of secondary data
- search the literature
- use the Harvard system of referencing
- review the literature
- identify your main research question(s).

5.1 Introduction

Before you can start the process of searching and reviewing the literature, you need to have identified a research topic. Most students have no difficulty in doing this because they have a particular interest in an aspect of one of the subjects they have studied. In some cases, the topic may be allocated. If you are having difficulty in identifying a research topic, try one of the techniques we explained in Chapter 2 to help you generate ideas.

The task of searching and reviewing the literature represents a significant proportion of the total time you will spend on your research and you need to start both activities as soon as possible. In this chapter, we will explain how to conduct a systematic literature search and a critical review of the literature that is relevant to your study. Many researchers do much of their searching on the Internet, using websites that give access to databases containing academic journal articles and other scholarly papers. We recommend that you are selective about the websites you search, to ensure that you only collect information from authoritative sources.

It is essential to keep accurate records so that you can acknowledge the sources of the information that provides the basis of your research. You will need to apply the rules of the bibliographic referencing system that is appropriate to your discipline and your supervisor. Once you have collected the literature that is relevant to your study, you will need to write a literature review that evaluates this body of knowledge. In this chapter we will explain what this entails.

5.2 Searching the literature

Your **literature search** can start as soon as you have your first thoughts on a potential topic and it will continue until you submit your dissertation or thesis. In this context, the **literature** refers to the existing body of knowledge. Therefore, a literature search can be defined as a systematic process with a view to identifying the existing body of knowledge on a particular topic. Knowledge is disseminated through various types of publication, which can be in hard copy or digital form, and the data can be qualitative (such as text or illustrations) or quantitative (such as tables or statistics).

A **literature search** is a systematic process with a view to identifying the existing body of knowledge on a particular topic.

The **literature** is all sources of published data on a particular topic.

The underlying purpose of the literature search is to collect as many relevant items of literature as possible and read them. In the process, you will learn more about the subject and the methodologies used in previous research, which is necessary before you can write a critical review of the literature. This will provide an analysis of what is already known about the phenomena you are going to study and also identify gaps and deficiencies in our knowledge, some aspects of which your study will address.

5.2.1 The literature

The literature refers to all sources of secondary data that are relevant to your study. Secondary data are data collected from an existing source, such as:

- e-resources, such as academic journal databases and the Internet
- research reported in books, articles, conference papers and reports
- books on the topic and on methodology
- coverage of business topics in professional journals, newspapers and broadcast media
- government and commercially produced statistics and industry data

- archives
- statutory and voluntary corporate reports
- internal documents and records of organizations.

At undergraduate level, it may be acceptable to refer to textbooks, but at Master's and doctoral level, you must locate original sources of knowledge referred to by the authors. By exploring what others have contributed to your area of interest, you will be in a better position to identify a particular research problem or issue to investigate. Your reading should help you understand the main issues within the topic and also the methodologies used in previous studies. If you are a positivist, you will be looking for theories and models so that you can develop a **theoretical framework** and hypotheses for your study. You can see how your ideas compare with what has gone before, and develop existing ideas or create new ones. Your literature search will continue throughout your study, so that your literature review will reflect the current state of knowledge and provide a rationale for your research question.

A **theoretical framework** is a collection of theories and models from the literature which underpins a positivist study. Theory can be generated from some interpretivist studies.

5.2.2 Procedure for a systematic literature search

In Chapter 1, we defined research as being systematic and methodical and you can demonstrate this in your methodology chapter when describing how you conducted your literature search. Initially, the subject of your research is likely to be fairly broad, which means your search will be in general terms only. Box 5.1 shows a general procedure for conducting a systematic literature search.

Box 5.1 Procedure for a systematic literature search

- Draw up a list of sources (journal databases, subject-related websites, bibliographic catalogues and other lists your business librarian suggests).
- Define the scope of the research.
- Determine keywords you can use for searching, including alternative spellings and synonyms.
- Search each source, keeping a record of your progress (for example: *Journal of Drinking Habits:* Searched 1990–2009 using keywords ...) and full details of relevant publications so that you can read them later and, if relevant, reference them in your work.
- Only collect literature that is relevant to your research in terms of the topic, theory and methodology. In the academic literature, select articles from high-quality journals that review the literature, describe the methods used, discuss the results and draw conclusions.
- Start with the most recent publications and work back in time, using the references at the end of relevant publications to lead you to previous studies.
- When you start to recognize the references cited in other works, you are nearing the end of your first search.
- To keep up to date, continue searching the literature throughout the project.

5.2.3 Defining the scope

The first step is to define the scope and context for your search, which will help limit the material you collect to that which is relevant. Limitations include:

- Time – for example, it may not be worth searching more than five years back if the phenomenon you are interested in is some kind of new technology. Find an appropriate cut-off date; it can be adjusted if necessary.
- Geography – for example a city, region, country or a comparison of two or more of these.
- Single or multidisciplinary approach – for example the development of new software programs in accountancy.
- Single discipline, but multi-concept approach – for example the role of employee appraisals in staff development.

The next step is to decide what sort of information you require. Very recent topics are not likely to be covered by books; journals and newspapers will be the most relevant places to look for information relating to recent events. You may find that some information, for example about a company's corporate strategy or organizational structure, may only be available in internal documents. These may be confidential or difficult to obtain. However, by considering carefully what type of information you expect to find, you can restrict your search to those types only, thus saving yourself valuable time.

You may be able to find much of the information you need from your own institution's library and subscriptions to databases. You need to read abstracts of articles and peruse the information from other sources; if the article or other item of literature is relevant to your research, you will need to print or photocopy a full copy. This may mean visiting another library, or requesting an inter-library loan, for which there may be a charge. You need to apportion plenty of time to allow for such delays.

5.2.4 Determining keywords

Once you have decided where to start searching, you must identify the **keywords** associated with your research topic that you will use to start off your first search. Keywords are the words used by software to search databases or by search engines to search websites on the Internet. Although you will gradually develop more words from reading the literature you find, you may need some lateral thinking to get you started, such as alternative English spellings and synonyms. For example, if your research is going to focus on the marketing of lager and beer in the UK, you might start your search using keywords such as 'marketing' 'advertising', 'lager', 'beer' and 'UK'. As you develop your literature search you may want to widen your search by including 'alcoholic beverages' or narrow it to 'mild', 'bitter', 'real ale' or 'stout'.

Keywords are words used by software to search databases or by search engines to search websites on the Internet for items containing those words.

When searching, you need to bear in mind that you are seeking authoritative sources. Although you might find it helpful, your supervisors and examiners are not likely to consider sources such as lecture notes (from your institution or another) and open resources such as Wikipedia as authoritative; you will need to seek out the original sources, to which their authors refer. You need to adopt a systematic approach and general surfing of the Internet is not advised. We recommend that you take advantage of any tutorials run by your library on how to access and search the e-resources to which your institution subscribes. You can also try academic search engines such as *Google Scholar,* the websites of national and international professional bodies, government departments and other organizations with activities that are relevant to your research topic.

Vox pop What has been the biggest challenge in your research so far?

Ben, MBA student investigating the impact of the credit crunch on access to finance for SMEs

I found there was a lot of literature on my research topic. This gave me a challenge as to which information to use as I had very limited time to complete my dissertation.

In a simple search, you enter all your keywords together in the search box. However, you may be overwhelmed by the thousands of 'hits'. We advise you to investigate the advanced search options that may be available. In many cases, this permits the use of what are known as Boolean proximity and adjacency operators. These simple words allow you to narrow the search or, in the case of too few 'hits', to broaden your search. Table 5.1 gives examples of the Boolean operators used in *ProQuest*, an e-resource that contains millions of articles from academic journals, and other publications.

Table 5.1 Examples of Boolean operators used in ProQuest

Operator	Description
AND	Find all the words. When searching for keywords in "Citation and Document Text," AND finds documents in which the words occur in the same paragraph (within approx. 1000 characters) or the words appear in any citation field. Use W/DOC in place of AND when searching for keywords within "Citation and Document Text," or "Document Text" to retrieve more comprehensive results. *Example:* Internet AND education
AND NOT	Find documents which have the first word, but not the second word. *Example:* Internet AND NOT html
OR	Find any of the words. *Example:* Internet OR intranet
W/#	Find documents where these words are within some number of words apart (either before or after). Use when searching for keywords within "Citation and Document Text" or "Document Text." *Example:* computer W/3 careers
W/PARA	Finds documents where these words are within the same paragraph (within approx. 1000 characters). Use when searching for keywords within "Document Text." *Example:* Internet W/PARA education
W/DOC	Find documents where all the words appear within the document text. Use W/DOC in place of AND when searching for keywords within "Citation and Document Text" or "Document Text" to retrieve more comprehensive results. *Example:* Internet W/DOC education
NOT W/#	Find documents where these words appear but are not within some number of words apart (either before or after). Use when searching for keywords within "Citation and Document Text" or "Document Text." *Example:* computer NOT W/2 careers
PRE/#	Find documents where the first word appears some number of words before the second word. Use when searching for keywords within "Citation and Document Text" or "Document Text." *Example:* world pre/3 web

Source: ProQuest, Advanced search tips. The content from ProQuest products is published with permission of ProQuest LLC. Further reproduction is prohibited without permission. www.proquest.com

The advantages of online searching of academic and other databases include:

- ease of access from your computer, wherever you have an Internet connection
- currency, since printed versions of journals and other documents take longer to reach the library shelves
- cross-disciplinary searching, since journals specializing in different subjects are held in the same publishers' database
- flexibility, as you can carry out a free-text search using any combination of terms and subjects, and you can develop your search strategy as you progress to focus on a particular research problem or issue of interest within the general topic area
- speed, since thousands of sources can be searched in seconds, compared with many hours searching a printed index and the library catalogue and then going to the library shelves to find the publication.

However, you need to bear in mind that searching can still be very time-consuming, particularly if you do not read what you are collecting and therefore do not focus your search at an early stage and adjust your search words accordingly. In addition, you will need to print the documents that are relevant to your research and this may incur some costs. You also need to remember that the results of your search will reflect the quality of the databases and other sources you search. You will know the end of your search is near when you start to recognize the references in the literature you are reading, but you should continue to search throughout your project to keep your knowledge up to date.

The following extended example is provided by Kevin (a third year PhD student investigating the personalization of products and services). Table 5.2 shows his keywords and search terms and Figure 5.2 shows how he combined his search terms.

Table 5.2 Kevin's keywords and search terms

Keyword	Search term
Engineer-to-order	Engineer-to-order OR ETO
Mass customization	mass customi* OR customer co-design* OR customer co-creation*
Mass personalization	mass personali*
Supply chain design	supply chain design* OR supply chain strate* OR supply chain architectur* OR supply chain manage* OR supply chain plan* OR SCM OR SCS OR supply chain manag* OR supply chain typolog* OR supply chain classi* OR Supply chain taxonom*
Product design	product develop* OR product design* OR product engineer* OR product architecture*
Flexible manufacturing	flexible manufactur*

The following illustrations show the results of Kevin's search of the ABI/INFORM Global database using *ProQuest* where he used a simple combination of his search terms (see Figure 5.1 which shows that 18 articles were identified) and subsequently a more sophisticated combination of search terms (see Figure 5.2 which shows that 74 articles were identified).

Kevin summarized the literature searching process he followed in a flow chart, which is shown in Figure 5.3.

In addition to the standard citation information, he made notes on the following features of each article. This process represents the thematic stage in the process.

- Rationale – the motivation for the article and an explanation of the issues addressed
- Arguments and findings – the focus of the article (categorized thematically)

- Context – any information that causes bias or limits comparability or generalization, such as location, sector, sampling method, sample size, response rate, unit of analysis
- Research method – type of methodology adopted
- Critique – evaluation of the methodology, arguments and conclusions (summarized in my own words).

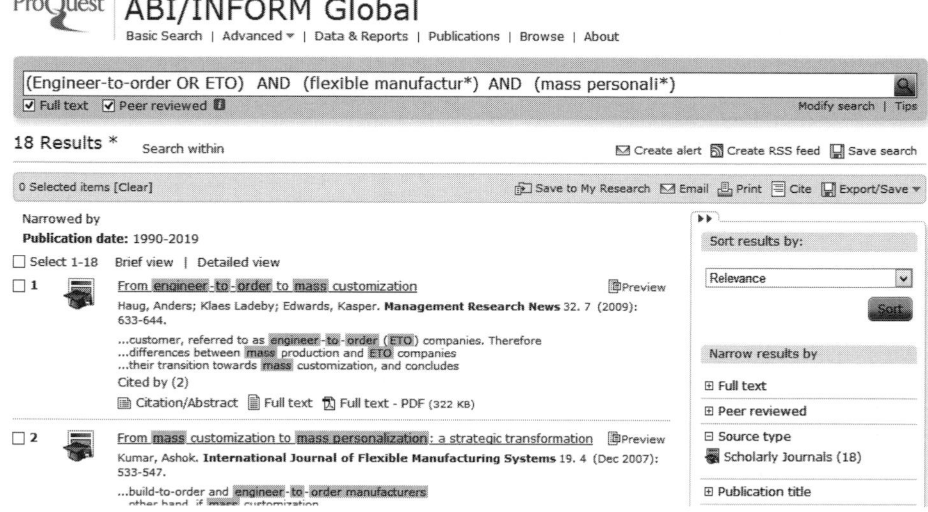

Figure 5.1 Kevin's initial search results

Source: ProQuest. The content from ProQuest products is published with permission of ProQuest LLC. Further reproduction is prohibited without permission. www.proquest.com

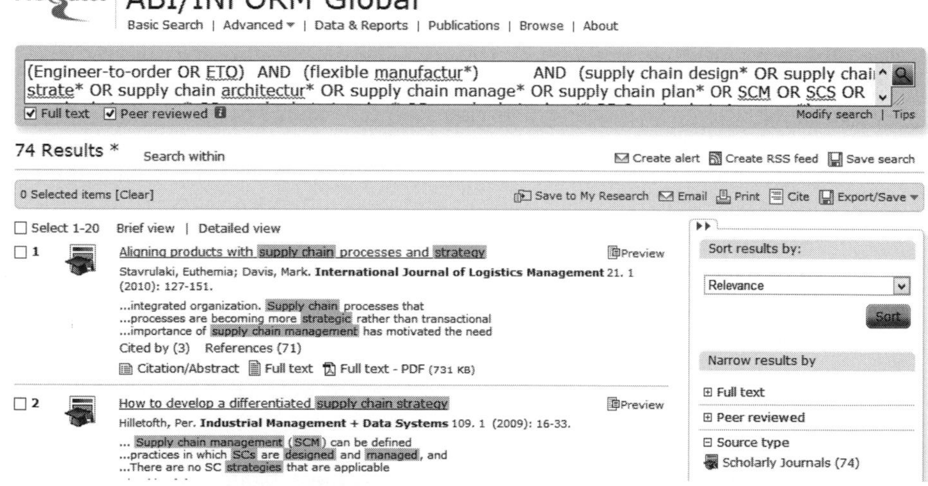

Figure 5.2 Kevin's subsequent search results

Source: ProQuest. The content from ProQuest products is published with permission of ProQuest LLC. Further reproduction is prohibited without permission. www.proquest.com

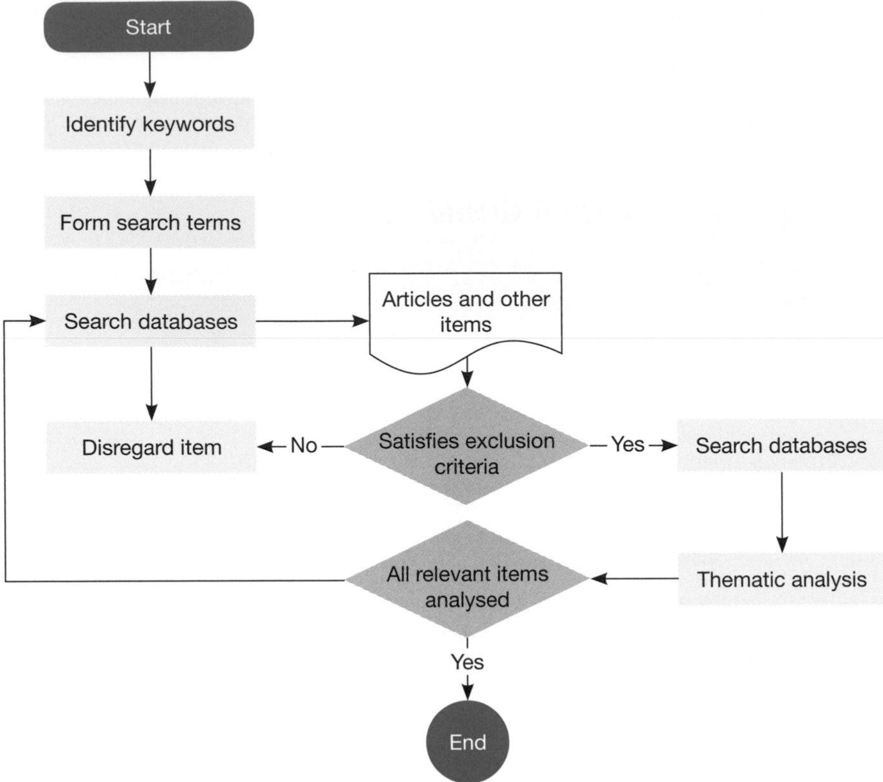

Figure 5.3 Flow chart of Kevin's literature search

With regard to the thematic analysis of the arguments and findings in each article, Kevin explains that the codes he used for categorizing the themes were based on definitive keywords that summarized the topic. The themes were then used to perform meta-analysis, construct a theoretical model and code the empirical data. This helped ensure that his theoretical model was grounded in the literature and his subsequent analysis of the research data he collected could be linked to the literature. Of course, doctoral students are more likely to have the time to develop the skills to conduct this high level of analysis and undergraduate students and those on taught Master's courses will not be expected to adopt such a detailed approach.

Vox pop What has been the biggest challenge in your research so far?

Mohamad, second year PhD student investigating failure of ICT projects in public sector organizations

The first five or six months you really like your ideas – you're running like a bullet, reading at least 10 articles every day – but after six months you know so much more and it gets complicated. At the beginning you think everything you know is right; afterwards you realize that you don't know whether it's right or not and the happy feeling really diminishes.

5.3 Referencing

Finding relevant information in the first place is hard enough, but finding it again later on can be even harder if you are not careful. It is good practice to make a note of everything you find, even if you eliminate it later because it is not relevant after all. In the long run this will save time by avoiding duplication and helping you with the selection and rejection of material. You will need to set up a filing system on your computer for storing copies of articles, notes, quotations and references (and a parallel system for hard copies you collect). You will soon find that your material can be collated into different categories, which you can place in folders with labels that help identify their contents.

You may have access to bibliographic software, such as *Reference Manager, ProCite, RefWorks* (Write-N-Cite). The main features of most bibliographic software are:

- References from most e-resources can be 'dragged' into your personalized database.
- You can also import charts, diagrams and images.
- You can cite publications you have in your database as you write, and the software will generate a list of references at the end of your document when you are ready.
- You can choose from a number of alternative formats for presenting the references, which is useful if you subsequently write articles for submission to journals that have different house styles.

It is by no means essential to use bibliographic software and some researchers find them time-consuming and inconvenient for relatively small studies. The alternative is to keep a list of your references in an ordinary *Microsoft Word* document (or equivalent) and store it in alphabetical order by author's surname. We suggest you do this in the format that is required for your dissertation or thesis. Whichever method of record keeping you adopt, the main reasons for maintaining accurate records are to:

- identify a particular item accurately so that you can locate it again online, in the library or order it through inter-library loan and avoid duplication of effort
- develop links between authors, topics, types of study, main findings and year published by searching your records
- allow you to use a citation in the text of your work to acknowledge the source of information taken from other authors
- allow your supervisor, examiner and other readers to find full bibliographic details of the works of the authors you have cited.

Table 5.3 gives examples of the data you need to record for a book or journal article.

Table 5.3 Data required for referencing

Books	Journal articles
Name(s) of author(s) or editor(s)	Name(s) of author(s)
Year of publication	Year of publication
Title of book	Title of article
Edition (if not the first)	Title of journal
Place of publication	Volume number and issue
Name of publisher	Page numbers

Whether you are an undergraduate, postgraduate or doctoral student, you must ensure that you follow one of the standard systems for referencing. All systems provide rules for making citations and references.

5.3.1 Citations and references

A **citation** is an acknowledgement in your text of the original source of information or ideas, whether reproduced exactly, paraphrased or summarized. This means the originator of theories, models and arguments, illustrations, diagrams, tables, statistics and any other information that you are using in your work must be acknowledged. Citations are important because they:

- provide evidence of your literature searching and the range of your reading
- help you support your arguments using the authority of the source you have cited
- help the reader to distinguish between your work and the existing body of knowledge, thus avoiding accusations of plagiarism.

References are a list containing the bibliographic details of the sources cited in the text. They are important because they:

- provide full bibliographic details that support the citations
- allow supervisors, examiners and other researchers to locate the source of the works you have cited.

A **citation** is an acknowledgement in the text of the original source from which information was obtained.

References are a list containing bibliographic details of the sources cited in the text.

We distinguish between a bibliography and a *list of references* because a bibliography can be a catalogue of publications, not a specific list of those that have been used and, therefore, cited. Some researchers use the terms interchangeably and you should check what the preferred terminology is in your institution.

There are two main groups of referencing systems: author–date systems, such as the Harvard system or the American Psychological Association (APA) system, and number-based systems, such as the Vancouver system. You will need to find out what is appropriate in your discipline and acceptable to your supervisor before deciding which method to adopt. The important thing to remember is to apply the rules consistently. This means you must first study the rules. Do not be tempted to copy someone else's style, as publishers often use adaptations to create their own house style. Of course, if you are submitting your work for publication, follow the journal's house style. The examples of the Harvard system we show in the next section are based on British Standards, BS 5605:1990.

5.3.2 The Harvard system

The Harvard system is widely used in most business and management research, and other social sciences. It is also used in anthropology and some of the life sciences. The APA system is more commonly used in North America. It is very similar to the Harvard system and both use the author–date system to acknowledge the source of information. Thus, citations in the text are shown as the surname of the author(s) and the date of publication, plus the page number if a quotation is used (or any other exact reproduction of data, such as a table, diagram or illustration). If a printed document or online material is not paginated or not dated, indicate this by using n.p. (no page number) or n.d. (no date) as appropriate. When citing more than one source, you should place the author–date information in chronological order (the oldest first).

There is no single authority on the Harvard system of referencing, so we are following the style defined in the widely used guide by Pears and Shields (2013). If there are more than three authors, cite the name of the first author followed by *et al.* This is the abbreviation of the Latin phrase *et alia*, which means 'and the others' (hence the abbreviation is in italic followed by a full stop). If you are citing more than one author with the same surname, you should include their initials in the text to avoid confusion. Box 5.2 shows a range of examples of how to make citations under the Harvard system.

Box 5.2 Citations under the Harvard system

Authors' words are paraphrased

There is evidence that the needs of micro-companies are very similar to the needs of non-micro small companies, and regulators should be wary of introducing concessions that discourage micro-companies from filing full, audited accounts if they so wish (Collis, 2012).

Or

Collis (2012) provides evidence that the needs of micro-companies are very similar to the needs of non-micro small companies, and regulators should be wary of introducing concessions that discourage micro-companies from filing full, audited accounts if they so wish.

Authors' words are quoted

'Regulation should not give the impression that there is no benefit to micro-companies from filing full audited accounts. The results of this study demonstrate non-micro small companies and micro-companies have assurance and reporting needs in common, although the specific drivers differ between the two size groups' (Collis, 2012, p. 463).

Citation for up to three authors

Using UK data, Collis, Jarvis and Skerratt (2004) identified a number of cost, management and agency factors.

Citation for more than three authors

Kitching *et al.* (2011) examined the value of the abbreviated accounts of small companies.

Multiple sources (in chronological order)

Other evidence indicates that small companies file voluntary audited accounts to maintain relationships with the bank (Collis and Jarvis, 2002; Collis, 2003; 2010; Collis, Jarvis and Skerratt, 2004).

A comprehensive example

Empirical evidence from the UK indicates that small companies file voluntary audited accounts to maintain relationships with the bank (Collis and Jarvis, 2002; Collis, 2003; 2010; Collis, Jarvis and Skerratt, 2004) and to send positive signals to lenders, suppliers and customers that the business is well managed (Marriott, Collis and Marriott, 2006). These findings are supported by a study in Finland (Ojala *et al.*, 2013), which found evidence of a relationship between capital structure and voluntary audit. Further research (Collis, 2012; 2013) finds that voluntary audit is the main predictor of the voluntary filing of full accounts by small companies.

Author with more than one publication in the same year

Latest statistics show that 87% of companies in the UK have fewer than 10 employees (BIS, 2012a) and the government is currently consulting on proposals to reduce regulatory burdens for these very small entities (BIS, 2012b).

Secondary citation

Findings from an empirical study by Collis and Jarvis (2000) (cited in Collis, Jarvis and Skerratt, 2004) suggest that …

Distinguishing authors with the same name

R. Hussey (2006) and A. Hussey (2006) examined the effect of …

Under the Harvard system, the bibliographic details of the sources cited in the text are presented in the list of references in alphabetical order by author's name. This list is shown at the end of the document, which means you can still use numbered footnotes or endnotes for providing explanatory information that would interrupt the flow of your main text. The list of references is not included in your word count.

Box 5.3 shows examples of references (and their punctuation) for different types of publication under the Harvard system and Box 5.4 illustrates how they are presented in alphabetical order in the list of references at the end of the document. With e-resources, you need to add the URL for the item (the web link) and date you accessed the item. The latter is shown in round brackets. You are advised to copy and paste the URL rather than retype it, as a full stop, comma or slash in the wrong place can lead to problems for you or anyone else wanting to locate the item. We also advise that you test the URL before submitting your work to ensure it does not need updating.

Box 5.3 Examples of references

Article in a journal

Collis, J. (2012) 'Determinants of voluntary audit and voluntary full accounts in micro- and non-micro small companies in the UK', *Accounting and Business Research,* 42(4), pp. 441–68.

Conference paper

Ojala, H., Niemi, L. and Collis, J. (2013) 'Determinants of audit effort in a changing audit environment', *49th BAFA Annual Conference,* Newcastle upon Tyne, 9–11 April.

Online report

Collis, J. (2008) *Directors' Views on Accounting and Auditing Requirements for SMEs.* London: BERR. Available at: http://www.bis.gov.uk/files/file50491.pdf (Accessed 14 February 2013).

Internet site

Collis, J. (2013) 'Why SMEs choose voluntary audit', *RealBusiness.* Available at: http://realbusiness.co.uk/article/17921-why-smes-choose-voluntary-audit (Accessed 20 February 2013).

Book

Collis, J. and Hussey, R. (2013) *Business Research.* 4th edn. Basingstoke: Palgrave Macmillan.

Chapter in a book

Collis, J., Dugdale, D. and Jarvis, R. (2001) 'Deregulation of Small Company Reporting in the UK', in McLeay, S. and Riccaboni, A. (eds) *Contemporary Issues in Accounting Regulation.* Boston: Kluwer, pp. 167–85.

Box 5.4 List of references under the Harvard system

References

BIS (2012a) *Business Population Estimates for the UK and the Regions.* Available at: http://www.bis.gov.uk/analysis/statistics/business-population-estimates (Accessed 14 February 2013).

BIS (2012b) *Company Law – Providing a Flexible Framework Which Allows Companies to Compete and Grow, A Discussion Paper.* Available at: http://www.bis.gov.uk/assets/biscore/business-law/docs/c/12-560-company-law-flexible-framework-discussion-paper (Accessed 20 February 2013).

Collis, J. (2003) *Directors' Views on Exemption from Statutory Audit,* URN 03/1342, October, London: DTI. Available at: http://www.berr.gov.uk/files/file25971.pdf (Accessed 20 February 2013).

Collis, J. (2008) *Directors' Views on Accounting and Auditing Requirements for SMEs,* London: BERR. Available at: http://www.bis.gov.uk/files/file50491.pdf (Accessed 20 February 2013).

Collis, J. (2010) 'Audit exemption and the demand for voluntary audit – a comparative analysis of the UK and Denmark', *International Journal of Auditing,* 14(2), pp. 211–31.

Collis, J. (2012) 'Determinants of voluntary audit and voluntary full accounts in micro- and non-micro small companies in the UK', *Accounting and Business Research,* 42(4), pp. 441–68.

Collis, J. (2013) 'Why SMEs choose voluntary audit', *RealBusiness.* Available at: http://realbusiness.co.uk/article/17921-why-smes-choose-voluntary-audit (Accessed 20 February 2013).

Collis, J. and Hussey, R. (2013) *Business Research.* 4th edn. Basingstoke: Palgrave Macmillan.

Collis, J. and Jarvis, R. (2000) *How owner-managers use accounts,* ICAEW Research Report, London: The Centre for Business Performance Research. ISBN 1841520500. Available at: http://www.icaew.com/index.cfm?route=111138 (Accessed 20 February 2013).

Collis, J. and Jarvis, R. (2002) 'Financial information and the management of small private companies', *Journal of Small Business and Enterprise Development,* 9(2), pp. 100–10.

Collis, J., Dugdale, D. and Jarvis, R. (2001) 'Deregulation of Small Company Reporting in the UK', in McLeay, S. and Riccaboni, A. (eds) *Contemporary Issues in Accounting Regulation,* Boston: Kluwer, pp. 167–85.

Collis, J., Jarvis, R. and Skerratt, L. (2004) 'The demand for the audit in small companies in the UK', *Accounting and Business Research,* 34(2), pp. 87–100.

Kitching, J., Kašperová, E., Blackburn, R. and Collis, J. (2011) *Small company abbreviated accounts: A regulatory burden or a vital disclosure?* Edinburgh: Institute of Chartered Accountants in Scotland. Available at: http://www.icas.org.uk/site/cms/contentviewarticle.asp?article=7529 (Accessed 20 February 2013).

Marriott, N., Collis, J. and Marriott, P. (2006) *Qualitative review of the accounting and auditing needs of small and medium-sized companies and their stakeholders,* London: Financial Reporting Council. Available at: http://www.frc.org.uk/documents/pagemanager/poba/Case%20studies%20report.pdf (Accessed 20 February 2013).

Ojala, H., Niemi, L. and Collis, J. (2013) 'Determinants of audit effort in a changing audit environment', *49th British Accounting and Finance Association Annual Conference,* Newcastle upon Tyne, April 9–11.

Note that in Box 5.4 we have used hanging paragraphs to present the list of references. This is not a requirement of the Harvard system and you may prefer to use block paragraphs. The main principle is that you should present the list in alphabetical order according to the name of the first author (use the AZ↓ tool in *Microsoft Word*). Do not use bullet points or number your list of references.

In this section we have concentrated on the most common needs of students when using the Harvard system of referencing, but you can find many more examples in Pears and Shields (2013). We also advise you to check the referencing guide provided by your university or supervisor.

5.4 Reviewing the literature

Once you have collected the literature that is relevant to your study, you will need to write a **literature review**. A literature review is a critical evaluation of the existing body of knowledge on a topic, which guides the research and demonstrates that relevant literature has been located and analysed. It should incorporate the latest literature and cover the major questions and issues in the field (Gill and Johnson, 2010).

A **literature review** is a critical evaluation of the existing body of knowledge on a topic, which guides the research and demonstrates that the relevant literature has been located and analysed.

At the proposal stage, a preliminary review of the literature helps develop your subject knowledge and provide a context for your research questions. A preliminary review is relatively brief and usually focuses on the seminal studies (the most influential previous research) and the main theories (if appropriate to your paradigm). When you write a full review of literature for your dissertation or thesis, you will also need to demonstrate an appropriate level of intellectual ability and scholarship. At that stage, your literature review will be large enough to occupy at least one chapter (more than one if the literature is large or your study has been designed as an exhaustive review of the literature).

5.4.1 Reading the literature

It may be very satisfying to know that you have a fine collection of literature neatly filed away (or piling up impressively in the corner), but you need to start reading and analysing it in order to develop your research proposal and design your study. As you read, you will learn more about the subject and the methodologies used in previous research.

Vox pop What has been the biggest challenge in your research so far?

Najma, UG student investigating views on Internet banking

The hardest part was reading all the journals!

It is important that you develop your skills as a critical reader. Drawing on Wallace and Wray (2011), Box 5.5 offers a checklist for reading the literature.

Box 5.5 Checklist for reading the literature

- What was the purpose of the study and how does it differ from other studies and your research?
- How does the author define key terms and are these terms used consistently?
- What is the structure of the argument?
- How was the research conducted and how do the methods differ from other studies and your research?
- What were the findings and how do they differ from other studies and your research?
- What claims does the author make and are they supported by appropriate evidence?
- Are there any underlying values that may be guiding the author and influencing these claims?
- Is there evidence to support any generalizations?
- What were the limitations and weaknesses of the study?
- Has any irrelevant material been included or has any necessary material been omitted?
- Does the author cite any literature that you need to locate and read?

5.4.2 Analysing the literature

You need to adopt a systematic approach when analysing your collection of articles and other items from the literature. Many researchers adopt a thematic approach, which involves categorizing the themes in the relevant literature. Both subject-related categories and methodology-related categories are likely to be broken down into various subgroups, which will emerge from your reading of the article. Without formally recognizing it, you will begin this process when you generate your keywords for searching the literature. Your thematic analysis of the literature can be facilitated if you record key details of the previous studies in a spreadsheet. This allows you to sort the data into different groups to help you structure your literature review (one article is likely to be included in many subgroups). Table 5.4 suggests a basic format, which you can adapt to suit your needs. We have included the standard author–date information to identify the publication, but also the date when the study was conducted, as many articles are not published for a year or more after the research has been completed.

Table 5.4 Recording and categorizing previous studies

Author and date	Subject categories	Methodology categories	Sample size	Response rate (if applicable)	Date of study	Location/ country

Ryan, Scapens and Theobald (2002) offer a structured approach to analysing the literature, using a network diagram where the articles in the literature are represented as a series of nodes in an interlinked network of theoretical and empirical developments. Box 5.6 summarizes the main steps.

Box 5.6 Procedure for generating a network of primary citations

1 From the literature you have collected, select all the articles that are published in what you consider are the top two or three journals among those represented. From these articles, select the most recent as you will analyse these articles first.
2 Examine each article and identify which of the previous studies or other items of literature mentioned is most important to the author's study. This is the primary citation for that article. Do the same for the other articles published that year.
3 Place all the primary citations for the most recent year as nodes in an oval text box at the bottom of your diagram and use Author (Date) to label them.
4 Repeat this process at five-yearly intervals to add new nodes to the diagram that reflect the year of publication. Draw links between nodes to identify the literary antecedents (similar to a family tree). Identify the node that lies at the core of the literature (the one with the most 'descendants') by putting it in a rectangular text box. This allows you to illustrate the theoretical framework that unites the literature.
5 The final step is to determine the motivation for each article, and the methodological rationale that links them.

5.4.3 Writing the literature review

Writing a literature review can seem a daunting task and you need to bear in mind what you are trying to achieve. According to Hart (1998), the purpose of the literature review is to:

- demonstrate skills in library searching
- show command of the subject area and understanding of the problem
- justify the research topic, design and methodology.

Creswell (2014) suggests that designing a map of the literature can be a useful preliminary step as it helps you summarize previous studies. You could use a mind map (see Chapter 2) or a hierarchical diagram that helps you organize the literature and shows where your study fits in.

Once you have reflected on your analysis, you are ready to start structuring and writing your review of the literature. We offer the following advice:

- Select only material that is relevant to the topic, industry, methodology and so on.
- Identify themes and group the material.
- Define key terms and draw out the important features.
- Compare results and methods of previous studies.
- Be critical and demonstrate relevance to your research.
- Set the context for your study (a deductive approach suggests you will identify a theoretical framework and hypotheses).
- Identify gaps or deficiencies in the literature that your study will address.
- Conclude with your research question(s).
- Acknowledge other people's contribution to knowledge using the Harvard system of referencing.

It is important that you develop your skills as a critical writer. Drawing on Wallace and Wray (2011), Box 5.7 offers a checklist for writing a critical review of the literature.

Box 5.7 Checklist for writing a critical literature review

- Have you stated what you are trying to achieve clearly?
- Have you defined key terms and used them consistently?
- Have you created a logical structure that helps the reader to follow your argument?
- How was the research conducted and how do the methods differ from other studies and your research?
- Have you stated your claims clearly and are they supported by appropriate evidence?
- Are you aware of how your values are reflected in what you write and have you made those values explicit where appropriate?
- Have you provided evidence to support any generalizations?
- Have you sustained focus, included all necessary material and avoided digressions and irrelevant material?
- Are your citations in the text and your list of references accurate and complete so that the reader can check your sources?

Vox pop What has been the biggest challenge in your research so far?

Mohamad, second year PhD student investigating failure of ICT projects in public sector organizations

Developing my conceptual (theoretical) framework. I've seen several theses where there's one chapter for the literature review and another chapter for the conceptual framework, but I can't see how to do that without a lot of repetition and it looks as though you almost have to know what your findings are before you've done the study.

If you are having difficulty in finding a theoretical framework, have a look at the advice in Chapter 14 (section 14.6).

You need to ensure that you have included all the major studies that are relevant to your study. You may also consider it diplomatic to refer to any relevant publication by your supervisor(s) and external examiners. A previous study may be relevant because it focuses on the same or a similar research problem or issue to the one you have in mind. Sometimes students become disillusioned because they think there is no literature on the issue they want to investigate. For example, if you are investigating labour turnover in hotels in Poland, perhaps you will not be able to find any other similar studies. However, you may find research has been done on this topic in other countries or there are studies of other HRM issues in Poland that illuminate your research. A second way in which previous research can be relevant is the methodology used. References to studies that have used the same methodology you plan to use or references to studies that have used a different research methodology in a similar subject area are essential. If you decide the item is not relevant, put it in a safe place in case you change your mind later.

A critical analysis of the literature identifies and appraises the contribution to knowledge made by others and comments on any weaknesses. Comments may focus on such matters as the reliability, validity and generalizability of the findings, which we discussed in Chapter 4. The gaps and deficiencies in the literature are relevant because they suggest the specific areas where further research is needed. Most researchers highlight the limitations of their work and suggest avenues for future research. If you have difficulty in identifying a specific research problem or issue, consider:

- testing a theory in a different setting
- making a new analysis of existing data
- replicating a previous study to provide up-to-date knowledge.

Reviewing the literature involves locating, reading and evaluating previous studies as well as reports of casual observation and opinion (Gall, Gall and Borg, 2003). Therefore, a literature review is not merely a description of previous studies and other material you collected during your literature search but requires a critical analysis. Unfortunately, some students do not recognize this, as Bruce (1994) found out. She analysed the views of 41 students at an early stage in their studies and identified six ways in which they viewed the literature review. It may be useful to think of these categories as being successive layers in a student's understanding of the nature and purpose of a literature review, with the deeper level of understanding captured by the last three descriptions:

- a list, with the primary focus on listing what was read, rather than extracting and using the knowledge in the literature
- a search, with the emphasis on finding the existing literature
- a survey, where the researcher is interested in the knowledge in the literature, but does not relate it to his or her own activities
- a vehicle for learning, where the researcher considers he or she is improving his or her own personal knowledge on the subject
- a research facilitator, where the researcher improves not only his or her own knowledge, but the literature has an impact on the research project itself
- a report, which is a synthesis of the literature and the earlier experiences with which the researcher has engaged.

Box 5.8 shows a simple example of how to avoid summarizing one article after another and turning your review into the equivalent of a shopping list.

Box 5.8 Avoiding a shopping list approach

Shopping list approach

Davis (2005) found that white rabbits bred more prolifically than those with dark coloured fur.

Smith (2006) argued that Davis (2005) had not defined 'dark' fur.

Jones (2007) used five well-defined colours of rabbit and found evidence that white rabbits are the most prolific breeders.

Attempt at synthesis

The identification of the colour of a rabbit's fur as a predictor of fertility is controversial. Although it has been claimed that white rabbits are better breeders than other colours (Davis, 2005), the reliability of this conclusion has been questioned on the grounds that non-white colours have not been clearly defined (Smith, 2006). Evidence from a recent study by Jones (2007) suggests that white rabbits are indeed more prolific breeders than four other well-defined colours of rabbit.

5.5 Avoiding plagiarism

Plagiarism is the act of taking someone's words, ideas or other information and passing them off as your own because you fail to acknowledge the original source. It is a form of academic misconduct that is taken very seriously, as it is the equivalent of stealing intellectual property.

Plagiarism is easily avoided if you follow the rules of one of the standard referencing systems, such as the Harvard system we have described in this chapter. In this chapter, we have emphasized the absolute necessity of applying the rules of the referencing system you are using when writing your literature review, but we would now like to emphasize that this is necessary throughout your work, whether you are writing your research proposal, the final dissertation or thesis, or an academic paper after you have completed your research.

The reason why it is imperative that you avoid plagiarism is that your supervisors, examiners and others evaluating your research need to distinguish between the contribution to knowledge made by others and the contribution made by your study. It is your responsibility to ensure that your work is meticulously referenced, that every quotation is enclosed in quotation marks and, whether it is text, a table, a diagram or other item that is reproduced, you show it exactly as it is in the original. This includes the punctuation, any emphasis (such as capital letters, italics or bold) and layout. This does not apply if you using your own words or developing someone else's table, diagram or other item, where you still acknowledge the source but can present the data as you choose.

We now want to explain a different example of plagiarism, which concerns submitting a piece of your own work for assessment if you have already received credits for it on another course. You cannot use the same research report you had assessed as part of a previous course or degree programme as your dissertation or thesis for a subsequent award.

It is not a defence to say you were not aware that you had committed plagiarism. Therefore, you need to familiarize yourself with the regulations (and penalties) that apply in your institution. If you are still in any doubt about what constitutes plagiarism, seek advice from your supervisor. To help you avoid the pitfalls, Box 5.9 provides a checklist for referencing.

Box 5.9 Checklist for referencing under the Harvard system

- Have I acknowledged other people's work, ideas and all sources of secondary data?
- Have I enclosed quotations in quotation marks and cited the author(s), date and page number in the original source?
- Have I acknowledged the source of all tables, diagrams and other items reproduced, including the number of the page in the original source?
- Have I applied the rules consistently?
- Have I included full bibliographic details for every source cited in my list of references?

5.6 Conclusions

Searching and reviewing the literature is a major part of your research and, although an intensive phase at the start of the project, will continue on a smaller scale until you submit your dissertation or thesis. Therefore, it is essential to start as soon as possible. This will be when you have chosen a general topic that is relevant to your course; it does not matter that you have not yet identified a particular research problem or issue to investigate, because you will identify this from studying the literature and identifying the need for your study. Most students will be required to incorporate a preliminary literature review in their research proposal, and this will be essential if you are applying for funding. All students will need to write a comprehensive critical literature review for their dissertation or thesis.

Searching the literature is time-consuming. It is rarely a problem locating literature but often a matter of not becoming overwhelmed by the number of items found. In this chapter we have given you guidance on how to define the scope of your research and narrow your search so that you focus as closely as possible on the relevant literature. You will then need to become familiar with the literature, which means setting aside plenty of time to read it, select what is relevant to your study and analyse it using a systematic method. You will write about the methods you used to search the literature (and what sources you searched) and how you analysed the material in your methodology chapter in your dissertation or thesis. In your proposal, you only need to indicate the main sources you will use, such as the journals and databases to which your institution subscribes.

In your literature review, and throughout your research, you must cite your sources correctly and provide full bibliographic details in your list of references. We have explained the principal rules of the Harvard system of referencing, but you must check which system you are expected to use. If your institution uses the APA system, you will find it is very similar to the Harvard system. More information on referencing will be available from your library and supervisor. It is your responsibility to ensure that you have not committed plagiarism. Many institutions use detection software to check for this and your supervisor will also be alert to this form of cheating. We have warned you about the dangers of plagiarism because it is taken very seriously and the penalties are harsh.

Remember that your literature review is not a shopping list and you must write a critical analysis that provides the context for your research, and concludes by identifying the need for your study and the main research question(s) it addresses. If you are a positivist, an important function of the literature review is to identify your theoretical framework and hypotheses. Box 5.10 shows a checklist for a literature review that draws together some of the main issues.

Box 5.10 Checklist for the literature review

- Have you cited the most important experts in your field?
- Have you referred to major research studies which have made a contribution to our knowledge?
- Have you referred to articles in the most important academic journals in your area?
- Have you identified any major government or other institutional study in your research field?
- Have you identified studies that use the same paradigms and methodologies you propose?
- Have you identified serious criticisms of any of the studies conducted?
- Have you avoided plagiarism?

References

Bruce, C. S. (1994) 'Research students' early experiences of the dissertation literature review', *Studies in Higher Education*, 9(2), pp. 217–29.

Creswell, J. W. (2014) *Research Design*, 4th edn. Thousand Oaks, CA: SAGE.

Gall, M. D., Gall, J. P. and Borg, W. R. (2003) *Educational Research: An Introduction*, 7th edn. Boston: Allyn & Bacon.

Gill, J. and Johnson, P. (2010) *Research Methods for Managers*, 4th edn. London: Paul Chapman.

Hart, C. (1998) *Doing a Literature Review.* London: SAGE.

Pears, R. and Shields, G. (2013) *Cite Them Right*, 9th edn. Basingstoke: Palgrave Macmillan.

Ryan, B., Scapens, R. W. and Theobald, M. (2002) *Research Method and Methodology in Finance and Accounting*, 2nd edn. London: Thomson.

Wallace, M. and Wray, A. (2011) *Critical Reading and Writing for Postgraduates*, 2nd edn. London: SAGE.

For Activities, see opposite.

Ready for more? Try the progress test online at www.palgrave.com/business/collis/br4/

Have a look at the Troubleshooting chapter and sections 14.2, 14.5, 14.6, 14.7, 14.9, 14.10, 14.14 in particular, which relate specifically to this chapter.

Activities

1. Take four different journals from different disciplines in your library and identify which system of referencing each journal uses.
2. Using an appropriate bibliographic database, search for information on a well-known company in your own country. Limit your results by date, country or any other variable available on the database. Repeat this with another database and compare the number of 'hits' you get and the features of the search facilities and presentation of the results.
3. Identify a major author in your field of research and conduct a search for all articles he or she has written. If any are co-authored, search for articles published by each author individually.
4. List the main findings of six key articles on your field of research. Then write a synthesis of the findings in no more than two paragraphs.
5. Literature review exercise
   The following reviews have been written by two students who have read the same articles. Which do you think is the better review and why?

Review 1

The popularity of roller-blading in the UK has its roots in the 1990s. Jane Iceslider (1990) describes roller-blading as a means of keeping fit for ice skating during the summer months. In a later article she reinforces this view, as evidenced by her comment, 'All my ice-skating friends use roller-blading as part of their fitness training' (Iceslider, 1992, p. 56).

Greg Sniffer, a reformed drug dealer, argues that roller-blades provide 'quick escape from any nosy cops' (Sniffer, 1998, p. 122).

Social worker, John Goodchild, describes roller-blading as 'a non-contact dance replacement activity for young people' (Goodchild, 1996, p. 29). He cites the growing popularity of children's roller discos in support of his claim. In a later article he notes that 'rollerblading is becoming an environmentally-friendly means of transportation in urban locations' (Goodchild, 1999, p. 30).

In his school magazine, Jason Scruff, describes roller-blading as being great fun, adding that all his mates go roller-blading (Scruff, J., 1996). In the same article he mentions how using roller-blades allows him to finish his paper round much faster than when walking. In an accompanying article, Melanie Scruff (Jason's sister), contends that 'roller discos are a great place to meet boys' (Scruff, M., 1996, p. 3) and that she would rather roller-blade into town to meet friends on a Saturday than walk or catch the bus.

Review 2

There is little agreement between authors for the reasons why people roller-blade in the UK. Initially it appears to have been a keep-fit activity (Iceslider, 1990 and 1992), but over time roller-blading appears to have become a fashionable activity (Goodchild, 1996), a social activity (Scruff, M., 1996) and a means of transport for work (Sniffer, 1998; Goodchild, 1999) and leisure (Scruff, M. 1996).

There is some evidence that young people have multiple reasons for roller-blading. For example, one teenager's motivation for roller-blading was in part due to following trends, but also to the speed of transportation compared to walking (Scruff, J., 1996).

Although it is possible that Goodchild (1996 and 1999) has based his conclusions on observation of particular cases of children's behaviour, there appears to have been no formal research into the reasons for the popularity of roller-blading in the UK. Therefore, there is scope for an exploratory study to identify the main motivations for the popularity of this activity.

References

Goodchild, J. D. (1996) 'The sociology of rollerblading', *Journal of Street Credibility*, 1(1), pp. 29–33.

Goodchild, J. D. (1999) 'Rollerblading to save the planet', *Journal of Street Credibility*, 3(3), pp. 8–9.

Iceslider, J. (1990) 'Why I rollerblade', *Journal of Fitness*, 3(2), pp. 21–2.

Iceslider, J. (1992) 'Rollerblade your way to fitness', *Journal of Fitness*, 5(1), pp. 53–6.

Scruff, J. (1996) 'Roller discos and Boys', *Kingston School Magazine*, Summer term, p. 4.

Scruff, M. (1996) 'Rollerblading is cool', *Kingston School Magazine*, Summer term, p. 3.

Sniffer, G. (1998) 'How I kicked the habit', *Rehabilitation Quarterly*, Winter, pp.122–5.

Adapted from 'A Mock Literature Review' (Anon.)

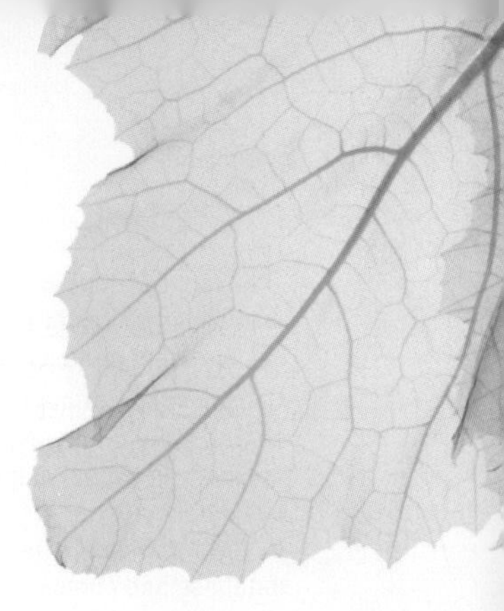

6

writing your research proposal

learning objectives

When you have studied this chapter, you should be able to:

- identify a research problem or issue
- determine the purpose of the research
- identify the main research question(s)
- determine the research design
- write a research proposal.

6.1 Introduction

Having identified your research paradigm, selected a research topic and begun to investigate the relevant literature, you are now ready to design your study and write your research proposal. If you are a student, the intellectual sophistication and length of your proposal will depend on the level and requirements of your programme, but once accepted by your supervisor(s), this critical document provides you with a detailed plan for your study. If you are bidding for research funds, your proposal will also play an important role.

This chapter draws together much of the information and guidance given in earlier chapters. For most students, writing their research proposal is the first formal milestone in their studies and paves the way for their dissertation or thesis. If you are studying for a Master's degree or a doctorate, it is likely that your research proposal will need to be more substantial than the proposal required for a Bachelor's degree. This means you will have to spend more time working on it to obtain the approval of your supervisor(s) and/or research committee. All students may find it useful to look at the examples of proposals at the end of the chapter.

We start by guiding you through the process of designing your research and then go on to explain how to communicate the main features of your proposed study in your research proposal. It is important to remember that we are only able to give general advice, and you will need to follow the specific requirements of your institution.

6.2 Overview of research design

Before you can write your research proposal, you must spend some time designing your proposed study. According to Vogt and Burke Johnson (2011), research design is the science and art of planning procedures for conducting studies so as to get the most valid findings. Determining your research design will give you a detailed plan, which you will use to guide and focus your research. Whether you are on an undergraduate course or are a postgraduate student, you will be expected to set out your research design in a document known as a research proposal. This is an important step because your research project will be accepted or rejected on the basis of your proposal.

McKerchar (2009) identifies the following characteristics of good research design:

- There is a good fit between the methodology and a paradigm that is understood and accepted by others, especially your supervisor.
- There is a fundamental framework or structure that guides the conduct of the research.
- Appropriate strategies of inquiry or research methods are employed.
- The design allows for knowledge claims to be made that are consistent with the strategy of inquiry.
- It allows the researcher to address the research question(s) and hence meet the aims and objectives of the study.

However, there are a number of constraints on achieving the optimal research design as Bono and McNamara (2011, p. 657) point out: 'The practical problem confronting researchers as they design studies is that (a) there are no hard and fast rules to apply; matching research design to research questions is as much art as science; and (b) external factors sometimes constrain researchers' ability to carry out optimal designs.'

Before you can begin designing your project, you need to have identified your research paradigm and chosen a research topic. You will remember that your choice of paradigm has important implications for your choice of methodology and the methods you will use to collect and analyse your research data. It also influences your choice of research problem and research questions. Figure 6.1 shows the main steps in research design. This simple model suggests the process is linear and moves smoothly from the research problem to the expected outcome. In practice, however, the process is often circular, reiterative and time-consuming, so do not be surprised if you find yourself constantly reviewing previous stages as you progress.

The **research problem** is the specific problem or issue that is the focus of the research.

The first step in designing your research is to identify a **research problem** or issue to investigate. However, you must remember that this does not take place in a vacuum, but in a particular context. Although you may have already determined your research paradigm, you might find that you have selected a research problem where you consider it is necessary to change some of your basic assumptions. Therefore, you may have to review your choice of paradigm and reflect on how appropriate it is to the problem you have identified. Another possibility is that you have picked a problem which is not acceptable to your supervisor or which for practical reasons cannot be investigated.

You will need to refine your research problem by providing a succinct purpose statement and developing research question(s). In a positivist study, you will develop a theoretical framework which will lead to hypotheses. In an interpretivist study, you are more likely to determine the purpose of your research and construct only one or two questions that you will refine and modify, and set within a theoretical context during the course of the research itself. The final stages of your research design will be defining terms, establishing your methodology and giving an indication of the expected outcome. It is important to remember that 'the more sophisticated and rigorous the research design is, the greater the time, costs, and other resources expended on it will be' (Sekaran, 2003, p. 118).

In the following sections we consider each of these activities separately. However, it is important to remember that although we have shown them in a linked sequence, in practice, research is seldom quite so straightforward and orderly. It is highly likely that you will have to retrace your steps and review some of the earlier stages as more information and more problems come to light in the later stages of constructing your research design. We will now examine each of the stages of research design shown in Figure 6.1 in detail.

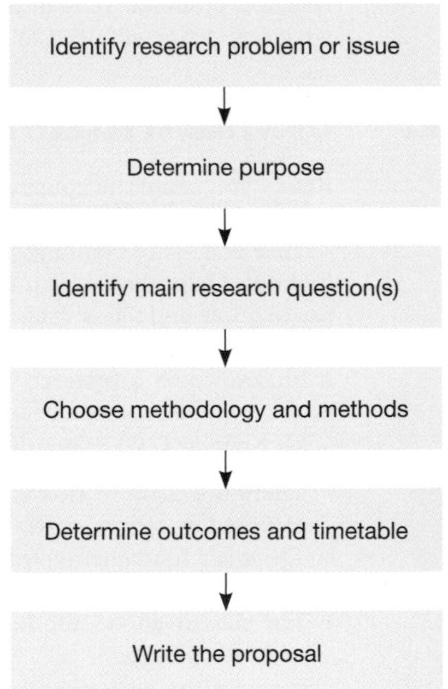

Figure 6.1 Main steps in research design

6.3 The research problem

6.3.1 Identifying a research problem

You will remember from previous chapters that a research project must focus on a specific problem or issue. If you are a student, this topic must be relevant to your degree programme and, if you are receiving funding, it must be relevant to your sponsor. Of course, it must also be a topic that is of interest to you!

When you have chosen your research problem, you will find it useful to write a simple statement describing it to help you to remain focused while planning the design of your research. Table 6.1 gives some examples of business research problems other students have identified.

Table 6.1 Examples of research problems

Research topic	Research problem
Accounting regulations	Whether accounting practices should be regulated by the government or by the accounting profession
Corporate governance	How corporate governance can be extended to employee communications
Financial accounting in the NHS	The use of financial accounting by doctors in general practice
Financial reporting	The most effective ways for communicating financial information to stakeholders
Environmental issues in accounting ethics	The criteria by which shareholders measure 'green' companies
Environmental issues in manufacturing	The influence of 'green' factors on supplier selection in the manufacturing sector
Gender issues in employment	The effect of career-break schemes on the recruitment and retention of skilled staff
Public service announcements as a method of communication	The effectiveness of public service announcements for communicating with students

Identifying a research problem or issue is always an exploratory and reiterative phase in your research. There are a number of ways in which you can develop your ideas within a general topic of interest. These include reading the relevant literature, discussions with your lecturers and other students, and looking at previous students' dissertations and theses. When choosing a research problem, you need to bear in mind that your study must be achievable in terms of the resources available, your skills and the time constraints imposed by the submission date. It must also be sufficiently challenging to meet the academic standards expected at your level of study.

The classic way in academic research is to read the literature on the topic of interest to you and identify any gaps and deficiencies in previous studies, since these will indicate opportunities for further research. Figure 6.2 shows a useful procedure for doing this. Identifying a research problem or issue can be a lengthy business since you have to keep revising your initial ideas and referring to the literature until you arrive at a business problem or issue you think will lead to a researchable project. You know that you are arriving at this stage when you can start generating suitable research questions.

Your initial search will probably result in three or four projects within your broad area of interest. You now need to compare them so that you can select one. At this stage it is helpful to eliminate any research problem that you consider is less likely to lead to a successful outcome. Although you may select a topic that is of great interest to you (and your supervisor), at the end of the day you will want to submit a research report which receives a high mark from the examiner or is accepted by the research/doctoral committee. Therefore, you need to examine your list of potential research problems critically and make certain that you select the one likely to give you the highest chance of success. We discuss the specific issues that give some indication of which of the research problems or issues you identify are likely to be the most researchable next.

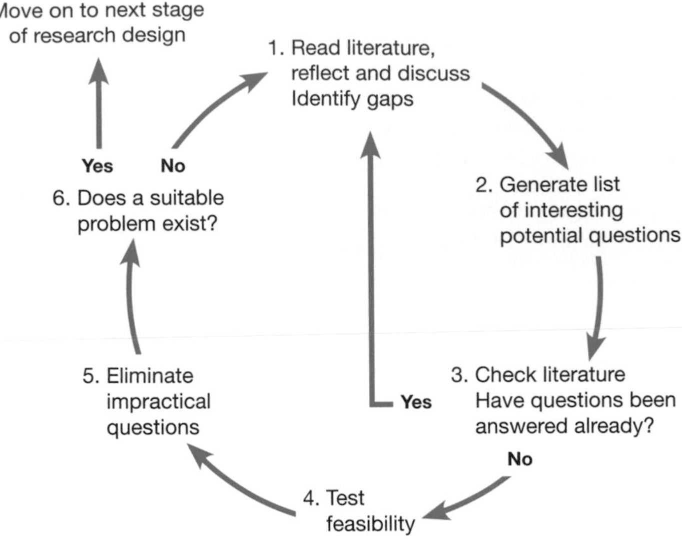

Figure 6.2 Identifying a research problem

6.3.2 Access to data

The availability of data is crucial to the successful outcome of your research. The term **data** refers to known facts or things used as a basis for inference or analysis. You will need to find out whether you will be able to have access to all the secondary and/or primary data you need for your study. Although you may be able to think of a number of interesting problems, your final choice may be constrained because the necessary data either are not available or are very difficult to collect.

Data are known facts or things used as a basis for inference or reckoning.

Many students fail to appreciate the barriers to collecting data. For example, postal questionnaire response rates are often very low; 20% is typical. Companies will rarely provide commercially sensitive information and in many cases may not have suitable records to allow them to give the required data. Therefore, before deciding on your research project, you must be sure that you will be able to get the data and other information you will need to conduct your research. Table 6.2 provides a checklist that you may find useful for assessing the availability of data.

Table 6.2 Assessing the availability of data

Type of data	Source
The literature	Check journal databases for academic articles, the library catalogue and Internet for other publications.
Official statistics	National jurisdictions, the European Commission and international organizations such as the World Bank publish statistics on their websites. Some may be available in your library.
Industry data	You may need background information about a particular industry. Check your library catalogue, databases and the Internet
Company data	Information may be available on the company's website and the company's annual report and accounts (which contains extensive narrative information in the case of listed companies). Check your library catalogue for other publications.

Type of data	Source
Internal data	List the information you require from the organization's records and get permission/confirmation of access in writing. Do not use unethical methods, such as asking a friend who happens to work in the accounts department!
People	How many will you need to see? Do you know them already? Have you got the necessary communication skills and recording equipment? Do you have sufficient funds and time?
Surveys	Where will you find a list of relevant organizations and contact details? How many interviews or questionnaires will you need for your analysis? What response rate do you anticipate? Do you have sufficient funds and time?

6.3.3 Your skills and resources

When planning your research, you need to consider what you will need to know and do to complete your research. You should be able to gain a reasonable understanding of your subject area by reading the relevant literature, but you will also need other skills, such as:

- IT skills for searching the literature and analysing data
- creative skills for designing questions and communicating concepts
- verbal communication skills for interviewing
- knowledge of statistics if you are planning a quantitative analysis
- general analytical skills if you are planning to interpret qualitative data
- verbal and written communication skills for presenting your research.

If you know that you have certain weaknesses, you need to assess whether you can overcome them in the time available. Your project is a period of development and you should welcome any opportunity to improve your skills and exploit your existing strengths.

When considering different research problems, it is useful to look at the implications of your choice. We summarize the main criteria for assessing potential research topics in Box 6.1.

Box 6.1 Criteria for assessing a research topic

- Is the topic relevant to your degree?
- Is the scope of the topic sufficiently narrow to make it feasible?
- Do you have access to the data you will need to research this topic?
- Do you have enough time to develop the knowledge and skills to research this topic?
- Is your interest in this topic sufficient to keep you motivated over the duration of the research?
- Is an article on this topic likely to be publishable in an academic journal (or attractive to a research committee)?
- Will the study fill a gap in knowledge, extend or replicate a previous study or develop new ideas in the literature?
- Will the study enhance your employability?

6.4 Purpose of the research

The **unit of analysis** is the phenomenon under study, about which data are collected and analysed.

Once you have chosen a suitable research problem or issue, your next task is to identify the overall purpose of the research and determine the **unit of analysis**. The unit of analysis is the phenomenon under study, about which data are collected and analysed, and is closely linked to the research problem and research questions. In business research, a unit of analysis might be a particular organization, division or department within an organization, or a more general group, such as business owners, managers, advisers or regulators. It could also be an inanimate object such as a particular type of event, decision, procedure, contract or communication (Blumberg, Cooper and Schindler, 2005).

Kervin (1992) suggests that it is generally best to select a unit of analysis at as low a level as possible. This should be at the level where decisions are made. Table 6.3 shows examples of different units of analysis, starting at the lowest and simplest level.

Table 6.3 Units of analysis

Unit of analysis	Example
An individual	A manager, employee, union member, investor, lender, supplier or customer
An event	A merger, strike, relocation, acquisition, change of leadership, change of strategy or decision to divest or close
An object	A machine, product, service or document
An organization or group of people	A type of business, division, department, committee or particular group of employees
A relationship	A manager/subordinate relationship, management/union relationship or head office/branch relationship, investor/manager relationship or customer/supplier relationship
An aggregate	A collection of undifferentiated individuals or bodies with no internal structure, such as companies in a certain industry, businesses of a certain size or in a particular location

Once you have determined your unit of analysis, you can state the purpose of your study clearly and succinctly. This can be achieved by writing two or three sentences that explain the main aim of the research and the more detailed objectives. The content depends on whether you are designing your research under a positivist or an interpretivist paradigm. You will use the future tense when explaining the purpose of the study in your proposal, but in your dissertation or thesis you will use the present or the past tense. Your writing style will reflect your rhetorical assumptions.

In a positivist study, the researcher adopts a formal style and uses the passive voice, accepted quantitative words and set definitions. For example, instead of writing 'I will hold interviews with ...' or 'I held interviews with ...' you will write 'Interviews will be held with ...' or 'Interviews were held with ...'. This is because positivists are trying to convey their rhetorical assumptions (see Chapter 4) and emphasize their independence and objectivity. The purpose statement needs to identify the sample, the unit of analysis and the variables to be studied. It may also be appropriate to identify key theory and the methods to be employed. The statement does not have to follow a formula. In the example in Box 6.2, the researcher explains the purpose of the research at the same time as describing the context and rationale for the study.

Box 6.2 Example of a purpose statement in a positivist study

This study focuses on a sample of 592 small companies in the UK, which includes 419 companies that are likely to be categorized as micro-companies under the European Commission's proposed Directive on accounting for 'micro-entities' (EC 2007, 2011). The sample represents a subset of private companies that took part in a survey commissioned by the Department for Business, Enterprise and Regulatory Reform (BERR) (Collis 2008). The purpose of this study is to contribute to the literature by investigating the determinants of two voluntary behaviours in micro- and non-micro small private companies: non-statutory audit and the filing of voluntary full accounts. The research examines the reasons for the auditing and filing decisions made in connection with the companies' financial statements for accounting periods ending in 2006 in the context of the UK raising the size thresholds for a small company to the EU maxima in 2004. It also explores the potential impact of the proposed Directive on accounting for 'micro-entities', which is intended to reduce accounting and financial reporting obligations for approximately 5.3 million companies, representing some 75% of entities within scope of the Fourth Company Law Directive (EC 2008a). It has the potential to affect some 60% of registered companies in the UK (BIS/FRC 2011).

Source: Collis (2012, pp. 1–2). Reprinted by permission of the publisher (Taylor & Francis Ltd, http://www.tandfonline.com).

In an interpretivist study it is normal to emphasize the methodology employed and to imply the inductive nature of the research. The central phenomenon being explored should be described as well as the location of the study. To reflect the rhetorical assumption of this paradigm, the researcher uses the personal voice, accepted qualitative terms and limited definitions. For example, instead of writing 'Interviews will be held with …' or 'Interviews were held with …', you will write 'I will hold interviews with …' or 'I held interviews with …'. This is because you are trying to convey the philosophical assumptions that are appropriate to your paradigm, emphasizing your involvement and subjectivity. In the example in Box 6.3, the researcher explains the purpose of the study and also gives details of the research questions.

Box 6.3 Example of a purpose statement in an interpretivist study

The purpose of this study is to address the gaps in the literature by providing empirical evidence on the value of the financial statements of incorporated and unincorporated SMEs in the context of trade credit decisions that support customer/supplier relationships. To obtain insights into potential international differences, we examine cases in Finland, the UK, South Africa and the USA in order to investigate the following research questions:

1. What are the main sources of information and types of information used by SMEs when making credit decisions in connection with new or existing customers?
2. What are the main sources and types of information used by credit rating agencies and credit insurers when making credit rating decisions?
3. In both cases, how is the information used and for what purposes?
4. In both cases, what other information would the decision maker like to see in the financial statements that would aid their decision?
5. What are the international similarities and differences in the findings in the context of institutional factors?

Source: Collis, Jarvis and Page (2013, p. 4).

6.5 The research questions

When you explain the purpose of your study, you may only give the general aims and objectives, but you can see from the example in Box 6.3 that the researchers have listed their **research questions**. A research question states the specific line of inquiry the research will investigate and attempt to answer. Therefore, your research questions provide a focus for your endeavours and are not the actual questions you might use in a questionnaire or interview. Identifying the research question(s) is a crucial stage in your research because it lies at the heart of your research design.

A **research question** is a specific question the research is designed to investigate and attempt to answer.

Figure 6.3 shows a simple model of how you can develop research questions. At each stage in the process you need to read, reflect and discuss what you are doing with others. The people you discuss your research with may be fellow students as well as your supervisor. We have already identified research as a process of inquiry, so the outcome of your investigation will be answers. However, you must ensure that the answers will be of interest or importance, otherwise your research will not receive much attention.

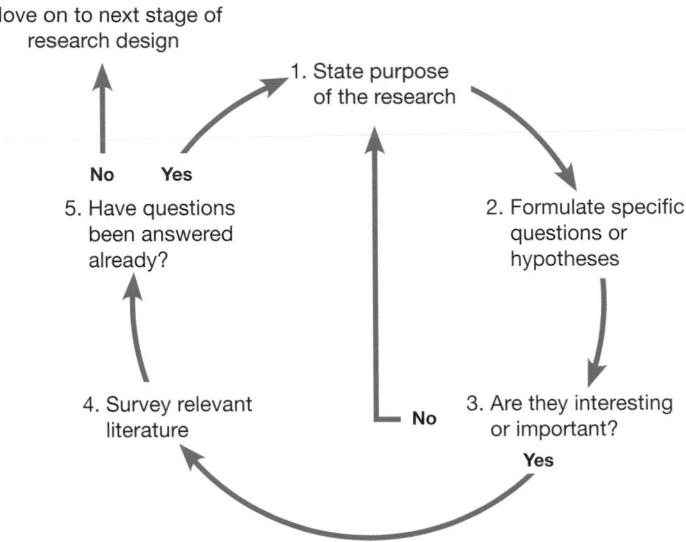

Figure 6.3 Identifying research questions

Before launching your investigations, you must search the relevant literature to see if anyone else has already answered your particular questions. If not, you can commence your research. However, if work has already been done in your chosen area, you may have to find ways of amending your proposed research so that it will produce new findings by extending or updating the existing body of knowledge.

6.5.1 Role of theory

A **theoretical framework** is a collection of theories and models from the *literature* which underpins a positivist study. Theory can be generated from some interpretivist studies.

A **theory** is a set of interrelated variables, definitions and propositions that specifies relationships among the variables.

A **hypothesis** is a proposition that can be tested for association or causality against empirical evidence.

According to Kerlinger and Lee (2000), a **theory** is a set of interrelated variables, definitions and propositions that presents a systematic view of phenomena by specifying relationships among variables with the purpose of explaining natural phenomena. On a more simple level, theories are 'explanations of how things function or why events occur' (Black, 1993, p. 25). A **theoretical framework** is a collection of theories and models from the literature. It is a fundamental part of most research studies and underpins the research questions. However, these can also be suggested by empirical evidence (from an exploratory study, for example), from which you subsequently develop a theory and construct propositions to test.

Although some applied research has no theoretical background, if theory exists, you can develop a testable **hypothesis**. A hypothesis is a proposition that can be tested for association or causality against empirical evidence using statistics. Thus, hypotheses are associated with the positivist paradigm where the logic of the research is deductive and quantitative methods of analysis are used. However, Blaikie (2000, p. 10) argues that in some studies 'the testing is more in terms of a discursive argument from evidence' and therefore does not involve the use of statistical tests.

According to Merriam (1988), theories can be classified into three types:

- grand theories, which are most often found in the natural sciences (such as the law of gravity)
- middle-range theories, which are placed higher than mere working hypotheses, but do not have the status of a grand theory
- substantive theories, which are developed within a certain context.

Laughlin (1995, p. 81) argues that in the social sciences it is not possible to have a grand theory, only skeletal theory, where 'empirical data will always be of importance to make the skeleton complete in particular contexts'. This does not mean that the theory will be changed or permanently completed, but will remain as a general framework within which a study can be conducted. Glaser and Strauss (1967) emphasize the importance of substantive theories, where theory is derived from the data, which they describe as *grounded theory* (see Chapter 9).

Given these differences of opinion, you may find it confusing trying to develop a theoretical framework. However, there are a number of theories, concepts and models from which you can draw, and you will discover them when you study the literature on your chosen topic. They are important in many studies because they provide possible explanations for what is observed.

6.5.2 Research questions in a positivist study

For a study designed under a positivist paradigm, Black (1993) recommends a specific research question, followed by a number of hypotheses. Kerlinger and Lee (2000) suggest that good research questions for a positivist study should:

- express a relationship between variables
- be stated in unambiguous terms in question form
- imply the possibility of empirical testing.

Your hypotheses will be based on theory. Each hypothesis is a proposition about the relationship between two variables that can be tested for association or causality against the empirical evidence you collect for your study.

Your hypothesis will identify the independent variable and the dependent variable. The null hypothesis (H_0) states that the two variables are independent of one another and the alternative hypothesis (H_1) states that they are associated with one another. For example, if you thought that older employees might work more slowly than young employees, your null and alternative hypotheses would be respectively:

H_0 There is no relationship between an employee's age and productivity.
H_1 There is a relationship between an employee's age and productivity.

In this example, age is the independent variable and productivity is the dependent variable. The purpose of your research will be to test specific aspects of any theory you may have found in the literature which suggests that there is a relationship between age and productivity level. Using the null hypothesis ensures that you adopt a cautious and critical approach when conducting statistical tests on your data.

Sometimes theory suggests that there is a possible direction for the relationship. In this case, you may decide to use a directional hypothesis. For example:

H_0 Productivity does not decrease as an employee increases in age.
H_1 Productivity decreases as an employee increases in age.

As you will have a number of hypotheses, it is important to use a formal, rhetorical style by repeating the same key phrases in the same order. For example:

There is no relationship between an employee's age and the level of productivity.
There is no relationship between an employee's age and the level of absenteeism.
There is no relationship between an employee's age and degree of skill.

You will subsequently use statistics to test whether there is evidence to reject the null hypothesis that states that there is no relationship (see Chapters 11 and 12). As you read the literature on your topic, note whether the authors have stated their hypotheses in the null or the alternative form. You may also wish to ask your supervisor whether he or she has a preference.

6.5.3 Research questions in an interpretivist study

In an interpretivist study, a theoretical framework may be less important or less clear in its structure. Some researchers attempt to approach their analysis with no prior theories, as they consider doing so would constrain and blinker them. Instead, they focus on trying to develop a theoretical framework, which is sometimes referred to as a model or substantive theory. It has been argued that 'even in wanting to escape theory, to be open-minded or wanting to believe that theorizing was unimportant to science, we would be practising a theory' (Slife and Williams, 1995, p. 9).

In some interpretivist studies, the research question takes the form of a grand tour question (Werner and Schoepfle, 1987), which is a single research question, posed in its most general form. For example, 'How do employees cope with redundancy in an area of high unemployment?' By doing this, the researcher does not block off any other potential lines of inquiry. This is necessary where an emerging methodology, such as grounded theory, is used and one stage of the research guides the next stage. Nevertheless, the aim of a grand tour question is to focus the study on certain phenomena or a particular direction. It may need to be refined during the course of the research and this may mean you need to change the title of your project to reflect the final research question(s). Creswell (2014) advises one or two grand tour questions, followed by no more than five to seven subsidiary questions.

The criteria for a good research question are less clear in interpretivist studies than in positivist studies. This is due to the importance of the interaction between the researcher and the subject of the study in the former. If you are planning to conduct an interpretivist study, you will find that your research questions often evolve during the process of research and may need to be refined or modified as the study progresses. You will find that there are different customs in different interpretivist methodologies, which will be apparent from the literature you read on your topic. The best advice is to concentrate on the language of the question. It is usual to begin the research questions with 'what' or 'how' and to avoid terms associated with positivism, such as 'cause', 'relationship' or 'association'. Creswell (2014) suggests that you should:

- avoid wording that suggests a relationship between variables, such as 'effect', 'influence', 'impact' or 'determine'

- use open-ended questions without reference to the literature or theory, unless otherwise dictated by the research design
- use a single focus and specify the research site.

Finally, you should not underestimate the influence of your paradigm on your research design. Box 6.4 illustrates this with two examples based on the same research problem and research questions.

Box 6.4 Example of the influence of paradigm on research design

Topic: Gender issues in employment
Research problem: The effect of the new career-break scheme in Firm A on the recruitment and retention of skilled staff

Research question: How has the new career-break scheme contributed to employment in Firm A?

- What is the nature of the scheme? (descriptive)
- What effect has it had on recruitment of male and female skilled staff? (analytical)
- What effect has it had on the retention of male and female skilled staff? (analytical)

Research design for a positivist study:

- Methodology: Case study
- Methods: Statistical analysis of (a) secondary data from staff employment records and (b) primary data from a self-completion questionnaire survey of staff

Research design for an interpretivist study:

- Methodology: Case study
- Methods: Thematic analysis of data from semi-structured interviews with staff (primary data)

6.6 Writing the research proposal

6.6.1 Overview

A **research proposal** is a document that sets out the research design for a proposed study. It explains what is already known about the research topic, the purpose of the research and the main research question(s). It also describes the proposed methodology (including justification for the methods used to select a sample, collect and analyse the research data), the scope of the research and any limitations. It should incorporate a timetable and often concludes with comments on the contribution of the proposed research (the expected outcomes).

A **research proposal** is a document that sets out the research design for a proposed study.

Most institutions have a formal process for submitting a research proposal and instructions concerning the contents and the maximum word count. Your supervisor and/or research committee will be looking at academic issues as well as the feasibility of the proposed study.

The main academic issues being assessed are whether:

- the proposed study is based on the literature and is academically robust. You do this by demonstrating that you are familiar with the literature and have identified a main research question.
- the methodology clearly states the source(s) from which you will collect the research data, why you are collecting the data, when you are going to collect the data, and how you are going to collect and analyse the data. Be careful not overlook the impor-

tance of explaining your method for selecting a sample or cases and your method(s) of analysis.
- the proposed study will make a contribution to knowledge (for postgraduate and doctoral students)
- the proposed study will provide opportunities to disseminate research via conference papers and academic journal articles (for doctoral students).

The main practical issues being assessed are whether:

- you have access to the research data (primary, secondary or both). If your research requires access to confidential data, you must provide documentary evidence from the organization(s) and/or individual(s) confirming that access has been granted.
- you have access to any finance needed to conduct the research and there are no major time constraints that would prevent the completion of the project. Therefore, if you are struggling on a student grant, do not design a study that requires extensive travelling to obtain your data that would be both time-consuming and expensive.
- the outcome is achievable.

Although it is best to use the standard format if your institution provides one, there is still plenty of flexibility to allow you to put your research proposal in its best light. Table 6.4 shows a typical *structure* of a research proposal, together with some guidance on the proportion of space you should consider devoting to each section.

Table 6.4 Indicative structure of a research proposal

	% of proposal
1. Introduction • The research problem or issue and the purpose of the study • Background to the study and why it is important or of interest • Structure of the remainder of the proposal	15
2. Preliminary review of the literature • Evaluation of key items in the literature • Theoretical framework (if applicable) • Where your research fits in and the main research question(s)	40
3. Methodology • Identification of paradigm • Justification for choice of methodology and methods • Scope of the research • Limitations of the research design and constraints relating to costs and other resources • Consideration of ethical issues	40
4. Outcomes and timetable	5
	100
References (do not number this section)	

The detailed content of your proposal will depend on the nature of your research project and how you intend to conduct it, but we are now ready to look at the main items.

6.6.2 Title

The title of your proposed study should be as brief as possible. Creswell (2014) advises that you use no more than 12 words, consider eliminating most articles and prepositions, and make sure that it includes the focus or topic of the study. There is no need to include unnecessary phrases, such as 'An approach to ...' or 'A study of ...'. If you are carrying out research in one particular company or industry, make this clear. You may find it useful to look at the working titles used in the sample of research proposals at the end of this chapter.

6.6.3 Introduction

The research problem or issue that is the focus of the study should be stated clearly in your introduction. It can usually be expressed in one or two sentences. Resist the temptation to write in sentences that are so long that no one can understand them! Try showing your explanation of the research problem to fellow students, family and friends; if they understand it, it is likely you will impress your supervisor with your clarity.

You may find it helpful to follow this with a little background explaining why this issue is important or of interest, and to whom. This would be an appropriate place to define key terms as they arise in your narrative. You could conclude the introduction by explaining the purpose of the proposed study (using one of the model purpose statements we illustrated earlier, if you find this helpful).

You should define key terms (and any common terms you are using in a novel way) on the first occasion that you use them. You should use a definition from an authoritative academic source, such as a specialist dictionary in your discipline. We do not advise you to use Wikipedia or online sources from websites that can be posted or edited by the public. Remember that the definition should be in quotation marks and you should cite the name of the author(s), the year of publication and page number(s) in brackets next to the quotation. In a positivist study, this is essential and enhances the precision and rigour of your research.

6.6.4 Preliminary literature review

Your preliminary review of the literature should be a critical analysis of the main studies in the literature that are relevant to your chosen research problem or issue you intend to investigate. Do not fall into the trap of taking a 'shopping list' approach to writing about the previous research you have identified in academic journals, books and other sources and remember that your lecturer's slides are not publications! At this stage, you are not expected to review the entire body of existing knowledge on the topic. Your supervisor will be familiar with the literature, so it is imperative that you cite the key authors and refer to the main theories and models. If you are using grounded theory in an interpretivist study, you will still write a preliminary review of the literature, but you will not need to identify a theoretical framework. If you are adopting a grounded theory methodology, you will need to provide a convincing argument for this choice in your methodology section.

Your preliminary review of the literature should conclude with an explanation of where your research fills any gaps or deficiencies in the literature (a gap in the literature is where no knowledge exists about a particular phenomenon in a particular context; a deficiency in the literature might be that the existing knowledge is out of date). This will lead you to state your main research questions and hypotheses (if applicable). Of course, your research questions must be feasible and relate to the research problem identified in the introduction section of your proposal. It is better to omit a question if you know it will be very difficult to address, rather than include it because it looks impressive.

As mentioned in Chapter 5, you may find it useful to design a map of the literature to guide the structure of your preliminary literature review. This map represents a plan (similar to writing an essay plan) and you do not include it in your literature review.

If you are having difficulty in finding articles and other publications on your research topic, or you are unable to write your preliminary literature review, have a look at the advice in Chapter 14 (section 14.9). If you are having difficulty in finding a theoretical framework, refer to section 14.6.

6.6.5 Methodology

The methodology section in your proposal is where you describe your proposed research design. This section is important because it shows how you intend to investigate your research questions. You should be aware by now that your choice is dictated by your research paradigm. Therefore, it is essential to recognize the paradigm you have adopted, but you do not need to justify it. However, you do need to explain and justify your methodology, the methods you will use to select a sample or cases and the methods you will use to collect and analyse your research data. You can provide a rationale for your choice by weighing up the advantages and disadvantages of alternatives. You must demonstrate that you have access to the research data you will need by stating the source of the data and the name of any external organization or contacts who have agreed to help you gain access to data. You also need to show that you have considered ethical issues and any constraints relating to costs and other resources (see Chapter 2).

Whatever the size of your proposed study, you will have to constrain your inquiries in a number of ways. Therefore, you will need to state the **delimitations** that establish the scope of your research. For example, you may confine your interviews to employees in Firm A or you may restrict your postal questionnaire to certain businesses in a particular geographical area. It can be more difficult to define the scope in an interpretivist study because the nature of the research is one of exploration and discovery.

An approach that can be used under either paradigm is to *deconstruct* your research question or hypothesis. Parker (1994) illustrates this with a hypothesis from a positivist study, which is shown in Figure 6.4. The process enables you to explain every term in considerable detail within the context of your proposed research. Not only does this give you considerable insight into your research, but you are in a better position to communicate it in your proposal (and in your dissertation or thesis).

Most students will need to discuss issues such as reliability, validity and generalizability, and all students should state the **limitations** of their study. A limitation describes a weakness or deficiency in the research. For example, you may be planning a small exploratory study, from which only tentative conclusions can be drawn. This might be because you are planning a positivist study using a convenience sample rather than a random sample, or you are planning an interpretivist study but do not have the resources to conduct an in-depth case study. Sometimes additional limitations become apparent after the proposal stage and you will need to comment on these when you write your dissertation or thesis.

A **delimitation** establishes the scope of the research.
A **limitation** is a weakness or deficiency in the research.

Students are often reluctant to mention problems with their research. There is no need to emphasize them at the proposal stage, and a comment is usually sufficient. However, you should not ignore them, as they serve two useful purposes:

- to identify potential difficulties, which can be discussed with your supervisor to ascertain whether they need to be resolved or whether they are acceptable in the context of your research design
- to signal at an early stage some of the issues you will need to address both during the course of the research and when writing it up.

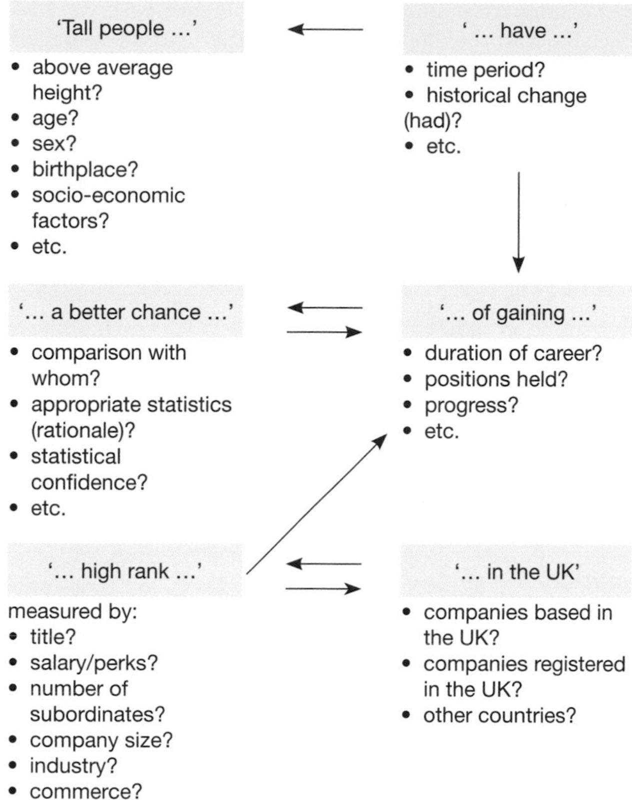

Figure 6.4 Example of deconstruction
'Tall people have a better chance of gaining high rank in the UK'
Source: Adapted from Parker (1994, p. 24).

If you are having difficulty in deciding which methodology and methods to use, have a look at the advice in Chapter 14 (sections 14.8, 14.10 and 14.12).

6.6.6 Contribution and timetable

At the proposal stage, you cannot describe the contribution of your research in terms of your findings. Therefore, the final section in your proposal is brief and will focus on the expected outcomes of the research. One way to express this is to refer to the purpose of the research. For example, if the purpose of your research is to investigate the impact of a new career-break scheme in Firm A, your expected outcomes are a description of the new scheme and an analysis of the impact of the scheme on the recruitment and retention of staff in Firm A. At all levels of research, but particularly at the doctoral level, it is important to emphasize that one outcome of the research is expected to be a contribution to knowledge. In your proposal, this can be stated in terms of the gaps and deficiencies you have identified in the literature.

Your proposed study must take account of the time constraints placed on the project by the submission date. You can use a *Gantt chart* with horizontal lines showing the timing of each stage to summarize your timetable (see Figure 6.5). We advise you to discuss your draft timetable with your supervisor. Even experienced researchers find that research always takes up more time than you think it will, so do allow a contingency for delays due to exams, job interviews, holidays, illness and so on. Jankowicz (1991) gives estimates of standard times for some project activities. These include one day for preparing a ten-question interview schedule and four weeks for piloting a large questionnaire. You must be realistic about the amount of time you have available and what you can achieve in that time.

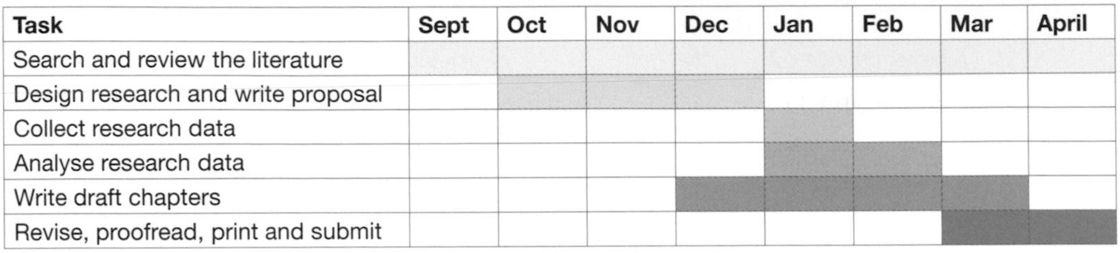

Task	Sept	Oct	Nov	Dec	Jan	Feb	Mar	April
Search and review the literature								
Design research and write proposal								
Collect research data								
Analyse research data								
Write draft chapters								
Revise, proofread, print and submit								

Figure 6.5 Example of a Gantt chart

6.6.7 Additional information

In some cases, you may need to include a statement of special resources required in your proposal (for example specialist software or access to particular libraries or organizations). If you are applying for funding, you will need to supply a budget for travelling to interviews, printing questionnaires, postage, purchasing reports and papers that are not available on loan and so on. Table 6.5 shows an example of how you might set out your budget (the figures are illustrative and the cost of the researcher's time is not included).

Table 6.5 Research budget

Expense	Basis of calculation	Cost	Comment
		€	
Travelling expenses	30 interviews @ €30	900	Car mileage from the university
Research reports	10 reports @ €15	150	Not available from library
Research assistant	100 hours @ €20 per hour	2,000	Data input and analysis
Conference	Fees, travel and accommodation	1,020	Dissemination of results
Submission of article	Submission fee	30	*World Journal of Management*
	Total	4,100	

If you are applying for funding, you may also be asked to provide a *statement of research activities and interests* to provide evidence of your suitability to carry out the proposed study. Box 6.5 shows an example of a suitable succinct statement that can be used as the basis for constructing your own.

Box 6.5 Statement of research activities and interests

For the past four years I have been very interested in the financial measures used to evaluate the performance of managers. This interest originated with my MBA. My dissertation, which received a distinction, was entitled '*The behavioural aspects of a budgetary control system in a small engineering company*'. From this I have developed three main areas of interest:

- Managerial performance measures in small manufacturing companies
- Managerial performance measures in financial services companies
- Managerial performance measures in charities

My research into these issues has resulted in five conference papers and two refereed journal articles, as shown in my CV. In the past two years I have spent approximately 70% of my research time conducting studies in XYZ Charity. This is a national charity to which I have full access, as confirmed in the attached letter from their CEO. My proposed research would take my previous research further by ...

6.6.8 References

The Harvard system of referencing is the method most commonly used in business and management. It allows you to avoid plagiarism by acknowledging all ideas and sources of information you have used in your work with a citation in the text and providing full bibliographic details at the end under the heading of references. Do not number the heading of this section and do not number the items listed, but place them in alphabetical order by author's name. This will allow any reader to locate and consult the original source of information; you can support all your assertions with an authoritative published source; and you can also show your supervisor the extent of your reading. Remember that however flattering it may be to your lecturers to be cited, their lecture slides are not a publication and you need to refer to the original publications to which they refer.

A citation is made whether the information from your reading of a publication takes the form of a quotation or is summarized in your own words. If you are quoting, or reproducing a table or figure, your citation must include the page number(s) as well as the name(s) of the author(s) and the year of publication (see Chapter 5). You should bear in mind that your ability to apply the accepted system of referencing is one of the criteria against which your proposal will be assessed.

The more academic articles, reports, books and other literature you have read on your research topic or on research methods, the more citations you will have made and the longer your list of references will be. Therefore, you need to keep careful records of all the hard copy and Internet sources you have used. Check that every citation in your proposal has a corresponding entry in your list of references and that you have not listed any items that you did not use and therefore did not cite. It is likely that your supervisor will do this when marking your proposal!

6.7 Evaluating your proposal

You will find that a considerable part of research involves reflecting on the work you have done. Designing your research is no exception. The most common reason for students failing at the proposal stage is because they have not been able to convert their general interest in a topic into the design of a study that will allow them to investigate a specific research problem. You must also ensure your design provides a good fit between your paradigm and the proposed methodology, and that the research process is logical. Your supervisor or sponsor will be looking at your research design from a practical point of view as well as an academic perspective, and will be assessing the feasibility of the design, given the resources available and the time constraints.

Feedback from peers and other researchers is very important and we strongly advise you to take every opportunity available to present your proposal to peers, at a research seminar or conference. A typical presentation would cover:

1 Title slide: Title of the study, your name and other pertinent details
2 Introduction: The purpose of the study (the aims and objectives) and the context
3 Preliminary literature review: An overview of the main previous studies (a map of the literature, it would provide a useful one-slide summary)
4 Proposed methodology: Sampling method, data collection and data analysis methods
5 Expected contribution.

As you get involved in selecting a suitable research problem and developing an appropriate research design, it is easy to forget the big picture. Here are some words of general advice:

- Don't be too ambitious. It is much better to submit a modest research proposal which you can achieve than to come to grief on a project which sets out to remedy all the problems of the world.
- Don't try to impress. The use of convoluted language and references to obscure articles does not help. Try to write simply and clearly so that any problems with your proposal can be identified and discussed with your supervisor.
- Discuss your proposal with friends and family. Although they may not be familiar with the subject matter, they can often ask the awkward question which you have not spotted.
- Be prepared to revise your proposal. It may be that you get part way through and realize that it is not possible to achieve all you set out to do. It is much better to correct this at the planning stage than to start the research and fail to complete it.
- Remember that your proposal is a plan. You will have done a considerable amount of work preparing it; do not throw it all away. You should use your proposal to guide and manage the research. This does not mean that you cannot adapt your work as the research progresses, but the proposal is a map which should indicate your course and allow you to decide why and when to depart from it.
- Allow time between completing your research proposal and submitting it so that you can reflect on it and make improvements.

If you are uncertain about how to write a research proposal that will be acceptable to your supervisor, have a look at the advice in Chapter 14 (section 14.7). Then use the checklist shown in Box 6.6 to evaluate it before your submit it to your supervisor (and/or potential sponsor).

Box 6.6 Project proposal checklist

1 Do you have, or can you acquire, the knowledge and skills to do the research?
2 Do you have the resources, such as computer facilities, travelling expenses?
3 Do you have access to the research data you need? If you need the cooperation of certain organizations or people, have you obtained their consent?
4 Does your title aptly describe your study?
5 Have you described the purpose and importance of your research?
6 Have you written a critical preliminary review of the literature and identified your main research question(s)?
7 Have you described and justified your methodology?
8 Is your timetable realistic?
9 Have you avoided plagiarism and checked that your work is correctly referenced?
10 Have you used the spelling and grammar check?

Just in case you are tempted to think that some of the items in the checklist are optional, Robson (2011) offers ten ways to get your proposal rejected. These are shown in Box 6.7.

Box 6.7 Ten ways to get your proposal turned down

1. Don't follow the directions or guidelines given for your kind of proposal. Omit information that is asked for. Ignore word limits.
2. Ensure the title has little relationship to the stated objectives; and that neither title nor objectives link to the proposed methods or techniques.
3. Produce woolly, ill-defined objectives.
4. Have the statement of the central problem or research focus vague, or obscure it by other discussion.
5. Leave the design and methodology implicit; let them guess.
6. Have some mundane task, routine consultancy or poorly conceptualized data trawl masquerade as a research project.
7. Be unrealistic in what can be achieved with the time and resources you have available.
8. Be either very brief, or preferably, long-winded and repetitive in your proposal. Rely on weight rather than quality.
9. Make it clear what the findings of your research are going to be, and demonstrate how your ideological stance makes this inevitable.
10. Don't worry about a theoretical or conceptual framework for your research. You want to do a down-to-earth study so you can forget all that fancy stuff.

Source: Robson (2011, p. 395). Reproduced with permission of Blackwell Publishing Ltd.

6.8 Conclusions

In this chapter we have built on your knowledge from studying the preceding chapters to explain how to design a research study and draw up a detailed plan for carrying out the study. We have explored ways in which you can identify a potential research problem by identifying gaps and deficiencies in the literature, and how the purpose of the research can be communicated succinctly through the use of a purpose statement. We have also discussed the role of the main research question(s), and the importance of determining your main research questions and a theoretical framework (the latter is not applicable if you are using a grounded theory methodology). We have looked at the role of hypotheses in a positivist study and the influence of your paradigm on your choice of methodology. Positivist and interpretivist studies will have different research designs. A positivist research design will incorporate a stronger theoretical basis and it will be necessary to develop hypotheses. There will be an emphasis on the proposed measurement and analysis of the research data. An interpretivist research design may incorporate a theoretical framework and set out various propositions, but the emphasis is more likely to be on the robustness of the methods that will be used to analyse the research data.

We have described how to write a research proposal, looked at a typical structure and suggested additional items that may need to be included, such as a statement of required resources, a budget or a statement of research activities and interests. Once your research proposal has been accepted, you can start collecting your research data. However, the acceptance of your proposal does not necessarily mean that your research project will be successful. A research proposal is merely a plan and the next step is to execute that plan. We explain how you can do this in the chapters that follow. You have already made a start because the majority of the sections you have written in your proposal will provide draft material for the chapters of your dissertation or thesis. During the course of your study, you should be adding to these draft chapters, discussing them with your supervisor(s) and making amendments.

Although every research proposal is unique, it is useful to look at other proposals. If you can obtain examples of successful proposals from your supervisor, these provide the best guide to what is acceptable at your own institution. The appendix at the end of this chapter contains a number of research proposals submitted by MPhil and PhD candidates. For the purpose of this book they have been abbreviated and therefore some of the richness of a full proposal is lost. Nevertheless, they provide useful illustrations of the style and content of postgraduate and doctoral proposals.

References

Black, T. R. (1993) *Evaluating Social Science Research.* London: SAGE.

Blaikie, N. (2000) *Designing Social Research.* Cambridge: Polity.

Blumberg, B., Cooper, D. R. and Schindler, P. S. (2005) Business Research Methods. Maidenhead: McGraw-Hill Education.

Bono, J. E. and McNamara, G. (2011) 'Publishing in *AMJ* – Part 2: Research Design, *Academy of Management Journal*, 54(4), pp. 657–60.

Collis, J. (2012) 'Determinants of voluntary audit and voluntary full accounts in micro- and non-micro small companies in the UK', *Accounting and Business Research,* 42(4), pp. 1–28.

Collis, J., Jarvis, R. and Page, M. (2013) *Value of the financial statements of SMEs to creditors,* ACCA Research Report. London: CAET.

Glaser, B. and Strauss, A. (1967) *The Discovery of Grounded Theory.* Chicago, IL: Aldine.

Jankowicz, A. D. (1991) *Business Research Projects for Students.* London: Chapman & Hall.

Kerlinger, F. N. and Lee, H. B. (2000) Foundations of *Behavioral Research,* 4th edn. Fort Worth, TX: Harcourt College Publishers.

Kervin, J. B. (1992) Methods for Business Research. New York: HarperCollins.

Laughlin, R. (1995) 'Methodological themes – empirical research in accounting: Alternative approaches and a case for "middle-range" thinking', *Accounting, Auditing and Accountability Journal,* 8(1), pp. 63–87.

McKerchar, M (2009) 'Philosophical Paradigms, Inquiry Strategies and Knowledge Claims: Applying the Principles of Research Design and Conduct to Taxation' *University of New South Wales Faculty of Law Research Series 2009, Working Paper 31.*

Merriam, S. B. (1988) *Case Study Research in Education: A Qualitative Approach.* San Francisco, CA: Jossey-Bass.

Parker, D. (1994) *Tackling Coursework.* London: DP Publications.

Robson, C. (2011) *Real World Research,* 3rd edn. Chichester: Wiley.

Sekaran, U. (2003) Research Methods for Business, 4th edn. New York: John Wiley.

Slife, B. D. and Williams, R. N. (1995) *What's Behind the Research: Discovering Hidden Assumptions in the Behavioural Sciences.* Thousand Oaks, CA: SAGE.

Vogt, W. P. and Burke Johnson, R. (2011) *Dictionary of Statistics & Methodology – A Nontechnical Guide for the Social Sciences,* 4th edn. Newbury Park, CA: SAGE.

Werner, O. and Schoepfle, G. (1987) *Systematic Fieldwork: Foundations of Ethnography and Interviewing.* Newbury Park, CA: SAGE.

Activities

1 Compare two potential research topics using the following criteria.

	Topic 1	Topic 2
a) Is the topic researchable, given time, resources, and availability of data?		
b) Is there a personal interest in the topic in order to sustain attention?		
c) Will the results from the study be of interest to others?		
d) Is the topic likely to be publishable in a scholarly journal or attractive to a research committee?		
e) Does the study fill a void, replicate, extend, or develop new ideas in the scholarly literature?		
f) Will the project contribute to career goals?		

2 Describe the purpose of your research by writing a positivist purpose statement using the guidelines in the chapter. Then rewrite it as an interpretivist purpose statement.

3 Set down your initial ideas for a proposed study by completing the following form.

Main research question	
a) What is your unit of analysis?	
b) What data are you going to collect?	
c) Why are you collecting the data?	
d) How will you collect the data?	
e) When will you collect the data?	
f) How will you analyse the data?	

4 Now deconstruct your research question as explained in this chapter.

5 Consolidate your answers to the previous questions and construct an outline research proposal. Evaluate the contents of your plan in accordance with the guidance given at the end of this chapter.

Now try the progress test online at www.palgrave.com/business/collis/br4/

Have a look at the Troubleshooting chapter and sections 14.2, 14.5, 14.6, 14.7, 14.8 in particular, which relate specifically to this chapter.

Appendix

Examples of business research proposals

Research area | Accounting decision making

Evaluating investment decisions in advanced manufacturing systems: a fuzzy set theory approach

Research problem and literature overview

An important function of management accounting systems is providing managers with models that evaluate all relevant information needed for making investment decisions (Accola, 1994). Although Discounted Cash Flow Models (DCFM) have been widely accepted by both academicians and practitioners as a sound approach to investment decisions (Klammer, Koch and Wilner, 1991; Wilner, Koch and Klammer, 1992; Cheung, 1993), many authors have criticized applying them to evaluate the investment in Advanced Manufacturing Systems (AMS) (for example Mensah and Miranti, 1989; Medearis, Helms and Ettkin, 1990) because these models are biased in favour of short-term investments whose benefits are more easily quantified than longer term projects. Consequently, these authors concluded that DCFM should not be applied to evaluate the investments in AMS. The most difficult task associated with applying DCFM in evaluating AMS investments lies in the existence of many variables which can hardly be measured and expressed in terms of cash flows, especially the benefits that the system will provide, such as greater manufacturing flexibility, learning effects, the effects on employee morale and decreased lead time.

Due to these criticisms some researchers (for example Medearis *et al.*, 1990; O'Brien and Smith, 1993) argue to ignore the financial analysis and regard the investment as a strategy that should be implemented regardless of the results of DCFM. Also, several authors suggested many approaches to evaluate the investment in AMS as a substitute of DCFM. These approaches are either numerical or non-numerical.

Thus, the main problem in the evaluation of investment decisions in AMS is how to quantify the expected benefits from these systems. In order to make these decisions in an objective manner, there is a need for a device that can properly treat qualitative variables in addition to quantitative variables. This suggests the use of fuzzy set theory (FST), which reduces the need for precise numerical inputs to decision analysis, in evaluating such decisions. FST provides a method of combining qualitative and quantitative variables for decision-making processes.

Research objective

The main objective of this research is introducing a suggested model for evaluating investment decisions in AMS considering qualitative and quantitative variables through the use of FST.

Methodology and work plan

The main aspects of the proposed research are: First, a model using the mathematical logic of FST will be constructed for evaluating the investment decisions of acquiring AMS. This will be carried on through an extensive theoretical study. So as to ensure that this model is applicable in the UK environment, a limited number of interviews with practitioners will be undertaken during the formulation of the model. Second, there will be an empirical study which can be used as a basis for evaluating the benefit and validity of the quantitative model. Input to the theoretical model will demand an in-depth understanding of particular investment decisions and the cooperation of key players in the decision-making process in order to establish 'fuzzy' variables. This data can only be collected in face-to-face interviews of a semi-structured nature.

References

Accola, W. L. (1994) 'Assessing risk and uncertainty in new technology investments', *Accounting Horizons*, 8(3) September, pp. 19–35.

Cheung, J. K. (1993) 'Management flexibility in capital investment decisions literature', *Journal of Accounting Literature*, 12, pp. 29–66.

Klammer, T., Koch, B. and Wilner, N. (1991) 'Capital budgeting practices: A survey of corporate use', *Journal of Management Accounting Research*, American Accounting Association, 3, Fall, pp. 113–30.

Medearis, H. D., Helms, M. M. and Ettkin, L. P. (1990) 'Justifying flexible manufacturing systems (FMS) from a strategic perspective', *Manufacturing Review*, 3(4) December, pp. 219–23.

Mensah, Y. M. and Miranti, P. J. (1989) 'Capital expenditure analysis and automated manufacturing systems: A review and synthesis', *Journal of Accounting Literature*, 8, pp. 181–207.

O'Brien, C. and Smith, J. E. (1993) 'Design of the decision process for strategic investment in advanced manufacturing systems', *International Journal of Production Economics*, 30–1, pp. 309–22.

Wilner, N., Koch, B. and Klammer, T. (1992) 'Justification of high technology capital investment – An empirical study', *The Engineering Economist*, 37(4), pp. 341–53.

Research area | Accounting regulation

The regulation of related party transactions

The problem

Related parties are an everyday occurrence in the business world and the transactions that take place between them are a natural process. However, in the UK, these transactions are not disclosed, which gives misleading information and enables companies the chance to act fraudulently (Mason, 1979). There are a number of cases of fraud using related parties including Pergamon Press (1969) and US Financial (1972) while more recently, the death of Robert Maxwell has revealed the syphoning of funds to related parties, effectively stealing people's pensions. For these reasons, it is essential that the disclosure of related party transactions should be regulated. Attempts to regulate these transactions have been made by the ASC with ED 46 (1989) but so far these have been unsuccessful.

Aim of the research

To enable any future standard concerned with the disclosure of related party transactions to be comprehensive and implementable, certain questions must be researched and answered:

1 Why was the earlier attempt at a standard unsuccessful?
2 How should 'related parties' be defined?
3 What information should be disclosed?
4 What should be the threshold of the influence of the resulting standard?
5 How valuable will the information be to the users of the accounts?

Methodology

The research will be conducted as a longitudinal investigation of the interest in related party transactions in the UK. This will include an extensive literature review of background papers (Brown, 1980), previous attempts at issuing a standard ED 46 (ASC,

1989) and comments made about the exposure draft (Hinton, 1989; ASC, 1990). A critique of ED 46 will be published as a major part of the research. The study will be conducted in the context of agency theory (Jenson and Meckling, 1976) and the 'market of excuses' thesis by Watts and Zimmerman (1979). A critical appraisal will also be made of the 'Nobes Cycle' (1991). The transfer to PhD will enable the research to include international experience, including IAS 24 (IASC, 1984) and SAS no. 6 (AICPA, 1975), conducted within the framework of international classification (Mueller, 1967; Nobes, 1992).

References

AICPA (1975) 'Statement on Auditing Standard No. 6', *Journal of Accountancy*, 140, September, pp. 82–5.
ASC (1989) Exposure Draft 46, *Related Party Transactions*, April.
ASC (1990) 'Comments received on ED 46'.
Brown, H. R. (1980) *Background paper on related party transactions*, ICAEW.
Hinton, R. (1989) 'Relating party transactions the UK way', *Accountancy*, 103(1150), pp. 26–7.
IASC (1984) IAS 24, *Related Party Disclosures*.
Jenson, M. C. and Meckling, W. H. (1976) 'Theory of the firm: Managerial behavior, agency costs and ownership structure', *Journal of Financial Economics*, 3(4), pp. 305–60.
Mason, A. K. (1979) *Related party transactions: A research study*, CICA.
Mueller, G. (1967) *International Accounting*, Part I, New York: Macmillan.
Nobes, C. (1992) *International Classification of Financial Reporting*, 2nd edn. Lava: Routledge.
Watts, R. L. and Zimmerman, J. L. (1979) 'The demand and supply of accounting theories: The market of excuses', *Accounting Review*, 54, April.

Research area | Auditing

An analytical study of the effect of confirmatory processes on auditors' decision-making and hypothesis updating

Research problem

Motivated in part by research findings in psychology, the auditing literature has recently begun to focus on auditors' use of confirmatory processes in evidence search and evaluation. Confirmatory processes mean that the auditor prefers to search for evidence confirming his initial hypotheses and also evaluates this evidence in a way that confirms his hypotheses (Church, 1990, p. 81). As the use of confirmatory processes is still a new trend in auditing, some problems are associated with the use of these processes, for example the impact of confirming and disconfirming approaches on auditors' decisions, the role of hypotheses formulation and the use of audit evidence in hypotheses updating.

Literature review

Most of the previous studies (for example Bedard and Biggs, 1991; McMillan and White, 1993) on the use of confirmatory processes in auditing focused on auditors' hypotheses formulation. These studies declared that auditors differ in their abilities to formulate correct or plausible hypotheses and these abilities are affected by various factors. Among these factors are expertise, source of hypotheses, hypotheses frame, professional scepticism, motivational factors and cognitive factors. The stated factors still need in-depth investigation in addition to determining what other factors can trigger the use of confirmatory processes in auditing. A few studies also examined the process of hypotheses updating. Einhorn and Hogarth (1985) formulated a model called 'Contrast/Surprise Model' which investigates the effect of confirming and/or disconfirming evidence on hypotheses updating. Ashton and Ashton (1988) investigated the validity of the previous model. However, their study is insufficient for investigating the process of hypotheses updating because they concentrated only on evidence order.

Research objective

The main objective of the proposed research is determining the effect of using confirmatory processes on auditor's decision-making, and investigating the process of hypotheses updating. The main research questions to be addressed are:

1 What factors trigger the use of confirmatory processes in auditing?
2 What is the process of hypotheses updating?
3 What theoretical models are relevant to the process of hypotheses updating?
4 What are the most appropriate circumstances for using confirmatory/disconfirmatory approaches?

Methodology

The research will be carried out through a theoretical and an empirical study. The empirical study will involve survey and experimental studies. The survey will be conducted through interviews with a number of auditors in auditing firms. It is intended to carry out 36 interviews in six auditing firms; two large, two medium and two small. Interviews will be held with two highly experienced, two medium experienced and two relatively inexperienced auditors in each firm. These interviews will help in determining factors affecting auditors' use of confirmatory processes. Following the analysis of this data, 18 experimental studies will be carried out to determine the validity of the proposed model. These experimental studies will be conducted in the same auditing firms as the interviews.

References

Ashton, A. H. and Ashton, R. H. (1988) 'Sequential belief revision in auditing', *Accounting Review*, October, pp. 623–41.

Bedard, J. C. and Biggs, S. F. (1991) 'Pattern recognition, hypotheses generation and auditor performance in an analytical task', *Accounting Review*, July, pp. 622–42.

Church, B. K. (1990) 'Auditors' use of confirmatory processes', *Journal of Accounting Literatures*, 9, pp. 81–112.

Einhorn, H. J. and Hogarth, R. M. (1985) *A Contrast/Surprise Model for Updating Beliefs*, Working Paper, April, Chicago: University of Chicago.

McMillan, J. J. and White, R. A. (1993) 'Auditors' belief revisions and evidence search: The effect of hypothesis frame, confirmation bias and professional skepticism', *Accounting Review*, July, pp. 443–65.

Research area | Buyer behaviour

The influence of children on the family purchase of environmentally friendly grocery products in South Wales

Previous studies of environmental consumerism have addressed the implications of the individual's buyer behaviour (Ottman, 1989; Charter, 1992) and changes in organizational management practices (Charter, 1992; Smith, 1993; Welford and Gouldson, 1993). The majority of studies in the area of green consumerism focus on the greening of the individual's buying behaviour, the development of green consumerism and the reactions of management in a wide sphere of industries. This research will take family buying behaviour models and build in an environmental perspective. The conceptual framework is presented briefly in Figure A.1.

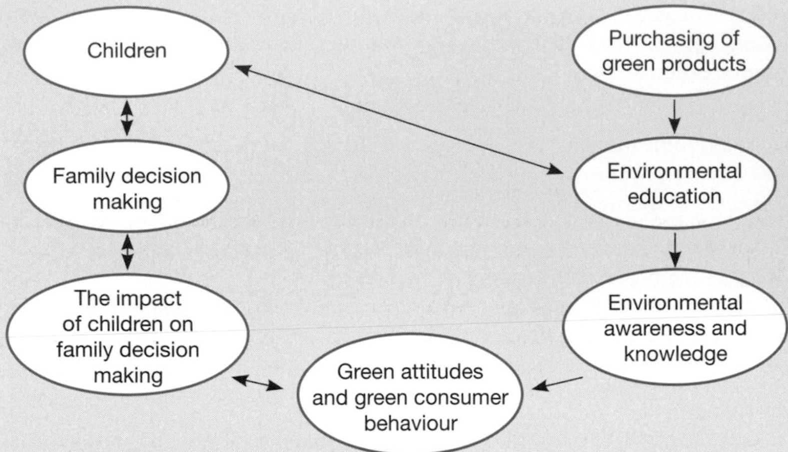

Figure A1. Diagrammatic conceptual framework

Research by Charter in 1992 revealed that environmental awareness is increasing in schools throughout Europe, with the introduction of environmental topics in a range of school syllabuses, together with wide recognition of the importance of environmental issues as a cross-curricular subject. This has resulted in environmental awareness and concern diffusing among children, with the direct result of children acting as important catalysts in raising the environmental awareness of the family group by reporting back what has been learned about the environment at school.

As Buttle (1993) discovered, consumer decisions are influenced by systematic relationships of the family which have a variable and determined effect upon the actions of individuals. Most researchers in environmentally responsive buyer behaviour have employed what Buttle (1993) describes as individualistic concepts and constructs. This research intends to take the interactive phenomena of the family and the influence of children on the purchase of environmentally responsible grocery products.

Aims

The purpose of the proposed study is to investigate the influence of children on the family purchase of environmentally friendly grocery products in South Wales with a focus on understanding of the influence that children have on family purchase of environmentally friendly grocery products. Grocery products have been selected because children have a major influence on product choice in this area, and are likely to be involved in product choice selection. The main aim of the study is to determine children's attitudes to and awareness of environmental concerns and the family–child interaction process within the context of environmentally responsive family buying behaviour.

Methodology

The first stage of this doctoral research has been a review of the existing literature on green consumerism, environmental education and children, and family buying behaviour. The literature review concentrates on several areas – first, on the diffusion of environmentally responsive buying behaviour; second, on the issues surrounding the development of children's attitudes and awareness of environmental concerns; and third, on the family–child interaction process within the context of family buying behaviour, as Figure A.1 illustrates.

The primary methodology consists of three stages: The exploratory research, which is underway, and consists of focus group sessions with primary school children in South Wales. The aims of the exploratory study are to determine the attitudes and behaviour of children towards environmental consumerism and how they believe they influence environmentally responsive family buying behaviour. The legal and ethical aspects of research with children will be adhered to.

Stage two will be an investigation of the family group through focus group sessions in South Wales, with the objective of establishing the actual interactive decision-making process within the sample families. This will be undertaken between September 1995 and March 1996.

The third stage of the research will consist of the development of case studies in order to investigate the holistic characteristics of the real-life situation. The case study sample will be developed from stage two of the research. The in-depth case study analysis will consist of semi-structured interviews and an observational study to be undertaken between March 1996 and March 1997.

Output

This research will contribute to family buyer behaviour knowledge and the understanding of environmentally responsive consumer behaviour; it will contribute to the understanding of the marketing implications of the influence of children in environmental decision-making and the ways in which decision-making is undertaken within the family group in the context of environmentally responsive buyer behaviour.

References

Buttle, F. (1993) The co-ordinated management of meaning: A case exemplar of a new consumer research paradigm, *European Journal of Marketing*, 28(8/9).

Charter, M. I. (1992) *Greener Marketing*. Sheffield: Greenleaf Publishing.

Ottman, J. (1989) 'Industries' response to green consumerism', *Journal of Business Strategy*, 13(4).

Smith, D. (1993) 'Purchasing department contributions to company environmental performance', *Purchasing Supply Management*, 20(1).

Welford, R. and Gouldson, A. (1993) *Environmental Management Business Strategy*. London: Pitman Publishing.

Research area | Organizational change

Changing the deal: The role of informal contracts in business transformation and organizational renewal

Introduction and literature review

In the last decade, the belief has grown among organizational theorists (Kanter, 1983; Handy, 1989; Pascale, 1990 and others) that in order to be successful in increasingly turbulent markets, organizations need to be able to assimilate, or better instigate, dramatic shifts in their industries. Change is becoming more discontinuous (Handy, 1989) or transformational in nature. The management of discontinuous change demands a more 'holistic approach' (Hinings and Greenwood, 1988) and an ability to recognize and, if appropriate, act on the limitations of the organization's existing paradigms (Morgan, 1986, 1993). It can also require organizations to build more flexibility into their structures and contractual arrangements (Atkinson, 1984). Roles may be restructured; jobs rescoped; new skills demanded; career paths obfuscated: in short, individuals are asked to undertake a radical rethink of their role, both within the organization and in a broader context. Formal contracts and cultures are being developed that aim to meet these challenges, but the informal side of organizational life cannot and should not be ignored.

A pilot project (in an operating company of a leading financial services group) conducted for this proposal, suggested that even when change is accepted at the 'rational' levels it may meet resistance if insufficient attention is paid to its broader implications (Jarvis, 1994). There is a growing need to understand the 'informal contract' between the employer and employee, if both parties' expectations are to be met.

A key output from the research will be a better understanding of the 'informal contract', and if and how it is evolving. At this stage, a working definition is being employed, as follows: 'the expectations – emotional and rational; conscious and unconscious – that employees bring to and take from their work and that are not covered by their job description and formal contract of employment'.

Research aim

The main aim of the MPhil stage of the project is to define the informal contract and establish its role in the implementation of major change programmes. The aim of the PhD stage of the research is to uncover if and how the informal contract can be 'managed' to support employees through major change.

Research methodology and proposed timetable

Primary research will be qualitative, collaborative inquiry (Reason, 1988) built around 6–8 case studies, each being conducted over a period of 18–24 months. This approach has been selected for its ability to yield data at the unconscious, as well as conscious, level. Hypotheses will be developed as the case study progresses and each case study will adopt four key research methods: interviews with senior management to provide an organizational context and an understanding of the aims and critical success factors for the change programme; depth interviews, with middle management grades and below, to provide context and a broad understanding of the individual meaning of the informal contract; individual diaries to provide a depth of information – 'felt' and rational – into the meaning of the informal contract to individuals; a series of inquiry groups to develop a shared meaning for the informal contract. Triangulation will be provided through this use of different methods and different sources, while an audit trail will ensure confirmability.

The PhD stage of the research will test hypotheses for transferability. As well as the opportunities for comparison provided by multiple case studies, it is envisaged that a series of cross-organizational groups, comprising senior managers, will be set up to look at how these hypotheses transfer from theory into practice.

References

Atkinson, J. (1984) *Emerging UK Work Patterns*, IMS Paper No. 145.
Handy, C. (1989) *The Age of Unreason*. Business Books Ltd.
Hinings, C. R. and Greenwood, R. (1988) *The Dynamics of Strategic Change*. Basil Blackwell.
Jarvis, C. (1994) *The Introduction of a Self-Assessment Appraisal System in to FSG OpCo*, unpublished.
Kanter, R. M. (1983) *The Changemasters*. Unwin Hyman.
Morgan, G. (1986) *Images of Organization*. SAGE.
Morgan, G. (1993) *Imaginization*. Penguin.
Pascale, R. (1990) *Managing on the Edge*. Penguin.
Reason, P. (1988) (ed.) *Human Inquiry in Action: Developments in New Paradigm Research*. London: SAGE.

Research area | Organizational culture

Evaluation of input and effectiveness of culture change on individuals and organizations

Background

I have run and co-tutored personal, management and organizational development courses for the last ten years. Co-tutoring has given me the opportunity to observe others' training, receive feedback and reflect on my own practice. The dominant thought area that has emerged from this reflection is that the quality of relationship between tutor and learner, and learner and learner, is of critical importance if lasting change and development is to occur.

As a participant in a self-managed learning group at Lancaster University (MAML), I found the experience challenging and, at times, frustrating. I believe this was due to the developmental relationships within the group. While this subject has emerged from reflecting on my own personal experience, I believe it is relevant to tutors, learners and managers. Effective 'engaging' between individuals could be a basis for effective managerial relationships.

Aim of the study

The study will explore the nature of 'engaging' (that is, effective developmental relationships) between tutors and learners, and learners and learners. The aim is to define and develop a working model of effective developmental relationships.

Theoretical context

Rowland (1993) has proposed a spectrum of tutoring relationships from 'didactic' to 'exploratory', with the middle ground being occupied by an 'interpretative' model. In his 'exploratory' and 'didactic' models the learning process is seen as being 'a black box, a kind of private psychological process in which the tutor cannot engage' (1993, p. 27). In the 'interpretative' models the tutor deliberately attempts to become part of the learning process. He characterizes the relationship as being one in which there is a free flow of learning and the tutor becomes an important part of the students' learning process. The psycho-therapeutic work of Rogers (1961) clearly defines the characteristics of what he terms a 'helping relationship'. This relationship creates a 'psychological climate' that ultimately releases human potential. Combining the work of Rowland (1993) and Rogers (1961) suggests a definition of 'engaging' as a relationship that creates a developmental psychological climate and a culture of support in which individuals develop shared meanings and collectively become an integral part of each other's reflective processes.

Using Reason's (1988) post-positivist research methodology of cooperative inquiry, I will work with groups to establish how individuals successfully 'engage'. Reason provides many useful insights into establishing cooperative inquiry groups including creating the 'right' atmosphere for people to examine processes, freely challenge and support one another. He suggests this is not easy and needs to emerge from the group as it matures towards truly authentic collaboration. This is another factor within the process of 'engaging' but between researcher and researched. Thus, the theoretical context of the research methodology parodies the area under study.

Methodology and research process

The proposed study will use a form of cooperative inquiry, which is ontologically based on a belief in a participatory universe and attempts to undertake research with people rather than on them. Cunningham (1988) suggests a broad model of cooperative inquiry which he calls 'interactive holistic research'. This non-linear, or as he puts it 'omni-focussed', model (p. 167) has four elements:

a) Collaborative inquiry – that is with people and either of Type I – in which the group explores its internal processes together – or Type II in which the group explores a process that happens outside the group.
b) Action research – research which is concerned with developing practical knowledge or praxis.
c) Experimental research – research which is concerned with how and what I experience.
d) Contextual locating – this represents the backdrop to the whole research study, whether intellectually, socially or emotionally.

Within the MPhil phase, I propose to establish a collaborative inquiry group with fellow tutors and learners to explore experiences of 'engaging' (Type II according to Cunningham, 1988). The purpose of this phase is to define and develop a model of 'engaging' between tutors and learners. This will be elaborated in the PhD phase by exploring the nature of developmental relationships within the group (Type I according to Cunningham, 1988) and to look further at this relationship in the context of managing. In this phase the objective is to define 'engaging' between learners and to develop a model of collaborative learning or development. The group will be assembled by invitation and consist of fellow tutors with an interest in exploring developmental relationships. Initial research with learners will be confined to participant observation to enable a working hypothesis to be established and will be undertaken with the many groups that I currently co-tutor. This will be replaced with a more formal collaborative inquiry which attempts to elicit a learner's perspective on 'engaging', initially free of any hypothesis, but later to explore a hypothesis which is either given or developed.

Research with fellow tutors and with learners will take place concurrently. The synthesis of these views will take place through a critical examination of my own practice and experience, through observation and critical subjectivity. Ideas that are developed will then be available for scrutiny and development with the collaborative inquiry group. In each of the groups (that is, learners and tutors) I will be the primary researcher.

References

Cunningham, I. (1988) 'Interactive Holistic Research: Researching Self-Managed Learning', in Reason, P. (1988) *Human Inquiry in Action – Developments in New Paradigm Research.* London: SAGE.

Reason, P. (1988) (ed.) *Human Inquiry in Action: Developments in New Paradigm Research.* London: SAGE.

Rogers, C. (1961) *On Becoming a Person.* London: Constable.

Rowland, S. (1993) *The Enquiring Tutor: Exploring the Process of Professional Learning.* London: Falmer Press.

Research area | Strategic management

Tacit knowledge and sustainable competitive advantage

Introduction and literature review

An enduring problem for strategic management is the sustainability of competitive advantage (Porter, 1985; Barney, 1991; Black and Boal, 1994). The proposed research is concerned with competitive advantage and the link between a heterogeneous firm resource (in this instance tacit knowledge) and the use of relatively homogeneous information technology (IT) assets. Much of the literature exploring the link between IT and competitive advantage, holds that innovatory systems are quickly and widely adopted and thus a source of enabling and not critical advantage (Banker and Kauffman, 1988; Ciborra, 1991). Contradictory research shows that this may not be the case as implementation of IT can produce unexpected outcomes (Ciborra, 1991). Other research (for example Cash and McFarlane, 1988; Kremar and Lucas, 1991; Lederer and Sethi, 1991) does not recognize the import of tacit knowledge and sees deviations in performance stemming from a lack of planning. However, recent additions to the literature question this logic, finding that intra-firm structural differences, the source of unexpected outcomes, can be combined with technology as complementary assets to confer a potential source of sustainable competitive advantage (Feeny and Ives, 1990; Clemons and Row, 1991; Heatley, Argarwal and Tanniru, 1995).

Inadequacy of current research

No empirical research has explored the role of tacit knowledge as a positive intra-firm structural differentiator in the implementation of IT. A priori observation seems to indicate that tacit knowledge is valuable, rare, imperfectly inimitable and non-transferable (Barney, 1991). Evaluating IT strategic successes, Ciborra (1991) identifies serendipity, trial and error, and bricolage as elements of a process of innovation in the use of systems. None of the literature explores the source, or the effects of this process. Thus, while the literature has speculated as to the role of tacit knowledge in creating sustainable competitive advantage (Spender, 1993), the empirical question, 'Can tacit knowledge provide a source of sustainable competitive advantage?' has not been addressed.

Aims and objectives of research

The research aims to fill this gap in the literature by examining the proposition that tacit knowledge is a source of competitive advantage, and asking, if it is, what the conditions are that are required to support it. The research also aims to answer the question of how tacit knowledge can provide a source of sustainable competitive advantage. This requires an examination of pre-emption, dynamic economies of learning and continuing innovation effects from using IT and tacit knowledge as complementary assets. Thus, the research will test the proposition that combinations of tacit knowledge and IT create core competencies that lead to superior performance, and that these competencies are inimitable in the sense used by Barney (1991). Barriers to imitation can be created by combining tacit knowledge and technology.

Methodology and plan of work

At the highest level of abstraction, it is proposed to use the resource-based view of the firm as a framework to understand asset combinations that can be the source of differences among firms. It is proposed that the research will operationalize measures developed by Sethi and King (1994) which were devised to assess the extent to which IT applications provide competitive advantage. In this research competitive advantage is driven by system performance, and this is the dependent variable in this study. The sample will be taken from the population of firms who use SAP business process software. The sample will be stratified for external validity according to Collis and Ghemawat's (1994) resource-based industry typology: along the dimensions of key resources and the nature of the production task. Construct validity will be established using pilot research; in-depth interviews.

The focus of the study will centre on deviations from expected performance of a tightly specified and robust business process oriented system which is widely used in a variety of industries. The unit of analysis is at the level of business processes. Deviations in performance between firms having the same IT system constitute differences in the dependent variable and this is a function of knowledge assets, their management and characteristics of the firm and system context. A research instrument will be designed which will be administered to collect cardinal and ordinal data on the dimensions of tacit knowledge, group dynamics, firm and system characteristics, including data collection on firm-specific technology trajectories.

References

Banker, R. and Kauffman, R. (1988) 'Strategic contributions of IT', *Proceedings of 9th International Conference on Information Systems*, pp. 141–50.

Barney, J. (1991) 'Firm resources and sustained competitive advantage', *Journal of Management*, 17(1), pp. 99–120.

Black, J. and Boal, K. (1994) 'Strategic resources: Traits, configuration and paths to sustainable competitive advantage', *Strategic Management Journal*, 15, pp. 131–48.

Cash, J. and McFarlane, F. (1988) *Competing Through Information Technology*. Harvard Business School Press.

Ciborra, C. U. (1991) 'The limits of strategic information systems', *International Journal of Information Resource Management*, 2(3), pp. 11–17.

Clemons, E. K. and Row, M. C. (1991) 'Sustaining IT: The role of structural differences', *MIS Quarterly*, September, pp. 275–92.

Collis, D. and Ghemawat, P. (1994) 'Industry Analysis: Understanding Industry Structure and Dynamics', in Fahey, L. and Randall, R. M. (eds) *The Portable MBA*, Wiley, pp. 171–93.

Feeny, D. and Ives, B. (1990) 'In search of sustainability: Reaping long-term advantage from investments in IT', *Journal of Management Information Systems*, 7(1), pp. 27–45.

Heatley, J., Agarwal, R. and Tanniru, M. (1995) 'An evaluation of innovative information technology', *Journal of Strategic Information Systems*, 4(3), pp. 255–77.

Kremar, H. and Lucas, H. (1991) 'Success factors for strategic IS', *Information and Management*, 21, pp. 137–45.

Lederer, A. and Sethi, V. (1991) 'Meeting the challenges of information systems planning', *Long Range Planning*, 25(2), pp. 69–80.

Porter, M. E. (1985) *Competitive Advantage*. Free Press.

Spender, J. C. (1993) 'Competitive advantage from tacit knowledge? Unpacking the concept and its strategic implications', *Academy of Management*, pp. 37–41.

Sethi, V. and King, W. (1994), 'Development of measures to assess the extent to which IT provides competitive advantage', *Management Science*, 40(12) pp. 1601–27.

7

collecting qualitative data

learning objectives

When you have studied this chapter, you should be able to:

- discuss the main issues in collecting qualitative data
- describe and apply methods based on interviews
- describe and apply methods based on diaries
- describe and apply methods based on observation
- compare the strengths and weaknesses of methods.

7.1 Introduction

In this chapter we focus on the main methods used to collect qualitative data. The methods are appropriate if you are planning to collect primary research data, such as the data you have generated from conducting interviews or focus groups. On the other hand, if you are planning to use secondary research data, which is data from an existing source such an archive or database, your main interest is likely to focus on the methods available to *analyse* qualitative data, which we cover in Chapter 8. This chapter will be of particular interest if you are designing a study under an interpretivist paradigm. As positivists often collect some qualitative data that need to be quantified, and because the research design may incorporate methodological triangulation (see Chapter 4, section 4.5), this chapter will also be of interest to those adopting a mixed methods approach. Some students describe their methods as 'quantitative methods' or 'qualitative methods'. We suggest that you avoid these ambiguous phrases as it is the data rather than the means of collecting the data that are in numerical or non-numerical form.

For each method we discuss, we start by explaining the nature of the method and how to use it before going on to give examples of how it has been applied in previous studies. We also examine the problems you may encounter and how they can be resolved. It is important to remember that if your research involves human participation or the collection and/or study of their data, organs and/or tissue, you will need to obtain ethical approval from your university (see Chapter 2).

7.2 Main issues in collecting qualitative data

Qualitative data are normally transient, understood only within context and are associated with an interpretivist methodology that usually results in findings with a high degree of **validity**. It contrasts with quantitative data, which are normally precise, can be captured at various points in time and in different contexts, and are associated with a positivist methodology that usually results in findings with a high degree of **reliability**. Examples of qualitative data include printed material such as text, figures, diagrams and other images, and audio and/or visual material such as recordings of interviews and focus groups, videos and broadcasts. All these forms of data may have been generated by you or by someone else, but the way in which they are collected needs to be systematic and methodical. The challenge for the researcher designing an interpretivist study is to apply method(s) that will retain the integrity of the data.

> **Reliability** refers to the absence of differences in the results if the research were repeated.
> **Validity** is the extent to which the research findings accurately reflect the phenomena under study.

Figure 7.1 shows an overview of the data collection process in an interpretivist study. However, it is important to realize that this is purely illustrative and the process is not as linear as the diagram suggests. Moreover, research data can be generated or collected from different sources and more than one method can be used.

7.2.1 Contextualization

Since qualitative data need to be understood within context, you need to collect some background information first. This is known as contextualization. Data about the context can relate to aspects such as time and location, or legal, social, political and economic influences. For example, a person working in a declining industry in a remote northern town in Canada, who is confronted with redundancy two weeks before the New Year starts, may have different views of the future than someone working in a booming high-tech industry in California. It is critical to your research that you establish and understand this contextual framework, as this will enhance your sensitivity to the qualitative research data you subsequently collect and aid your interpretation. When we say that you 'understand' the context, we mean that you make reference to it when you analyse and interpret your data and when you draw conclusions. This will add to the richness and depth of your findings.

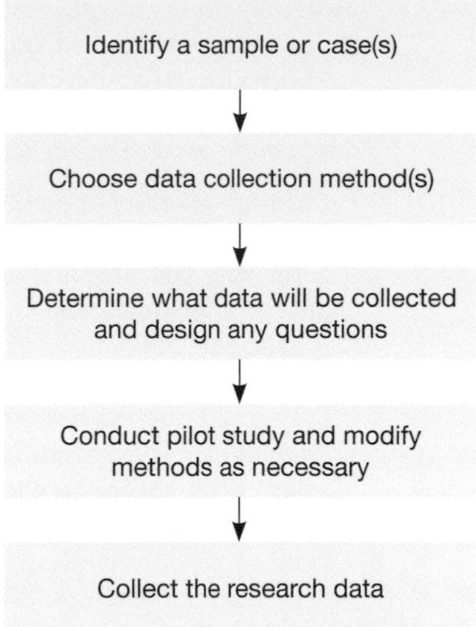

Figure 7.1 Overview of data collection in an interpretivist study

Much of the contextualizing data will be found in the literature. Do not ignore statistical data simply because they are quantitative. Information such as the level of unemployment in an area, the economic performance of an industry or employment patterns in a particular company can contribute to setting the framework within which you will be doing your research. Local newspapers are also important, but quite often take a political stance. It is sometimes more revealing to read the letters from readers than the editorials, as the readers' letters usually express the opinions and feelings of people who are part of the phenomenon you are studying.

Having established the context, you need to collect data relating to the location of your study and any events taking place before you collect the data. Therefore, equipment such as a camera, video recorder, audio recorder and a notebook will be needed. The notes taken while collecting primary research data are sometimes referred to as *field notes*, a term borrowed from the natural sciences.

7.2.2 Selecting a sample under an interpretivist paradigm

A **sampling frame** is a record of the population from which a sample can be drawn. A **population** is a body of people or collection of items under consideration and a **sample** is a subset of the population. If the population is relatively small, you can select the whole population; otherwise, you will need to select a sample.

A **sampling frame** is a record of the population from which a sample can be drawn.

A **population** is a body of people or collection of items under consideration for statistical purposes.

A **sample** is a subset of a population.

Under an interpretivist paradigm, the research data will not be analysed statistically with a view to generalizing from the sample to the population. Therefore, you do not need to select a random sample. For example, you may be designing an interpretivist study that investigates the experiences of entrepreneurs seeking finance to start or expand their businesses. In most countries, 99% of businesses are small or medium-sized firms and there is a constant churning of businesses being set up and businesses closing for one reason or another. This makes it extremely difficult to trace them all, so you would need to identify a method for selecting a manageable number for the study. One way to do it is to narrow the scope of your study to a particular location (for example an industrial estate in your location that has a number of small business units), or to select only the small businesses who are members of a local professional group. Perhaps you are interested in the views of students attending a series of workshops offered by your university on improving employability skills. As you are not able to attend all the workshops, you could restrict your sample to those attending the same workshops as you.

You will need to describe your population and any sampling methods used in your methodology chapter. If generalization is not your aim, there are a number of methods that can be used to select a non-random sample:

- *Snowball sampling* or *networking* is used in studies where it is essential to include people with experience of the phenomenon being studied in the sample. For example, supposing you are interested in how people cope with redundancy. Perhaps you are able to find some people who have experienced being made redundant who are willing to take part in your survey. One of the questions you would ask them would be whether they know of anyone else who has also been through the same experience with whom they could put you in touch. In this way, you can extend your sample of participants.
- *Judgemental* or *purposive sampling* is similar to snowball sampling as the participants are selected by the researcher on the strength of their experience of the phenomenon under study. However, in judgemental sampling the researcher makes the decision prior to the commencement of the survey and does not pursue other contacts that may arise during the course of the study.
- *Natural sampling* occurs when the researcher has little influence on the composition of the sample. The sample is sometimes referred to as a *convenience sample*. For example, only particular employees are involved in the phenomenon being investigated or only certain employees are available at the time of the study.

Vox pop What has been the biggest challenge in your research so far?

Sharif, undergraduate student investigating how car dealerships have survived during the recession

My biggest challenge has been getting the interviews. I was relying on my next door neighbour to give me the first interview, but although he's given me a day several times, when the time comes he says he's too busy. I was hoping it would snowball from there and he'd introduce me to his contacts. I'm going to have to start cold calling.

Hany, final year PhD student investigating the ERP impact on the internal audit function

Collecting sensitive data wasn't an easy task at all! My research depended on interviews with internal auditors, but permission was refused by more than 20 organizations before I found four that would agree to give me access. So my initial plan of conducting a comparative study between two countries had to be altered to a comparative study between sectors within one country.

It can be difficult to find willing participants who fit your selection criteria and this is often a problem for undergraduate students and those on taught Master's programmes, who have tight time constraints and few external contacts. The following approaches may be useful:

- Advertising can be used in local or national newspapers, or you can visit locations where members of your population are likely to congregate. For example, if you wish to find out how people cope with unemployment, you might find a suitable sample of individuals who are currently experiencing this by visiting your local Job Centre or an employment bureau.

- If you are in full or part-time employment, or you are a member of a club, society or online social group, you may find that you already have access to a suitable sample. For example, if you are a member of a gym, you might meet people who use exercise as a means of controlling stress at work; if you are a member of a trekking club or a sailing club, you might meet people who are willing to share their views on environmental issues related to their sport.
- *Piggybacking* is where you extract your sample from an existing survey or use another survey to obtain your population simultaneously.
- Finally, you can use *screening* as a method for finding a sample. For example, if you were interested in why people purchase a particular product, you would interview a large number of people and select only those who buy the product.

If you are designing a study under a positivist paradigm, you will be interested in generalizing from your sample to the population. If that is the case, you must not use any of these methods but refer to the methods for selecting a random sample in Chapter 10.

We will now move on to examine some of the main methods for collecting data for qualitative analysis. It is important to remember that the methods associated with interpretivist paradigms often allow the researcher to collect and analyse the research data in one process. This contrasts with methodologies associated with positivist paradigms, where statistical methods are used to analyse the data. If you are designing a study under an interpretivist paradigm, you will need to read this chapter in conjunction with Chapter 9; if you are designing a study under a positivist paradigm, you will need to read this chapter in conjunction with Chapter 10 and the appropriate chapter(s) on statistical analysis.

7.3 Interviews

Interviews are a method for collecting data in which selected participants (the interviewees) are asked questions to find out what they do, think or feel. Verbal or visual prompts may be required. Under an interpretivist paradigm, interviews are concerned with exploring 'data on understandings, opinions, what people remember doing, attitudes, feelings and the like, that people have in common' (Arksey and Knight, 1999, p. 2) and will be unstructured or semi-structured.

In an unstructured interview, none of the questions are prepared in advance but evolve during the course of the interview. The researcher uses open-ended questions, which cannot be answered with a simple 'yes' or 'no' or a short factual answer; instead, an **open question** requires a longer, developed answer. A **closed question** is one that requires a 'yes' or 'no' answer or a very brief factual answer, or it requires the respondent to choose from a list of predetermined answers. Closed questions are quick and simple to answer, whereas open questions take longer to answer and require the respondent to think and reflect. Open questions are used to obtain opinions or information about experiences, and feelings, such as 'What are the benefits of working for this company?' The researcher may also use probes to explore the interviewee's answers in more depth.

In a semi-structured interview, the researcher prepares some questions to encourage the interviewee to talk about the main topics of interest and develops other questions during the course of the interview.

An **interview** is a method for collecting primary data in which a sample of interviewees are asked questions to find out what they think, do or feel.

An **open question** is one that cannot be answered with a simple 'yes' or 'no' or a very brief factual answer, but requires a longer, developed answer.

A **closed question** is one that requires a 'yes' or 'no' answer or a very brief factual answer, or requires the respondent to choose from a list of predetermined answers.

The order in which the questions are asked is flexible and the researcher may not need to ask all the pre-prepared questions because the interviewee may have provided the relevant information when answering another question. Under a positivist paradigm, interviews are structured, which means the questions are planned in advance and each interviewee is asked the questions in the same order (see Chapter 10).

Easterby-Smith, Thorpe and Jackson (2012, p. 132) suggest that unstructured or semi-structured interviews are appropriate when:

- it is necessary to understand the personal constructs (sets of concepts or ideas) used by the interviewee as a basis for his or her opinions and beliefs
- the purpose is to develop an understanding of the respondent's 'world' so that the researcher might influence it (for example through action research)
- the logic of a situation is not clear
- the subject matter is highly confidential or commercially sensitive, or there are issues about which the interviewee may be reluctant to be truthful.

7.3.1 Using interviews under an interpretivist paradigm

Interviews are a popular method for collecting research data and you may think that all you have to do is talk to someone. Unfortunately, it is not quite as simple as that. You need to clarify what information you want and this may be guided by a conceptual framework you have developed from the literature. In addition, you need to think about how to get access to people who can supply the information you need and how to select a sample. Once you have resolved those issues, you need to consider how you can encourage the interviewees to give you the information you need and how you will record the interview. Some students use a mobile phone to record the interview as an alternative to buying a specific audio recorder. The main consideration is the sound quality.

Interviews can be conducted with individuals or groups, using a variety of methods. Each method has different strengths and weaknesses. Cost is often an important factor and the best method for a particular study may depend on the size, location and accessibility of the sample.

- *Face-to-face* – This is the traditional approach and the interview can be conducted with participants in the street, at their homes, in the workplace or any convenient place. Interviewing is time-consuming and can be expensive if you have to travel any distance to meet participants. However, this method offers the advantage that comprehensive data can be collected and it may be useful if you need to ask complex or sensitive questions. Where the interview is conducted outside working hours, it may be possible to conduct a longer interview than is possible during the busy working day. It is important that you take precautions to ensure your personal safety when meeting participants (see Chapter 2).
- *Telephone* – This is also a widely used method and offers the advantage that it reduces the cost of travel while still allowing personal contact. It may not be possible to conduct such a long interview as you could using the face-to-face method if the interview is conducted during working hours, but there are fewer constraints on the geographical location of the sample. However, you may need to consider the cost of buying specialist recording equipment and possibly the cost of the calls.
- *Online* – Web-based methods of video conferencing such as *Skype* overcome some of the cost constraints associated with face-to-face and telephone interviews. However, online methods introduce limitations on your choice of sample, as interviewees must

have access to the Internet and be willing and able to use this type of software. Moreover, you will need to plan how you will record the interviews.

The most common form of interview is one-to-one, but some researchers find it useful to have two interviewers to help ensure that all the issues are fully explored and notes are kept of nuances, gestures and interruptions in addition to an audio recording of what is said during the interview. It is helpful to have a record of what occurred during the interview as it can be used to extract a more robust and comprehensive interpretation.

Unstructured interviews are very time-consuming and there may be problems controlling the range of topics and recording the questions and answers. You may also have problems when it comes to analysing the data as the questions raised and the matters explored vary from one interview to another as different aspects of the topic are revealed. This process of open discovery is the strength of such interviews, but it is important to recognize that the emphasis and balance of the emerging issues may depend on the order in which your participants are interviewed. We discuss the methods for analysing interview data in the next chapter.

7.3.2 Designing questions for interviews under an interpretivist paradigm

In this section, we focus on designing interview questions where the research data generated will be analysed using non-numerical methods. Before you can start designing any questions, you need to have gained considerable knowledge about your topic from reading the literature. The only exception to this is would be if you are designing an inductive study using a methodology such as grounded theory. We discuss this in Chapter 9.

Table 7.1 shows examples of different types of interview question and their uses.

Table 7.1 Types of interview question

Type of question	Useful for	Not useful for
Open question (e.g. Tell me what happened when ...)	Most openings to explore and gather broad information	Very talkative people
Closed question (e.g. Who did you consult?)	Getting factual information	Getting broad information
Multiple questions (more than one in a sentence)	Never useful	Never useful
Probes (e.g. What happened next?)	Establishing sequence of events or gathering details	Exploring sensitive events
Hypothetical question (e.g. What might happen that could change your opinion?)	Encouraging broader thinking	Situations beyond the interviewee's scope
Comparison question (e.g. Do you prefer weekly or fortnightly team meetings?)	Exploring needs and values	Unrealistic alternatives
Summary question (e.g. So, am I right in thinking that the main issues are ...?)	Avoiding ambiguity, validating data and linking answers	Premature or frequent use

To ensure that you gain maximum information, it is essential that you probe the interviewee by asking questions that require them to elaborate on their initial statement. There are a number of qualitative characteristics relating to the answers that you must establish and Table 7.2 shows examples of the probes you can use to elicit such data.

Probes are questions you ask in response to what the interviewee has said. They are asked so that you can gain greater understanding of the issue under study and are the beginning of the data analysis stage. They are used in an unstructured or semi-structured interview. If you are thinking of asking prepared questions only, you would be using a structured interview, which is a method associated with a positivist paradigm.

Table 7.2 Examples of probes

Characteristic	Probe
Clarity	Can you give me an example of this? What do you mean? Can you explain that again?
Relevance	How do you think that relates to the issue? Can you explain how these factors influence each other?
Depth	Can you explain that in more detail? Can you give me examples?
Dimension	Is it possible to look at this another way? Do you think that is a commonly held opinion?
Significance	How much does this affect you? What do you think is the most important? Would you change your opinion if X was to happen?
Comparison	Can you give me an example where this did not happen? Can you give me an example of a different situation? In what way does your opinion differ from the views of other people?
Bias	Why do you hold this opinion? What might happen that could change your opinion?

You should bear in mind that recent events may affect the interviewee's responses. For example, he or she may have just received news of a promotion or a salary increase; alternatively, the interviewee may have just received a reprimand or bad news about a friend or relative. If time allows, you will find it useful to arrive at the interview venue 15 minutes beforehand to assimilate the atmosphere and the environment, and spend the first few minutes putting the interviewee at ease. It is difficult to predict or measure bias, but you should be alert to the fact that it can distort your data and hence your findings.

You must always ask the interviewee for permission to record the interview using an audio recorder and taking notes. After putting your interviewee at ease, you may find it useful to spend a little time establishing a rapport before starting to record. You can offer to switch the recorder off if your interviewee wants to discuss confidential or sensitive information but seek permission to continue to take notes. You may find that this encourages a higher degree of frankness. We discussed the issue of confidentiality in Chapter 2.

Questions should be presented in a logical order and it is often beneficial to move from general to specific topics. It is important to remember that you should only ask questions that are relevant to your study. *Classification questions* collect data about the characteristics of the unit of analysis, such as the interviewee's job title, age or education; or the geographical region, industry, size or age of the business. If you wish to make comparisons with previous studies, government statistics or other publications, it is essential to use probes to ensure that you have enough information to categorize the information correctly so that you can describe your sample. There is some debate over the best location for classification questions. Some researchers believe they are best placed at the beginning so that the interviewee gains confidence in answering easy questions; others prefer to place them at the end so that the interview starts with the more interesting questions. If your questions are of a sensitive nature, it can be beneficial to start with the non-threatening classification questions. On the other hand, if you have a large number of classification questions, it could be better to ask them at the end, so that the interviewee is not deterred at the start.

Some research projects include the investigation of sensitive issues such as equality, health, redundancy, financial loss or safety. Lee (1993) offers the following advice on asking *sensitive questions*:

- Use words that are non-threatening and familiar to the respondents. For example, when explaining the purpose of the questionnaire, say you are looking at working patterns rather than investigating absenteeism in their place of work.
- Lead up to any sensitive question slowly.
- You may find that participants will answer questions about past indiscretions more readily than questions about current behaviour. For example, they may admit to stealing from their employer at some time in the past, but be unwilling to disclose that they have done so recently.

These suggestions raise ethical issues and you must determine your own position on this. If you find your interviewee is showing signs of resisting some topics, the best advice is to drop those questions. However, this will alert you to the likelihood that these may be interesting and important issues and you may wish to find an alternative way of collecting the data, such as diary methods or observation (see sections 7.7 and 7.8 respectively).

You need to let the interviewee know that the interview is coming to an end. One way of doing so is to say that you have asked all the questions you had in mind and ask whether he or she has any final comments. You should then conclude by thanking them and reassuring them that you will be treating what they have told you as confidential. If you want to improve the validity of your findings, you should arrange to send a summary of your findings to the interviewee for feedback on your interpretation. When you have left the interview, you should spend as much time as possible immediately afterwards adding to your notes. You will find it helpful if you can share your insights and reflections with your supervisor or fellow students.

Vox pop What has been the highpoint of your research so far?

Pippa, final year PhD student investigating how a small town is affected by increased tourism

The experiences of towing a campervan to remote places for my fieldwork and meeting a lot of wonderful people who gave me a lot of time.

Nesrine, fourth year PhD student investigating supply chain agility

Solving my data collection problem! I'd started collecting primary data [via face-to-face interviews] in Egypt when the 'Arab Spring' happened and it wasn't safe to go there. I thought it would mean that I had to start all over again in another country. Then at last, after several months, I was able to go back to Cairo again and carry on!

7.3.3 Examples of studies using interviews

In this section we examine two examples where all the interviewees in each study were asked the same set of questions and were able to answer them in their own words. The first study (Brockman *et al.*, 2010) investigated the level of personal cohesiveness in new product development teams. The researchers obtained agreement to work with 12 teams and the team leader of each team was interviewed first. Next, two members from each team were interviewed and this provided a total of 36 interviews. There were approximately equal numbers of men and women in the sample and each interview lasted around 45 minutes. Therefore the total time taken for the 36 interviews was more than 25 hours.

You can appreciate that the researchers had carefully planned the sampling and sequencing of the interviews. This was important as they spent 25 hours conducting the interviews. If you are planning to use a similar approach, you must make sure you are fully prepared. Do not to be too ambitious about the number of interviews but decide how many people you will interview on the basis of their position and expertise/knowledge. Brockman *et al.* (2010) used predetermined questions, but every question was open-ended. As the researchers observed, this meant that the data analysis took a considerable amount of time. Therefore, this is not an approach that is suitable if you have tight time constraints.

The second study (Lengnick-Hall, Gaunt and Kulkarni, 2008) focused on the employment of people with disabilities and sought the opinions of 38 executives in small (0–49 employees), medium (50–499 employees) and large (500 or more employees) companies. The interviews took place in the participants' offices; typically with no one else present. To determine what questions should be asked, the researchers conducted a thorough review of the existing literature. As the subject of the research might be considered sensitive, the questions were designed at the industry level, rather than focusing on the employee's company, with a view to eliciting more candid answers.

Both studies demonstrate the necessity of being very careful in selecting the sample and planning the interviews. The researchers in the second study state that the interview questions were derived from the literature. Even with a team of experienced researchers, preparing the questions and conducting the interviews takes a lot time and the subsequent transcribing and analysis of the data is likely to take even longer. You must bear this in mind if you are planning to use interviews as part of your research design.

7.3.4 Potential problems

Sometimes the interviewee is accompanied by another person (often to ensure that all the questions you ask can be answered). You must be alert to the fact that if there is more than one interviewer or interviewee it will change the dynamics of the interview. Another situation that can arise is that your interviewee may be wearing 'two hats' (in other words, have multiple roles). For example, the finance director of a company you are interviewing may also be on an advisory group that influences EU company law; a factory employee may also be a trade union official. Therefore, when asking questions, you must determine whether he or she is giving a personal opinion or making a policy statement Another problem is that the interviewee may have certain expectations and give what he or she considers is the 'correct' or 'acceptable' answer to the question. Lee (1993) suggests that, to some extent, this can be overcome by increasing the depth of the interview.

When asking questions, you need to be aware of the potential for inadvertent class, race or gender *bias*. For example, a study that examined sex bias more than 40 years ago (Rosenthal, 1966) found that male and female researchers obtained significantly different data from their subjects. The following tendencies were observed:

- Female subjects were treated more attentively and considerately than male subjects.
- Female researchers smiled more often than male researchers.
- Male researchers placed themselves closer to male subjects than female researchers did.

- Male researchers showed higher levels of body activity than female researchers did. When the subject was male, both male and female researchers showed higher levels of body activity than they did with female subjects.
- Female subjects rated male researchers as being friendlier than female researchers, and as having more pleasant and expressive voices than female researchers.
- Both male and female researchers generally behaved more warmly towards female subjects than they did towards male subjects, with male researchers being the warmer of the two.

Vox pop What has been the highpoint in your research so far?

Chris, undergraduate student investigating environmental implications of logistics in the grocery market

Finishing my interviews, but now I realize that I'm going to have transcribe them all!

7.4 Critical incident technique

Unstructured interviews are not merely idle conversations. It is your role to encourage the participant to tell his or her story in his or her own words, while keeping the interviewee to the relevant issues. You are trying to obtain in-depth and authentic knowledge of people's life experiences (Gubrium and Holstein, 2001). One way to do this is to use **critical incident technique.** This method is based on the participant's recollections of key facts and can be used to collect data about a specific activity or event. It was originally developed by Flanagan (1954) as a method to be used under a positivist paradigm, but principles can be modified and adapted according to the circumstances. This makes it very useful for designing interview questions in an interpretivist methodology.

Critical incident technique is a method for collecting data about a defined activity or event based on the participant's recollections of key facts.

7.4.1 Using critical incident technique

Flanagan intended the researcher to collect critical incidents using a form such as the one in Box 7.1, but his questions could form the basis of a semi-structured interview.

Box 7.1 Example of how to collect effective critical incidents

"Think of the last time you saw one of your subordinates do something that was very helpful to your group in meeting your production schedule." (Pause until he indicates that he has such an incident in mind.) "Did his action result in increase in production of as much as one per cent for that day? – or some similar period?"

(If the answer is "no", say) "I wonder if you can think of the last time that someone did something that did have this much of an effect in increasing production." (When he indicates he has such a situation in mind, say) "What were the general circumstances leading up to this incident?"

....

....

"Tell me exactly what this person did that was so helpful at that time." ....

....

"Why was this so helpful in getting your group's job done?" ....

....

"When did this incident happen?" ....

"What was this person's job?" ....

"How long has he been on this job?" ....

"How old is he?" ....

Source: Flanagan (1954, p. 342). This content is now in the public domain.

Critical incident technique helps interviewees to talk about issues in the context of their own experience and discourages them from talking about hypothetical situations or other people's experiences. For example, if you are using interviews with owners of small businesses to investigate a research problem relating to access to finance, the critical incident might focus on their experiences at the start-up stage. You could follow this up by asking them to tell you about the next time they can remember needing capital and what happened, until you have covered all the occasions. If there are a great many of the type of critical incidents you are interested in, it is best to ask about the most recent or to ask the interviewee afterwards why he or she chose that particular event.

7.4.2 Examples of studies using critical incident technique

In this section we examine the way in which critical incident technique is used in three published studies. The first study (Meldrum and McCarvill, 2010) focuses on employees with part-time, seasonal or temporary contracts in the leisure industry. The sample was obtained by asking students on relevant academic courses to complete a short screening questionnaire and this produced 168 responses. One of the questions asked respondents if they were willing to participate in an interview to discuss their work experiences and, if so, to provide their contact details. The results of the screening survey were used to identify students with a range of work experiences (ranging from high to low commitment), job types and settings, and the number of jobs they had. A total of 24 students with the appropriate experience were identified and subsequently these students took part in individual semi-structured interviews.

The questions selected were used to measure the affective dimensions of commitment to the organization, occupation, supervisor, work group and customers. They were asked to describe significant events (the critical incidents) when others' actions (fellow workers or customers) seemed particularly effective or ineffective in achieving organizational goals. A less effective alternative might be to ask: 'Are your fellow workers effective in achieving organizational goals?' but the answers may have been based merely on vicarious knowledge or unsupported evidence. From this you can see that asking the participant to think of a specific event is crucial to the technique.

The second example (Johnstone, Wilkinson and Ackers, 2010) is a study that investigated the work agreement between employer and employees. The aim of the study was to gather opinions of those involved in the partnership agreement rather than vague recollections of organizational events. By using critical incident technique, those interviewed were encouraged to identify some of the main organizational and employment relations issues/incidents over the past five years (or since they joined the organization if less than five years). The researchers asked what happened, how it was managed, who said what and to whom, how the interviewee felt at each stage and how he or she perceived the outcome. A total of six long interviews were conducted with managers, three with employee representatives and three with full-time union officials. The interview data were supplemented with data from focus groups with employees.

In the third example (Chen-Tsang and Ching-Shu, 2009), the researchers used a questionnaire to collect data rather than holding interviews. The aim of the study was to identify the seriousness of service failures in restaurants, any corrective action taken and the response of the customer. The researchers sent a questionnaire to a sample of customers who had visited any chain restaurant during the previous six months and who had experienced a service failure. A total of 500 incidents were identified and 431 of them matched the researchers' definition of a service failure. The questionnaire covered the following topics and some of questions were based on a rating scale and therefore yielded quantitative data:

1 A detailed description of the failure that occurred.
2 The perceived magnitude of the failure on a scale of 1–10, where 1 = a minor mistake and 10 = a major mistake.
3 A detailed description of what measure the restaurateur took to compensate for the failure.
4 The degree of satisfaction for the compensation, where 1 = very unsatisfied and 10 = very satisfied.
5 The type of chain restaurant.
6 Whether the incident caused them to cease patronage at the restaurant.
7 Demographic information about the respondent such as age, gender and level of education.

A recurring theme with the studies we have discussed is the care that the researchers took in selecting people they wished to interview. Although each study focuses on a different topic, all three benefited from using critical incident technique as it helps create focus. Although the number of interviews is not large, considerable insights can be gained from using this technique in a small number of in-depth interviews.

7.4.3 Potential problems

If you have limited knowledge of the phenomenon under study, you may find it difficult to determine what constitutes a critical incident. A search of the literature will help you. One problem associated with any method based on memory is that the participant may have forgotten important facts. There is also the problem of post-rationalization, where the interviewee recounts the events with a degree of logic and coherence that did not exist at the time. In common with all types of interview, critical incident technique may generate a considerable amount of data that will take some time to analyse.

7.5 Focus groups

A **focus group** is a method for collecting data whereby selected participants discuss their reactions and feelings about a product, service, situation or concept, under the guidance of a group leader.

Focus groups are used to gather data relating to the feelings and opinions of a group of people who are involved in a common situation or discussing the same phenomenon. Focus groups combine interviewing (see section 7.3) and observation (see section 7.8), but allow fresh data to be generated through the interaction of the group. They can be used in an interpretivist methodology but are also used by positivists before or after conducting a survey.

Under the guidance of a group leader, selected participants are encouraged to discuss their opinions, reactions and feelings about a product, service, and type of situation or concept. For example, you might wish to get a group of employees from a company together to discuss what they feel about the profit-sharing scheme in operation, or a group of consumers to discuss their views on a particular brand of mobile phone or a television programme. Listening to other group members' views stimulates participants to voice their own opinions. This helps produce data that would be less accessible without this group interaction (Morgan, 1997).

Focus groups have a long history and were used during the Second World War to examine the effectiveness of propaganda (Merton and Kendall, 1946). In business research, focus groups have long been popular in marketing research, but are increasingly being used in other disciplines.

Focus groups can be useful for a number of purposes, such as to:

- develop knowledge of a new phenomenon
- generate propositions from the issues that emerge
- develop questions for a survey
- obtain feedback on the findings of research in which the focus group members participated.

7.5.1 Using focus groups

If you are planning to hold a focus group, you will need to enlist help. You will probably want to facilitate the meeting yourself, which means you will need someone else to take detailed notes and another person to manage the audio and/or video recording. Many researchers find it essential to make a video recording of the discussions as the visual cues can be even more revealing than the audio or written records. You will need to prepare a list of issues you want to cover and, if you are the facilitator, you will find it useful to take brief notes of the main points as they emerge. It is very difficult (but not impossible) to run a focus group by yourself, but there is a risk is that data you collect will not have the breadth and depth you are seeking. Box 7.2 shows the main steps involved.

Box 7.2 Procedure for a focus group

1 Prepare a list of issues you want to cover.
2 Invite a group of people with sufficient experiences in common on the research problem to meet at a neutral location.
3 Create a relaxed atmosphere when introducing the group members and explaining the purpose of the focus group and how it will be conducted.
4 Start the session with a broad, open question. This can be displayed on an overhead projector or flip chart. If possible, give visual explanations or examples.
5 Allow the group to discuss the issue(s) as you introduce them without intervention from you, except to ensure that all members have an opportunity to contribute to the discussion and all the issues are covered.

An alternative group method is the *Delphi method*, which is used to establish communication between geographically dispersed experts to allow them to deal with a complex problem in a systematic, methodological way. Originally developed in the USA for coordinating statements by experts in the context of predicting likely war scenarios, the method takes its name from the oracle of Delphi in ancient Greece, through whom the gods were believed to give prophecies about the future. It is now widely used to collect 'judgements on a particular topic through a set of carefully designed sequential questionnaires interspersed with summarized information and feedback of opinions derived from earlier responses' (Delbecq, Van den Ven and Gustafson, 1975). The questionnaire can be administered in face-to-face interviews or by email (hence the term e-Delphi). Like focus groups, it is widely used as a forecasting technique in marketing and policy-based research. The advantages of the Delphi method are that it generates decisions from a structured group rather than an unstructured focus group and avoids the problem of peer pressure that can be present in a focus group (Lindqvist and Nordänger, 2007).

7.5.2 Examples of using focus groups

Again we have examples from two studies. The first study (Brüggen and Willems, 2009) compares different types of focus group: offline and online focus groups, and the e-Delphi method. The methods were compared in terms of their depth, breadth, efficiency, group dynamics, non-verbal impressions and attitudes of participants. We will concentrate on the investigation of the offline and online focus groups. Online focus groups take place in a virtual room where participants can view and react to the comments of other group members and the moderator. All participants are online at the same time, which allows for direct interactions and a synchronous group discussion.

The study concluded that offline focus groups had the highest depth and breadth and that they are most efficient, leading to high quality outcomes when compared with online focus groups. Although they may take some effort to set up, as a student you may find online focus groups a novel method for collecting data in your field. If you could also conduct some offline focus groups, your project could incorporate an interesting comparison of the findings from the two approaches.

The second study (Kerrigan and Graham, 2010) not only describes focus groups but also suggests potential avenues for research. The study examines regional news media, which face an uncertain future as the Internet allows bloggers and amateur journalists to provide alternative sources of news and comment. Two data collection methods were used: 15 semi-structured interviews followed by one focus group with five participants in order to gain further insights. During the focus group, three key questions were posed. The first focused on the level of disruption in the media sector as a result of the development of social media and the second related to the potential for wealth/value creation through the social space being generated in these networks. The third question concentrated on the organization, control, and management of the interactions between the media organizations.

7.5.3 Potential problems

Focus groups are fairly inexpensive to set up. This has resulted in their extensive use to examine industrial, economic and social problems, but the results are sometimes nothing more than the opinions of a small group of people and offer little in the way of deep insights or illumination of the issues under study. To be credible as a data collection technique, focus groups must be properly managed.

One approach is to run a series of groups comprising major categories and compare your findings. For example, you may have separate groups of permanent employees, part-time employees and retired employees discussing their opinion of their employer. Another approach is to have one group containing members from each category. It can be difficult to obtain sufficient volunteers. Too few participants would not generate sufficient data, and too many might mean some do not participate fully; if they do, a large group may be hard to manage. You must remember that you are not trying to obtain a sample from which you can generalize, but to obtain as full a range of perceptions and experiences as possible of the issue or phenomenon of interest to you. Therefore, we advise five to ten participants, but we advise that you try to get acceptances from about fifteen to allow for non-attendance on the day.

If the research problem or issue is of interest and relevance to the group, it should not be difficult to generate relevant discussions. In consumer research, participants are invited to try sample goods. This is difficult to replicate when the topic concerns something intangible, such as ethical or equality issues, regulation or corporate governance. It helps if the subject is controversial and often a short documentary will generate discussions. However, sometimes the focus group does not work because one member is highly vociferous and dominates the discussion. Therefore, the researcher needs to explain the purpose of the focus group meeting and how it will be conducted at the onset, and prepare a strategy for encouraging everyone to make a contribution if some remain silent. One approach is to thank the dominant individual for his or her contribution and take the lead for a moment by summarizing the points he or she has made and writing them on a flip chart. Then the rest of the group are invited to give their opinions on these points and add others.

7.6 Protocol analysis

Protocol analysis is a data collection method used to identify the mental processes in problem solving, and is usually associated with an interpretivist methodology. The aim of the method is to find out how people behave and think in a particular situation, particularly in solving a complex problem. Smagorinsky (1989, p. 475) describes protocol analysis as 'an expensive and meticulous research method that has had its share of growing pains'. However, the method offers a tool for the researcher who is interested in how individuals solve business problems.

Protocol analysis is a method for collecting data used to identify a practitioner's mental processes in solving a problem in a particular situation, including the logic and methods used.

The researcher gives some form of written problem to a practitioner who is experienced in that field. As the practitioner addresses the problem, he or she gives verbal explanations of how he or she is doing it and the researcher records the process. Sometimes the practitioner generates further questions, which form the basis of a subsequent stage in the research.

Protocol analysis studies tend to be small, involving fewer than a dozen participants. The process of constructing the problem that is given to the practitioners is difficult and is part of the research process. The researcher must seek to contrive a realistic problem and address the fundamental issues, and also define the scope of the study. Furthermore, the researcher must have sufficient knowledge to be able to understand and interpret the logic and methods the practitioner uses to address the problem (it cannot be assumed that a solution is always found).

7.6.1 Using protocol analysis

There are a number of ways in which the verbal data can be generated. *Retrospective verbalization* takes place when the participant is asked to describe processes after they have occurred. *Concurrent verbalization* takes place when the participant is asked to describe and explain their thoughts as they undertake a task. There are two types of concurrent verbalization: directed reports and think-aloud protocol. The former result when participants are asked to describe only specific behaviours and the latter when they are asked to relay every thought that comes into their heads. Figure 7.2 summarizes the different types of protocol.

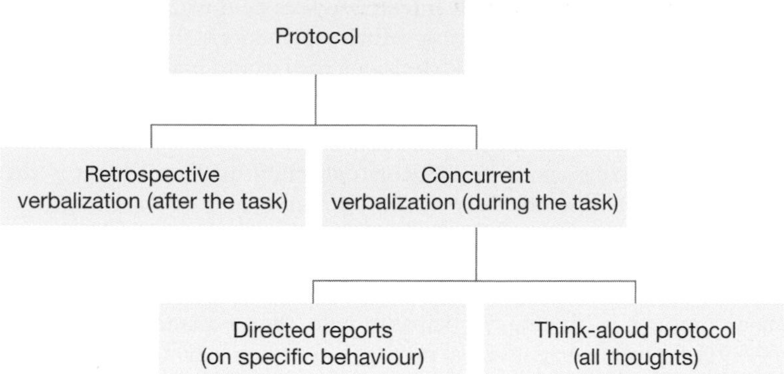

Figure 7.2 Types of protocol

Day (1986) identified the following advantages of using protocol analysis:

- It helps to reduce the problem of interviewer bias.
- The possibility of omitting potentially important areas or aspects is reduced.
- The technique is open-ended and provides considerable flexibility.

7.6.2 Examples of studies using protocol analysis

In this section we examine the way in which protocol analysis is used in two published studies. The first study (Deakins, Whittam and Wyper, 2010) investigated how bank managers made lending decisions in connection with actual business propositions. The researchers explain the stages involved in preparing the materials before the interviews took place:

- The first stage was to obtain examples of good propositions for banks loans which had been refused.
- From these examples, the researchers developed seven cases which were examined by a bank lending expert; five cases were considered suitable for the research.
- These cases were then sent to eight bank managers who had agreed to participate in the research so that they could study the cases in advance.
- Subsequently, each bank manager took part in an interview lasting approximately two hours. The interviewer asked the bank manager to 'think aloud' by talking through the decision-making process for each case study.

As the authors note, protocol analysis interviews are open-ended and require a considerable time commitment from the interviewee together with considerable skills and knowledge on the part of the interviewer.

The second study (Read *et al.*, 2009) was much larger and compared the ways in which a group of 27 experienced entrepreneurs and a group of 37 managers with little entrepreneurial experience approached marketing decisions when there was considerable uncertainty. All were asked to think aloud when making marketing decisions in exactly the same business situation (the case). The researchers describe the following stages in the research:

- The sample was selected by determining what is meant by entrepreneurial expertise.
- A case study scenario was developed that described an uncertain situation and the information seeking tasks required to develop a market for the product.

- Having studied the case, individual interviews were held with all the participants, who were asked to 'think aloud' by giving verbal explanations about the information they would require and the details of the decisions they would make.
- The recordings of the interviews were subsequently coded and analysed.

This study also emphasizes the care you must take when designing a study. One of the common problems experienced by students collecting qualitative data is that they are unable to analyse it successfully due to lack of planning at the design stage.

7.6.3 Potential problems

One major problem is finding participants with the necessary knowledge and time. Bolton (1991) used concurrent verbal protocols to test questionnaires and identify questions associated with information problems. However, he warns that it is 'time consuming and labour intensive' (Bolton, 1991, p. 565). Day (1986, p. 296) points out that a major drawback of using retrospective verbalization is that it does not consider 'a real-time situation, but rather an action replay'. On the other hand, concurrent verbalization requires the researcher maintaining a continuous presence and is usually too time-consuming and disruptive to be considered a feasible choice.

7.7 Diary methods

A **diary** is a method for collecting data where selected participants are asked to record relevant information in diary forms or booklets over a specified period of time.

Diaries are a method for collecting written data that can be used under both an interpretivist and a positivist methodology. A diary is a record of events or thoughts and is typically used to capture and record what people do, think and feel. Participants are asked to record relevant information in diary forms or booklets over a specified period of time.

7.7.1 Using diary methods

Plummer (1983) distinguishes between three types of diary:

- A *log* is a detailed diary in which participants keep a record of the time they spend on their activities. This is a method of collecting quantitative data and is normally used in a positivist study.
- A *diary* is where participants keep descriptive records of their day-to-day lives. These are free-form and present the researcher with several challenges, but also tremendous insights. The diarist should be encouraged to write his or her thoughts as if the diary is secret and to be read by nobody else. This will encourage illuminating revelations but these can be difficult to interpret. It is also challenging to make comparisons if several participants are keeping diaries about the same phenomenon. You may even question whether they are in fact observing the same events, as their perceptions can differ so much.
- A *diary-interview* has the advantage of allowing the researcher to progress to another level of inquiry. The participants are asked to keep a diary in a particular format for a short period. Detailed questions are subsequently developed from the diaries and form the basis of an in-depth interview with the diarist. The extent to which the researcher determines the format is a matter of judgement, but it is one that you must be able to defend. If there is time, we recommend that unstructured interviews are held to agree the format with the participants. Typical formats include those based on time (where the diarist records what they do, think or feel at specific times of the day), events

(where the diarist makes the record whenever the activity, thought or feeling occurs) and random (where the diarist makes the choice).

Diary methods offer the advantage of allowing the perspectives of different diarists to be compared. They can be a useful means of gaining sensitive information or an alternative to using direct observation. In contrast to participant observation, where the researcher is involved in the research, in a diary study, data are collected and presented largely within the diarist's frame of reference. Stewart (1965) used diaries as part of a study of managers' jobs and cites the following main advantages:

- Diaries greatly increase the possible coverage of numbers and types of participants, and their geographical and industrial distribution.
- The data can be collected simultaneously, which is less time-consuming than observation.
- The classification of activities is made by the diarist rather than the observer, who may be unfamiliar with the technical aspects of the job.
- The diarist can record all activities, whereas an observer may be excluded from confidential discussions.

7.7.2 Examples of using diary methods

Neither of the examples we are going to examine relates to a business topic, but they have been chosen because they represent modern adaptations of traditional diary methods. The first study (Ronka *et al.*, 2010) focuses on the daily dynamics in two families in Finland. The family members participating in the research were required to send text messages (SMSs) in answer to structured diary questions three times a day over a one-week period. They also kept records in written diaries. The researchers found that the mobile phone method of data collection facilitated the recording of participants' answers at the agreed times and the participants reported that answering was easy and did not take up too much time. A major limitation with SMSs is the constraint on the number of characters in each text message when the participant replies. Therefore, if you are considering using this method, you must ensure that the questions posed will elicit reliable and valid responses.

In the second study (Boddy and Smith, 2008), written diaries and telephone interviews were used to collect data from a sample of 82 mothers about the minor injuries experienced by their eight-year-old children. The mothers were asked to keep a structured incident diary for nine days and participate in a daily structured telephone interview over that period. The researchers found that telephone interviews resulted in more missing data than the diary records and reported that the participants preferred the diary method. This comparison of the two methods offers insights into their potential benefits and drawbacks for this particular group of subjects and is a reminder of the importance of choosing methods that are appropriate to the research question but also appropriate to the participants. Here, we can see that the use of methodological triangulation improved the validity of the findings.

7.7.3 Potential problems

Practical problems associated with diary studies include selecting participants who can express themselves well in writing, focusing the diary (what should be recorded and when) and providing encouragement over the record-keeping period. You will also find that setting up a diary study involves considerable time and effort. As with many other methods of data collection, there is also the issue of confidentiality. Stewart (1965) points out other disadvantages:

- There are severe limitations if the study is concerned with comparability, although these are reduced if the participants are a homogeneous group.
- There may be difficulty in finding a suitable sample and the researcher may have to rely on volunteers.
- There will always be some unreliability in what is recorded.

This last point can be extended to the bias that can occur in the diarists' record keeping. For example, the participants may want to give a favourable impression by claiming to work harder, longer and more efficiently than they did. They may be inclined to omit information that they perceive as giving a negative impression, such as taking a two-hour lunch break instead of the usual one-hour break. There is also the problem that participants might be tempted to modify their normal behaviour during the study to provide the information they think you want. If participants misreport their activities or change their behaviour to give a false impression, it greatly reduces the reliability of the findings. This can also happen when a researcher is using observation as a technique for collecting research data. We examine this next.

7.8 Observation

Observation is a method for collecting data used in a laboratory or natural setting to observe and record people's actions and behaviour.

Observation can take place in an artificial (laboratory) setting or in a natural setting (a real life situation). Observing people in a natural setting is often referred to as fieldwork. A natural setting is preferred in a study designed under an interpretivist paradigm because of the importance of context and its influence on the phenomenon being studied. This does not necessarily preclude the use of a laboratory setting, if that is an integral part of the research design.

7.8.1 Using observation methods

The most common type of observation in business research is non-participant observation where the researcher observes and records what people say or do without being involved. The subjects of the research may not be aware that they are being observed, especially if they are being recorded on video or captured in photographs. If the focus of the research is dialogue, audio recordings can be made. As with all data collection methods, permission must be sought from the subjects in advance. If the recording equipment is reliable and can be set up in such a way that the observer does not need to be present, it means that he or she is not distracted by having to write notes, which could also influence the subjects' behaviour. However, that does not remove the possibility that the subjects may alter their behaviour because they know they are being observed and/or recorded.

Under an interpretivist design, the themes relating to the actions and dialogue will emerge during the analysis of the recordings. However, in a study designed under a positivist paradigm, the observer may go on to measure the frequency of occurrence, time of duration or other quantitative data. Alternatively, a positivist observer may have prepared a schedule of phenomena of interest from the literature.

The second type of observation is participant observation. In this method, the researcher is fully involved with the participants and the phenomena being researched. The aim is to provide the means of obtaining a detailed understanding of the values, motives and practices of those being observed. The main factors to be considered with this method of observation are the:

- purpose of the research
- cost of the research
- extent to which access can be gained
- extent to which the researcher would be comfortable in the role
- amount of time the researcher has available.

7.8.2 Examples of using observation methods

In this section we examine examples of participant and non-participant observation. Both reflect the need for an opportunity to use observation. Essentially, something must be happening and the researcher must be there to see it. In our first example (Bowen, 2008), the researcher was a member of a party of tourists taking a two-week tour from the UK to Malaysia and Singapore. The holiday included a variety of tourist venues and activities such as walks and boat trips in the rainforest, snorkelling off the coast and the islands, and cultural visits. The researcher provides the following list of requirements for conducting participant observation:

- the phenomenon under study is observable within an everyday setting
- the researcher has access to an appropriate setting
- the phenomenon is sufficiently limited in size and location to be studied as a case
- the research questions are appropriate for a case study
- the research problem can be investigated by collecting qualitative data from direct observation and other means that are relevant to the setting.

With participant observation research there is an ethical dilemma: should you declare what you are doing or hide it from the other members of the group? In this study, the researcher revealed that he was a university lecturer and declared his research interest. If you are planning to use participant or non-participant observation, we strongly advise you to discuss this important ethical issue with your supervisor at an early stage.

Our second example (Findlay *et al.*, 2009) is a large project that involved the use of non-participant observation to examine the formal negotiation process between management and unions. The researchers were non-participant observers of the negotiations and they also conducted 90 formal interviews with key players before, during and after agreement was reached.

The research team was fortunate in having access to every stage of the bargaining process and was able to observe both formal and informal meetings between management and union negotiators. As a student, you will find that access is often a major challenge. If you are conducting a study using non-participant observation, make sure you have full agreement from all the parties concerned. In addition, you need to clarify how long that agreement will last, any barriers to your attendance and whether there are any restrictions on how you write up the research. This last point is important because in some cases the people being observed may want the right to edit your work, which would not be acceptable.

7.8.3 Potential problems

There are a number of problems associated with observation techniques. One problem is that you cannot control variables in a natural setting, but by observing the behaviour in two different settings you can draw comparisons. Other problems are concerned with ethics, objectivity, visibility, technology for recording what people say and/or do, boredom with the task and the difficulty of concentrating for long periods of time, and the impact the researcher has on those observed. Problems of observer bias may arise, such as when one observer interprets an action differently from a colleague. Another problem can be that the observer fails to observe some activities because of distractions. In addition, the grid designed for recording observations may be deficient because it is ambiguous or incomplete.

Observing people in any setting is likely to make them wonder what you are doing. Knowing that they are being observed, may make them change their behaviour by becoming more productive than usual; more docile than usual; take more risks than usual; be less decisive than usual and so on. These are known as *demand characteristics*, because you are making demands on the individual, and this may affect the research. It may be possible to minimize the demand characteristics by not stating the exact purpose of the research. For example, instead of saying you are studying the effect of supervision on the level of productivity, you could say that you are investigating the effect of different environments on job satisfaction.

Many years ago such an approach might have been acceptable and after the observation the researcher would have explained the true purpose of the research. However, the ethical codes now used by many countries and universities state it is not acceptable to mislead the participants. It is usually necessary for you to explain beforehand the purpose of the research to the participants and to ensure that they understand it. In some universities it is necessary to obtain the signed consent of the participant. The ethics rules in most countries do not allow you to observe people without their prior permission and without explaining the purpose of your research.

7.9 Conclusions

The collection of qualitative data under an interpretativist paradigm cannot be separated from the analysis. Although for the purposes of explanation we are discussing collection and analysis in separate chapters, in practice the analytical process starts as soon as you begin collecting qualitative data. If you are collecting qualitative data as part of a positivist study, you will choose quantifying methods in the next stage, followed by statistical analysis. We cover this in the next few chapters. Whichever paradigm you have adopted, it is essential that you do not collect data until you have decided on the method of analysis.

All researchers must consider the ethical issues involved. As a general rule you should inform the participants of the purpose of the research and, where practicable, obtain their written consent to take part. Most of the methods in this chapter are based on the researcher recording the data (interviews, critical incident technique, focus groups, protocol analysis and observation) or the participant recording the data (diary methods). We have also mentioned grounded theory methodology again, where any interpretivist method(s) can be used. Some of the methods in this chapter are associated with specific analytical methods, which we discuss in the next chapter.

It is also essential that you use rigorous methods for recording research data that also provide evidence of the source. Note-taking allows you to jot down the main points, which is starting off the analysis process. However, it would be difficult to write comprehensive notes and you may miss important information because you are busy writing. Most note-taking involves a degree of instant analysis, which can lead to omissions, distortions, errors and bias as you subjectively filter what data you record. Moreover, even shorthand writers may sometimes find it difficult to decipher their notes afterwards.

Audio or video recording overcomes these problems and leaves you free to concentrate on taking notes of other aspects, such as attitude, behaviour and body language. A specific recording device can be used, or the facilities on your telephone or laptop. The important thing to remember is that you need to obtain the participant's agreement to being recorded. Although new technology has made video easier to use, the cost of the equipment may be a problem. The advantage of video is the relative completeness and complexity of the data thus captured and the permanence of the record it provides. The subsequent analysis can be conducted in any order and at different speeds.

References

Arksey, H. and Knight, P. (1999) *Interviewing for Social Scientists.* London: SAGE.

Bolton, R. N. (1991) 'An exploratory investigation of questionnaire pretesting with verbal protocol analysis', *Advances in Consumer Research*, 18, pp. 558–65.

Boddy, J. and Smith, M. (2008) 'Asking the experts: Developing and validating parental diaries to assess children's minor injuries', *International Journal of Social Research Methodology*, 11(1), pp. 63–77.

Bowen, D. (2008) 'Consumer thoughts, actions, and feelings from within the service experience', *The Service Industries Journal*, 28(10), pp. 1515–30.

Brockman, B. K., Rawlston, M. E., Jones, M. A. and Halstead, D. (2010) 'An exploratory model of interpersonal cohesiveness in new product development teams', *The Journal of Product Innovation Management*, 27(2), pp. 201–19.

Brüggen, E. and Willems, P. (2009) 'A critical comparison of offline focus groups, online focus groups and e-Delphi', *International Journal of Market Research*, 51(3), pp. 363–81.

Chen-Tsang, S. and Ching-Shu, S. (2009) 'Service failures and recovery strategies of chain restaurants in Taiwan', *The Service Industries Journal*, 29(12), pp. 1779–96.

Day, J. (1986) 'The use of annual reports by UK investment analysts', *Accounting & Business Research*, Autumn, pp. 295–307.

Deakins, D., Whittam, G. and Wyper, J. (2010) 'SMEs' access to bank finance in Scotland: an analysis of bank manager decision making', *Venture Capital*, 12(3), pp. 193–209.

Delbecq, N. C., Van den Ven, A. H. and Gustafson, D. H. (1975) *Group techniques for program planning: A guide to nominal group and Delphi processes*, Glenview, IL: Scott Foresman, cited in Lindqvist, P. and Nordänger, U. K. (2007) '(Mis- ?) using the E-Delphi Method: An attempt to articulate the practical knowledge of teaching', *Journal of Research Methods and Methodological Issues*, 1(1), pp. 1–13.

Easterby-Smith, M., Thorpe, R. and Jackson, P. (2012) *Management Research*, 4th edn. London: SAGE.

Findlay, F., McKinlay, A., Marks, A. and Thompson, P. (2009) 'Collective bargaining and new work regimes: 'too important to be left to bosses', *Industrial Relations Journal*, 40(3), pp. 235–51.

Flanagan, J. C. (1954) 'The critical incident technique', *Psychological Bulletin*, 51(4), July, pp. 327–58.

Gubrium, J. F. and Holstein, J. A. (eds) (2001) *Handbook of Interview Research.* Thousand Oaks, CA: SAGE.

Johnstone, S., Wilkinson, A. and Ackers, P. (2010) 'Critical incidents of partnership: five years' experience at NatBank', *Industrial Relations Journal*, 41(4), pp. 382–98.

Kerrigan, F. and Graham, G. (2010) 'Interaction of regional news-media production and consumption through the social space', *Journal of Marketing Management*, 26(3-A), pp. 302–20.

Lee, R. M. (1993) *Doing Research on Sensitive Topics.* London: SAGE.

Lengnick-Hall, M. L., Gaunt, P. M. and Kulkarni, M. (2008) 'Overlooked and underutilized: people with disabilities are an untapped human resource', *Human Resource Management*, 47(2), pp. 255–73.

Lindqvist, P. and Nordänger, U. K. (2007) '(Mis- ?) using the E-Delphi Method: An attempt to articulate the practical knowledge of teaching', *Journal of Research Methods and Methodological Issues*, 1(1), pp. 1–13.

Meldrum, J. T. and McCarvill, R. (2010) 'Understanding commitment within the leisure service contingent workforce', *Managing Leisure*, 15, pp. 48–66.

Merton, R. K. and Kendall, P. L. (1946) 'The focussed interview', *American Journal of Sociology*, 51, pp. 541–57.

Morgan, D. L. (1997) *Focus Groups as Qualitative Research*, 2nd edn. Thousand Oaks, CA: SAGE.

Plummer, K. (1983) *Documents of Life: An Introduction to the Problems and Literature of a Humanistic Method.* London: Allen & Unwin.

Read, S., Dew, D., Sarasvathy, S. D., Song, M. and Wiltbank, R. (2009) 'Marketing under uncertainty: The logic of an effectual approach', *Journal of Marketing*, 73(3), pp. 1–18.

Ronka, A., Malinen, K., Kinnunen, U., Tolvanen, A. and Lamsa, T. (2010) 'Capturing daily family dynamics via text messages: development of the mobile diary', *Community, Work & Family*, 13(1), pp. 5–21.

Rosenthal, R. (1966) *Experimenter Effects in Behavioural Research.* New York: Appleton-Century-Crofts.

Smagorinsky, P. (1989) 'The reliability and validity of protocol analysis', *Written Communication*, 6(4), pp. 463–79.

Stewart, R. (1965) 'The use of diaries to study managers' jobs', *Journal of Management Studies*, 2, pp. 228–35.

Activities

1. You intend to conduct research to examine the study habits of your fellow students. Select two data collection methods you could use and discuss their advantages and disadvantages.
2. You want to identify the features that employees most like about their workplace. Explain how you would do this.
3. You ask an interviewee the following question: 'How much do you like your job?' The interviewee has replied, 'Not much'. List the probes you would use to improve the quality of his or her answer.
4. Working in small groups (or pairs), one person mimes an action, such as playing a computer game, studying for an examination, carrying out a domestic chore or a work-related task, while the others write down their interpretations and subsequently compare them.
5. You intend to use participant observation to examine the study habits of your fellow students in lectures. In pairs, design a form on which you will record your observations. (Hint: Which students will you focus on? What behaviour will you record? What else might you record?) Reflect on the advantages and disadvantages of this method and how you could overcome the main challenges.

Check how you're getting on with the online progress test at www.palgrave.com/business/collis/br4/

Have a look at the Troubleshooting chapter and sections 14.2, 14.5, 14.7, 14.10, 14.11 in particular, which relate specifically to this chapter.

8

analysing qualitative data

learning objectives

When you have studied this chapter, you should be able to:

- discuss the main issues in analysing qualitative data
- describe and apply a general analytical procedure
- describe and apply content analysis
- describe and apply discourse analysis
- compare the strengths and weaknesses of methods.

8.1 Introduction

Your choice of method for analysing your research data depends on your paradigm and on whether the data are quantitative or qualitative; indeed, you may have collected some of each type. In this chapter we consider the main methods by which qualitative data can be analysed. The methods we describe that focus on quantifying the research data will be of interest to you if you are designing a study under a positivist paradigm, whereas the non-quantifying methods will be of interest to those adopting an interpretivist paradigm.

The research data may represent secondary data such as emails, letters, reports, articles, advertisements, broadcasts or films, or primary data such as field notes, interview transcripts, audio or video recordings, photographs, images or diagrams. It is challenging to manage the analysis of a large amount of data and therefore we describe the main methods that allow you to analysis your data in a rigorous and systematic manner. We also discuss the use of software as an aid to managing the process. As we have pointed out before, it is essential that you describe and justify your method(s) in your proposal, and subsequently in your dissertation or thesis.

If you have collected a large volume of qualitative research data, you may find the analysis stage much more difficult than the collection stage. Therefore, we have referred to studies that illustrate how other researchers analysed qualitative data successfully. We advise that you obtain a copy of these studies before you start collecting data. This should help you avoid the problem of collecting the data and then finding that you do not know how to interpret it.

We have already noted that researchers may use more than one method to collect their research data and you can also use multiple methods to analyse your data. This is useful if the methods are complementary and add to the interpretation. In the next chapter we examine integrated methods where the analysis stage is incorporated into the collection stage.

8.2 Main issues in analysing qualitative data

Analysing qualitative data presents both positivists and interpretivists with a number of challenges. One of these challenges is that there is 'no clear and universally accepted set of conventions for analysis corresponding to those observed with quantitative data' (Robson, 2011, p. 466). Another challenge is that the data collection method can also incorporate the basis of the analysis, which makes it difficult to distinguish methods by purpose. Furthermore, in some published studies, it is difficult to appreciate how the researcher structured and summarized hundreds of pages of qualitative data to arrive at the findings. This accounts for the criticism that 'brief conversations, snippets from unstructured interviews, or examples of a particular activity are used to provide evidence for a particular contention … [and] the representativeness or generality of these fragments is rarely addressed' (Bryman, 1988, p. 77). Others comment on the lack of instruction in methods for analysing qualitative data. We agree with Morse (1994, p. 23), who laments that 'despite the proliferation of qualitative methodology texts detailing techniques for conducting a qualitative project, the actual process of data analysis remains poorly described'.

8.2.1 Managing the data

New researchers have a tendency to design very ambitious studies. If you are designing your study under an interpretivist paradigm, you are seeking depth and richness of data, so you should limit the scope of your study. This will provide more focus and help reduce the amount of qualitative data you collect. You can also reduce the amount of data you collect by conducting fewer interviews, focus groups, observations and so on. The breadth of scope of your study depends on the level of your course, what is normal in your discipline and what is acceptable to your supervisor, research committee and/or sponsors.

Morse (1994) suggests that all the different approaches to analysing qualitative data are based on four key elements in the process, although the emphasis varies according to the methodology used:

- *Comprehending* is acquiring a full understanding of the setting, culture and study topic before the research commences. There is considerable debate in interpretivist research on how much prior knowledge the researcher should have. There are those who believe that the researcher should not approach the study with pre-knowledge and the mind should be uncluttered by previous theories and concepts which might block out new perspectives and discoveries. Morse argues that the researcher does need to be familiar with the literature at the commencement of the study, but should remain distanced from it so that new discoveries can be made without being contaminated by preconceptions.
- *Synthesizing* is the drawing together of different themes and concepts from the research and forming them into new, integrated patterns. It is where items of data are reduced and sifted to give a general explanation of what is occurring.
- *Theorizing* is the 'constant development and manipulation of malleable theoretical schemes until the best theoretical scheme is developed' (Morse, 1994, p. 32). Theory gives qualitative data structure and application. It involves confronting the data with alternative explanations. Causal links or patterns can be hypothesized and 'tested' with selected informants who may refute or verify them. There are three ways of developing theory:
  - identify the beliefs and values in the data and attempt to make links with theory
  - use lateral thinking by examining and comparing the concepts and data from other settings
  - construct theory from the data by induction.
- *Recontextualizing* the data through the process of generalization, so that the theory emerging from the study can be applied to other settings and populations. In the process the researcher will return to existing theories to place the results in a context and establish new developments and models or new links.

Vox pop What has been the biggest challenge in your research so far?

Nawi, final year PhD student investigating the determinants of financial structure in SMEs

For me, it's staying focused. It's quite a tough task for me to organize all the data I've collected around the research questions. But I have to do it!

If you are having difficulty in organizing your qualitative research data or you do not know when to start the analysis, have a look at Chapter 14 (section 14.11).

8.2.2 Using qualitative data analysis software

Qualitative data analysis (QDA) software, such as *NVivo* and *ATLAS.ti* is widely available and can be very useful in managing the analysis of a large amount of qualitative data. Dembowski and Hanmer-Lloyd (1995) identified the following ways in which QDA software can assist the interpretivist:

- importing and storing text
- coding the data
- searching and retrieving text segments
- stimulating interaction with the data
- relationship building within the data.

It is important to realize that the software does not remove the chore of transcribing audio recordings of interviews or video recordings of focus groups, for example. You can only import textual data for analysis. As Wolfe, Gephardt and Johnson (1993) point out, the software can only support the process of analysis and it is the researcher who conducts the analysis and interprets the data. Critics argue that using software distances the researcher from the data and encourages a mechanical approach to the analysis. This may, indeed, be a problem for new researchers. Gilbert (2002) identifies three stages that researchers experience in the use of software for analysing qualitative data:

- the tactile–digital divide where the researcher must get used to working with the data on the computer screen rather than hard copy
- the coding trap where the researcher finds the software brings him or her too close to the detail of the data and too much time is spent coding without taking a broader, more reflective view
- the meta-cognitive shift where the researcher learns to reflect on how and why he or she works in a particular way and what impact this has on the analysis.

If you are planning to use QDA software you will experience these challenges yourself. Remember that the software will not do the analysis for you, but it will help you with the process of structuring, coding and summarizing the data. You need to allow time to follow the online tutorials and become familiar with the software. You may find it useful to keep a research journal in the software program as this allows students 'to rapidly and openly record their thoughts, questions, reflections and emergent theoretical ideas to a central executive point in the program' (Johnston, 2006, p. 387).

If you have applied your method(s) of data collection rigorously, you may feel somewhat overwhelmed by the amount of material you have to analyse and need to reduce the volume by restructuring and summarizing the data. If you are designing a study under an interpretivist paradigm, you will want to use non-quantifying methods and we look at a method for doing this next.

8.2.3 Quantifying methods

If you are designing a study under a positivist paradigm, you will probably collect most of your data in numerical form (via a questionnaire, for example), which you will analyse statistically. However, you may have collected a small amount of qualitative data from responses to open-ended questions, which means you need a method to convert that data to a numerical form. Alternatively, you may decide not to quantify the data, but use them to provide quotations to support your interpretation of your statistical analysis of the quantitative data. If you are using *methodological triangulation* (see Chapter 4, section 4.5), you will not necessarily want to quantify certain qualitative data. Typical examples are where you collect data from exploratory interviews to help you identify variables for developing hypotheses, or conduct post-survey interviews with a small number of respondents to aid the interpretation and validity of the results. However, other studies require the quantification of very large amounts of data (for example the analysis of documents).

Positivists may use *informal methods* to quantify small amounts of qualitative research data, such as counting the frequency of occurrence of the phenomena under study. This allows them to examine 'such things as repetitive or patterned behaviours' (Lindlof, 1995, p. 216). If the action, event or other phenomenon occurs frequently in the data, you might decide to omit some references to it to avoid repetition. This is not a shortcut because every occurrence must be counted to determine which data should be omitted. Frequency of occurrence can also be used to investigate whether an action, event or other phenomenon of interest is a common or rare occurrence. Another way of selecting data of interest is to designate items as 'important' and therefore retained in the analysis, or 'not important' and therefore ignored when counting the frequency of occurrence. You will need to be careful not to lose the richness and detail of the data in the process.

If you use informal methods to quantify your qualitative research data, it is essential that you explain the criteria for including and discarding data in your methodology chapter so that your supervisor and others can see that you have applied your methods systematically and rigorously. In addition, you must be clear about why the method is appropriate, as you will need to justify your choice. This will entail comparing its advantages and disadvantages with appropriate alternatives.

We will now examine some of the main non-quantifying methods used to analyse qualitative research data.

8.3 General analytical procedure

Miles and Huberman (1994) describe a widely used general procedure for analysing qualitative data, which is useful because it is not tied to a particular data collection method, and will help you conduct your analysis in a systematic way that you can describe in your dissertation or thesis. Their advice is derived from an extensive study of the literature, a survey of researchers using methods of qualitative inquiry and an examination of the examples and exhibits the respondents provided that showed how they applied their methods. They concluded that qualitative data analysis involves three simultaneous flows of activity:

- reducing the data
- displaying the data
- drawing conclusions and verifying the validity of those conclusions.

Figure 8.1 illustrates the overlapping nature of these elements and how they take place both during the data collection period and afterwards. Indeed, some data reduction may take place in advance of the data collection period when the researcher chooses the conceptual framework, research questions and participants or cases. You need to remember that these processes rely on the fact that you are very familiar with your data and require a systematic approach. We will now look at the first three stages in detail.

8.3.1 Data reduction

Data reduction is a stage in the data analysis process that involves selecting, discarding, simplifying, summarizing and reorganizing qualitative research data.

In an interpretivist study, you will have collected a mass of qualitative data such as published documents, field notes and interview transcripts that must be reviewed, analysed and interpreted. Whichever method(s) you decide to use for analysing your data, it will involve reducing the data. **Data reduction** is 'the process of selecting, focusing, simplifying, abstracting, and transforming the data that appear in written-up field notes or transcriptions' (Miles and Huberman, 1994, p. 10). It is the

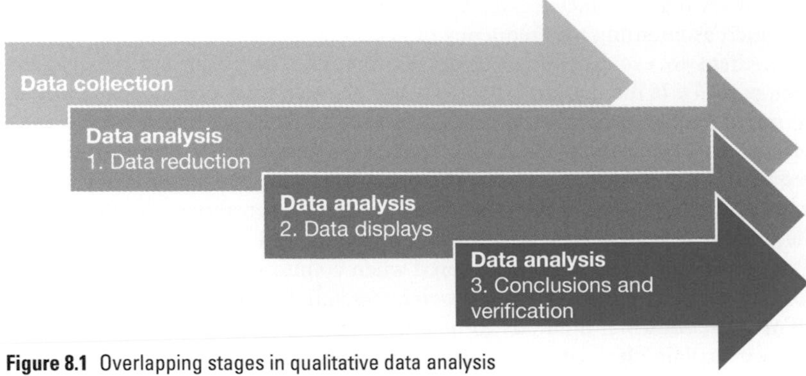

Figure 8.1 Overlapping stages in qualitative data analysis

Vox pop What has been the highpoint of your research so far?

Hany, final year PhD student investigating the ERP impact on the internal audit function

The final stage of the qualitative data analysis when the findings started to be clear to me. Although the analysis of around 50 interviews was a very exhausting task that took a long time, the process and the findings turned out to be very interesting.

Kevin, final year PhD student investigating the personalization of products and services

When I conducted my pilot study and found the information the interviewees gave actually confirmed my conceptual framework – even the answers I didn't anticipate confirmed it! My first thought was 'At least I won't have to go back to the drawing board', quickly followed by 'I hope no one else has the same idea and starts writing about it before I do!'

first stage in the analysis process. *Continuous* data reduction involves discarding irrelevant data and collating data where relationships of interest exist. *Anticipatory* data reduction occurs when the researcher uses a theoretical framework or highly structured research instrument that leads to certain data being ignored. This is not usually a feature of an interpretivist study as it restricts collection of rich data and limits deep understanding of the phenomena under study.

You would be right in thinking that data reduction means that you will ignore some of the data you have collected. This is because it is not until you are familiar with your data that you can determine what is relevant and what is not. Consequently, *reflection* is a key part of an interpretivist methodology. Imagine you are from another planet and you are watching one of the events at the Olympic Games. Until you have spent a considerable amount of time analysing and reflecting on what you observe, you would find it very difficult to make sense of the behaviour of the participants.

Data reduction can be achieved by *restructuring the data*. The data may have been collected in a chronological form dictated by the method of collection (diary methods and observation, for example) or because it is a convenient framework for asking questions (in interviews, for example). If you are using a theoretical framework, this will provide categories into which the data can be fitted. If you are not using a theoretical framework, a suitable structure may emerge during the data collection stage.

Data reduction of text can be achieved by *detextualizing the data*. This simply means summarizing the data in the form of a diagram. For example, if a diarist or interviewee gave you information about who he or she communicated with during the previous day in the office, you could summarize these interactions by drawing a network diagram.

We summarize the main features of data reduction in Box 8.1. Although we have explained that data reduction is a key part of analysing qualitative data, it is important that you keep all the data you have collected so that you can provide your supervisor and/or sponsor with an audit trail showing the process you followed to arrive at your conclusions. You will use some of the data to provide quotations or examples to illustrate your findings.

Box 8.1 Main features of data reduction

- Reducing the data – finding a systematic way to select relevant data, often through the use of coding.
- Restructuring the data – using a pre-existing theoretical framework or one that emerges during the data collection stage to provide categories into which the data can be fitted.
- Detextualizing the data – summarizing data in the form of a diagram.

8.3.2 Data displays

A **data display** is a summary of data in a diagrammatic form that allows the user to draw valid conclusions.

Diagrammatic analysis makes use of **data displays** to summarize complex data. Data displays are 'a visual format that presents information systematically, so the user can draw valid conclusions and take needed action' (Miles and Huberman, 1994, p. 91). Examples include a network diagram, matrix, chart or graph.

Miles and Huberman (1994) provide a comprehensive guide to using data displays and their approach spans not only the analysis of qualitative data, but the entire research design from the beginning to the writing of the final report. In this section we describe some of their suggestions for data displays for the analysis of qualitative data.

There are no limits to the types of displays that can be generated from qualitative data, but they fall into two major categories: networks and matrices:

- A *network* has a series of labelled nodes with links between them, which represent relationships.
- A *matrix* is a table with defined columns and rows and appropriate headings. If the matrix displays a chronological sequence of events, the headings of the columns show the dates and the row labels show the event, action or other phenomenon of interest. If time information is not relevant, another simple form of matrix might show partially ordered data that is little more than a checklist. A complex matrix may illustrate variables, periods of time and conditions, as well as the researcher's thoughts and evaluations. Whether a matrix is simple or complex, you will have to spend considerable time designing it and summarizing your raw data.

We summarize Miles and Huberman's general advice for constructing data displays in Box 8.2.

Box 8.2 General advice for constructing data displays

- Consider what appropriate displays can be used to bring together qualitative data so that conclusions can be drawn.
- Be inventive in using displays; there are no limits on the types of diagrams and illustrations which can be used.
- Constructing displays is an iterative process where you construct an initial display and draw some tentative conclusions, which will be modified, or even overturned, as new items of data become available and new displays are constructed.
- Be systematic in your approach to constructing displays and analysing data, but be aware that by becoming more formal in your approach there are the dangers of becoming narrow, obsessive or blind to new meaning which might emerge from the data.
- Use mixed models in your analysis and draw from different methodologies and approaches in your analysis.
- Remain self-aware of the entire research process and use supportive friends to act as critical voices on matters and issues you are taking for granted.
- Communicate what you learn with colleagues who are interested in qualitative studies. In particular share your analytical experiences.

An *events flow network* is useful for displaying a complex sequence of events, in terms of both chronological order and relationships. It will also lay the foundation for a causal analysis: 'what events led to what further events and what mechanisms underlay those associations' (Miles and Huberman, 1994, p. 113). Figure 8.2 shows an example of an events flow network relating to the experiences of a university student who had interrupted his/her studies. The student's experiences are presented in the boxes in the left-hand column, and the researcher's summary of the major forces moving the student to the next experience are shown on the right. The '+' signs indicate the strength of the various forces; the '–' signs, the strength of the student's dissatisfaction with the succeeding experiences.

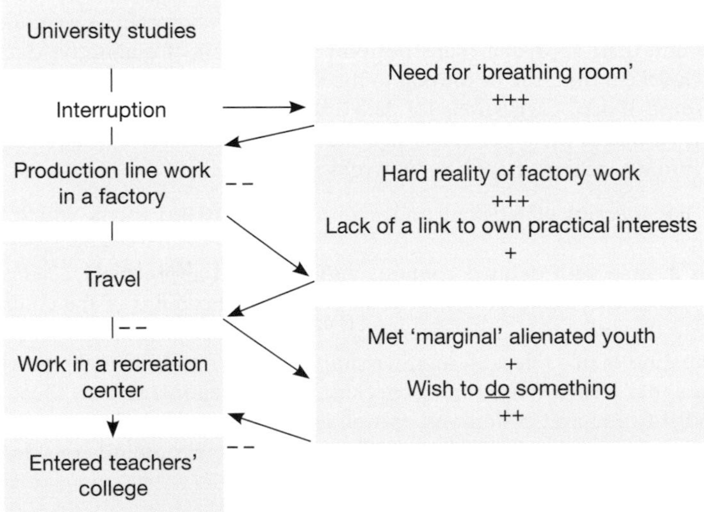

Figure 8.2 Events flow network: A student's learning and work experience

Source: Miles and Huberman (1994, p. 114). Reproduced with permission of SAGE Publications.

An *effects matrix* is useful for selecting and displaying data that represent the changed state of individuals, relationships, groups or organizations. Box 8.3 shows an example of an effects matrix summarizing data on one or more outcomes where the researcher was examining organizational change in a school. The researcher has divided the outcome of change at the school into structural changes, procedural or operating changes and more general relational or social climate changes, where the conceptual sequence is from 'hard' to 'soft' change. In addition, these aspects are displayed separately for the early use period (the first and second years) and the later use period (the third year). The researcher also distinguishes between primary changes, which followed directly from the requirements of change, and 'spin-offs', some of which had not been fully anticipated. Thus, the matrix displays effects, time of use and primary as well as spin-off outcomes.

Box 8.3 Effects matrix

Organization changes after implementation of the ECRI Program

	Early use 1st and 2nd yrs.		Later use 3rd yr.	
EFFECT TYPES	PRIMARY CHANGES	SPIN-OFFS	PRIMARY CHANGES	SPIN-OFFS
Structural	Scheduling: ECRI all morning, rescheduling music, phys. ed. Helping teacher named: has dual status(teach/ admin)	Cutting back on math, optional activities Two separate regimens in school Ambiguity of status and role	Integrated scheduling, cross-age grouping in grades 2–6	Less individual latitude: classroom problems become organizational problems
Procedural	No letter grades, no norms	Parents uneasy 2 regimens in class Teachers insecure Loosens age-grading system	ECRI evaluation sheets, tightening supervision	Teachers more visible, inspectable
	Institutionalizing assistance via helping teacher	In-house assistance mechanism implanted	More uniformity in work in all classes	Problems, solution more common, public
Relations/ Climate	Users are minority, band together	Cliques, friction between users, non-users	Tighter academic press	Reduction in "fun activities", projects (eg Xmas)
			Perception by teachers of collective venture	More lateral help More 'public' distress

Source: Miles and Huberman (1994, p. 138). Reproduced with permission of SAGE Publications.

Both the events flow network and the effects matrix are examples of simple diagrams and it is possible to construct far more complex displays. It is important to remember that constructing the display is only one aspect of the analytical process. The first step in constructing any type of display is to become familiar with your data; then construct your display and, finally, write up your conclusions.

8.3.3 Using a general analytical procedure

Miles and Huberman (1994, p. 9) identified a number of common features in the procedures used by those analysing qualitative data:

- giving labels (codes) to words, phrases, paragraphs and son, and labelling them as examples of a particular 'thing' which may be of interest in the initial set of materials obtained from observation, interviews, documentary analysis and so on
- adding comments, reflections and so on (commonly referred to as 'memos')
- going through the materials trying to identify similar phrases, patterns, themes, relationships, sequences, differences between subgroups and so on
- using these patterns, themes and so on to help focus further data collection
- gradually developing a small set of generalizations that cover the consistencies found in the data and linking these generalizations to a formalized body of knowledge in the form of constructs (sets of concepts or ideas) or theories.

Coding your data allows you to group data into categories that share a common characteristic. In this context, a *code* is 'a word or short phrase that symbolically assigns a summative, salient, essence-capturing, and/or evocative attribute for a portion of language-based or visual data' (Saldaña, 2013, p. 3). The codes are generated by the researcher and provide a link between the data that have been collected and the researcher's analysis and interpretation of the data.

All qualitative data collection methods generate a considerable volume of material and the procedure shown in Box 8.4 offers a method by which it can be managed and controlled.

Box 8.4 General analytical procedure for qualitative data

1 Convert any rough field notes into a written record that you and your supervisors will still be able to understand later on. You may wish to add your own thoughts and reflections. This will be the start of your tentative analysis. You should distinguish your interpretation and speculations from your factual field notes.

2 Ensure that any material you have collected from interviews, observations or original documents is properly referenced. The reference should indicate who was involved, the date and time, the context, the circumstances leading to the data collection and the possible implications for the research. You may find it useful to record your references on a pro forma summary sheet, which you can store in an indexed system for ease of retrieval.

3 Start coding the data as soon as possible. This will involve allocating a specific code to each variable, concept or theme that you wish to identify. The code can be allocated to a specific word or to a phrase. The use of exemplars is helpful when applying the code and explaining its significance in your dissertation or thesis. The code will allow you to store, retrieve and reorganize data in a variety of ways. You will find it easier if you start with as many codes as you feel necessary and later collapse them into a smaller number.

4 You can then start grouping the codes into small categories according to patterns or themes which emerge. This is not a mechanical task, but will require considerable reflection. If you are not using a theoretical framework, do not attempt to impose categories, but allow them to emerge from the data. Compare new items of data as they are collected with your existing codes and categories, and modify them as required.

5 At various stages, write summaries of your findings at that point. The discipline of putting your thoughts on paper will help with your analysis and highlight any deficiencies to be remedied.

6 Use your summaries to construct generalizations that you can use to confront existing theories or to construct a new theory.
7 Continue until you are satisfied that the generalizations are sufficiently robust to stand the analysis of existing theories or the construction of a new theory.

Box 8.5 shows an example of coding on an extract from an interview transcript, where the researcher (R) is investigating the role of credit in small firms. The interviewee (I) is the owner-manager of a company that creates online training courses. The researcher has identified the codes in the right-hand margin.

Box 8.5 Example of coding

Transcript	Codes
R: I'd now like to focus on credit decisions made in connection with customers. Approximately how many and what proportion of your customers are given credit?	
I: Almost all of them. Well, all of them except for those few credit card individuals – everybody else is given credit.	
R: So how do you decide whether to give credit?	
I: We don't think of it like that. I guess we decide to take someone on as a client and implicit in that is the fact that we're going to give them credit because it's the only way it's going to work. And our concern is very rarely their ability to pay but the time it might take to get the money.	IMPLICIT DECISION CREDIT PERIOD
R: Is that because of the nature of the people you're dealing with?	
I: Yeah, they're large businesses that … I mean they might go out of business, but credit checking them probably isn't going to tell me anything about that … so my concerns are how Byzantine are the approval mechanisms for getting paid and is there some kind of weird purchase order system that I haven't been made privy to or whatever. That's one concern and the other one is whether there's something about the work that we're being commissioned to do that might leave open to doubt whether we have satisfactorily completed it. Should there be a change of personnel or a falling out, could they say 'Well you haven't done it,' and because what we're creating is something that's virtual, then would that then be difficult? You haven't got a bunch of stuff you can kick and say 'Look, here it is. I made it; I delivered the goods; pay me; I created this course for you.' 'Well it's rubbish.' 'No, it's not. It's really high standard.' That's an unpleasant debate to have to have if you're not getting paid.	CREDIT CHECKS NOT USEFUL RISK OF LATE PAYMENT
R: So would you normally be in that sort of discussion with the person who wants the product rather than any credit people?	
I: Yeah, I've never spoken to anyone. Our bookkeeper would chase an invoice with the accounts department, but no, I sit down with the person who commissions us and we scope the project out and we agree a schedule and within that discussion there is an invoicing schedule.	CREDIT CONTROL STAGE PAYMENTS
R: Is there any discussion about the terms of reference?	
I: No, I unilaterally put a payment period onto the first invoice and I won't discuss that.	
R: Does the value of the contract affect any credit decisions?	
I: Generally, no. We've had some very big contracts. We do control how much money someone owes us, not because we have a concern about whether they might never pay us, but because we just need	IMPORTANCE OF CASH FLOW

to get the cash in. So we're quite keen to agree milestones within a project. Our whole approach to managing a project is designed to say there will be this initial scoping and the price for that is X and we'll invoice you at this point. Then there'll be stage one, stage two, stage three, stage four invoices that will come out. Sometimes we'll end up having to agree to raise those on satisfactory completion of the work, but quite often we can manage to build a time frame where – how can I explain this? Imagine that we scope a piece of work that has an initial prototype or whatever and then there are five chunks of it left. We say 'Okay, we'll do the five chunks. It'll take five months and we'll invoice you for each one at the end of the month,' and we put the dates in; and then the client doesn't provide the content we need [for the online training programme] ... In some cases we'll still raise the invoices and say, 'Look, we'll do the work when it comes in, but I have staff sitting here waiting for it.' And they'll say, 'That's fine, we don't mind paying as long as you say you'll do it.' TRUST

Coding the data helps you group the coded data into categories and start seeing patterns in the data. For example, the researcher in the example in Box 8.3 might create the following category and interconnected subcategories from the codes in that part of the transcript:

Category: Credit decisions in connection with customers

Subcategory: Management policy

Code: IMPLICIT DECISION
Code: CREDIT CHECKS NOT USEFUL
Code: TRUST

Subcategory: Importance of cash flow

Code: PAYMENT PERIOD
Code: CREDIT PERIOD
Code: STAGE PAYMENTS
Code: CREDIT CONTROL
Code: RISK OF LATE PAYMENT

Coding must be conducted with care and requires immersing yourself in the data. By that we mean, reading and re-reading the material and identifying categories that capture elements of the phenomena under study. Some researchers develop codes based on those used in previous studies or on their theoretical framework; others develop codes purely on the basis of the patterns they find in the data. During your study of the literature you will come across articles and other papers where the researchers claim to have used grounded theory. Developed by Glaser and Strauss (1967) and elaborated by Strauss and Corbin (1998) and Corbin and Strauss (2008), it involves a highly systematic approach to applying specific types of codes at several stages in the coding cycle. This leads to the development of theory that is 'grounded' in the data – hence the name of the methodology. Some researchers have loosely applied some of the procedures and yet still claim to have used grounded theory, so you must be wary of falling into the same trap. If you are interested in using grounded theory, you will find a detailed description in Chapter 9.

8.3.4 Examples of studies using general analytical procedures

The extent to which your analysis is structured will depend on the extent to which you structured the collection of your data. We will now look at two examples.

A highly structured analysis is described in an evaluation conducted in an international business setting by Jinkerson *et al.* (1992). The study was complex. It was concerned with the analysis of training needs in the tax practice of a firm of consultants and involved a number of researchers using personal interviews, telephone interviews and a postal questionnaire survey in 14 European countries. Two specific research instruments were used: a master questionnaire, which provided the conceptual framework for data collection, and a data checklist to track the collection of data from respondents. The questionnaire identified themes, key points and questions and each received a unique code, as did each country, office and participant. The data checklist was completed by the project researchers at the end of an interview or on receipt of data from respondents and showed the data collected. This permitted any missing data to be identified and subsequently collected. The researchers maintained six sets of files for the study and these are described in Table 8.1.

Table 8.1 Files documenting the study

File type	Description of contents
Raw data	Interview notes: documents describing existing training strategies, etc: completed questionnaires: Work paper 1
Data summaries	Summaries of raw data: Workbook 2
Data reconstruction	Relationship with and across countries on key themes; notes about insights. Hunches, developing interpretations; drafts of reports including findings and conclusions; Workbooks 3, 4, and 5
Methodology	Descriptions of methodology and its limitations; description of instrument development processes and procedures for administration; correspondence with management about the study
Plans, proposal and budget	Work programme and timeliness, proposal, budget for personnel level, payroll and non-payroll
Instruments and tools	Data collection and analysis tools

Source: Jinkerson *et al.* (1992, p. 278). With permission from Elsevier.

The process of research was conducted through the use of work papers which were contained in the first three files:

- Work paper 1 contained the raw data from interview notes.
- Work paper 2 summarized the raw data in Workbook 1 for each of the main points for each of the offices in the study.
- Work paper 3 reconstructed the data in Workbook 2 to create a picture across all key points within a single theme for all offices in each country.
- Work paper 4 was a country summary where the researchers wrote an overall assessment of the tax practice and training situation in that country.
- Work paper 5 contained the findings of the research and the recommendations.

This may appear to be a very elaborate system, but it must be remembered that this was a particularly large and complex project. In addition to illustrating the use of systems and procedures to manage and analyse qualitative data, this example demonstrates the amount of planning and management required for a research project.

The second example (Demangeot and Broderick, 2010) was a study that investigated online shopping and the data were analysed using *QSR NUD*IST v.6* software. The analysis sought to uncover recurring patterns in data that related to instances of online exploration activity by participants through description of their motives, the environmental stimuli or online actions taken and the expected consequences of those actions. The analysis generated a large number of categories. A process that involved constantly going through the data, and referring the literature, identified seven categories of shopping motives, twelve environmental stimuli and eight consequences.

8.3.5 Potential problems

Our first recommendation is that you do not collect too much data. This is particularly important for students on undergraduate and taught Master's programmes where there are tight time constraints. For example, it is easy to underestimate how long it takes to arrange, conduct and transcribe interviews, and then find you have very little time left to analyse the data. It is very important that you adopt a systematic approach and keep a record of the analytical procedures you have used, so that you can explain and justify your method(s) in your dissertation or thesis.

The next issue is determining the categories. One approach is to go through the literature and extract categories from there or see what others have done. It is common to start with a large number of categories and then, through a process of re-categorization, gradually collapse them as you become more familiar with the data. We discuss issues relating to categorization in more detail in the next chapter when we examine grounded theory.

In this section we have focused on methods of analysing qualitative data through coding, summarizing, categorizing and identifying patterns or themes. Some qualitative researchers prefer a more intuitive approach to data analysis and 'assume that through continued readings of the source material and through vigilance over one's presuppositions, one can capture the essence of an account' (Miles and Huberman, 1994, p. 8). Although we have suggested ways in which you can analyse the qualitative data you have collected, the value of the analysis will depend on the quality of your interpretation.

8.4 Content analysis

Content analysis is a method by which selected items of qualitative data are systematically converted to numerical data for analysis.

Content analysis is a widely used method for quantifying qualitative data. It is usually associated with a positivist paradigm, although it has been described as 'the diagnostic tool of qualitative researchers' (Mostyn, 1985, p. 117) for analysing a large amount of open-ended material and reducing it to manageable amounts for analysis. Content analysis is a method by which selected items of qualitative data are systematically converted to numerical data. Normally a document is examined, although the technique can be used to analyse other forms of communication, such as newspapers, broadcasts, audio recordings of interviews, and video recordings of non-participant observations and focus groups. Mostyn (1985) claims the technique was used to analyse communications as early as 1740.

According to Beck, Campbell and Shrives (2010), two main approaches to content analysis are found in the financial reporting literature: mechanistic and interpretative. Mechanistic approaches can be divided into form-orientated content analysis, which focuses on counting the frequency of words or concrete references, and meaning-orientated content analysis, which focuses on the underlying themes in the text. The general purpose of interpretative approaches is to capture meaning by disaggregating the text into its constituent parts and subsequently describing the contents of each component to increase understanding of what is communicated and how.

8.4.1 Using content analysis

If you have a large amount of data to analyse, the first step is to determine the basis for selecting a sample. However, if the amount of data is manageable and you have sufficient time, you can analyse all the data. The next step is to determine the coding units, such as a particular word, character, item or theme that is found in the material. Table 8.2 shows examples of coding units.

Table 8.2 Examples of coding units

Coding unit	Example
Words/phrases	Examine minutes of company/union meetings for the word 'dispute' Examine circulars and press releases to shareholders for the phrase 'increased dividends'
Theme	Examine minutes of company/union meetings for examples where agreement was reached Examine circulars and press releases to shareholders examples where increases in productivity are linked to increased profits
Item	Examine newspapers for articles focusing on small businesses Examine company reports for items dealing with environmental issues
Time	Measure the time allocated to business news items on the news bulletins of different television channels

Once you have determined the coding units, you can construct a coding frame, which lists the coding units in the first column, leaving room for the analysis of each communication to be added on the horizontal axis. The analysis can be based on the frequency of occurrence and/or other factors. For example, if you were examining the *Financial Times* for articles focusing on small businesses, you might want to analyse such things as the date of the paper, the page number, the length of the article, the author, the main issues in the article, names of firms, owners and so on. Under a positivist paradigm, the data could then be further analysed using statistics.

The choice of coding units can be confusing and you must consider the implications for your findings. For example, if you choose words instead of sentences or you count pages or sections on a particular theme, you could arrive at different conclusions. In addition, if you ignore figures, tables and images, you will not capture the messages they communicate that may be relevant to the phenomena under study. These issues are discussed by Hooks and Van Staden (2011) in the context of the environmental reporting by companies. They conclude that the quality of environmental disclosure is highly correlated with disclosures counted by sentence count. They also propose a quality per sentence measure.

If you are analysing secondary data, content analysis offers a number of advantages to researchers over other methods because you need only select a population or sample, and you have a permanent record which can be examined many times. You can avoid the time and expense associated with setting up and conducting questionnaire surveys, unstructured interviews, focus groups or observation. This leaves you free to spend more time on your analysis. It is also a non-obtrusive method, which means that the subjects of the study are not likely to be aware of or influenced by your interest. Finally, the systems and procedures for carrying out content analysis are very clear, so researchers who are concerned with the reliability and validity of their study will find the method highly acceptable.

Vox pop What has been the highpoint of your research so far?

Jennifer, undergraduate student investigating extent of environmental reporting in FTSE 100 companies

Finding a journal article on my topic that describes the coding frame [the authors] used for their content analysis!

8.4.2 Examples of studies using content analysis

If you are planning to use content analysis, we advise you to read the following studies, which we have selected because the researchers explain their methods. Czepiec (1993) examined advertising traits by analysing 454 advertisements appearing in the *People's Daily* between 1980 and 1989 to determine which factors Chinese businessmen consider most important when promoting their industrial products. She analysed the text of the advertisements for mention of 21 advertising traits which had been generated from previous studies concerned with buying behaviour.

Pullman, McGuire and Cleveland (2005) analysed customers' comments from a hotel satisfaction survey. They provide a thorough guide to the methods used to count words and determine association between certain words. They also explain how they used linguistic analysis to explore the semantics, syntax and context of comments, which led to the identification of key ideas, evaluation of their relative importance and predictions of customer behaviour. The authors also provide worked examples of various software programs that support content analysis.

Mehdizadeh (2010) used content analysis to examine traits of narcissism and self-esteem demonstrated by fellow undergraduate students at York University with active accounts on the social networking website, Facebook.com. A random sample of 100 students (50 female and 50 male) agreed to participate and signed a waiver form allowing their Facebook pages to be rated by the researcher. The aim of the study was to assess the amount of self-promotion, which was defined as any descriptive or visual information that appeared to attempt to persuade others about one's own positive qualities. The pages analysed were the About Me section, the Main Photo, the first 20 pictures on the View Photos of Me section, the Notes section, and the Status Updates section.

The aim of a study by Peetz and Reams (2011) was to gain an understanding of the existing body of knowledge on sport marketing. To do this they conducted a content analysis of *Sport Marketing Quarterly* from its inception in September 1992 (Volume 1, Issue 1) to June 2011 (Volume 20, Issue 2). The study analysed the authors by gender, institutional affiliation, location, number of authors per paper and the ordering of the authors. It also analysed the editorial board (the editor, associate editor, guest editor, section editor and reviewers) by number, gender, and editorial position. In addition, categories were established to determine the type of research and the type of methodology employed.

8.4.3 Potential problems

If content analysis is appropriate for your paradigm, it can be a useful way of systematically analysing qualitative data by converting the material into quantitative data. However, content analysis suffers from a number of problems. Silverman (2013) contends that its theoretical basis is unclear and the conclusions drawn can be trivial and of little consequence. There is also the concern that if you select only the words or phrases you have determined are of interest, you may ignore large amounts of data that could help you understand the phenomena under study at a deeper level.

Another problem is concerned with the availability of published data. For example, perhaps you want to analyse quarterly data for the past five years, but subsequently find that one quarter's data are not available. You also need to remember that if you are analysing secondary data, the material will have been written for another purpose and audience, and this influences its content and wording. With large amounts of data, the method can be time-consuming and tedious, and it requires a consistent approach and high levels of concentration.

8.5 Discourse analysis

Discourse analysis is a term that describes a number of approaches to analysing the use of language in a social-psychological context. The focus is on examining the language of social interactions in the context in which they take place. It contrasts with linguistics, which is a study of the language itself. Potter (1997, p. 146) explains that discourse analysis 'emphasizes the way versions of the world, of society, events and inner psychological worlds are produced in discourse'. According to Cunliffe (2008, p. 80), 'discourse is viewed in various ways as talk, written text, social practice and/or physical and symbolic artefacts'. In organizational and business research, it can be used to analyse naturally occurring talk (for example conversations), but also contrived forms of talk and texts (for example interviews, emails and other written forms of communication exchanged between organizational members).

Discourse analysis refers to a number of approaches to analysing the use of language in a social-psychological context.

Discourse analysis allows the researcher to investigate how language both constructs and reflects reality. We discussed the philosophical assumptions associated with different research paradigms in Chapter 3. The proponents of discourse analysis reject the notion that knowledge can only be generated through scientific objectivity since most people, including researchers, are not objective. Instead, they adopt a social constructionist perspective, which acknowledges that we all have our own expectations, beliefs, and cultural values. Consequently, we all construct our own versions of reality, which we convey through our use of language. Whereas discourse analysis can be described as adopting a constructionist perspective, in *critical discourse analysis* the researcher adopts a poststructuralist point of view and examines discourse from the perspective of rhetoric and focuses on where power lies within relationships.

The most prominent academic associated with the development of discourse analysis is Foucault (1972, 1977 and 1980). Saussure (1974) argues that language creates social identities and social relationships and thus provides us with a perspective of the world we inhabit. This theme has been taken up by many others, including Johnston (2002), who contends that discourse analysis is concerned with what is happening when people exchange information, make decisions and form relationships. However, Scollen and Scollen (2012) suggest that differences in communication are less to do with cultural reasons and more to do with being members of different corporate and professional groups.

8.5.1 Using discourse analysis

Discourse analysis is not merely a general analysis of transcripts or other documents. Irrespective of what form the discourse takes (for example talk or written communication), the person is trying to achieve something and the analysis focuses on trying to identify the strategies being used to achieve the particular outcome. Potter (2004, p. 609) suggests there are three basic questions that need to be addressed:

- What is this discourse doing?
- How is this discourse constructed to make this happen?
- What resources are available to perform this activity?

The first step is to transcribe any audio recordings that are to be analysed. You can then start the process of identifying characteristics in the transcripts and/or other documents under analysis that will form the particular themes or discourses. Potter and Wetherell (1988, p. 171) identify the following interconnected concepts:

- *function* refers to the practical ways discourse might be used, for example, to explain, justify or excuse, as well as to legitimize the power of particular management groups
- *variability* refers to the fact that the same event, the same social group or the same personality may be used to describe the same thing in many different ways as *function* changes
- *construction* relates to the notion that discourses are manufactured out of pre-existing linguistic resources and in this manufacturing process an active selection process takes place whereby some formulations will be chosen and others will not.

If you are planning to use discourse analysis as a method for examining organizations and individuals, we advise you to discuss it fully with your supervisor at an early stage. We suggest that it is more suitable for PhD students than for undergraduates or students on a taught Master's programme.

8.5.2 Examples of studies using discourse analysis

There is considerable literature on discourse analysis in the social sciences, including several articles that examine business issues. Stead and Bakker (2010) provide a comprehensive guide to the literature and the authors make a strong argument for the use of discourse analysis as a process of critical self-reflection in career counselling and development so as to enhance ethical, fair and inclusive practices. We have selected articles that provide explanations of the method and how it is applied. We emphasize that in our opinion this is a method that is best suited for the advanced researcher.

Our first study (Hrynyshyn and Ross, 2011) provides a good discussion of the technique and explains how the researchers applied it in a study of the Canadian Auto Workers Union (CAW). The purpose of the study was to investigate how the CAW, and particularly its leadership, actively defines or frames workers' interests, problems and solutions and, as a result, how it forms its strategy on the environment and climate change. The researchers conducted a critical discourse analysis of the union's policy documents and leadership statements with a view to uncovering implicit meanings in verbal and written communications, and visual representations. They contend that the systematic study of implicit meanings, through examination of the choice of words and symbols, helped reveal the actors' motivations for their activity, whether consciously articulated or not. In our opinion, the research adopted a hermeneutics methodology, which we discussed in Chapter 4. The analysis is based on the interpretation and understanding of text in the context of underlying historical and social forces.

The next study (Parkinson and Howorth, 2008) focuses on social entrepreneurs. The researchers provide a comprehensive discussion of this term, but as we are only concerned with their methods, we can regard it as referring to people who deliver community services using a business approach. Five local agencies (funders, intermediaries and support agencies) were asked to identify and nominate social entrepreneurs. The researchers collected their data through 20 tape-recorded, unstructured interviews, each lasting 45 to 60 minutes. The interviews were relaxed and conversational, starting with the request: 'Tell me what you do.' Prompts, such as 'how' and 'why' were used to facilitate reflection.

The first stage of the analysis of the 20 interviews used *Wmatrix* software to determine which linguistic features should be investigated further. A sample of five of the interviews was then selected for critical discourse analysis due to time constraints. These interviews were chosen to reflect differences that might be expected to influence the language used. The five interviews included differences in terms of the gender of the interviewee (three women and two men), local origin (three local and two newcomers), nature of their social enterprise activity and apparent high affinity or resistance to the enterprise discourse from an initial reading. Sections for analysis were selected either because of their relevance to the research question or because they contained moments of apparent crisis or cruces such as hesitation, redefinition, repetition, contestation or deliberation.

The critical discourse analysis of the five interviews took place in three stages:

1 The researchers took a broad view of the context in which the statements were made, how they connected to other debates and how the interviewees generally framed their spoken texts.
2 More detailed text analysis then looked at the micro-processes of discourse that shaped the text including text cohesion, ethos, grammar, theme, modality and word meaning.
3 The researchers examined social practice, which is concerned with how the interviewees reproduce or transform social structures in their spoken text and the intended and unintended effect of the texts on wider power relations and ideologies. The researchers concluded people 'doing' social enterprise appropriate or rewrite the discourse to articulate their own realities.

Our final study (Harkness *et al.*, 2005) examines stress in the workplace. The purpose of the study was to describe how female clerical workers make sense of their experiences at work, while also considering the discursive world that they inhabit. A total of 22 female clerical workers from a large western Canadian city participated in seven focus groups (averaging three to four participants in each group) which lasted approximately two hours.

The researchers drew upon a number of other studies to establish the following procedures:

1 Coding through reading the transcripts repeatedly and taking note of illustrative quotes.
2 Categorizing codes through rereading transcripts repetitively, looking for patterns, themes, and a limited number of interpretative repertoires (that is, alternative ways of describing experiences of stress).
3 Identifying ideological dilemmas, subject positions, and discursive strategies.
4 Extracting quotations from the transcripts to support the findings.
5 Refining the analysis and documentation in parallel.

8.5.3 Potential problems

Although discourse analysis offers a range of approaches to analysing the relationship between the use of language, social action and social theory, it is not without its problems. The main problem is that it is a time-consuming and specialized technique. You may find it hard to identify the context and the various interpretivist repertoires, and match them to each other to develop an understanding of the function of the stories from the perspective of the speaker/author. It can be argued that there is much more to the world and meaning than what we talk about, and 'care must be taken not to imply that language users are merely conduits of socially constructed meanings and interests' (Cunliffe, 2008, p. 81).

8.6 Evaluating your analysis

Once you have selected a method of analysis and applied it, you will want to know how to evaluate your analysis. A number of authors have suggested various criteria that can be used to evaluate an interpretivist study in its entirety and these can be used to assess the quality of your analysis. Lincoln and Guba (1985) suggest that four criteria should be used:

- *Credibility* is concerned with whether the research was conducted in such a manner that the subject of the inquiry was correctly identified and described. Credibility can be improved by the researcher involving him or herself in the study for a prolonged period of time, by persistent observation of the subject under study to obtain depth of understanding, by triangulation by using different sources and collection methods of data, and by peer debriefing by colleagues on a continuous basis.
- *Transferability* is concerned with whether the findings can be applied to another situation that is sufficiently similar to permit *generalization*.
- *Dependability* focuses on whether the research processes are systematic, rigorous and well documented.
- *Confirmability* refers to whether the research process has been described fully and it is possible to assess whether the findings flow from the data.

Leininger (1994) developed six criteria:

- Credibility
- Confirmability
- Transferability
- Saturation
- Meaning-in-context
- Recurrent patterning.

Although there are some differences between her definitions of the first three terms and those of Lincoln and Guba, the general themes are similar. *Saturation* is concerned with the researcher being fully immersed and understanding the project. This is very similar to the recommendations used by Lincoln and Guba to enhance credibility. *Meaning-in-context* 'refers to data that have become understandable within holistic contexts or with special referent meanings to the informants or people studied in different or similar environmental contexts' (Leininger, 1994, p. 106). *Recurrent patterning* refers to the repetition of experiences, expressions and events that reflect identifiable patterns of sequenced behaviour, expressions or actions over time.

The above recommendations stress how important it is that you are highly familiar with the qualitative data you have collected. You will need to be systematic and rigorous in your approach to the analysis, which means you must be clear about your methodology, methods for collecting data and the techniques you use to analyse the data. One procedure adopted by a number of researchers at the analysis stage is concerned with obtaining respondent validity. This involves discussing your findings with participants to obtain their reactions and opinions. This can give you greater confidence in the validity of your conclusions.

8.7 Conclusions

In this chapter we have examined a number of different methods of analysing qualitative data. If you are conducting your research under an interpretivist paradigm, the majority of the data you will have collected are likely to be in a qualitative form. Even if you have taken a positivist approach, some of the data you have collected may be qualitative. The main challenges when attempting to analyse qualitative data are how to reduce and restructure the data in a form other than extended text, both in the analysis and when presenting the findings. Unfortunately, few researchers describe their methods in enough detail to provide a comprehensive guide.

There are a number of methods and techniques which can be used to quantify the data. If that is not possible, or is philosophically unacceptable, you must devise some form of coding to represent the data to aid storage, retrievability and reconstruction. The synthesis and reorganization of data should lead to the development of themes and patterns that can be confronted by existing theories or used to construct new theories. Many researchers find that the use of displays is extremely valuable for part, if not all, of their data analysis. Others decide a particular technique is more appropriate. Whichever approach you adopt, it is essential that you establish systems and procedures to allow you to manage and organize the raw data you have collected.

You need to remember that your purpose, when analysing the data, is to find answers to your research questions. Therefore, you need to keep your research questions at the front of your mind while you are conducting the analysis. No matter how good the techniques and procedures you adopt are, the quality of your analysis will depend on the quality of the data you have collected and your interpretation.

References

Beck, A. C., Campbell, D. and Shrives, P. J (2010) 'Content analysis in environmental reporting research: Enrichment and rehearsal of the method in a British–German context', *The British Accounting Review,* 42(3), pp. 207–22.

Bryman, A. (1988) *Quantity and Quality in Social Research.* London: Unwin Hyman.

Corbin, J. and Strauss, A. (2008) *Basics of Qualitative Research: Techniques and Procedures for Developing Grounded Theory,* 3rd edn. Thousand Oaks, CA: SAGE.

Cunliffe, A. L. (2008) 'Discourse Analysis', in Thorpe, R. and Holt, R. (eds), *The SAGE Dictionary of Qualitative Management Research.* London: SAGE, pp. 81–2.

Czepiec, H. (1993) 'Promoting industrial goods in China: Identifying the key appeals', *International Journal of Advertising,* 13, pp. 257–64.

Demangeot, D. and Broderick, A. J. (2010) 'Exploration and its manifestations in the context of online shopping', *Journal of Marketing Management,* 26(13–14), pp. 1256–78.

Dembowski, S. and Hanmer-Lloyd, S. (1995) 'Computer applications – A new road to qualitative data analysis', *European Journal of Marketing,* 29(11), pp. 50–62.

Foucault, M. (1972) *The Archaeology of Knowledge.* Translated by A. M. Sheridan. London: Tavistock.

Foucault, M. (1977) *Discipline and Punish: The Birth of the Prison.* Translated by A. M. Sheridan. New York, NY: Pantheon Books.

Foucault, M. (1980) *Power/knowledge: Selected interviews and other writings, 1972–1977.* Edited by C. Gordon. Brighton: Harvester Press.

Gilbert, L. S. (2002) 'Going the distance: 'Closeness' in qualitative data analysis software', *International Journal of Social Research Methodology,* 5(3), pp. 215–28.

Glaser, B. G. and Strauss, A. L. (1967) *The Discovery of Grounded Theory: Strategies for Qualitative Research.* New York: Aldine de Gruyter.

Harkness, A. M. B., Long, B. C., Bermbach, N., Patterson, K., Jordan, S. and Kahn, H. (2005) 'Talking about work stress: Discourse analysis and implications for stress interventions', *Work & Stress,* 19(2), pp. 121–36.

Hooks, J. and van Staden, C. J. (2011) 'Evaluating environmental disclosures: The relationship between quality an extent measures', *The British Accounting Review.* 43(3), pp. 200–13.

Hrynyshyn, D. and Ross, S. (2011) 'Canadian autoworkers,

the climate crisis, and the contradictions of social unionism', *Labor Studies Journal*, 3(1), pp. 5–36.

Jinkerson, D. L., Cummings, O. W., Neisendorf, B. J. and Schwandt, T. A. (1992) 'A case study of methodological issues in cross-cultural evaluation', *Evaluation and Program Planning*, 15, pp. 273–85.

Johnston, H. (2002) 'Verification and Proof in Frame and Discourse Analysis', in Klandermans, B. and Staggenborg, S. (eds), *Methods of Social Movement Research.* Minneapolis: University of Minnesota Press, pp. 62–91.

Johnston, L. (2006) 'Software and method: Reflections on teaching and using QSR NVivo in doctoral research', *International Journal of Social Research Methodology*, 9(5), pp. 379–91.

Leininger, M. (1994) 'Evaluation Criteria and Critique of Qualitative Research Studies', in Morse, J. M. (ed.) *Critical Issues in Qualitative Research Methods.* Thousand Oaks, CA: SAGE, pp. 95–115.

Lincoln, Y. S. and Guba, E. G. (1985) *Naturalistic Enquiry.* Newbury Park, CA: SAGE.

Lindlof, T. R. (1995) *Qualitative Communication Research Methods.* Thousand Oaks, CA: SAGE.

Mehdizadeh, S. (2010) 'Self-Presentation 2.0: Narcissism and self-esteem on Facebook', *CyberPsychology, Behavior & Social Networking*, 13(4), pp. 357–64.

Miles, M. B. and Huberman, A. M. (1994) *Qualitative Data Analysis.* Thousand Oaks, CA: SAGE.

Morse, J. M. (1994) 'Emerging From the Data: The Cognitive Processes of Analysis in Qualitative Inquiry' in Morse, J. M. (ed.) *Critical Issues in Qualitative Research Methods.* Thousand Oaks, CA: SAGE, pp. 23–43.

Mostyn, B. (1985) 'The Content Analysis of Qualitative Research Data: A Dynamic Approach', in Brenner, M., Brown, J. and Canter, D. (eds) *The Research Interview, Uses and Approaches.* London: Academic Press, pp. 115–46.

Parkinson, P. and Howorth, C. (2008) 'The language of social entrepreneurs', *Entrepreneurship & Regional Development,* 20, pp. 285–309.

Peetz, T. B. and Reams, L. (2011) 'A Content Analysis of *Sport Marketing Quarterly*: 1992–2011', *Sport Marketing Quarterly,* 20(4), pp. 209–18.

Potter, J. (1997) 'Discourse Analysis as a Way of Analysing Naturally Occurring Talk', in Silverman, D. (ed.) *Qualitative Research: Theory, Method and Practice.* London: SAGE.

Potter, J. (2004) 'Discourse Analysis', in Hardy, M. and Bryman, A. (eds), *Handbook of Data Analysis.* London: SAGE.

Potter, J. and Wetherell, M. (1988) *Discourse and Social Psychology: Beyond Attitudes and Behaviour.* London: SAGE.

Pullman, M., McGuire, K. and Cleveland, C. (2005) 'Let me count the words: Quantifying open-ended interactions with guests', *Cornell Hotel & Restaurant Administration Quarterly*, 46(3), pp. 323–45.

Robson, C. (2011) *Real World Research.* Chichester: Wiley.

Saldaña, J. (2013) *The Coding Manual for Qualitative Researchers*, 2nd edn. Thousand Oaks, CA: SAGE.

Saussure, F. de (1974) *Course in General Linguistics.* Edited by C. Bally and A. Sechehaye in collaboration with A. Riedlinger. Translated by W. Baskin. London: Fontana.

Scollen, R., Scollen, S. W. (2012 *Intercultural communication – A Discourse Approach,* 3rd edn. Oxford: Wiley-Blackwell.

Silverman, D. (2013) *Doing Qualitative Research*, 4th edn. London: SAGE.

Strauss, A. L. and Corbin, J. (1998) *Basics of Qualitative Research: Techniques and Procedures for Developing Grounded Theory*, 2nd edn. Thousand Oaks, CA: SAGE.

Stead, G. B. and Bakker, T. M. (2010) 'Discourse analysis in career counseling and development', *The Career Development Quarterly*, 59(1), pp. 72–86.

Wolfe, R. A., Gephardt, R. P. and Johnson, T. E. (1993) 'Computer-facilitated data analysis: Potential contributions to management research', *Journal of Management,* 19(3), pp. 637–60.

Activities

1 You intend to conduct research to examine the study habits of your fellow students. In the previous chapter you discussed the advantages and disadvantages of two data collection methods you could use. Build on this by discussing the advantages and disadvantages of any two methods you could use to analyse the data.

2 You are interested in environmental issues. Using content analysis, construct a coding frame and analyse the contents of a national newspaper that provides international news coverage (today's copy). Use a data display to summarize the data resulting from your content analysis.

3 Take the same coding frame and analyse the website for a television news channel with international coverage. Use a data display to summarize your findings. Are you surprised by the differences and how would you explain them?

4 Run the tutorial on the qualitative data analysis (QDA) software to which you have access

(for example *NVivo*). Import an essay or paper you have written. Code the themes in each paragraph and indicate the relationships between themes. Generate a diagram. If you do not have access to QDA software, you can perform this task by hand. Print the paper in double spacing to allow room for codes and use different coloured highlighter pens to indicate themes. You can generate a diagram in *Microsoft Word* using SmartArt, Shapes, Tables, and so on, from the Insert menu.

5 If you have done Activities 2–4, choose one of them and write notes on the transferability, dependability and confirmability of your analysis (see section 8.6).

To access the online progress test visit www.palgrave.com/business/collis/br4/

Have a look at the Troubleshooting chapter and sections 14.2, 14.5, 14.7, 14.10, 14.11, 14.12 in particular, which relate specifically to this chapter.

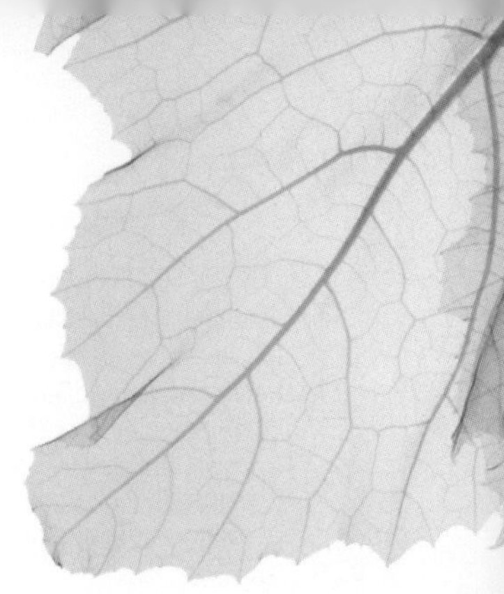

9

integrated collection and analysis methods

learning objectives

When you have studied this chapter, you should be able to:

- discuss the main issues in using integrated collection and analysis methods
- describe and apply the principles of grounded theory
- describe and apply repertory grid technique
- describe and apply cognitive mapping
- compare the strengths and weaknesses of methods.

9.1 Introduction

The collection of qualitative data under an interpretative paradigm cannot be separated from the analysis. Although we have discussed the methods of collection and analysis separately in Chapters 7 and 8, in practice the analytical process starts as soon as you begin collecting qualitative data. In this chapter we examine integrated methods for collecting and analysing qualitative data where collection and analysis are intertwined.

The first method we discuss is grounded theory. It can be described as an integrated method because it entails an iterative process of data collection, data analysis and theory building, which leads to further data collection and analysis, and so on. This generates theory that is 'grounded' in the research data. The second method is repertory grid technique, where the personal constructs (sets of concepts and ideas) of the interviewee regarding certain elements relating to the phenomenon under study are used to generate relationships between pairs of elements and constructs. This generates quantitative data on a matrix (the grid) for subsequent analysis. We also describe a method known as cognitive mapping, which is also based on the personal constructs of the interview, but this time the method summarizes the relationships between constructs in a diagram (the map). All these methods are rigorous and systematic and can be used independently or in research design that incorporates methodological triangulation (see Chapter 4, section 4.5).

This chapter will help you to understand the close relationship between data collection and analysis in integrated methods and show you how to present the findings in your dissertation or thesis.

9.2 Grounded theory

You will remember that we mentioned grounded theory in our discussion of the main methodologies in Chapter 4. Widely used in business research as well as other social sciences, **grounded theory** is associated with Glaser and Strauss (1967) and their contention that research should be conducted without a priori theory in order to build theory that is faithful to the phenomena under investigation and which illuminates the research problem or issue. 'Joint collection, coding and analysis of data is the underlying operation. The generation of theory, coupled with the notion of theory as process, requires that all three operations be done together as much as possible' (Glaser and Strauss, 1967, p. 43). Glaser (1978) suggests that the researcher should enter the research setting with as few predetermined ideas as possible. Of course, no one can completely distance themselves from the beliefs or the structures with which they have grown up or have developed since. However, the researcher needs to be aware of the presence of such prejudices. Once a prejudice has been recognized, its validity can be questioned, and it no longer remains a bias.

Grounded theory is a framework in which there is joint collection, coding and analysis of data using a systematic set of procedures to develop an inductively derived theory.

Drawing on Hutchinson, Johnston and Breckon (2010, p. 284), the key characteristics of grounded theory are:

- *Iteration* – Grounded theory is an iterative process in which early data collection and analysis inform subsequent sampling and analytical procedures, requiring concurrent involvement in data collection and analysis.
- *Purposive and theoretical sampling* – Sampling decisions are a function of the research question and the continuing development of theory.
- *Coding* – Analysis is achieved through coding and categorizing the codes relating to concepts and their attributes identified from a wide range of observations.

- *Theorizing* – The choice of technique for advancing theory development throughout the process depends on the epistemological and theoretical stance of the researcher.
- *Making comparisons* – Systematic comparisons are made within and between cases, or over time, to identify variations in the patterns.
- *Theoretical density* – There needs to be evidence of depth to the observations presented leading to theory from which hypotheses can be generated, in addition to evidence of *theoretical saturation* where new data no longer reveal any further theoretical insights.

You may be aware that after years of collaboration, there was public academic disagreement between Glaser and Strauss about how grounded theory should be developed and the two researchers decided to go their separate ways. Glaser continued with his approach and his work is usually referred to as classic grounded theory or Glaserian grounded theory. In the meantime, Strauss began to collaborate with Corbin in a direction that they considered to be more fruitful. Both approaches have their followers, but you need to understand that these are two very different ways of conducting research. Therefore, if you are planning to use grounded theory, you must discuss your choice with your supervisor and find out which he or she recommends. If you are on an undergraduate or taught Master's programme, it is not likely that you will have sufficient time or experience to use Glaserian grounded theory. This is more appropriate for doctoral students, who have time to gain the necessary knowledge of philosophy and the philosophical assumptions of the methodology. We will now explain grounded theory as espoused by Strauss and Corbin, which does not require detailed knowledge of philosophy.

9.2.1 Using grounded theory

Strauss and Corbin (1990, p. 24) describe grounded theory as 'a systematic set of procedures to develop an inductively derived grounded theory about a phenomenon. The findings of the research constitute a theoretical formulation of the reality under investigation, rather than consisting of a set of numbers, or a group of loosely related themes'. Grounded theory is normally used in conjunction with interviews but can also be used with data collected from observation or any data collection method associated with an interpretivist paradigm. It is important not to impose boundaries set by prior theory. It is difficult for researchers to rid themselves of the theoretical models and concepts they are familiar with that help them make sense of the world and the way it works. Once more, imagine you are watching one of the events at the Olympic Games. Try to ignore your existing knowledge about what the competitors, officials and audience are doing by pretending you are from another planet. Now start reflecting and analysing what you observe. It would require substantial study and reflection on your part to arrive at an explanatory theory that all the participants could understand. Perhaps the best advice is to approach the research, not with an empty mind, but with an open mind. Therefore, all data can be relevant in illuminating the study.

Coding

The first stage of analysis under a grounded theory methodology is coding. The codes are labels that enable the qualitative data to be separated, compiled and organized. According to Strauss and Corbin (1990, pp. 61, 96 and 116) there are three levels of coding:

- *Open coding* is 'the process of breaking down, examining, comparing, conceptualizing and categorizing data'. It represents the basic level, where the codes are simple and topical.

- *Axial coding* is 'a set of procedures whereby data are put back together in new ways after open coding, by making connections between categories'. This is a more conceptual level than open coding and links the codes to contexts, consequences, patterns of interaction and causes. The codes are more abstract.
- *Selective coding* is 'the procedure of selecting the core category, systematically relating it to other categories, validating those relationships, and filling in categories that need further refinement and development'. This provides the storyline that frames the account.

It is important to emphasize that grounded theory requires the discovery and creation of codes from interpretation of the data. This contrasts with the approach under a positivist paradigm, where coding requires logically deduced, predetermined codes into which the data are placed.

The relationships between categories and subcategories discovered during the research should result from the information contained within the data or from deductive reasoning that is verified within the data. Relationships should not arise from previous assumptions that are not supported by the information in the data. Any views held by the researcher prior to the study may restrict his or her perceptions of the phenomenon under investigation. This might lead to important links and relationships remaining undiscovered or inaccurate deductions about the data, for example.

We will now examine the process in a little more detail. Open coding of raw data involves a number of processes. First, the researcher breaks down and labels the individual elements of information, making the data more easily recognizable and less complicated to manage. These codes are then organized into a pattern of concepts and categories, together with their properties. This is accomplished by classifying the different elements into distinct ideas (the concepts) and grouping similar concepts into categories and subcategories. The properties are those characteristics and attributes by which the concepts and categories can be recognized. The properties of each category of concepts must be defined along a continuum.

The labels by which the concepts and categories of concepts are known are entirely subjective (chosen by the researcher). However, the label should reflect their nature and content. As the concepts are grouped into more abstract categories, so too should the labels become more conceptual. The labels can come from a variety of sources; for example technical literature, interviewees and informants – *in vivo* codes (Glaser, 1978; Strauss, 1987) – or from the researcher's own imagination and vocabulary. However, the labels should be explained. Labels with technical content or unfamiliar jargon can cause problems of interpretation to readers outside the field. Other problems can arise when common terms are used as codes; sometimes readers can be biased by a prior knowledge or understanding of a term which conflicts with or does not reflect what is intended by the researcher. Therefore, it is important that the researcher's interpretation of the code labels is given.

In practice, open coding and axial coding may take place concurrently. Axial coding is an extension of open coding that involves connecting categories and subcategories on a more conceptual level than was adopted at the open coding stage. Whereas the earlier stage of coding involved the breaking down and separation of individual elements, axial coding is the restructuring of the data and developing various patterns with the intention of revealing links and relationships. The process includes the development of the properties of concepts and categories of concepts, and linking them at the dimensional level. At this stage, the researcher will construct mini-theories about the relationships which might exist within the data and which need to be verified. Although the overall theoretical framework will not be discovered during axial coding, the mini-theories can be incorporated into and form part of the overall paradigm model that is being developed alongside the research. Box 9.1 shows the main stages of axial coding.

Box 9.1 Main stages in axial coding

1 Identifying the phenomenon: The phenomenon should be defined in terms of the conditions that give rise to its existence, and what causes its presence. It should be characterized in terms of the context in which it is situated. The action and interactional strategies that are used to manage the phenomenon should be developed and linked to the phenomenon, as well as the consequences of those strategies. This will form a pattern showing the relationships between specific categories, as follows:

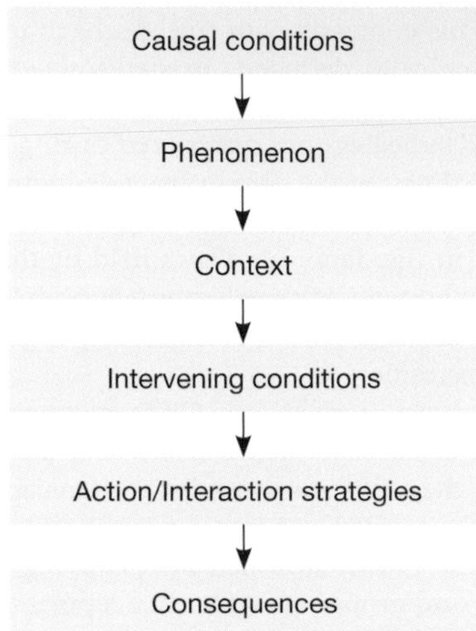

2 Linking and developing by means of the paradigm: This is achieved through rigorous questioning and reflection, and by continually making comparisons. By identifying and defining the phenomenon, the researcher has already asked questions about the possible relationship between certain categories and subcategories and has linked them together in the sequence shown above. These statements, which relate to categories and subcategories, must be verified against data. This is part of the inductive/deductive process of grounded theory. Where further data support the statements of relationships, the researcher can turn the statements into hypotheses.

3 Further development of categories and subcategories in terms of properties and dimensions: This develops the ideas already generated within the identification of the phenomenon. It builds on the relationships discovered and purposefully tracks down other relationships, some of which will fall outside the paradigm model. The categories should be linked at the dimensional level. Within this further development is the recognition of the complexity of the real world. Although relationships are being discovered, not all the data will apply to the theory at all times. These anomalies must not only be accepted, but must be incorporated into the research.

Selective coding is the process of selecting the core category, systematically relating it to other categories, validating these relationships and filling in categories that need further refinement. This process enables themes to be generated that can then be 'grounded' by referring to the original data.

Box 9.2 shows an example of coded concepts in an interview transcript.

Box 9.2 Example of coding from hazardous waste study

Paragraphs from an interview relating to Hazardous Waste case-study

Interview S, 27 April

Paragraph 8
I don't think there is any doubt that on this job I readily accepted the advice of the civil engineering consultant, L, and didn't have the experience to question that advice adequately. I was not aware of the appropriate site investigation procedure, and was more than willing to be seduced by the idea that we could cut corners to save time and money.

Paragraph 9
But L's motives were entirely honorable in this respect. He had done a bit of prior work on a site nearby. And his whole approach was based upon the expectation that there would be fairly massive gravel beds lying over the clay valley bottom, and the fundamental question in that area was to establish what depth of piling was required for the factory foundations. He was assuming all along that piling was the problem. And he was not (and he knew he was not) experienced in looking for trouble for roads. His experience said that we merely needed a flight auger test to establish the pile depths.

Source: Architect S, a member of the design team involved in the incident, describing the decision of the civil engineering consultant, L, restricting the scope of the initial site investigation to the question of the need to have piled foundations for warehouse units.

Significant concepts identified within paragraphs

Paragraph 8
Accepting professional advice
Criticizing others' work
Cutting corners
Experience

Paragraph 9
Knowledge of local conditions
Selective problem representation obscures wider view
Experience

Source: Pidgeon, Turner and Blockley (1991, p. 160). With permission from Elsevier.

Theorizing

The theoretical framework is developed by the researcher alternating between inductive and deductive thought. First, the researcher inductively gains information that is apparent in the research data. Next, a deductive approach is used to allow the researcher to turn away from the data, think rationally about the missing information and form logical conclusions. When conclusions have been drawn, the researcher reverts to an inductive approach and tests these tentative hypotheses with existing or new data. By returning to the data, the deducted suggestions can be supported, refuted or modified. Then, supported or modified suggestions can be used to form hypotheses and investigated more fully. It is this inductive/deductive approach and the constant reference to the data that helps ground the theory. Figure 9.1 illustrates the iterative nature of the process.

Figure 9.1 emphasizes the relationship between data collection, coding, analysis and theoretical development. As you can see, the interviews (or observations) are not completed altogether at the start of the study, but proceed throughout the research. If

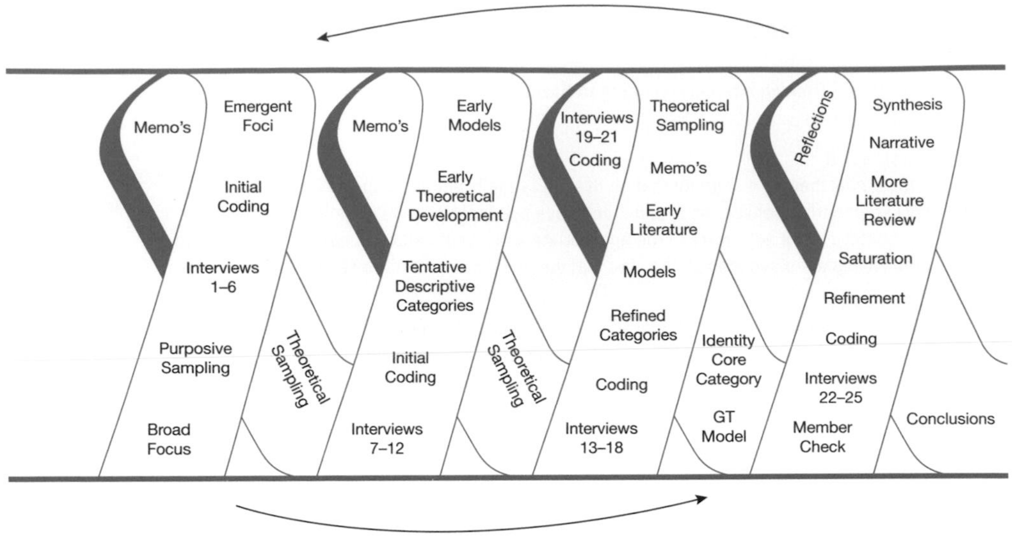

Figure 9.1 Developing grounded theory

Source: Hutchinson, Johnston and Breckon (2010, p. 286). Reprinted by permission of the publisher (Taylor & Francis Ltd, http://www.tandf.co.uk/journals).

you use this method, you may find that you have to return to individuals and check your first assumptions or to collect more data. This leads to uncertainty over when you should stop collecting data. The answer is that you carry on until you have reached **theoretical saturation.** 'This means, until (a) no new or relevant data seems to be emerging regarding a category, (b) the category is well developed in terms of its properties and dimensions demonstrating variation, and (c) the relationships among categories are well established and validated' (Strauss and Corbin, 1998, p. 212).

Theoretical saturation is when the inclusion of new data does not add to your knowledge of the phenomenon under study.

9.2.2 Studies using grounded theory

Grounded theory methodology is becoming increasingly popular in business research. Many researchers using grounded theory provide diagrams to explain the theory they have generated, as in our first example. Hussey and Ong (2005) investigated the financial reporting practices in one large organization and identified three functions of financial reporting that were formed through the interplay between the objectives of the preparers and the stakeholders, together with political and environmental determinants. This affected the type of financial information that was disclosed, to whom it was disclosed and the mode of communication. The researchers identified a reinforcement effect or a destabilizer effect following the dissemination of the financial report, according to the extent to which the preparers and stakeholders were satisfied with the fulfilment of the desired function. The aftermath influences the determinants to formulate the function of the financial report in future years. Figure 9.2 illustrates this.

Our second example (Kihl, Richardson and Campisi, 2008) is a study that investigated some of the issues faced by student athletes when there is an instance of academic corruption. The researchers identified three main consequences that led to harmful

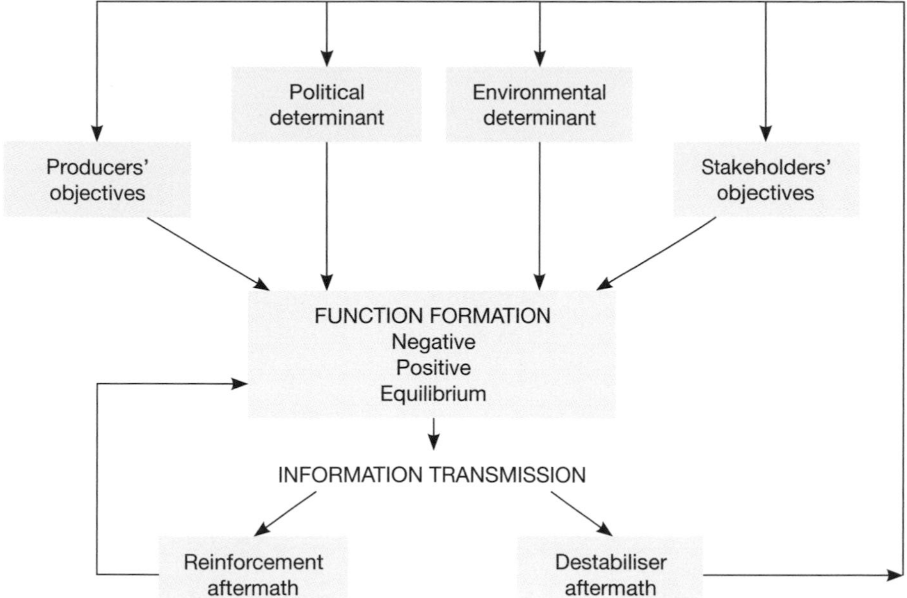

Figure 9.2 Substantive model of financial reporting
Source: Hussey and Ong (2005, p. 158).

outcomes (negative treatment, sanctions and a sense of loss) in addition to some positive outcomes. Figure 9.3 shows the flow diagram that summarizes their theoretical model.

9.2.3 Potential problems

Grounded theory presents a number of problems, which include the difficulty of dealing with the considerable amount of data generated and the generalizability of the findings. Not only is the research process very time-consuming, but it is set within a particular context, which may limited the generalizability of the findings. In such cases, the researchers may refer to the development of a *substantive model* based on the observable themes and patterns within the setting of the study rather than a theory.

Although coding plays a significant role in the analysis of qualitative data, you need to remember that this is only part of grounded theory methodology. If you only intend to use the coding procedures from grounded theory, in your methodology chapter you will need to explain why you have not incorporated the generation of theory. This may be difficult since there are a number of alternative analytical procedures you might use. At the undergraduate level, your supervisor may only require you to demonstrate some of the important concepts and variables that would be part of a theory.

We emphasize that if you are planning to use grounded theory, you must discuss it with your supervisor at an early stage. Jones (2009) describes the experiences of a doctoral student who had to convince the committee that such a methodology was acceptable. His argument was that all other methodologies were inappropriate, which eliminated them as alternatives, leaving grounded theory as the only choice.

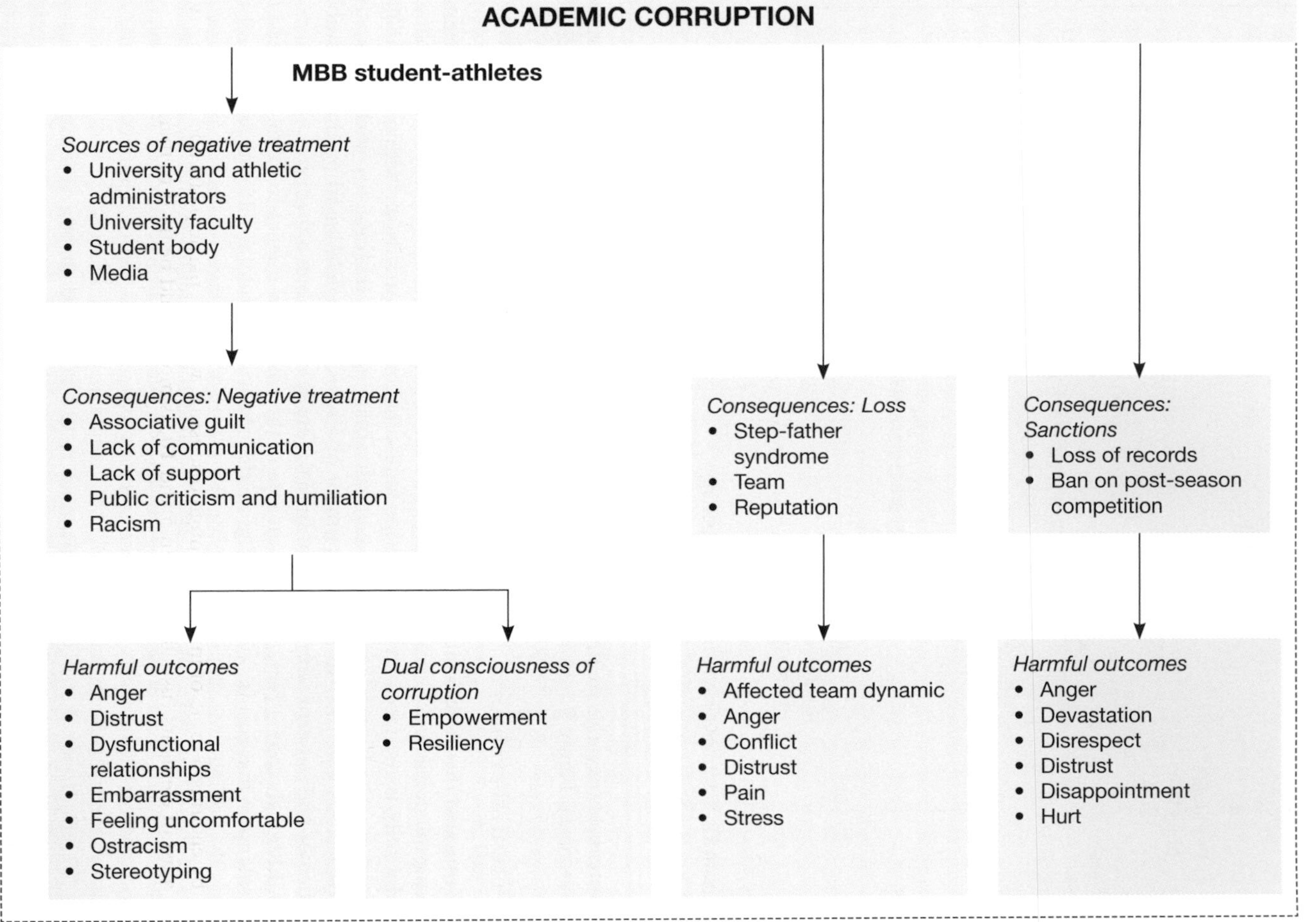

Figure 9.3 Theoretical model of academic corruption

Source: Kihl, Richardson and Campisi (2008, p. 284). With permission of Human Kinetics.

9.3 Repertory grid technique

Based on personal construct theory (Kelly, 1955), **repertory grid technique** is a form of structured interview during which a matrix (the grid) is developed that contains a mathematical representation of the perceptions and constructs a person uses to understand and manage his or her world. The technique 'allows the interviewer to get a mental map of how the interviewee views the world, and to write this map with the minimum of observer bias' (Stewart and Stewart, 1981, p. 5).

Repertory grid technique is a method based on personal construct theory that generates a mathematical representation of a participant's perceptions and constructs.

A **personal construct** is a set of concepts or general notions and ideas a person has in his or her mind about certain things.

A **personal construct** is a set of concepts or general notions and ideas a person has in his or her mind about certain things. The underlying theory is that 'people strive to make sense of their world by developing a personal construct system: a network of hypotheses about how the world works' (Hankinson, 2004, p. 146). Our personal constructs are not necessarily fixed; as we gain new knowledge and experience, we develop new models to help us make sense of the world. Our construct system represents reality as we know it. Others may share our view of reality or perhaps only part of it if their construct systems overlap with ours. Inconsistencies in our personal construct systems help explain why we might view other people's behaviour as being at odds with ours.

9.3.1 Using repertory grid technique

It can be argued that at one level a repertory grid 'is nothing more than a labelled set of numbers' (Taylor, 1990, p. 105). However, it provides a structured way for interpretivists to assess individuals' perceptions and gather data that permits themes and patterns to be discerned based on quantitative data measured on an *ordinal scale* (see Chapter 10, section 10.3.1) that readily lends itself to statistical analysis. That would appeal if you are planning a positivist study, but if you are designing your study under an interpretivist paradigm, it is essential to seek explanation of the constructs, elements and scores from the interviewee at the time. In all cases, we recommend that you ask permission to audio record the interview and take notes.

Repertory grid technique requires the identification of *elements* and *constructs*, and a procedure for enabling participants to relate the constructs to the elements. The elements on the grid are the objects or concepts under discussion, and constructs are the characteristics or attributes of the elements. Following Kelly's original approach, many studies have used people as elements, but other studies have used occupations and work activities (for example Hunter, 1997) and organizations (for example Barton-Cunningham and Gerrard, 2000; Dackert *et al.*, 2003).

Elements can be generated in several ways:

- by eliciting a topic of interest through discussion with the participants and drawing up a list of elements (usually between 5 and 10, as more could be hard to manage)
- by describing a situation and allowing the participant to identify the elements
- by providing a pool of elements and asking the participant to select a certain number of elements
- by providing predetermined elements.

A separate card is used to show the name of each element and these cards are used to elicit the constructs, using *triads* or *dyads*. The classical approach is to use triads, where the interviewer selects three cards at random to show the interviewee. He or she is first asked to decide which two are similar and what differentiates them from the third and then to think of a word or phrase for each similarity or difference between pairs in the triad. The process is repeated until a comprehensive list of personal constructs is obtained. The alternative approach is to use dyads, where pairs of cards are selected at random and the interviewee is asked to provide a word or phrase that describes each similarity or difference. We advise you to choose the method that is the most appropriate for exploring the participant's view of the phenomena under study.

The main stages in repertory grid technique are summarized in Box 9.3.

Box 9.3 Procedure for repertory grid technique

1 Determine the focus of the grid.
2 Determine the elements in advance or agree them with each interviewee (approximately 5–10).
3 Write each element on a separate card.
4 Decide whether to use triads or dyads.
5 Select the appropriate number of cards at random.
6 Ask the interviewee to provide a word or phrase that describes each similarity and difference between the pairs of elements.
7 Use these words or phrases as the constructs on the grid.
8 Explain the rating scale to the interviewee (for example 5 = high, 1 = low)
9 Ask the interviewee to indicate the number closest to his or her view and explain the reason.
10 Construct a grid for each interviewee based on his or her responses and scores.

In an *ideographic approach*, the grid is based on the unique elements and personal constructs elicited from the interviewee, and the scores he or she gives that measure relationships between each element and construct. These describe his or her world and the grid may have very little in common with the grids of other interviewees. In a *nomothetic approach*, predetermined elements and/or constructs are used, which facilitate comparison across cases and aggregation of the scores in the grids (Tan and Hunter, 2002). At a very simple level you can detect emerging patterns, but in a positivist study you might want to take a statistical approach.

9.3.2 Examples of studies using repertory grid technique

Our first example is a study that used repertory grid technique to investigate employees' constructs in relation to a set of elements based on organizational systems (Dunn and Ginsberg, 1986). Box 9.4 shows an example of the repertory grid for one of the employees interviewed. If you refer to the article, you will see that the researchers used the data from the repertory grids to calculate three indices of cognitive content, which allowed them to measure differences in the structure and content of reference frames.

A second example is a study by Brook (1986), who used repertory grid technique in conjunction with interviews and questionnaires (methodological triangulation) to measure the effectiveness of a management training programme. The grid was based on typical interpersonal situations encountered by managers in their daily work, together with two elements referring to performance before and after training, and two elements relating to examples of their best and worst performance. The situations she used to elicit the elements were:

1 A time when I delegated an important task to a co-worker
2 The time when I actively opposed the ideas of my controlling officer (or someone in authority)

3 A time I had to deal with a problem brought to me by a member of my staff
4 A time I had to make an important decision concerning my research (or other work)
5 A time when I had a professional association with some outside organization (business, industry, etc.)
6 The occasion when I made (or proposed) changes in the running and conduct of section meetings or other procedures of a similar nature
7 An occasion when I felt most satisfied with my work performance
8 An occasion when I felt least satisfied with my work performance
9 My professional self *now*
10 My professional self *a year ago.* (Brook, 1986, Table 3, p. 495)

She found that the repertory grids provided 'rich and varied data on individual subjects which could then be validated against other information obtained from before-and-after interviews and questionnaires' (Brook, 1986, p. 495).

Box 9.4 Sample individual repertory grid

Constructs	**Elements**					
Rating scale 1–7	Inventory management system	Strategic planning system	Office automation	Decision support system	Quality working circle	Collateral organization
Technical quality	6	5	4	2	1	3
Cost	2	1	4	6	5	3
Challenge to status quo	6	1	2	4	5	3
Actionability	1	6	2	4	5	3
Evaluability	6	1	2	5	4	3

Source: Based on Dunn and Ginsberg (1986, p. 964). Reproduced with permission of SAGE Publications.

The next study (Lemke, Clark and Wilson, 2011) used repertory grid technique during 40 interviews with customers to examine the quality of their experience. The researchers identified nine suppliers as the elements of the grid and then used the triadic method to establish the constructs. During the interview the customer was shown three cards, each of which displayed the name of one of the nine suppliers. The customers were asked how two of the suppliers differed from the third. This generated the first construct. Next, the interviewee was asked to state the opposite of this construct, so that the labels could be used as the anchors on either end of a scale. The interviewee was then asked to rate all nine suppliers on this construct using a five-point scale. The interviewee was shown another three cards displaying the names of another triad of suppliers and asked to explain how two of them differed from the third, but using a different reason from the explanation given for the first construct. This process continued until no further constructs could be identified. Not surprisingly, several constructs appeared in more than one interview and it was possible to reduce the total number of constructs to 119. These were then categorized into 17 experience categories. To ensure the reliability of the categorization process, not only did the research team meet to discuss and agree the categories, but they also called upon the help of two independent scholars to ensure the analysis was managed appropriately.

This was a major study involving three experienced researchers and two independent scholars, and conducting 40 interviews would be too time-consuming for an undergraduate or taught Master's student. To avoid this problem, some researchers use a literature search or a sample of interviewees to establish the constructs. Some academics may be opposed to this, so if you are planning to do this, it is important that you discuss it with your supervisor first.

Identifying the elements and constructs and then completing the grid with the ratings given by the interviewees is only part of the method. Interpretivists will be interested in gaining an understanding of the scores on the grids from a qualitative analysis of the explanations given by the interviewees when they were completing the grid. If the researcher has not used a standard set of elements and constructs for all interviewees, *content analysis* can be used to count the frequency of occurrence of elements and constructs with a view to identifying common trends. It is also possible to compare individuals' grids for cognitive content and structure.

The scores on the repertory grid can be analysed statistically. The particular statistics used should be appropriate for variables measured on an *ordinal scale* (see Chapters 10 and 11). If you have sufficient data, cluster analysis and factor analysis may be useful for aiding the interpretation of the data. You need to remember that if your hypotheses are not underpinned by theory or deductive reasoning, a mathematical 'relationship' may be found that is entirely spurious.

9.3.3 Potential problems

The main practical problems with repertory grid technique are that it is very time-consuming and participants may find it difficult to compare and contrast the triads or dyads of the elements, and describe constructs in the prescribed manner. There is also the challenge of how to aggregate data from individual grids. It is possible to examine a relatively small matrix for patterns and differences between constructs and elements. However, a large matrix would require the use of software to generate the grid and analyse the data. A follow-up interview with the participant increases the validity of the statistical analysis, but you will need to bear in mind that the meaning given to events and experiences can change over time.

Although repertory grid technique has been used in positivist studies, it is argued that the foundations of personal construct theory lie within the interpretivist paradigm (Reason and Rowan, 1981). If you want to use repertory grid technique to collect quantitative data for statistical purposes, you are designing your study under a positivist paradigm and you need to be aware that there is some debate over this when you justify your methodology in your dissertation or thesis.

9.4 Cognitive mapping

Cognitive mapping is a method based on personal construct theory that structures a participant's perceptions in the form of a diagram.

Cognitive mapping attempts to extend personal construct theory (Kelly, 1955) and is widely used in business research to analyse and structure written or verbal accounts of problem solving. The underlying theory is that different people interpret data in different ways and therefore they solve problems in different ways. As already explained, people make sense of the world by developing a network diagram of personal constructs that help them understand it. When decision makers have to resolve new and complex problems they cannot process all information that would be relevant, but can reflect on their existing cognitive maps to determine what action should be taken. From a researcher's point of view, if we can gain understanding of the decision maker's cognitive map, we will be in a better position to understand his or her decision-making process.

9.4.1 Using cognitive mapping

Cognitive mapping is often used in projects concerned with the development of strategy and can be useful in action research. It can be used to summarize interview transcripts or other documentary data in a way that promotes reflection and analysis of the problem, leading to potential solutions. If interviews are used to gather the data, the questions asked should focus on the factors that affect the problem, the concepts relating to the problem, why those concepts are important to the interviewee and how they are related. The main stages in cognitive mapping are as follows:

- An account of the problem is broken into phrases of about ten words which retain the language of the person providing the account. These are treated as distinct concepts which are then reconnected to represent the account in a graphical format. This reveals the pattern of reasoning about a problem in a way that linear text cannot.
- Pairs of phrases can be united in a single concept where one provides a meaningful contrast to the other. These phrases are the personal constructs in Kelly's theory, where meaning is retained through contrast.
- The distinct phrases are linked to form a hierarchy of means and ends; essentially explanations leading to consequences. This involves deciding on the status of one concept relative to another. There are a number of categories or levels defined in a notional hierarchy that help the user make these decisions. Meaning is retained through the context.

Drawing on Ackermann, Eden and Cropper (1990), Box 9.5 shows a procedure for cognitive mapping that focuses on strategic issues.

Box 9.5 Procedure for cognitive mapping

1. Construct your map on a single A4 page so that links can be made.
2. Start mapping about two-thirds of the way up the paper in the middle, displaying the concepts in small rectangles of text.
3. Separate the sentences into phrases.
4. Build up a hierarchy.
5. Identify goals and potential strategic issues as the discussion unfolds.
6. Retain opposite poles for additional clarification.
7. Add meaning to concepts by placing them in the imperative form; include actors and actions if possible.
8. Retain validity by not abbreviating words and phrases used by the problem owner.
9. Identify the option and outcome within each pair of concepts.
10. Ensure that a generic concept is superordinate to specific items that contribute to it.
11. Code the first pole as the one that the problem owner sees as the primary idea.
12. Tidy up the map to provide a more complete understanding of the problem.

Source: Ackermann, Eden and Cropper (1990). With permission. For further information on mapping for research, see: Eden, C. and Ackermann, F. (1998) 'Analysing and Comparing Idiographic Causal Maps' in Eden, C. and Spender, J-C (eds), *Managerial and Organizational Cognition*. London: SAGE, pp. 192–209.

Cope is a software program that has been developed to aid cognitive mapping. There is no pre-set framework, other than the nodes and linkages convention. This means the researcher can impose any structuring convention that seems appropriate. The program can handle complex data, which are held in a database in a form that is amenable to analysis and presentation. As its name suggests, *Cope* aids the management of large amounts of data, but it also reduces the need for early data reduction and compels the researcher to be explicit about the assumptions he or she is using to structure and analyse the data. It can be used to build models that retain the meaning of the data and aid 'the development of theoretical accounts of phenomena' (Cropper, Eden and Ackermann, 1990, p. 347). This makes it a useful tool for researchers using grounded theory or the general analytical procedure associated with Miles and Huberman (1994). Figure 9.4 shows an example of a cognitive map using *Cope*.

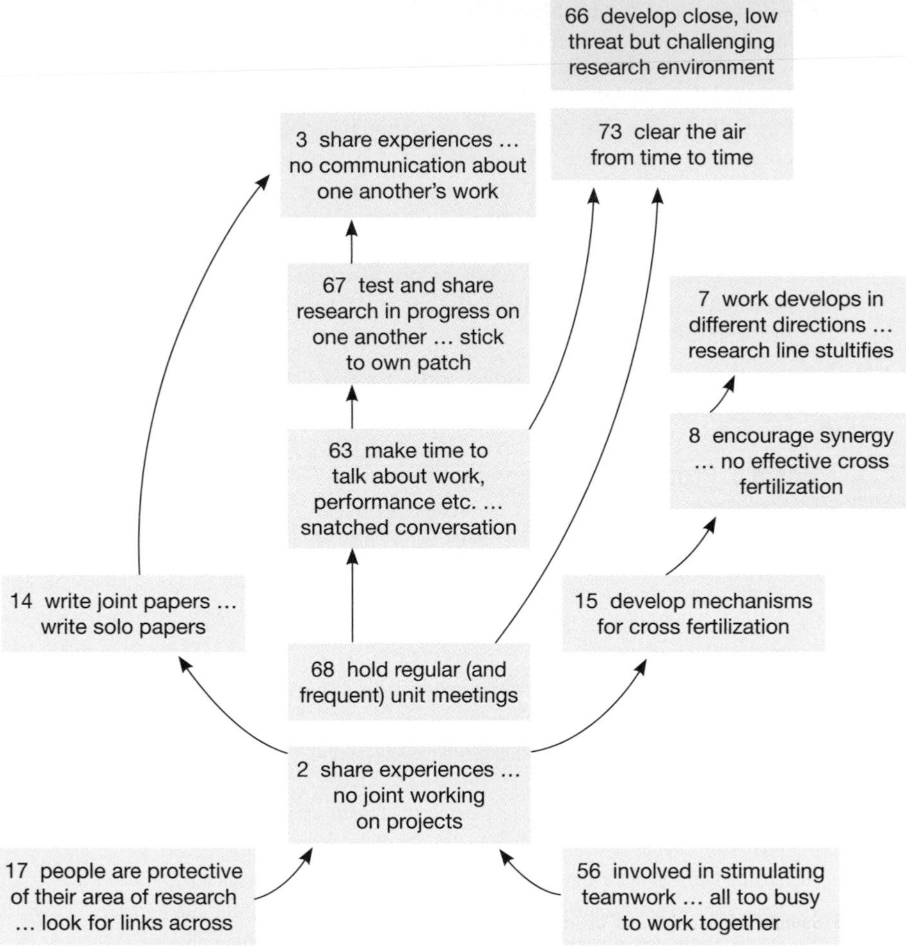

Figure 9.4 Example of a cognitive map

Source: Cropper, Eden and Ackermann (1990, p. 350). Reproduced with permission of SAGE Publications.

9.4.2 Example of a study using cognitive mapping

Boujena, Johnston and Merunka (2009) used interviews in combination with cognitive mapping to investigate customers' reactions to sales force automation systems (software information system used to automate some sales and sales force management functions in a business). The researchers conducted semi-structured interviews with seven buyers from different industries. The interviewees were asked to identify the benefits they perceived when dealing with a salesperson using a sales force automation system. The first stage of the analysis was to identify themes in the interview data using the general analytic procedure described by Miles and Huberman (1994). The themes were then refined by referring to the literature to construct meta-categories (a meta-category is a category about categories).

The researchers also conducted a lexical analysis by counting the words used most frequently by buyers when identifying benefits and presenting the frequencies and frequency percentages in a simple table. To obtain an in-depth understanding of customers' perceptions, a cognitive map was generated for each interviewee and all the maps were subsequently aggregated to a single cognitive map. To ensure validity, each individual was shown their map and asked if it accurately represented the causal relationships. Figure 9.5 shows the causal map for one of the customers.

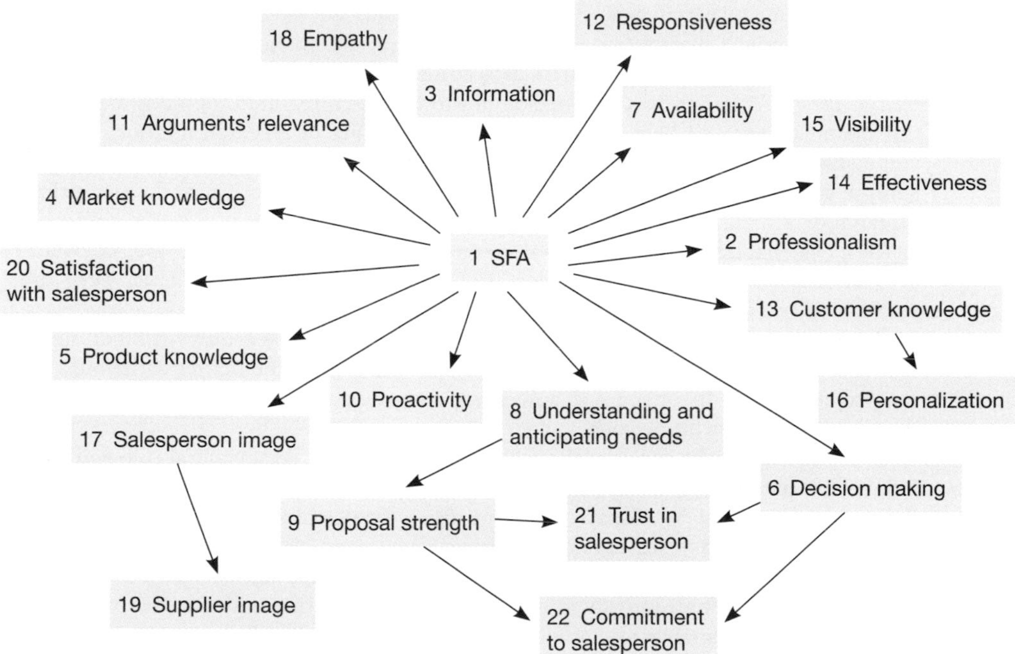

Figure 9.5 Sample individual causal cognitive map

Source: From *Journal of Personal Selling & Sales Management* 29, no. 2 (Spring 2009), 143. Copyright © 2009 by PSE National Educational Foundation. Reprinted with permission of M.E. Sharpe, Inc. All Rights Reserved. Not for Reproduction.

This research incorporates many of the lessons that we have discussed in this chapter and the previous two. To conduct a successful qualitative research project, you do not need to collect a large amount of data: the number of interviews or observations can be small. However, the data you collect must be as complete as possible and qualitative researchers will often refer to the data being 'rich'.

9.4.3 Potential problems

Cognitive mapping shares some of the problems of repertory grid technique: it is time-consuming and if you are using interview data, you may need to conduct a follow-up interview with the participant to increase the validity of the analysis. When reflecting on the generalizability of your findings, you will need to remember that the map represents the participant's thinking about a particular problem at a particular point in time. The links representing relationships between concepts reveal patterns rather than causality. If you are analysing interview data, the map is a product of the researcher's analysis of data produced from interaction between the researcher and the participant. The use of qualitative data analysis (QDA) software, such as *Cope*, addresses the challenge of how to manage the data and facilitates the generations of a professional looking cognitive map.

9.5 Conclusions

Whichever paradigm you have adopted, it is essential that you know how you are going to analyse your research data. Some of the methods we have covered in this chapter demonstrate how a matrix (repertory grid techniques) or diagram (cognitive mapping) can be used to analyse your research data and summarize the findings in your dissertation or thesis. Although you may decide not to use the integrated methods explained in this chapter, they will help deepen your understanding of research methods and help you justify the choices you have made. It is essential that you know how you are going to analyse your research data, regardless of whether these are secondary data or primary research data.

We advise caution if you are an undergraduate or a student on a taught Master's programme who is considering using grounded theory. The approach is very time-consuming and the development of a new theory is a difficult task. It can be made easier by the use of diagrams as you proceed with your research. If you are an MPhil or doctoral student planning to use grounded theory, you should discuss the matter with your supervisor to ensure that he or she is in agreement with the particular approach you intend to take when using this framework.

All researchers must consider the ethical issues involved. As a general rule you should inform the participants of the purpose of the research and, where practicable, obtain their written consent to take part. You must ask for permission if you are planning to takes notes or record observations or interviews you conduct as part of a study based on grounded theory, repertory grid technique or cognitive mapping.

Deciding to adopt an integrated approach to the collection and analysis of data does not preclude other analytical methods in your research project (methodological triangulation). The more you analyse the data, the more you will extract interesting insights and illumination of the phenomenon you are studying. If your supervisor agrees, you may decide to include both qualitative and quantitative analyses and we will start our discussion on collecting data for statistical analysis in the next chapter.

References

Ackermann, F., Eden, C. and Cropper, S. (1990) 'Cognitive Mapping: A User Guide', *Working Paper No. 12.* Glasgow: Strathclyde University, Department of Management Science.

Barton-Cunningham, J and Gerrard, P. (2000) 'Characteristics of well-performing organisations in Singapore', *Singapore Management Review*, 22(1), pp. 35–65.

Boujena, O., Johnston, W. J. and Merunka, D. A. (2009) 'The benefits of sales force automation: A customer's perspective', *Journal of Personal Sales and Sales Management*. XXIX(2), pp. 137–50.

Brook, J. A. (1986) 'Research applications of the repertory grid technique', *International Review of Applied Psychology*, 35, pp. 489–500.

Cropper, S., Eden, C. and Ackermann, F. (1990) 'Keeping sense of accounts using computer-based cognitive maps', *Social Science Computer Review*, 8(3), pp. 345–66.

Dackert, I., Jackson P. R., Brenner, S. O. and Johansson, C. R. (2003) 'Eliciting and analyzing employees' expectations of a merger', *Human Relations*, 56(6), pp. 705–13.

Dunn, W. and Ginsberg, A. (1986) 'A sociocognitive network approach to organisational analysis', *Human Relations*, 40(11), pp. 955–76.

Glaser, B. (1978) *Theoretical Sensitivity*. Mill Valley, CA: Sociology Press.

Glaser, B. and Strauss, A. (1967) *The Discovery of Grounded Theory*. Chicago, IL: Aldine.

Hankinson, G. (2004) 'Repertory grid analysis: An application to the measurement of distant images', *International Journal of Nonprofit and Voluntary Sector Marketing*, 9(2), pp. 145–54.

Hunter, M. G. (1997) 'The use of RepGrids to gather interview data about information system analysts', *Information Systems Journal*, 7, pp. 67–81.

Hussey, R. and Ong, A. (2005) 'A substantive model of the annual financial reporting exercise in a non-market corporate', *Qualitative Research in Accounting and Management*, 2(2) pp. 152–70.

Hutchinson, A. J., Johnston, L. H. and Breckon, J. D. (2010) 'Using QSR-NVivo to facilitate the development of a grounded theory project: an account of a worked example', *International Journal of Social Research Methodology*, 13(4), pp. 283–302.

Jones, J. W. (2009) 'Selection of grounded theory as an appropriate research methodology for a dissertation: One student's perspective', *The Grounded Theory Review*, 8(2), pp. 23–34.

Kelly, G. A. (1955) *The Psychology of Personal Constructs: A Theory of Personality*. New York: Norton.

Kihl, L. A., Richardson, T. and Campisi, C. (2008) 'Toward a grounded theory of student athletes suffering and dealing with academic corruption', *Journal of Sport Management*, 22(3), pp. 273–302.

Lemke, F., Clark, M. and Wilson, H. (2011) 'Customer experience quality: an exploration in business and customer contexts using repertory grid', *Journal of the Academy of Marketing Science*, 39(6), pp. 846–68.

Miles, M. B. and Huberman, A. M. (1994) *Qualitative Data Analysis*. Thousand Oaks, CA: SAGE.

Pidgeon, N. F., Turner, B. A. and Blockley, D. I. (1991) 'The use of grounded theory for conceptual analysis in knowledge elicitation', *International Journal of Man–Machine Studies*, 35, pp. 151–73.

Reason, P. and Rowan, J. (1981) *Human Inquiry: A Sourcebook of New Paradigm Research*. Chichester: John Wiley.

Stewart, V. and Stewart, A. (1981) *Business Applications of Repertory Grid*. Maidenhead: McGraw-Hill.

Strauss, A. (1987) *Qualitative Analysis for Social Scientists*. New York: Cambridge University Press.

Strauss, A. and Corbin, J. (1990) *Basics of Qualitative Research: Grounded Theory Procedures and Techniques*. Newbury Park, CA: SAGE.

Strauss, A. and Corbin, J. (1998) *Basics of Qualitative Research: Grounded Theory Procedures and Techniques*, 2nd edn. Newbury Park, CA: SAGE.

Tan, F. and Hunter, M. G. (2002) 'The repertory grid technique: A method for the study of cognition in information systems', *MIS Quarterly*, 26(1), pp. 39–57.

Taylor, D. S. (1990) 'Making the most of your matrices: Hermeneutics, statistics and the repertory grid', *International Journal of Personal Construct Psychology*, 3, pp. 105–19.

Activities

1 In pairs, use repertory grid technique to examine students' study habits. Select roles (researcher or interviewee) and agree the elements. Start designing the grid with the elements as the headings of the columns. Write each element on a card or small piece of paper. Using dyads, randomly select two cards and ask the interviewee to provide a word or phrase that describes each similarity and difference between the pairs of elements. Use these words or phrases as the constructs on the grid. Take a copy of the blank grid (for the next exercise). Using a rating scale of 1 to 5 (where 5 = high, 1 = low), ask the interviewee to indicate the number closest to his or her view and explain the reason. Take notes of the reasons. Complete the grid by adding the scores.

2 Continue the exercise by swapping roles and complete the second grid using the same rating scale of 1 to 5. Reflect on the similarities and differences in the scores. How would you explain them?

3 Divide into two groups and debate the motion that repertory grid technique is a suitable method for interpretivists. One group argues for the motion and the other against it.
4 Compare repertory grid technique and cognitive mapping in the context of the validity and generalizability of the findings.
5 Discuss the advantages and disadvantages of grounded theory as a framework for business research

Now try the progress test online at www.palgrave.com/business/collis/br4/

Have a look at the Troubleshooting chapter and sections 14.2, 14.5, 14.7, 14.10, 14.11 in particular, which relate specifically to this chapter.

10

collecting data for statistical analysis

learning objectives

When you have studied this chapter, you should be able to:

- select a random sample
- classify variables according to their level of measurement
- describe the main methods for collecting data for statistical analysis
- discuss the strengths and weaknesses of different methods
- design questions for questionnaire and interview surveys.

10.1 Introduction

You may be reading this chapter because you are designing a positivist study and you need to identify and discuss your intended method(s) of data collection to finalize your proposal. Alternatively, you may be reading this chapter because your proposal has been accepted, and you are now ready to start collecting primary research data for statistical analysis. In either case, this chapter will help guide you. We would emphasize that we do not recommend that you use the terms 'quantitative methods' or 'qualitative methods' as it is the data rather than the means of collecting the data that are in numerical or non-numerical form. You can read this chapter quite independently from Chapter 7, which focuses on the collection of qualitative data. In this chapter, we focus on methods used to collect data for statistical analysis. If you have already studied Chapter 7, you will notice that some of the methods we describe are similar as they can also be adapted for use under a positivist paradigm.

You will remember from Chapter 4 that the two main methodologies associated with positivism are experimental studies and surveys. Since experimental studies are not widely used in business research for practical and ethical reasons, we focus on the methods used to collect primary research data when a survey methodology is adopted. We start by examining the main issues, which include methods for selecting a sample. This is followed by a section that explains the different types of variables about which data will be collected. This paves the way for a detailed discussion of the use of self-completion questionnaires and interviews. We also describe critical incident technique, which can be incorporated in either method.

The close relationship between collecting and analysing the research data means it is important to think ahead to the type of statistical analysis you will use when designing the actual questions for self-completion questionnaires and interviews. Therefore, we examine the issues relating to designing questions separately.

10.2 Main issues in collecting data for statistical analysis

Researchers are interested in collecting **data** about the phenomena they are studying. You will remember that in Chapter 1 we defined data as known facts or things used as a basis for inference or reckoning. Some authors distinguish between data and **information**, by defining information as the knowledge created by organizing data into a useful form. This obviously depends on how items of data are perceived and how they are used. For example, if you are a positivist, you may have collected data relating to the variables under study via a questionnaire survey, which you subsequently analysed using statistics. You probably consider that this process allowed you to turn data into information that makes a small contribution to knowledge. On the other hand, your respondents may consider that what they gave was information in the first place.

Your research data can be *quantitative* (in numerical form) or *qualitative* (in non-numerical form, such as text or images). Data can also be classified by source. Your study may be based on an analysis of **secondary data** (data collected from an existing source) or on an analysis of **primary data** (data you have generated by collecting them from an original source, such as an experiment or survey). Typical sources of secondary research data include archives, commercial databases, government and commercially produced statistics and industry data,

Data are known facts or things used as a basis for inference or reckoning.

Information is the knowledge created by organizing data into a useful form.

Secondary data are collected from an existing source, such as publications, databases and internal records.

Primary data are generated from an original source, such as your own experiments, surveys, interviews or focus groups.

statutory and voluntary corporate reports, internal documents and records of organizations, and information in printed and web-based publications. Your university's business librarian will be able to tell you more about the archives and databases available in your university.

Figure 10.1 shows an overview of the data collection process in a positivist study. However, it is important to realize that this is purely illustrative and the process is not as linear as the diagram suggests. Moreover, research data can be generated or collected from different sources and more than one method can be used.

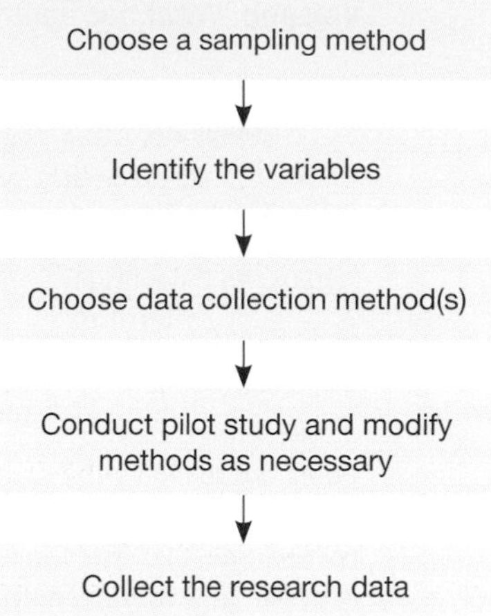
Choose a sampling method
Identify the variables
Choose data collection method(s)
Conduct pilot study and modify methods as necessary
Collect the research data

Figure 10.1 Overview of data collection for a positivist study

10.2.1 Selecting a sample for a positivist study

A **sampling frame** is a record of the population from which a **sample** can be drawn. A **population** is a body of people or collection of items under consideration for statistical purposes. If the population is relatively small, you can select the whole population; otherwise, you will need to select a random sample. Under a positivist paradigm, a sample is an unbiased subset that represents the population. 'It is vital to obtain a random sample to get some idea of variation ... To build general conclusions on ... limited data is a bit like a lazy evolutionist biologist finding a few mutant finches ... in a population on day one of a field outing then returning home to claim that all finches of this species display the same properties' (Alexander, 2006, p. 20).

A **random sample** is one where every member of the population has a chance of being chosen. Therefore, a random sample is an unbiased subset of the population, which allows the results obtained for the sample to be taken as being true for the whole population; in other words, the results from the sample are generalizable to the population.

To find out how many items there are in the population, you need to find a suitable sampling frame. For example, if you were conducting research where employees are the unit of analysis, the human resources (HR) department of the business may be willing to supply a staff list. However, if businesses are your unit of analysis, you will need to look for a suitable database, such as *Fame* or *Dun & Bradstreet* or *DataStream*. For example, perhaps your research focuses on the financial structure of small companies in the paper recycling industry in the London postal area. Your unit of analysis is a small company, which you decide to define as a private limited company with up to 50 employees. You decide to use the *Fame* database to identify companies that fit your criteria and your investigations show that there are 32 such companies. If you conduct your research on these 32 companies, your research findings will relate only to paper recycling companies of this size in London and you will not be able to generalize the results of your study to any larger companies in that sector in London or to companies outside London.

On the other hand, perhaps you are investigating the performance of all small companies in all industries throughout the UK. In this case, your unit of analysis is still a small company and you can still use the

A **population** is a body of people or collection of items under consideration for statistical purposes.

A **sampling frame** is a record of the population from which a sample can be drawn.

A **sample** is a subset of a population.

A **random sample** is an unbiased subset of a population that is representative of the population because every member had an equal chance of being selected.

Vox pop What has been the biggest challenge in your research so far?

Maysara, MBA student investigating healthcare systems management in occupied Palestinian territory

I could not find any publications on my subject in the Middle East so I was hoping to conduct a survey of a random sample of the Palestinian public. But this was not possible due to the politico/demographic set-up of the Palestinian territories. So I ended up doing an online survey which could only target a specific group of the Palestinian public.

Fame database as the sampling frame, but this time you find that there are thousands of companies that fit your criteria. To save the expense and inconvenience of investigating all these companies, it is acceptable to reduce the number to a manageable size by selecting a random sample. Figure 10.2 shows the main steps in selecting a random sample.

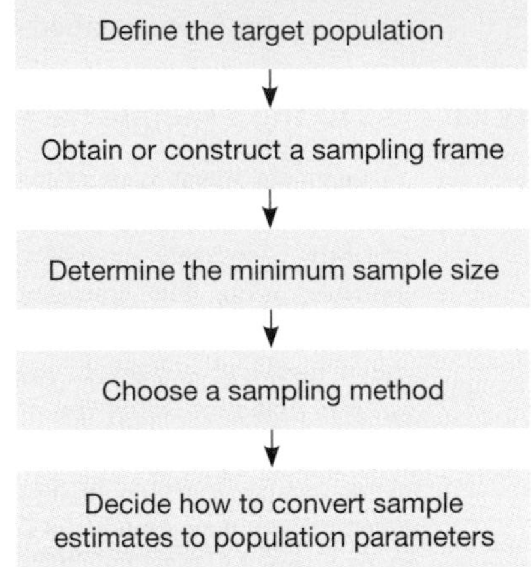
Define the target population
Obtain or construct a sampling frame
Determine the minimum sample size
Choose a sampling method
Decide how to convert sample estimates to population parameters

Figure 10.2 Main steps in selecting a random sample

10.2.2 Sample size

For an undergraduate or taught Master's dissertation or thesis, it is common to accept a degree of uncertainty in the conclusions you draw, so selecting a sufficiently large random sample to allow your results to be generalized to the population may not be vital to your study. Nevertheless, you still need a large enough sample to address your research questions because if your sample is too small, it may preclude some important statistical tests among the subsets within it (for example looking for differences between industry sectors). Therefore, the greater the expected variation within the sample, the larger the sample required.

In addition, you need to remember that the larger the sample, the better it will represent the population. Therefore, if you want to generalize from your results, you must determine the minimum sample size to reflect the size of the population. In a questionnaire survey, you will also need to take account of your expected *response rate*, which may be 10% or less. Recent surveys in your field or your own pilot survey will give you some idea of the response rate you can expect.

The minimum sample size to allow results from a random sample to be generalized to the population is much higher for a small population than it is for a large population. 'As the population increases, the sample size increases at a diminishing rate and remains relatively constant at slightly more than 380 cases' (Krejcie and Morgan, 1970, p. 610). This is illustrated in Table 10.1.

Clegg (1990) suggests the three main considerations are:

- the statistical analysis planned
- the expected variability within subsets in the sample
- the tradition in your research area regarding what constitutes an appropriate sample size.

The factors that must be considered when determining the appropriate number of subjects to include in a sample are discussed in detail by Czaja and Blair (1996); essentially, it is a question of deciding how accurate you want your results to be and how confident you want to be in that answer.

Table 10.1 Determining sample size from a given population

Population	Sample size
10	10
100	80
200	132
300	169
400	196
500	217
700	248
1,000	278
2,000	322
3,000	341
4,000	351
5,000	357
7,000	364
10,000	370
20,000	377
50,000	381
75,000	382
≥1,000,000	384

Source: Adapted from Krejcie and Morgan (1970, p. 608), with permission of SAGE Publications.

10.2.3 Methods for selecting a random sample

A sample that is chosen randomly is the equivalent of a lottery where every number has a chance of being drawn. The sample will be biased if the researcher or someone else chooses it or asks for volunteers, or if inducements are offered, because the sample may have characteristics that others in the population do not possess.

One way to select a random sample is to allocate a number to every member of the population and select a sample based on the numbers given in a random number table (see Appendix at the end of this book) or random numbers created by a computer. To generate random numbers in *Microsoft Excel*, open a spreadsheet and click on the cell where you want the random number to be shown (for example A1 in Figure 10.3). From the menu at the top, select Formulas and then Math & Trig. This opens a drop-down list of mathematical functions. Scroll down and select RAND and then click OK. A random number between 0 and 1 will appear in cell A1 and the complete function =RAND () appears in the formula bar. Generate another random number by moving to another cell and pressing F9 on the keyboard.

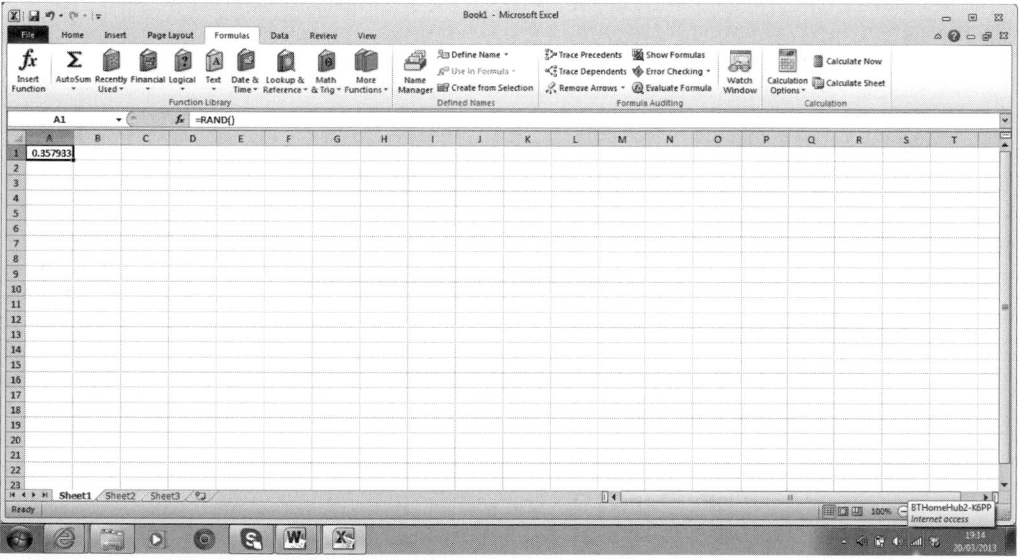

Figure 10.3 Generating a random number in Microsoft Excel

Source: Used with permission from Microsoft.

If you want to select a random number between 0 and 100, click on the cell where you want the random number to be shown and type =RAND*100 into the formula bar. If you want a random number between 0 and 1,000, type =RAND*1000. If you want a random number between 500 and 1,000, type =RANDBETWEEN(500, 1000).*1000.

In *systematic sampling*, the population is divided by the required sample size (n) and the sample chosen by taking every 'nth' subject, as illustrated in Box 10.1.

Box 10.1 Systematic sampling

Example
Population: 10,000
Sample size: 370

Divide the population by the required sample size:

$$\frac{10{,}000}{370} = 27$$

Select a randomly chosen number between 1 and the required sample size of 27 (we have chosen 3). List the subjects in the population and number them. Then select the 3rd subject and every 27th one thereafter until 370 subjects have been selected:

3, 30, 57, 84, 111, 138, 165 and so on

Stratified sampling overcomes the problem that a simple random sample might result in some members of the population being significantly under- or over-represented. It does this by taking account of each identifiable strata of the population. For example, if your sampling frame consists of all the employees in an insurance company, you may identify the following strata: senior managers, supervisors and clerical staff. You would then need to find out how many there were in each category and work out what percentage of the whole this represents, so that you can ensure that the same proportions are reflected in the sample. Box 10.2 shows an example.

Box 10.2 Stratified sampling

Example
Population: 500 (1% senior managers, 5% supervisors, 94% clerical staff)
Sample size: 217

217 x 1% = 2 senior managers
217 x 5% = 11 supervisors
217 x 94% = 204 clerical staff
Total 217

Other sampling methods include:

- *Quota sampling* involves giving interviewers quotas of different types of people to question, for example 25 men under the age of 21; 30 women over 50 and so on. It is widely used in marketing research.
- *Cluster sampling* involves making a random selection from a sampling frame listing groups of units rather than individual units. Every individual belonging to the selected groups is then interviewed or examined. This can be a useful approach, particularly for face-to-face interviews, where for time or economy reasons it is necessary to reduce the physical areas covered. For example, a certain number of project teams within a company might be selected and every member of the selected teams interviewed.

- *Multi-stage sampling* is used where the groups selected in a cluster sample are so large that a sub-sample must be selected from each group. For example, first select a sample of companies. From each company, select a sample of departments and from each department select a sample of managers to survey.

10.3 Variables

Once you have determined which method you will use to select a sample, you will need to turn your attention to the variables about which you will collect data. You will remember that under positivism, research is deductive and one of the purposes of the literature review is to identify a **theory** or set of theories (a theoretical framework) for your study. As explained in Chapter 3, a theory is a set of interrelated variables, definitions and propositions that specifies relationships among the variables. A **variable** is an attribute or characteristic of the phenomenon under study that can be observed and measured. Researchers collect data relating to each variable and use this **empirical evidence** to test their **hypotheses**.

A **theory** is a set of interrelated variables, definitions and propositions that specifies relationships among the variables.

A **variable** is a characteristic of a phenomenon that can be observed or measured.

Empirical evidence is data based on observation or experience.

A **hypothesis** is a proposition that can be tested for association or causality against empirical evidence.

Before you can collect any research data, you need to understand the properties of the variables relating to the phenomena you are studying. We have just described a variable as an attribute or characteristic of the phenomenon under study that can be observed and measured. You can see from this definition that variables are usually taken to be numerical and this is because any non-numerical observations can be quantified by allocating a numerical code (Upton and Cook, 2006). For example, the responses to open questions in a survey can be examined to identify the main themes and then a number given to each theme or category.

10.3.1 Measurement levels

The level at which a variable is measured has important implications for your subsequent choice of statistical methods. 'A level of measurement is the scale that represents a hierarchy of precision on which a variable might be assessed' (Salkind, 2006, p. 100). There are four levels of measurement, which we will examine in decreasing order of precision:

- A **ratio variable** is a quantitative variable measured on a mathematical scale with equal intervals between points and a fixed zero point. The fixed zero point permits the highest level of precision in the measurement and allows us to say how much of the variable exists (it could be none) and compare one value with another. For example, using sea level as the fixed zero point, we can measure altitude in feet or metres. This means we can say that one aeroplane is flying at an altitude measured in metres that is twice as high as another aeroplane. If we use kilometres as the measurement scale, we can measure the distance by train from London to Brussels. If we use time as the measurement scale, we would designate the time of departure from London as the fixed zero point and compare the average time of the journey by high speed train with the time by air. This allows us to say that, the *mean* (average) train journey is only 10% longer than by air.

A **ratio variable** is measured on a mathematical scale with equal intervals and a fixed zero point.

An **interval variable** is measured on a mathematical scale with equal intervals and an arbitrary zero point.

- An **interval variable** is a grouped quantitative variable measured on a mathematical scale that has equal intervals between points and an arbitrary zero point. This means you can place each data item precisely on the scale and compare the values. For example, the interval between an IQ score of 100 and 115 is the same as the interval between 110 and 125, but it is not possible to say that someone with an IQ of 120 is twice as intelligent as someone with an IQ of 60. Temperature is another example: If the temperature was 1° centigrade yesterday and 2° centigrade today, we know that today is warmer by an interval of 1°, but we cannot say that today is twice as warm as yesterday because 0° centigrade does not mean there is no temperature! With only an arbitrary zero point, we cannot say that the difference between two points on the scale is a precise representation of the variable under study.

- An **ordinal variable** is measured using numerical codes to identify order (ranks). This allows you to see whether one observation is ranked more highly than another observation. For example, degree classifications of candidates applying for a job (1, 2.1, 2.2 or 3), their location preferences (1st, 2nd or 3rd) or their rating of their key skills (using a scale of 1 to 5, where 5 = high and 1 = low). Therefore, ordinal variables provide categorical measures.
- A **nominal variable** is measured using numerical codes to identify named categories. For this reason, it is described as a 'categorical' variable. Each observation is placed in one of the categories. For example, you may have a variable for the gender of an applicant for a job (two categories), ethnicity (several categories) and qualifications (several categories). If it is not possible to anticipate all the categories, you can include a category labelled 'Other'. This is also used if you subsequently find some of your named categories contain very few observations.

An **ordinal variable** is measured using numerical codes to identify order or rank.

A **nominal variable** is measured using numerical codes to identify named categories.

One of the reasons why it is important to identify the level of measurement of variables is that it has implications for your statistical analysis. If you have collected data from ratio or interval variables, and the data meet certain distributional assumptions, you can use *parametric* statistic tests, which are based on the mean. On the other hand, if your data come from ordinal or nominal variables you will need to use the less powerful non-parametric methods. We examine this further in the next two chapters.

10.3.2 Discrete and continuous quantitative variables

Quantitative variables measured on a ratio or interval scale can be discrete or continuous. A **discrete variable** can take only one value on the scale. For example, the number of sales assistants in a baker's shop on different days of the week might range from 1 to 5 and the variable can only take the values 0, 1, 2, 3, 4 or 5. Therefore, a value of 1.3 or 4.6 sales assistants is not possible.

A **discrete variable** is a ratio or interval variable measured on a scale that can take only one of a range of distinct values, such as number of employees.

A **continuous variable** is a ratio or interval variable measured on a scale where the data can take any value within a given range, such as time or length.

On the other hand, a **continuous variable** can take any value between the start and end of a scale. For example, the amount of fruit and vegetables wasted in a hotel kitchen each day might vary from 0 kg to 10 kg and the variable can take any value between the start and end of the scale. Therefore, the data for Monday could be 3 kg exactly, but on Tuesday it could be 3.5 kg and on Wednesday 2.75 kg. In practice, there is considerable blurring of these definitions. For example, it can be argued that income is a discrete ratio variable, because income is a specific value within a range of values. However, because there are so many different possibilities when incomes are taken down to the last penny or cent, income is generally considered to be a continuous variable. Weight is certainly a continuous variable, but if the weighing scales are only accurate to the nearest tenth of a kilogram, the results will be from the distinct range of values, 0.1, 0.2, 0.3, 0.4 and so on.

10.3.3 Dichotomous and dummy variables

A **dichotomous variable** is a variable that has only two possible categories, each with an assigned value. 'Gender' is an example of a natural dichotomous variable where the two groups are male and female and can be described as a categorical variable. Sometimes a variable that is not a natural dichotomy can be recoded into a new dummy variable. A **dummy variable** is a dichotomous quantitative variable coded 1 if the characteristic is present and 0 if the characteristic is absent. Perhaps you have collected data relating to the variable 'age', which measures the number of years since the business was started in five-year periods (< 5 years, 6–10 years, 11–15 years, 16–20 years and so on). You could collapse this variable into a new dummy variable called Maturity with two groups coded as 1 = Mature (≥ 5 years old) and 0 = Otherwise. If you do this, keep the original variable with its precise information in case you need it, because one of the disadvantages of recoding it into a dichotomous variable is that all this detail is lost.

A **dichotomous variable** is a variable that has only two possible categories, such as gender.

A **dummy variable** is a dichotomous quantitative variable coded 1 if the characteristic is present and 0 if the characteristic is absent.

Kervin (1992) suggests a number of arguments to support how you can treat a dichotomous variable in terms of the level of measurement. Using the above example of 'maturity', you might say that since the values represent a named category, it is a nominal variable with two groups named 'young' and 'mature'. Alternatively, you could argue that since the mature group has more of the original variable than the young group, it is an ordinal variable. Since there are only two values, you might decide to ignore the question of equal intervals and treat it as an interval variable. Finally, you might conclude that the 0 represents a natural zero point indicating that the business is not a mature business; in other words, the variable is a dummy variable where 0 = the characteristic of maturity is absent and 1 = the characteristic is present. Therefore, you treat it as a ratio variable. However, you are only likely to find support for the first of these arguments and we advise that you discuss the others with your supervisor before using them to justify your choice of statistical methods in your proposal.

10.3.4 Hypothetical constructs

Finding a measurement scale for variables such as the age of the businesses in your study or financial variables is not difficult, as there are widely accepted measures such as the number of years since the business was started and monetary measures respectively. However, if your variables were abstract ideas such as intelligence or honesty, you will need to search the literature to find a suitable measurement scale or develop your own **hypothetical construct**. A construct is a set of concepts or general notions and ideas a person has about certain things. Because a construct is a mental image or abstract idea, it cannot be observed and it is difficult to measure. Consequently, positivists develop a category or numerical scale to measure opinion and other abstract ideas. For example, intelligence has been measured by psychologists as a numerical hypothetical construct called intelligence quotient (IQ), which is based on the individual's score from a carefully designed test.

A **hypothetical construct** is an explanatory variable that is based on a scale that measures opinion or other abstract ideas that are not directly observable.

Apart from saving you time, the main advantages of finding an existing hypothetical construct, rather than developing your own, are that the validity of the measure is likely to have been tested and you can compare your results with others based on the same construct. Examples include social stratification categories, frequency categories, ranking and rating scales (see section 10.5.4).

10.3.5 Dependent and independent variables

In many statistical tests it is necessary to identify the **dependent variable** (DV) and the **independent variable** (IV). A dependent variable is a variable whose values are influenced by one or more independent variables. Conversely, an independent variable is a variable that influences the values of a dependent variable. For example, in an experimental study, the intensity of lighting (IV) in the workplace might be manipulated to observe the effect on the productivity levels (DV), or a stressful situation might be created by generating random loud noises (IV) outside the workplace window to observe the effect on the completion of complex tasks (DV).

A **dependent variable** is a variable whose values are influenced by one or more independent variables.

An **independent variable** is a variable that influences the values of a dependent variable.

An extraneous variable is any variable other than the independent variable that might have an effect on the dependent variable. For example, if your study involves an investigation of the relationship between productivity and motivation, you may find it difficult to exclude the effect of other factors, such as a heatwave, a work-to-rule, a takeover or anxiety caused by personal problems. A confounding variable is one that obscures the effect of another variable. For example, employees' behaviour may be affected by the novelty of being the centre of the researcher's attention or by working in an unfamiliar place for the purposes of a controlled experiment.

10.4 Data collection methods

The two main data collection methods we discuss in this section are self-completion questionnaires and interviews. We also describe critical incident technique, which can be incorporated in either method. These are widely used methods in positivist studies, but you should also explore other methods mentioned in previous studies in your field. Before you start collecting any data, you need to have a list of the population of people or collection of items under consideration. If the population is too large to include them all in your questionnaire or interview survey, you will need to decide on a method for selecting a suitable sample. Remember that you must also obtain ethical approval if your study involves human participants.

In Chapter 7, we drew attention to the importance of using rigorous methods for recording research data that also provide evidence of the source. If the participant is not providing written responses, you will need to jot down the main points in a notebook. This necessarily means leaving out items and all the details, which can lead to distortions, errors and bias. Even shorthand writers sometimes have a problem in deciphering their notes afterwards and you need to be aware that relying on your notes will be inadequate. Audio and/or video recording overcomes these problems and leaves you free to concentrate on taking notes of other aspects, such as attitude, behaviour and body language, if these are relevant to your understanding of the phenomena under study. You can use a specific recording device or the facilities on your telephone or laptop. The important thing to remember is that you need to obtain the participant's agreement to being recorded.

10.4.1 Questionnaires

A **questionnaire** is a list of carefully structured questions, which have been chosen after considerable testing with a view to eliciting reliable responses from a particular group of people. The aim is to find out what they think, do or feel because this will help you address your research questions. Of course, this raises the issue of *confidentiality*, which we examined in Chapter 2. When a questionnaire is used in an interview, many researchers call it an *interview schedule*. You may also come across the term *research instrument*, which is a questionnaire or interview schedule that has been used and tested in a number of different studies. In a face-to-face or telephone interview, the answers to the questions are recorded by the interviewer. However, in a postal or online survey, the questionnaire is completed by the respondent. This is cheaper and less time-consuming, but there are a number of other factors that you should be aware of if you are conducting an interview survey and we discuss these in the next section.

A **questionnaire** is a method for collecting primary data in which a sample of respondents are asked a list of carefully structured questions chosen after considerable testing, with a view to eliciting reliable responses.

Questionnaires or interview schedules are also used in a *Delphi study*, where the aim is to gather opinions from a carefully selected group of experts. Once the responses have been summarized, the results are returned to the participants so that they can re-evaluate their original answers once they have seen the responses of the group. This process is repeated a number of times until there is a consensus. Unlike a focus group, the experts do not meet or know the identities of the other group members.

The main steps involved in designing a questionnaire are summarized in Figure 10.4.

Question design is concerned with the type of questions, their wording, the order in which they are presented and the reliability and validity of the responses. We discuss this in detail in section 10.5. You will need to explain the purpose of the study, since the respondents need to know the context in which the questions are being posed. This can be achieved by starting the questionnaire with an explanation or attaching a covering letter. It is very important that you apply the principles for ethical research we explained in Chapter 2.

It is essential that you pilot or test your questionnaire as fully as possible before distributing it. At the undergraduate level, you could ask your supervisor, friends and family to play the role of respondents. Even if they know little about the subject, they can still be very helpful in spotting a range of potential problems (see section 10.5). However, the best advice is to try your questionnaire out on people who are similar to those in your sample. If you are a Master's or doctoral student, you may find it takes several drafts, with tests at every stage, until you are satisfied, so allow plenty of time for this important part of the process.

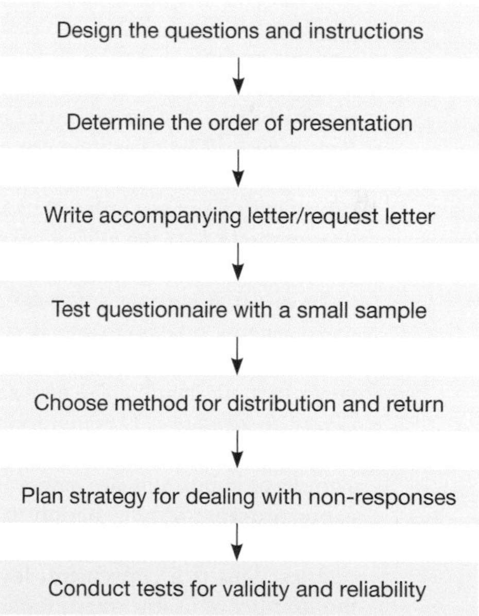

Figure 10.4 Designing a questionnaire

Although we discussed *distribution* methods in the context of interviews in Chapter 7, we revisit them here in the context of a questionnaire survey. You will see that each method has strengths and weaknesses. Cost is often an important factor and the best method for a particular study often depends on the size and location of the sample.

- *By post* – This is a commonly used method of distribution that is fairly easy to administer. The questionnaire and covering letter are posted to the population or the sample, usually with a prepaid envelope for returning the completed questionnaire. If you are conducting an internal survey in a particular company, it may be possible to use the internal mail. If it is a large survey, you will need to consider the cost of printing, postage and stationery. You should also leave plenty of time for getting the questionnaire printed, folding and inserting the contents, sealing the envelopes and franking or stamping them. However, one of the drawbacks is that response rates of 10% or less are not uncommon and this introduces the problem of sample bias because those who respond may not be representative of the population. Response rates can be increased by keeping the questionnaire as short as possible (for example two sides of A4) and using closed questions of a simple and non-sensitive nature.
- *By telephone* – This is also a widely used method to employ as it reduces the costs associated with face-to-face interviews, but still allows some aspect of personal contact. A relatively long questionnaire can be used and it can be helpful with sensitive and complex questions. However, achieving the desired number of responses may require a very large sampling frame and you may need to consider the cost of buying specialist recording equipment and possibly the cost of a great many telephone calls. Moreover, your results may be biased towards people who are available and willing to answer questions in this way.
- *Online* – Web-based tools, such as *SurveyMonkey, Kwiksurveys, Freeonlinesurveys and Qualtrics*, allow you to create your own survey and email it to potential respondents. You can view the preliminary results as they come in and the data file can be exported to *Microsoft Excel, IBM® SPSS® Statistics software (SPSS)* and other software packages for analysis. Like the last two methods of distribution, online surveys are now so widely used that obtaining sufficient responses may take some time and the results may be biased. If your survey is large, you may have to pay a fee to the service provider.
- *Face-to-face* – The questionnaire can be presented to respondents in the street, at their homes, in the workplace or any convenient place. It is time-consuming and can be expensive if you have to travel to a particular location to meet an interviewee. However, this method offers the advantage that response rates can be fairly high and comprehensive data can be collected. It is often very useful if sensitive or complex questions need to be asked. Where the interview is conducted outside working hours, it is possible to use a lengthy questionnaire. It is important that you take precautions to ensure your personal safety when using the face-to-face method (see Chapter 2). We look at interviews in more detail in the next section.
- *Group distribution* – This method is only appropriate where the survey is conducted in a small number of locations or a single location. You may be able to agree that the sample or subgroups are assembled in the same room at the same time, such as the canteen during a quiet period in the afternoon. You can then explain the purpose of the survey and how to complete the questionnaire, while being available to answer any queries. This is a convenient, low-cost method for administering questionnaires and the number of usable questionnaires is likely to be high.
- *Individual distribution* – This is a variation of group distribution. If the sample is situated in one location, it may be possible to distribute, and collect, the questionnaires individually. As well as a place of work, this approach can be used in theatres, restau-

rants and even on trains and buses. It is normally necessary to supply pens or pencils for the completion of the questionnaires. You may encounter problems with sample bias if you use this method; for example, you may only capture patrons who visit a theatre on a Monday, or travel at a particular time. However, if properly designed, this method can be very precise in targeting the most appropriate sample.

There are two major problems associated with questionnaire surveys. The first is *questionnaire fatigue*. This refers to the reluctance of many people to respond to questionnaire surveys because they are inundated with unsolicited requests by post, email, telephone and in the street. The second problem is what to do about *non-response bias*, which can be present if some questionnaires are not returned. Non-response bias is crucial in a survey because your research design will be based on the fact that you are going to generalize from the sample to the population. The most common way of dealing with these problems is to send a follow-up request to non-respondents. If you intend to do this, you will need to keep a record of who replies and when. If you are conducting a postal questionnaire survey, we advise you to send a fresh copy of the questionnaire (perhaps printed on different coloured paper or with an identifying symbol in addition to the unique reference number). In Chapter 12 we explain how you can use a generalizability test to check for non-response bias in your sample. Later on in this chapter, we discuss the problem of item non-response (non-response to particular questions) and the need for a reliability test.

10.4.2 Using interviews under a positivist paradigm

As explained in Chapter 7, **interviews** are a method for collecting data in which selected participants (the interviewees) are asked questions to find out what they do, think or feel. Verbal or visual prompts may be required. Under a positivist paradigm the interview is likely to be based on a questionnaire (also referred to as an interview schedule), which means the questions are planned in advance and each interviewee is asked the questions in the same order. Interviews can be conducted with individuals or groups using face-to-face, telephone or video conferencing methods (although video conferencing is not likely to be feasible for a large-scale survey).

An **interview** is a method for collecting primary data in which a sample of interviewees are asked questions to find out what they think, do or feel.

In a structured interview, these questions are likely to be *closed questions*, each of which has a set of predetermined answers. There may be some *open questions*, which allow the respondent to answer in his or her own words. In a large structured or semi-structured face-to-face or telephone interview, a questionnaire is prepared in advance and is completed by the interviewer from the responses given by the interviewee (for example interviews used in a market research surveys). In a semi-structured interview, some of the questions are pre-prepared, but the interviewer is able to add additional questions in order to obtain more detailed information about a particular answer or to explore new (but relevant) issues that arise from a particular answer. Unstructured interviews are associated with an interpretivist paradigm (see Chapter 7).

In a large interview survey, many interviewees are needed and this gives rise to the problem of obtaining access to an appropriate sample. You will need to explain the purpose of the study, since the interviewees need to know the subject of the interview and the context in which you will ask your questions. Obtaining a sample and conducting the interviews can be very time-consuming and there may be travel and hospitality costs to consider. In some studies, a self-completion questionnaire may be more appropriate.

Structured interviews make it easy to compare answers because each interviewee is asked the same questions. However, in a semi-structured interview the issues discussed, the questions raised and the matters explored change from one interview to the next as different aspects of the topic are revealed. This process of discovery is the strength of such interviews, but it is important to recognize that the emphasis and balance of the issues that emerge may depend on the order in which you interview the participants. In semi-structured interviews, it may be difficult to keep a note of the questions and answers, controlling the range of topics and, later, analysing the data.

You must ask the interviewee's permission to record the interview using an audio recorder. After putting your interviewee at ease, you may find it useful to spend a little time establishing a rapport before starting to record. You can offer to switch the recorder off if your interviewee wants to discuss confidential or sensitive information and seek permission to continue to take notes. You may find that this encourages a higher degree of frankness. We discussed the issue of confidentiality in Chapter 2. Lee (1993) offers the following advice if you are asking *sensitive questions*:

- Use words that are non-threatening and familiar to the respondents. For example, when explaining the purpose of the questionnaire, rather than saying you are conducting research into absenteeism in their workplace, say you are looking at working patterns.
- Lead up to any sensitive question slowly.
- You may find that participants will answer questions about past indiscretions more readily than questions about current behaviour. For example, they may admit to stealing from their employer at some time in the past, but be unwilling to disclose that they have done so recently.

These suggestions raise ethical issues and you must determine your own position on this. If you find your interviewee is showing signs of resisting some topics, the best advice is to drop those questions. However, this will alert you to the likelihood that these may be interesting and important issues and you may wish to find an alternative way of collecting the data, such as diary methods or observation (see Chapter 7).

In a positivist study, you will need to ensure that all the interviews are conducted in the same way to avoid *interviewer bias*. This means that not only should the same questions be asked, but also that they should be posed in the same way. Furthermore, you must ensure that each respondent will understand the question in the same way. This is known as *stimulus equivalence* and demands considerable thought and skill in question design. Drawing on Brenner (1985), Box 10.3 shows a checklist for reducing interviewer bias.

Box 10.3 Checklist for reducing interviewer bias

- Read each question exactly as worded in the questionnaire.
- Read each question slowly, using the same intonation and emphasis.
- Ask the questions in the same order.
- Ask every question that applies.
- Use the same response cards (if required as part of the design).
- Record exactly what the respondent says.
- Do not answer the question for the respondent.
- Show interest by paying attention when the respondent is answering, but do not show approval or disapproval.
- Make sure you have understood each answer and that the answer is adequate.

Source: Brenner (1985), with permission.

There is also potential for inadvertent class, race or sex bias. Another problem is that the interviewee may have certain expectations about the interview and give what he or she considers is the 'correct' or 'acceptable' answer to the question. Lee (1993) suggests that, to some extent, this can be overcome by increasing the depth of the interview. You should bear in mind that recent events may also affect the interviewee's responses. For example, he or she may have just received news of a promotion, a salary increase, a cut in hours, a reprimand or bad news about a member of the family. If time allows, you will find it useful to arrive at the interview venue 15 minutes beforehand to assimilate the atmosphere and the environment, and spend the first few minutes putting the interviewee at ease. It is difficult to predict or measure bias. Nevertheless, you should be alert to the fact that it can distort your data and hence your findings.

The most common form of interview is one-to-one, but some researchers find it useful to have two interviewers to help ensure that all the issues are fully explored and notes are kept of nuances and relevant non-verbal factors. Sometimes the interviewee is accompanied by another person (often to ensure that all the questions you ask can be answered). You must be alert to the fact that more than one interviewer or interviewee will change the dynamics of the interview. Another problem is that an interviewee may be 'wearing two hats'. For example, the finance director of a company may also be a director of other companies or involved in other organizations; an employee may also be a trade unionist or a shareholder. When you are asking questions, you must determine which 'hat' the interviewee is wearing, and whether he or she is giving a personal opinion or making a policy statement.

As well as deciding on the structure and recording of an interview, you must also be able to bring it to a satisfactory conclusion and let the interviewee know that it is ending. One device is to say that you have asked all the questions you had in mind and ask whether the interviewee has any final comments. You should then conclude by thanking them and reassuring them that you will be treating what they have told you as confidential. After you have left the interview, it is beneficial to add further notes.

Despite some disadvantages, interviews permit the researcher to ask complex questions and ask follow-up questions, which is not possible in a self-completion questionnaire. Thus, further information can be obtained. An interview may permit a higher degree of confidence in the replies than responses to a self-completion questionnaire and can take account of non-verbal communications such as the attitude and behaviour of the interviewee.

10.4.3 Critical incident technique

Critical incident technique is a method for collecting data about a defined activity or event based on the participant's recollections of key facts.

Critical incident technique is a method for collecting data about a defined activity or event based on the participant's recollections of key facts. Developed by Flanagan (1954), it allows important facts to be gathered about behaviour in defined situations 'in a rather objective fashion with only a minimum of inferences and interpretation of a more subjective nature' (p. 335). Although it is called a technique, it is not a set of rigid rules, but a flexible set of principles that can be modified and adapted according to the circumstances. In Chapter 7, we explained how it can be used as the basis for a semi-structured interview under an interpretivist paradigm and we will now look at its use under a positivist paradigm.

Flanagan recommended that only simple types of judgements should be required of observers, who should be qualified. All observations should be evaluated by the observer in terms of an agreed statement of the purpose of the activity. The procedure for establishing the general aims of an activity, the training of the interviewers and the manner in which observations should be made are all predetermined. What is of prime interest to researchers is the way in which Flanagan concentrates on an observable activity (the incident), where the intended purpose seems to be clear and the effect appears to be logical; hence, the incident is critical.

We showed Flanagan's example of a form for collected effective critical incidents in Chapter 7. In this chapter we will look at an example taken from a questionnaire survey of householders (MacKinlay, 1986), which contained six open questions. The questionnaire allowed a third of an A4 page per question for the reply, but some respondents added additional sheets. The questions were preceded by an explanation, as shown in Box 10.4.

Box 10.4 Critical incident technique in a survey

These questions are open-ended and I have kept them to a few vital areas of interest. All will require you to reflect back on decisions and reasons for decisions you have made.

1 Please think about an occasion when you improved your home. What improvements did you make?
2 On that occasion what made you do it?
3 Did you receive any help? If 'yes', please explain what help you received.
4 Have you wanted to improve your home in any other way but could not?
5 What improvements did you wish to make?
6 What stopped you from doing it?

Source: MacKinlay (1986) cited in Easterby-Smith, Thorpe and Lowe (1991, p. 84).

It is likely that many researchers use this approach without realizing it. One of the benefits is that it allows the researcher to collect data about events chosen by the respondent because they are memorable, rather than general impressions of events or vicarious knowledge of events. In interviews, it can be of considerable value in generating data where there is a lack of focus or the interviewee has difficulty in expressing an opinion.

One of the problems associated with methods based on memory is that the participant may have forgotten important facts. In addition, there is the problem of post-rationalization, where the interviewee recounts the events with a degree of logic and coherence that did not exist at the time.

10.5 Designing questions

Once you have decided on the method and you have identified the variables about which you need to collect data to test your hypotheses, you are ready to start designing the actual questions you will ask. In this section, we focus on designing questions for a positivist study, where the research data generated will be analysed using statistical methods. Before you can decide what the most appropriate questions will be, you must gain a considerable amount of knowledge about your subject to allow you to develop a theoretical or conceptual framework and formulate the hypotheses you will test. Your subject knowledge will come from your taught and/or independent studies; your theoretical framework (sometimes referred to as a conceptual framework) that underpins the hypotheses you will test will be drawn from your literature review. The statistical methods you will use will be described in your methodology chapter.

Questions should be presented in a logical order and it is often beneficial to move from general to specific topics. This is known as funnelling. In complex questionnaires, it may be necessary to use filter questions, where respondents who have given a certain answer are directed to skip a question or batch of questions. For example, 'Do you normally do the household shopping? *If YES, go to next question; if NO, go to Question 17.*'

In addition to designing the questions themselves, in a self-completion questionnaire you also give precise *instructions* (for example whether to tick one or more boxes, or whether a number or word should be circled to indicate the response). The clarity of the instructions and the ordering and presentation of the questions can do much to encourage and help respondents. These factors also make the subsequent analysis of the data easier.

Classification questions collect data about the characteristics of the unit of analysis, such as the respondent's job title, age or education; or the geographical region, industry, size or age of the business. If you wish to make comparisons with previous studies, government statistics or other publications, it is essential to use the same categories. Classification questions collect data that will enable you to describe your sample and examine relationships between subsets of your sample. Remember, you should only collect data about variables you will use in your analysis.

There is some debate over the best location for classification questions. Some authors believe that they are best placed at the beginning, so that respondents gain confidence in answering easy questions; others prefer to place them at the end, so that the respondent starts with the more interesting questions. If your questions are of a sensitive nature, it may be best to start with the non-threatening classification questions. If you have a large number of classification questions, it could be better to put them at the end, so that the respondent is not deterred at the start. Remember to allocate a unique reference number to each questionnaire. This will enable you to maintain control of the project and, if appropriate, you will be able to identify which respondents have replied and send follow-up letters to those who have not. If you are using triangulation, you will also be able to match data about the unit of analysis from different sources.

10.5.1 General rules

It is essential to bear your target audience in mind when designing your questions. If your sample is composed of intelligent people, who are likely to be knowledgeable about the topic, you can aim for a fairly high level of complexity, but the general rule is to keep your questions simple. Box 10.5 summarizes the general rules for designing questions.

Box 10.5 General rules for designing questions

- Provide a context by briefly explaining the purpose of the research.
- Only ask questions that are needed for the analysis.
- Keep each question as short and as simple as possible.
- Only ask one question at a time.
- Include questions that serve as cross-checks on answers to other questions.
- Avoid jargon, ambiguity and negative questions.
- Avoid leading questions and value-laden questions that suggest a 'correct' answer.
- Avoid calculations and memory tests.
- Avoid questions that could cause offence or embarrassment.

These fundamental aspects of question design are important, because once you have asked the questions there is often little you can do to enhance the quality of the answers. It can be helpful to the respondent if you qualify your questions in some way, perhaps by referring to a specific time period, rather than requiring the respondent to search their memory for an answer. For example, instead of asking, 'Have you ever bought Fair Trade coffee?' you might ask, 'Have you bought Fair Trade coffee in the past three weeks?' A question can also be qualified by referring to a particular place. For example, 'What are your views on the choice of Fair Trade coffee in your local supermarket?'

If the issue addressed in the question is complex or rigid, we might wish to add some generality to it. For example, 'Do you travel to work in your own car?' might be taken to mean every day. This can be generalized by inserting the word 'normally' or 'usually', thus: 'Do you normally travel to work in your own car?' A question can also be made more general by inserting the word 'overall' or the term 'in general'. For example, 'In general, are you satisfied with the level of service you obtain from the company?' However, in some questions precision may be important and desirable.

Coolican (2009) identifies a number of pitfalls to avoid when deciding on the order in which questions should be asked, which we now examine:

- Respondents have a tendency to agree rather than disagree with statements (known as response acquiescence). Therefore, you should mix positive and negative questions to keep them thinking about their answers.
- The respondent may try to interpret the aim of the question or questionnaire, or set up emotional blocks to some questions. Therefore, you should ensure that both positive and negative items appear and that less extreme statements are presented first.
- Some answers may be considered more socially desirable than others. For example, if you want to ask 'How often do you take a bath/shower each week?' respondents who do not wash very often may not give a valid answer, but one that fits the image they wish to present. You can try to address this problem by putting in some statements that only those respondents who are answering to impress would choose (for example more than twice a day), but if your pilot test produces too many of these responses, you should discard your questionnaire or interview schedule.

In the remainder of this section, we examine the different types of questions you can ask and the importance of incorporating features that will enhance your results and assist in the later analysis of the responses you receive.

10.5.2 Open and closed questions

A **closed question** requires a 'yes' or 'no' answer or a very brief factual answer, or requires the respondent to choose from a list of predetermined answers.

An **open question** cannot be answered with a simple 'yes' or 'no' or a very brief factual answer, but requires a longer, developed answer.

A positivist approach suggests **closed questions**, which allow the respondent to choose from predetermined answers. For example, questions seeking facts, such as the respondent's age (where the predetermined answers are given in age bands) or job title (where the respondent chooses from a list). Other closed questions may seek opinions (for example a question where the predetermined answers are given in the form of statements with which the respondent can agree or disagree).

However, there may be some **open questions**, which allow the respondents to answer in their own words. Subsequently, each response is examined carefully to identify the key words, phrases or themes across the answers, and placed in a category with a numerical code, which represents a nominal variable. For example, in a survey of the directors of small companies, question 3 asked whether they would have the accounts audited even if the company were not legally required to do so, and were given a choice of 'yes' (coded 1 or 2 as shown in Box 10.6) or 'no' (coded 0). Box 10.6 shows this closed question and the open question that followed, which asked them to give their reasons and provided space for the answer. An initial analysis identified nine categories across the responses and the following values allocated to each, with no order implied: 1 = cost savings, 2 = no benefit, 3 = check, 4 = good practice/governance, 5 = assurance for shareholders, 6 = assurance for customers/suppliers, 7 = assurance for bank/lenders, 8 = exit plans, 9 = other.

Box 10.6 Open and closed questions

3. Would you have the accounts audited if not legally required to do so? *(Tick one box only)*

Yes, the accounts are already audited voluntarily	☐	(1)
Yes, the accounts would be audited voluntarily	☐	(2)
No	☐	(0)

Please give reasons for either answer

....

....

Source: Adapted from Collis (2003).

Closed questions are very convenient and are usually easy to analyse, since the range of potential answers is limited and can be coded in advance. On the other hand, open questions offer the advantage that the respondents are able to give their opinions as precisely as possible in their own words. For undergraduates and Master's students, who often have to work within a tight time frame, it is advisable to keep the number of open-ended questions to the minimum in a large survey. Moreover, all researchers need to be aware that a large number of open questions may deter busy respondents from replying.

10.5.3 Multiple choice questions

Multiple choice questions are those where the participant is asked a closed question and selects his or her answer from a list of predetermined responses or categories. It may be difficult to provide sufficient, unambiguous categories to allow the respondent to give an unequivocal answer. An example of this is a question that seeks to ascertain respondents' occupations. Even in a fairly small organization there may be quite a wide range of occupations; you cannot provide a full list because it would take up too much room. As a general guide, approximately six predetermined responses or categories are usually sufficient. In interviews, you will find it helpful to have a printed copy of the choice of answers to show the interviewee. This means he or she can study the list rather than have to memorize all the alternatives. The interviewee then simply tells you his or her choice.

When deciding on categories, you must take care to use terms that mean something to the participants, so that you can have confidence in their replies. For example, you may use the term 'Accountant' as one of your job title categories, meaning a person who has passed the necessary exams to become a member of one of the accountancy bodies. However, some respondents may attribute a wider meaning to this term and you may find that a bookkeeper or credit controller sees himself or herself as a belonging to this category.

In a single organization, it is usually possible to construct categories for factual questions that people will understand. If you are taking a random sample of the population, it becomes much harder. If you are uncertain that you have covered all possibilities, you should add an 'Other' category that allows the respondent to provide their own category and a 'Don't know' category if this is likely to apply.

Box 10.7 shows two examples of multiple choice questions and their associated answers. Whereas question 1 expects only one response, question 5 asks respondents to tick as many boxes as apply. It is important to give clear instructions.

Box 10.7 Multiple choice (fact)

1. Is the company a family-owned business? *(Tick one box only)*

Wholly family-owned (or only 1 owner)	☐	(1)
Partly family-owned	☐	(2)
None of the shareholders are related	☐	(0)

5. Apart from Companies House, who normally receives a copy of the company's statutory accounts? *(Tick as many boxes as apply)*

(a) Shareholders	☐
(b) Bank and other providers of finance	☐
(c) Directors/managers who are not shareholders	☐
(d) Employees who are not shareholders	☐
(e) Major suppliers and trade creditors	☐
(f) Major customers	☐
(g) Tax authorities	☐
(h) Other *(Please state)*	☐

Source: Adapted from Collis (2003).

Sometimes a question is phrased so that the respondent is presented with a range of opinions and has to select the one that most closely resembles their own. The drawback with this type of question is that it takes up considerable space and does not capture the respondents' opinions in their own words. As a result, you cannot be certain about how closely it matches their opinions. However, it can sometimes be useful for dealing with sensitive issues, since it identifies different responses. It can also be useful as a means of cross-checking other questions by presenting the situation in a different way. Box 10.8 shows an example of a question that could be used to evaluate how well students worked together on a group assignment.

Box 10.8 Multiple choice (opinion)

Thinking about your assignment group, which of the following statements is closest to your view? *(Tick one box only)*

(a) We are a very happy and friendly group	☐	(1)
(b) We get on better than most of the other groups	☐	(2)
(c) We have our ups and downs like any other group	☐	(3)
(d) We tend to be less argumentative than other groups	☐	(4)
(e) We have had some unresolved conflicts	☐	(5)

10.5.4 Ranking and rating scales

Another approach is to ask respondents to rank a list of items and Box 10.9 shows an example. Unfortunately, the responses to such questions can be disappointing. Often respondents will not have gone through this type of exercise before and may be unwilling to spare the time to think about it. You may find that after ranking the first three, they leave the others blank because they have been unwilling or unable to decide a rank for the remaining items. If you would like to include a ranking question, keep the number of items as low as possible (preferably no more than six).

Box 10.9 Ranking

Rank the following five learning resources
(Rank the most useful resource as 1, the next most useful as 2, and so on)

The activities during the lectures	☐
The activities during the tutorials	☐
The lecture notes on *Blackboard*	☐
The recommended textbook	☐
Feedback from the progress tests	☐

The most straightforward way to collect opinions is to set a simple question requiring a 'Yes' or 'No' response. This elicits a clear response, but does not offer any flexibility and may force respondents into giving an opinion when they do not hold one. Because opinion and other abstract ideas are difficult to observe and measure, you may decide to use a rating scale, to measure intensity of opinion and other abstract ideas. This allows respondents to give a more discriminating response and allows them to indicate if they feel neutral. Box 10.10 shows an example where respondents are asked to indicate their level of agreement with a set of statements using a rating scale of 1 to 5. If there had been more room, each number might have had a label (for example 5 = Strongly agree, 4 = Agree, 3 = Neutral, 2 = Disagree, 1 = Strongly disagree). Unlike ranking, where 1 represents the top of the scale, you will find it useful to follow the convention of allocating 1 to the lowest level of agreement, importance, usefulness, or whatever it is your rating scale is measuring. This will make it easier to interpret the results of your statistical analysis.

Box 10.10 Intensity rating scale

4. What are your views on the following statements regarding the audit?
(Circle the number closest to your view)

	Agree				Disagree
(a) Provides a check on accounting records and systems	5	4	3	2	1
(b) Improves the quality of the financial information	5	4	3	2	1
(c) Improves the credibility of the financial information	5	4	3	2	1
(d) Has a positive effect on company's credit rating score	5	4	3	2	1

The example in Box 10.10 shows a particular type of intensity rating scale known as a *Likert scale* that is often used in multiple item measures of attitudes. Sometimes the midpoint on the scale is omitted to force the choice between agreeing and disagreeing.

An advantage of using ranking and rating scales is that a number of different statements can be provided in a list, which makes economical use of the space and is easy for the respondent to complete. Moreover, these ordinal variables are measured at a higher level than a nominal variable requiring a simple 'Yes' or 'No' answer, which has implications for the type of statistic tests that can be used in your analysis. Box 10.11 gives examples of commonly used scales.

Box 10.11 Examples of intensity, frequency and evaluation rating scales

General adjectives
5 Very/Extremely/Strongly satisfied/important/agree, etc.
4 Fairly/Quite/Moderately
3 Slightly/Weakly
2 Not very/Hardly
1 Not at all satisfied/important/agree, etc.

Directional general adjectives
5 Very/Extremely/Strongly satisfied, important, agree, etc.
4 Moderately/Fairly/Mostly
3 Neutral/Undecided/Unsure
2 Moderately/Fairly/Mostly
1 Very/Extremely/Strongly dissatisfied/unimportant/disagree, etc.

Directional comparisons
5 Much better
4 Better
3 About the same
2 Worse
1 Much worse

Frequency
5 All the time
4 Most of the time
3 Sometimes
2 Seldom/Rarely
1 Never/Not at all

Evaluation
5 Excellent
4 Very good
3 Average
2 Poor
1 Very poor

A *semantic differential rating scale* is a type of rating scale that is used to capture underlying attitudes and feelings. The respondent is asked to rate a single phenomenon on a series of dimensions. Each dimension is described by a pair of bipolar adjectives placed at each end of a line which usually has seven points placed evenly along it. The respondents are asked to indicate their opinion by placing a cross on one of the seven points on the scale. Box 10.12 shows an example that might be familiar to you. You will see that the respondent is encouraged to read each dimension carefully because the positive end of the scale is not always on the right-hand side.

Box 10.12 Semantic differential rating scale

Think of the last lecture you attended. For each of the following dimensions, place a cross (x) on one of the 7 points on the line that best indicates your experience (the first item shows an example).

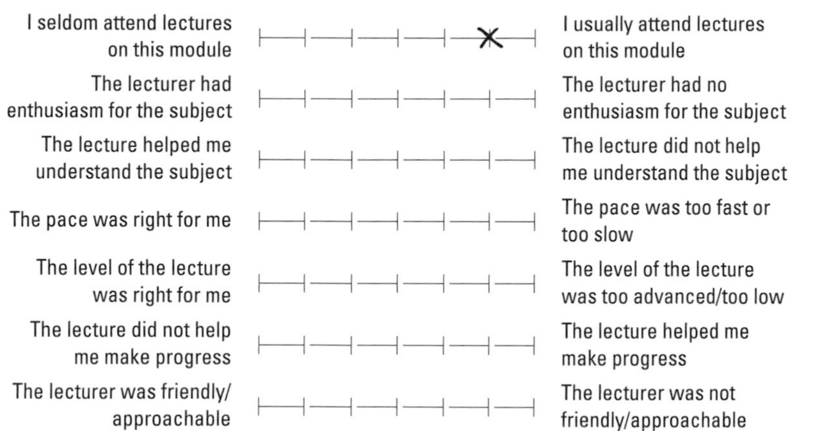

I seldom attend lectures on this module	I usually attend lectures on this module
The lecturer had enthusiasm for the subject	The lecturer had no enthusiasm for the subject
The lecture helped me understand the subject	The lecture did not help me understand the subject
The pace was right for me	The pace was too fast or too slow
The level of the lecture was right for me	The level of the lecture was too advanced/too low
The lecture did not help me make progress	The lecture helped me make progress
The lecturer was friendly/ approachable	The lecturer was not friendly/approachable

10.5.5 Reliability and validity

If you decide to use a rating scale to measure an abstract concept such as an ability or trait that is not directly observable (in other words, your explanatory variable is a hypothetical construct), you will want to be sure that the scale will measure the respondents' views reliably. Reliability refers to the accuracy and precision of the measurement and absence of differences in the results if the research were repeated. Perhaps you want to investigate the abstract concept of professionalism among qualified accountants. You search the literature and decide to use the five dimensions of professionalism identified by Hall (1968):

- The use of the professional organization as a major reference
- A belief in service to the public
- Belief in self-regulation
- A sense of calling to the field
- Autonomy.

You then conduct interviews with accountants and generate a number of indicators for each dimension. These form the basis of the statements you ask respondents to rate in your questionnaire, such as the following which relate to the first dimension (the professional organization as a major reference):

- I attend the local meetings of my professional body
- I participate in professional development workshops for members
- I read the newsletters and reports sent by my professional body
- I read about new issues on the website of my professional body
- I use the technical information on the website of my professional body
- I use the technical information on the websites of other professional bodies
- I can contact my professional body if I need technical support

Reliability is important, even if the concepts, dimensions and scales have been used by many other researchers because your sample is likely to differ in some respects from the samples of other studies.

The validity of the measure is also important. This is concerned with the extent to which the measure actually does capture the concept you are trying to measure; in other words, whether the data collected represent a true picture of the concept. The reason why there may be doubt lies in the problem that our questions may contain errors (perhaps they are worded ambiguously), the respondent may become bored or there may be antagonism between the researcher and the participants leading to *item non-response*. Typical examples include failing to answer questions that apply or not following instructions by ticking more than one box when only one choice was allowed. There are a number of ways of dealing with such problems, such as making an educated guess based on the respondent's other answers or using statistical methods. If you have a large number of non-responses to a particular question across the sample, it usually means the question design was at fault and the data from that question should not be used in your analysis. If a respondent returns an incomplete questionnaire or one where questions that are crucial to your analysis are not answered, you will have to discard it.

In Chapter 12 (section 12.5.4) we explain how you can use a *reliability test* to check the reliability of the rating scale. The important thing to remember is that the responses to your questions may turn out to be highly reliable, but the validity of your results will be very low if your questions do not measure what you intended them to measure. Therefore, it is important that the questions you ask correspond with the explanation you give respondents regarding the purpose of your study; otherwise, the questions may seem irrelevant and they may lose interest in answering them.

10.5.6 Eliminating questions

Having decided on the questions you wish to ask, it is common to find that you have far too many. Use the checklist given in Figure 10.5 to help you determine which questions you should retain and which you should drop.

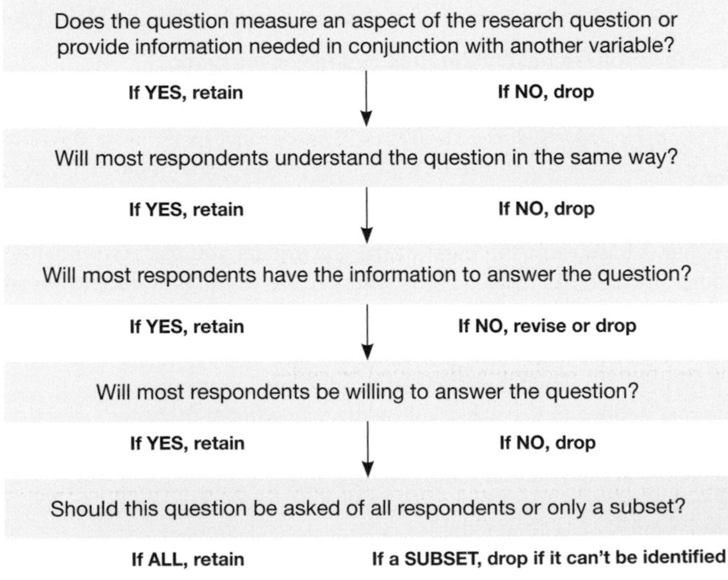

Figure 10.5 Checklist for eliminating questions

You must be alert to the possibility that some of the issues you wish to investigate may be offensive or embarrassing to the respondents. We do not recommend you ask any *sensitive questions* in a self-completion questionnaire. Not only is it likely to deter respondents from answering the sensitive question, but it may discourage them from participating at all.

10.6 Coding questions

Although coding is more closely related to data analysis than to data collection, it is important to consider at this stage how you will analyse your research data and what software is available to help you with this task (for example *Microsoft Excel*, *Minitab* and *IBM® SPSS® Statistics*). *SPSS* is widely used in business research because it can process large amounts of data and we will be introducing the principles of data entry and analysis using *SPSS* in the next chapter.

10.6.1 Coding closed questions

Pre-coding questions for statistical analysis as part of the questionnaire design makes the subsequent data entry easier and less prone to error. Where this is not possible, it is important to remember to keep a record of the codes used for each question and what they signify. This is essential should you decide to use a third party to input your data, and also for when you start to interpret the analysed data.

It is usual to reserve certain code numbers for particular purposes. For nominal variables where only one can be selected, allocate a different code to each so that the answer can be identified. For nominal variables where more than one answer may apply, each variable is treated independently: use 1 to indicate the box has been ticked (the characteristic is present) and leave blank if it has not been ticked. This will be interpreted by *SPSS* as a 'missing' data, which means a non-response. Depending on your planned analysis, you may wish to use 0 if the box has not been ticked (the characteristic is not present). Similarly, it is usual to code the answer 'yes' as 1 and the answer 'no' as 0. There is no need to pre-code ordinal variables because they use a numerical rating scale.

You may have noticed that the examples of questions we used in this chapter were pre-coded. Box 10.13 shows an example of a completed questionnaire. Look carefully at the way in which the potential answers have been coded. Each code is discretely shown in brackets next to the relevant box. There are no hard and fast rules about where to place the codes and you may find that it makes more sense to put the codes at the top of a column of boxes for some sets of variables. You simply need to adopt a location that improves the accuracy and efficiency of processing the data, while not confusing the respondent. In this example, a smaller, lighter font has been used to reduce the likelihood of the respondent becoming distracted by codes.

Earlier in this chapter, we suggested that you should pilot your questions before commencing your data collection in earnest. We also recommend that once you have your test data, you also pilot your coding. Amending coding errors now will save you valuable time and effort later when errors can only be painstakingly corrected by hand on every record sheet or questionnaire.

Box 10.13 A pre-coded questionnaire

URN 42

1. Is the company a family-owned business? *(Tick one box only)*

Wholly family-owned (or only 1 owner)	☐	(1)
Partly family-owned	☐	(2)
None of the shareholders are related	☐	(0)

2. How many shareholders (owners) does the company have?

(a) Total number of shareholders ☐

Breakdown:

(b) Number of shareholders with access to internal financial information ☐

(c) Number of shareholders without access to internal financial information ☐

3. Would you have the accounts audited if not legally required to do so?
(Tick one box only)

Yes, the accounts are already audited voluntarily	☐	(1)
Yes, the accounts would be audited voluntarily	☐	(2)
No	☐	(0)

Please give reasons for either answer

....

....

4. What are your views on the following statements regarding the audit?
(Circle number closest to your view)

	Agree				Disagree
(a) Provides a check on accounting records and systems	5	4	3	2	1
(b) Improves the quality of the financial information	5	4	3	2	1
(c) Improves the credibility of the financial information	5	4	3	2	1
(d) Has a positive effect on company's credit rating score	5	4	3	2	1

5. Apart from Companies House, who normally receives a copy of the company's statutory accounts? *(Tick as many boxes as apply)*

(a) Shareholders ☐

(b) Bank and other providers of finance ☐

(c) Employees who are not shareholders ☐

(d) Major suppliers and trade creditors ☐

(e) Major customers ☐

(f) Tax authorities ☐

(g) Other *(Please state)*.. ☐

6. Do you have any of the following qualifications/training?
(Tick as many boxes as apply)

(a) Undergraduate or postgraduate degree ☐

(b) Professional/vocational qualification ☐

(c) Study/training in business/management subjects ☐

Source: Adapted from Collis (2003).

10.6.2 Coding open questions

Statistical analysis can only be conducted on quantitative data. Open questions where the answer takes a numerical value do not need to be coded (for example dates or financial data). However, open questions where you are unable to anticipate the response (including those where you provide an 'Other' category) will result in qualitative data that cannot be coded until all the replies have been received. The task of recording and counting frequencies accurately and methodically can be helped by using tallies. A tally is just a simple stroke used to count the frequency of occurrence of a value or category in a variable. You jot down one upright stroke for each occurrence until you have four; the fifth is drawn horizontally across the group, like a five bar gate. You can then count in fives until you get to the single tallies. Box 10.14 shows tallies being used to help record the frequencies for the second part of question 3, which was designed as an open question to capture the respondents' reasons for a particular action.

Box 10.14 Using tallies to count frequencies

3. Would you have the accounts audited if not legally required to do so?
(Tick one box only)

Yes, the accounts are already audited voluntarily ☐ (1)
Yes, the accounts would be audited voluntarily ☐ (2)
No ☐ (0)

Please give reasons for either answer

Voluntary audit

Assurance for third party ~~||||~~ ~~||||~~ ~~||||~~ ~~||||~~ ~~||||~~ ~~||||~~ ~~||||~~ 35

Good practice ~~||||~~ ~~||||~~ ~~||||~~ |||| 19

No audit

No benefit/no need ~~||||~~ ~~||||~~ ~~||||~~ ~~||||~~ ~~||||~~ ~~||||~~ ~~||||~~ | 36

Cost savings ~~||||~~ ~~||||~~ ~~||||~~ ~~||||~~ ~~||||~~ ~~||||~~ || 32

10.7 Conclusions

In this chapter, we have discussed the methods you can use to select a sample under a positivist paradigm, if the population is too large to be used. If you want to generalize the results from the sample to the population, you must select a random sample of sufficient size to represent the population and allow you to address your research questions. We have also investigated the main methods for collecting primary data under a positivist paradigm. You should now be in a position to make an informed choice, bearing in mind that some methods can be adapted for use under either paradigm and you can use more than one method. You must obtain ethical approval from your university before you collect any data if your study involves human participants.

We have also examined how you can classify variables according to their level of measurement, which has important implications for how you design your questions and the statistical tests you can use to analyse your research data. There are a number of ways in which questions can be designed, including the use of hypothetical constructs to measure abstract ideas. We have discussed these matters and explained how questions in questionnaires and other data record sheets can be pre-coded for subsequent statistical analysis.

There is considerable choice in methods for distributing questionnaires. If you are using interviews, you must use rigorous methods to record the research data that provide evidence of the source. The important thing to remember is that you need to obtain the participant's agreement if you intend to audio record the interview and take notes.

References

Alexander, D. (2006) 'The devil with Dawkins', *Times Higher Education*. London: TSL Education, 3 February, p. 20.

Brenner, M. (1985) 'Survey Interviewing', in Brenner, M., Brown, J. and Canter, D. (eds) *The Research Interview: Uses and Approaches*. New York: Academic Press, pp. 9–36.

Clegg, F. G. (1990) *Simple Statistics*. Cambridge: Cambridge University Press.

Collis, J. (2003) *Directors' Views on Exemption from Statutory Audit*, URN 03/1342, October, London: DTI. [Online]. Available at: http://www.berr.gov.uk/files/file25971.pdf (Accessed 20 February 2013).

Coolican, H. (2009) *Research Methods and Statistics in Psychology*, 5th edn. London: Hodder Arnold.

Czaja, R. and Blair, J. (1996) *Designing Surveys: A Guide to Decisions and Procedures*. Thousand Oaks, CA: Pine Forge Press.

Flanagan, J. C. (1954) 'The critical incident technique', *Psychological Bulletin*, 51(4), July, pp. 327–58.

Hall, R. H. (1968) 'Professionalism and bureaucratization', *American Sociological Review*, 33, pp. 92–104.

Kervin, J. B. (1992) *Methods for Business Research*. New York: HarperCollins.

Krejcie, R. V. and Morgan, D. W. (1970) 'Determining sample size for research activities', *Educational and Psychological Measurement*, 30, pp. 607–10.

Lee, R. M. (1993) *Doing Research on Sensitive Topics*. London: SAGE.

MacKinlay, T. (1986) *The Development of a Personal Strategy of Management*, M.Sc. thesis, Manchester Polytechnic, Department of Management, cited in Easterby-Smith, M., Thorpe, R. and Lowe, A. (1991) *Management Research*. London: SAGE.

Salkind, N. J. (2006) *Exploring Research*. Upper Saddle River, NJ: Pearson International.

Upton, G. and Cook, I. (2006) *Oxford Dictionary of Statistics*, 2nd edn. Oxford: Oxford University Press.

Activities

1 You are interested in environmental issues. Discuss the advantages and disadvantages of collecting secondary data, such as the newspaper or television news coverage, compared with primary data.

2 General lecture questionnaire
Think about the last lecture you attended and complete the following questionnaire. This is just an exercise and you won't be asked to identify the lecture or the lecturer or reveal your ratings. When you've finished, jot down what you like or dislike about the questionnaire from your perspective as a 'respondent'. Then form a group to discuss your views on the instructions, the layout and the questions.

GENERAL LECTURE QUESTIONNAIRE

The purpose of this questionnaire is to obtain your views and opinions about the lectures you have been given during the course from this lecturer to help him evaluate his teaching.

Please ring the response that you think is the most appropriate to each statement. If you wish to make any comments in addition to those ratings please do so on the back page.

The lecturer	Strongly agree	Agree	Neither agree nor disagree	Disagree	Strongly disagree
1. Encourages student participation in lectures	5	4	3	2	1
2. Allows opportunities for asking questions	5	4	3	2	1
3. Has a good lecture delivery	5	4	3	2	1
4. Has good rapport with students	5	4	3	2	1
5. Is approachable and friendly with students	5	4	3	2	1
6. Is respectful towards students	5	4	3	2	1
7. Is able to reach student level	5	4	3	2	1
8. Enables easy note taking	5	4	3	2	1
9. Provides useful printed notes*	5	4	3	2	1
10. Would help students by providing printed notes	5	4	3	2	1
11. Has a good knowledge of his subject	5	4	3	2	1
12. Maintains student interest during lectures	5	4	3	2	1
13. Gives varied, lively lectures	5	4	3	2	1
14. Is clear and comprehensible in lectures	5	4	3	2	1
15. Gives lectures which are too fast to take in	5	4	3	2	1
16. Gives audible lectures	5	4	3	2	1
17. Gives structured, organized lectures	5	4	3	2	1
18. Appears to be enthusiastic for his subject	5	4	3	2	1

*Please answer if applicable

Source: Anon.

3 Now put on your researcher's hat and redesign the general lecture questionnaire and pilot it with two fellow students. Stay with them while they complete it so you can ask them how useful they found the instructions and how easy they found it to answer the questions. Ask them what they liked and did not like about it.

4 Design a one-page, self-completion questionnaire to find out what brand of toothpaste people normally buy and their reasons. If you did this activity in Chapter 4, you may want to make some improvements with the new knowledge you have gained from studying this chapter. It is likely that your first question will list various brands of toothpaste and ask the respondent to indicate the one he or she normally uses. Base your subsequent questions on the information you can extract from the following interview transcript.

Interviewer: Why did you buy the brand of toothpaste you are using at present?

Respondent: Well, my wife and I usually get the one that's on special offer. It's not that money is tight – that's what she chooses to do. So we tend to get the one where there's money off, 25% extra free, two for the price of one, and so on. But last week the brand on special offer was a new one – we hadn't seen it before. It's really good because it has a strong minty taste. I don't like the ones with fancy fruit flavours. This new one's good – I like it a lot. [Pause] What's it called, now? I can't remember the name of it at the moment. [Pause] That's funny because I clean my teeth at least twice a day, so I see the tube often enough! Anyway, my wife likes it too and I think we'll buy it again, even if it's not discounted when we need to the next tube. When you get to my age it is important to look after your teeth, you know!

- Number each question and pre-code your variables (apart from any open questions).
- Make a note of whether the level of measurement of each variable is nominal, ordinal, interval or ratio.
- Identify your dependent variable and independent variables.

5 Pilot your toothpaste questionnaire with two fellow students. Stay with them while they complete it so you can ask them how useful they found the instructions and how easy they found it to answer the questions. Ask them what they liked and did not like about it.

Check your understanding with the online progress test at www.palgrave.com/business/collis/br4/

Have a look at the Troubleshooting chapter and sections 14.2, 14.5, 14.7, 14.10, 14.12, 14.13 in particular, which relate specifically to this chapter.

11

analysing data using descriptive statistics

learning objectives

When you have studied this chapter, you should be able to:

- differentiate between descriptive statistics and inferential statistics
- enter data into *SPSS*, recode variables and create new variables
- generate frequency tables, charts and other diagrams
- generate measures of central tendency and dispersion
- generate measures of normality.

11.1 Introduction

If you have adopted a positivist paradigm, you will have collected quantitative data and you will need to quantify any qualitative research data. If your knowledge of statistics is somewhat rusty, you should find this chapter useful as it contains key formulae for some of the basic techniques, together with step-by-step instructions and worked examples. However, you may prefer to enter your data into a software program, such as *Microsoft Excel*, *Minitab* or *SPSS*. In this chapter, we introduce you to *IBM® SPSS® Statistics software (SPSS)*, which is widely used in business research because it can process a large amount of data.

SPSS provides a data file where data can be stored, which is similar to a spreadsheet. Once the data have been entered or imported into *SPSS*, frequency tables, charts, cross-tabulations and a range of statistical tests can be performed quickly and accurately. The resulting output can then be pasted into your dissertation or thesis. Whether you decide to calculate the statistics yourself or use software, you will need to determine which statistics are appropriate for the data you have collected and how to interpret the results. This chapter and the next will give you guidance.

11.2 Key concepts in statistics

The term **statistics** was introduced by Sir Ronald Fisher in 1922 (Upton and Cook, 2006) and refers to the body of methods and theory that is applied to quantitative data. Moore *et al.* (2009, p. 210) define a **statistic** as 'a number that describes a sample'. For example, you could calculate the mean number of employees in a sample of companies to describe the average size of the sample. A statistic can be used to estimate an unknown **parameter**, which is a number that describes a population. Thus, if you had a random sample that was a representative of the population, you could use the sample mean to estimate the average number of employees in the population of companies. A random sample is a representative subset of the population where observations are made and a population includes the totality of observations that might be made (as in a census).

Research data can be secondary data (for example a survey of a sample of annual reports using content analysis), primary data (for example a survey of a sample of companies using questionnaires) or both. In addition to quantitative data, you may have collected some qualitative data (for example themes you have identified in the narrative sections of the annual reports or categories you have identified from responses to open questions in the questionnaire survey). You can see from the definition of statistics that statistical methods can only be applied to quantitative data, so you will need to quantify any qualitative data beforehand. You can do this by identifying each nominal variable and recording the frequency of occurrence of each category it contains. You will remember that in the previous chapter we recommended using *tallies* to aid the counting of frequencies.

Statisticians commonly draw a distinction between **descriptive statistics** and **inferential statistics.** Descriptive statistics are used to summarize the data in a more compact form and can be presented in tables, charts and other graphical forms. This allows patterns to be discerned that are not apparent in the raw data and 'positively aids subsequent hypothesis detection/confirmation' (Lovie, 1986, p. 165). Inferential statistics are

A **statistic** is a number that describes a sample.

Statistics is a body of methods and theory that is applied to quantitative data.

A **parameter** is a number that describes a population.

Descriptive statistics are a group of statistical methods used to summarize, describe or display quantitative data.

Inferential statistics are a group of statistical methods and models used to draw conclusions about a population from quantitative data relating to a random sample.

'statistical tests that lead to conclusions about a target population based on a random sample and the concept of sampling distribution' (Kervin, 1992, p. 727).

Univariate analysis is the analysis of data relating to one variable.

Bivariate analysis is the analysis of data relating to two variables.

Multivariate analysis is the analysis of data relating to three or more variables.

In an undergraduate dissertation, the research may be designed as a small, descriptive study. If so, you may be able to address your research questions by using descriptive statistics to explore the data from individual variables (hence the term **univariate analysis**). However, at postgraduate level, you are likely to design an analytical study. Therefore, you are more likely to use descriptive statistics at the initial stage and then go on to use inferential statistics (or other techniques) in a bivariate and/or multivariate analysis. We will examine the statistics used in **bivariate analysis** (analysis of data relating to two variables) and **multivariate analysis** (analysis of data relating to three or more variables) in the next chapter.

11.3 Getting started with *SPSS*

11.3.1 The research data

We are going to use real business data collected for a postal questionnaire survey of the directors of small private companies (Collis, 2003) that focused on their option to forgo the statutory audit of their accounts. Do not worry if you know nothing about this topic, as no prior knowledge is required (you may remember seeing extracts from the questionnaire as some of the questions were used as examples in the previous chapter). The survey was commissioned by the government as part of the consultation on raising the turnover threshold for audit exemption in UK company law from £1 million to £4.8 million, which would extend this regulatory relaxation to a greater number of small companies. The literature showed that although some of the companies that already qualified for audit exemption made use of it, others apparently chose to continue having their accounts audited. This led to the following research question: What are the factors that have a significant influence on the directors' decision to have a voluntary audit?

Very briefly, the theoretical framework for the study was that the emphasis on turnover in company law at that time implied a relationship between size and whether the cost of audit exceeded the benefits. Agency theory (Jensen and Meckling, 1976) suggests that audit would be required where there was information asymmetry between 'agent' and 'principal' (for example the directors managing the company and external owners, or between the directors and the company's lenders and creditors).

Based on this framework, a number of hypotheses were formulated. Each hypothesis is a statement about a relationship between two variables. The *null hypothesis* (H_0) states that the two variables are independent of one another (there is no relationship) and the *alternative hypothesis* (H_1) states that the two variables are associated with one another (there is a relationship). Using inferential statistics, the hypotheses are tested against the empirical data and the alternative hypothesis is accepted if there is statistically significant evidence to reject the null hypothesis (in other words, the null hypothesis is the default). Here is the first hypothesis in the null and the alternative form:

H_0 Voluntary audit does not increase with company size, as measured by turnover.
H_1 Voluntary audit increases with company size as measured by turnover.

You should ask your supervisor whether he or she would prefer you to state your hypotheses in the null or the alternative form. Box 11.1 lists the nine hypotheses, which are stated in the alternative form.

Box 11.1 Hypotheses to be tested

H1 Voluntary audit is positively associated with turnover.
H2 Voluntary audit is positively associated with agreement that the audit provides a check on accounting records and systems.
H3 Voluntary audit is positively associated with agreement that it improves the quality of the financial information.
H4 Voluntary audit is positively associated with agreement that it improves the credibility of the financial information.
H5 Voluntary audit is positively associated with agreement that it has a positive effect on the credit rating score.
H6 Voluntary audit is positively associated with the company being family-owned.
H7 Voluntary audit is positively associated with the company having shareholders without access to internal financial information.
H8 Voluntary audit is positively associated with demand from the bank and other lenders.
H9 Voluntary audit is positively associated with the directors having qualifications or training in business or management.

The sampling frame used was *Fame*. This is a database containing financial and other information from the annual reports and accounts of more than 8 million companies in the UK and Ireland. At any one moment in time, some of these companies are dormant, some are in the process of liquidation, some have not yet registered their accounts for the latest year and some do not qualify for audit exemption on the grounds of the public interest (for example listed companies and those in the financial services sector). A search of the database identified a population of 2,633 active companies within the scope of the study in 2003 (likely to qualify for audit exemption if the turnover threshold were raised), and which had registered their accounts for 2002. The questionnaire was sent to the principal director of each company with an accompanying letter explaining the purpose of the research and that it had been commissioned by the then Department for Trade and Industry.[1] After one reminder, 790 completed questionnaires were received, giving a response rate of 30%. This unexpectedly high rate was undoubtedly due to the use of the government logo on the questionnaire, since response rates from small businesses are usually considerably lower. We are going to use this survey data to illustrate some of the key features of *SPSS*. The data file is available at www.palgrave.com/business/collis/br4/.

The identity of the respondents will not be revealed as they were assured anonymity. This was achieved through the use of a unique reference number (URN) known only to the researcher. Box 11.2 shows the responses given by respondent 42.

11.3.2 Labelling variables and entering the data

Our illustrations are based on *IBM® SPSS® Statistics software v20*. You run the program in the same way as any other software. For example, *start* ⇒ All Programs ⇒ [name of the version available to you]. If your programs are on a local area network, *SPSS* may be in a separate folder for mathematical and/or statistics packages. The program usually opens with a screen inviting you to choose what you would like to do. Select Type in data and *SPSS* Data Editor will then open a new data file in Data View (see Figure 11.1), in which each row of cells represents a different case (for example a respondent to a questionnaire

1 In subsequent restructuring, the Department of Trade and Industry was replaced by the Department for Business, Enterprise and Regulatory Reform, which itself was replaced by the Department of Business, Innovation and Skills.

Box 11.2 Questionnaire completed by respondent 42

URN 42

1. Is the company a family-owned business? *(Tick one box only)*

Wholly family-owned (or only 1 owner)	☑	(1)
Partly family-owned	☐	(2)
None of the shareholders are related	☐	(0)

2. How many shareholders (owners) does the company have?

(a) Total number of shareholders [2]

Breakdown:

(b) Number of shareholders with access to internal financial information [2]

(c) Number of shareholders without access to internal financial information [0]

3. Would you have the accounts audited if not legally required to do so?
(Tick one box only)

Yes, the accounts are already audited voluntarily	☐	(1)
Yes, the accounts would be audited voluntarily	☐	(2)
No	☑	(0)

Please give reasons for either answer

....

....

4. What are your views on the following statements regarding the audit?
(Circle number closest to your view)

	Agree				Disagree
(a) Provides a check on accounting records and systems	5	4	(3)	2	1
(b) Improves the quality of the financial information	5	4	3	(2)	1
(c) Improves the credibility of the financial information	5	4	3	(2)	1
(d) Has a positive effect on company's credit rating score	5	4	3	(2)	1

5. Apart from Companies House, who normally receives a copy of the company's statutory accounts? *(Tick as many boxes as apply)*

(a) Shareholders ☑

(b) Bank and other providers of finance ☐

(Other variables omitted from this example)

6. Do you have any of the following qualifications/training?
(Tick as many boxes as apply)

(a) Undergraduate or postgraduate degree ☐

(b) Professional/vocational qualification ☐

(c) Study/training in business/management subjects ☐

Turnover data taken from 2002 accounts on Fame: £74.411k

Source: Adapted from Collis (2003).

survey) and each column represents a different variable. If you are using secondary research data that you have exported to a *Microsoft Excel* spreadsheet, you can simply copy and paste it into the *SPSS* Data Editor.

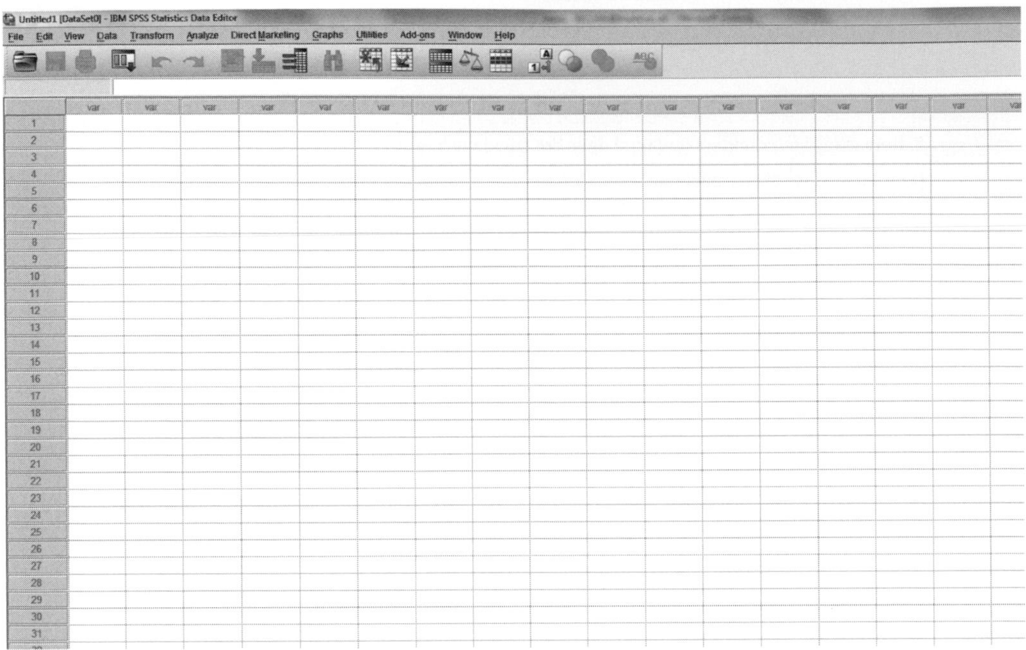

Figure 11.1 *SPSS* Data Editor

Now switch from Data View to Variable View by clicking on the tab at the bottom left of the screen and you can start naming and labelling your variables:

- Under Name, type a short word to identify the variable. In this survey, each respondent was given a unique reference number (URN) so that primary data from the questionnaire survey could be matched to secondary data from *Fame*. Therefore, you might decide to type URN as the name for the first variable. The second variable relates to the first question, so you might want to name it Q1. You will find that *SPSS* prevents you from using a number as the first character or any spaces. Initially you will find this a quick and easy way to name your variables.
- Under Decimals, amend the default to reflect the number of decimal places in the data for that variable. For example, for Q1 you will select 0 decimal places, whereas for turnover you will need to select 3 decimal places.
- Under Labels, type a word or two that adds information to the name of the variable. For example, Family ownership for Q1; Total owners for Q2a; With internal info for Q2b; Without internal info for Q2c. For Q4, you might decide to use a keyword, such as Check for Q4a; Quality for Q4b; Credibility for Q4c; Credit score for Q4d.
- Under Values, enter the codes and what they signify. For example, in Q4, 1 = Disagree and 5 = Agree (once you have entered this information, you can copy and paste it to other variables using the same codes); for Q6, 1 = Yes and 0 = Otherwise. TURNOVER does not need any codes entered because it is a ratio variable.

SPSS provides a default measure for missing data (or no response), so unless you have a particular reason to enter a code for a non-response, move on to Measurement. *SPSS* gives you a choice of Scale (use for ratio or interval variables), Ordinal or Nominal. If you need to jog your memory to make these decisions, refer to Chapter 10, section 10.3.1).

At this point, save the file (File, Save As) and name it Data for URN 42.sav. Figure 11.2 shows the screen at this stage in the process.

Data for URN 42.sav [DataSet1] - IBM SPSS Statistics Data Editor

File Edit View Data Transform Analyze Direct Marketing Graphs Utilities Add-ons Window Help

	Name	Type	Width	Decimals	Label	Values	Missing	Columns	Align	Measure	Role
1	URN	Numeric	4	0		None	None	5	Right	Nominal	Input
2	Q1	Numeric	6	0	Family ownership	{0, Not relat...	None	5	Right	Nominal	Input
3	Q2a	Numeric	6	0	Total owners	None	None	5	Right	Scale	Input
4	Q2b	Numeric	6	0	With internal info	None	None	5	Right	Scale	Input
5	Q2c	Numeric	6	0	Without internal...	None	None	5	Right	Scale	Input
6	Q3	Numeric	6	0	Future decision	{0, No}...	None	5	Right	Nominal	Input
7	Q4a	Numeric	6	0	Check	{1, Disagree...	None	5	Right	Ordinal	Input
8	Q4b	Numeric	6	0	Quality	{1, Disagree...	None	5	Right	Ordinal	Input
9	Q4c	Numeric	6	0	Credibility	{1, Disagree...	None	5	Right	Ordinal	Input
10	Q4d	Numeric	6	0	Credit score	{1, Not impo...	None	5	Right	Ordinal	Input
11	Q5a	Numeric	6	0	Bank	{0, Otherwis...	None	5	Right	Nominal	Input
12	Q6a	Numeric	6	0	Degree	None	None	5	Right	Nominal	Input
13	Q6b	Numeric	6	0	Prof/voc qualific...	None	None	5	Right	Nominal	Input
14	Q6c	Numeric	6	0	Studied bus/mg...	None	None	5	Right	Nominal	Input
15	TURNOVER	Numeric	12	3	Turnover £k	None	None	8	Right	Scale	Input

Figure 11.2 Variable View of Data for URN 42.sav

Next return to Data View and enter the data values (the observations) for respondent 42, including the data for turnover, which for the convenience of this exercise is shown as a note at the end of the questionnaire. Notice that if you place your cursor over the name of a variable, *SPSS* will reveal the label you added in Variable View. For example, by placing the cursor on the variable Q4a, the label Check is displayed, which was used to remind us that this variable relates to the role of the audit as a check on accounting records and systems (see Figure 11.3). This is a very useful feature that helps ensure you enter the data in the appropriate column.

11.3.3 Recoding variables

A **dummy variable** is a dichotomous quantitative variable coded 1 if the characteristic is present and 0 if the characteristic is absent.

A **dichotomous variable** is a variable that has only two possible categories, such as gender.

In the previous chapter, we mentioned situations where you might have collected data in a particular form for one purpose, but you subsequently want to recode the data and create a different variable in a new, simpler form called a **dummy variable**. This is a **dichotomous variable** containing only two categories, where 1 = the characteristic is present and 0 = the characteristic is absent. It is important to keep the original variable in case you need the more detailed and precise information for another purpose. We will illustrate how to recode a variable with Q1, which collected data about the extent to which the company is family-

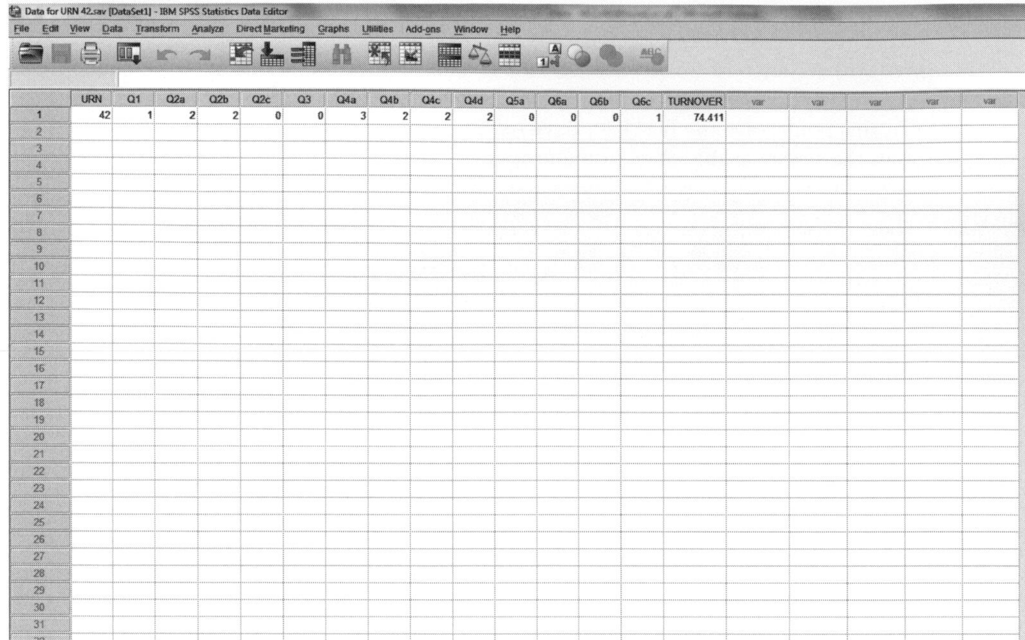

Figure 11.3 Data View of Data for URN 42.sav

owned. We are going to recode it into a new variable called FAMILY, which will have two groups: companies that are wholly family-owned (or have only one owner) and those that are not.

In Variable View select the whole of row 3 to position the new variable above it:

- From the menu, select Edit ⇒ Insert Variable.
- Name the new variable FAMILY and label it as Q1.
- Under Values, enter the details for the two groups: 1 = Wholly family-owned, 0 = Otherwise.
- Change the number of decimal places to 0 and change the measurement level to nominal.

From the menu, select Transform ⇒ Recode into Different Variables.

- From the list of variables on the left, select Q1 and use the arrow button ➡ to move it into the Input Variable --> Output Variable box.
- Type FAMILY in the Output Variable Name box and click Old and New Values.
- Under Old value, click System-missing and under New value click System-missing and then click Add.
- Under Old value, type 1 and under New value, type 1 and click Add.
- Under Old value, click All other values and under New value, type 0 and click Add ⇒ Continue ⇒ Change and OK.

Figure 11.4 illustrates the recoding process.

When you have finished, return to Data View and carry out a visual check that the value 1 in the new dummy variable coincides with the value 1 in the original variable. This is just an exercise, but when you enter your own research data, you will not start

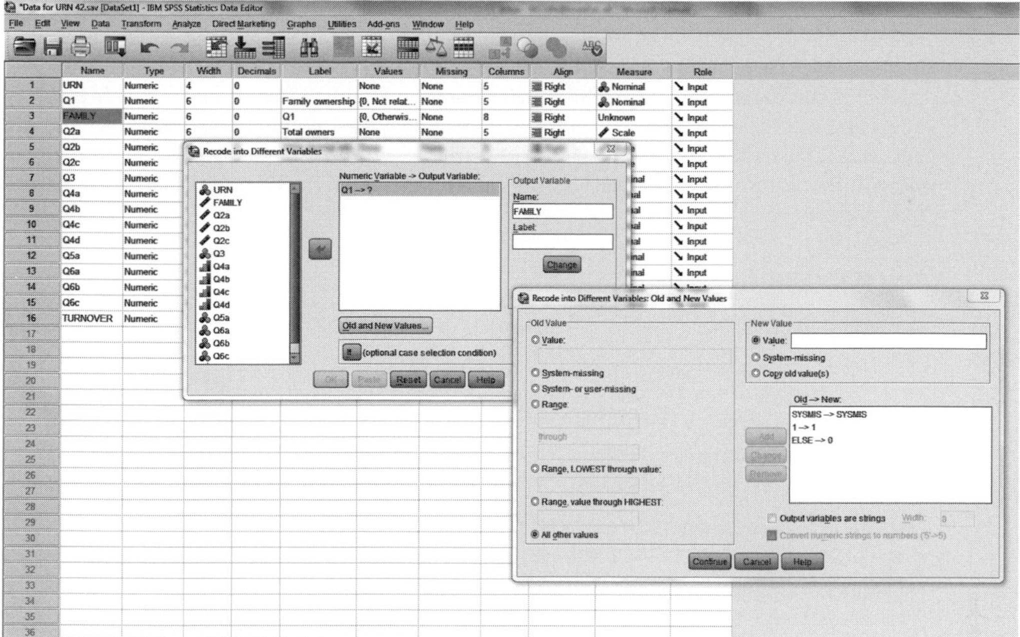

Figure 11.4 Recoding into a different variable

recoding any variables until you have finished entering all the observations for your sample. Remember that it is essential to verify the accuracy of your recoding instructions by checking the outcome. With a large number of cases, it is not practical to use a visual check and we suggest you compare the total frequencies for each category in the old and new variables instead. We will show you how to generate frequency tables in the next section. If you find you have made a mistake, simply go through the steps for recoding the variable again.

You can reinforce and extend your knowledge of recoding by creating three more dummy variables:

- Recode Q2c into EXOWNERS, where 1 = External owners, 0 = Otherwise. Do this by recoding SYSMIS --> SYSMIS, 0 --> 0, ELSE --> 1.
- Recode Q3 into VOLAUDIT, where 1 = Yes, 0 = No. Do this by recoding SYSMIS --> SYSMIS, 0 --> 0, ELSE --> 1.
- Recode Q6a, Q6b and Q6c into EDUCATION, where 1 = Degree, qualifications or training, 0 = Otherwise. This is a bit more complicated. As each variable will make a contribution to the new variable, recode 1 --> 1 for each variable in turn. Then check Data View to see the new variable accurately reflects your instructions. If so, from the menu select Transform ⇒ Recode ⇒ Into same variable and after selecting Education, recode 1 --> 1, ELSE --> 0. Then in Data View carry out a last visual check on the accuracy of the outcome. As already mentioned, this is essential when working with your own data, as you will not do any recoding until you have finished entering the data for your entire sample.

At this point, you may have begun to think that it would be more convenient if the names we used for the four variables in Q4 were more informative, like the names of the new variables you have created. Renaming them is easy. Go into Variable View and under Name, type CHECK instead of Q4a and under Label, type Q4a instead of Check. Carry out a similar reversal for Q4b, Q4c and Q4d. Although using the question numbers was useful at the data entry stage, this small change will aid the next stage, which involves analysing the variables and interpreting the results. When you have finished, save the file and exit. Table 11.1 now summarizes the variables in the analysis, where for some tests we will be describing VOLAUDIT as the dependent variable (DV) and the others as the independent variables (IVs).

Table 11.1 Variables in the analysis

Variable	Definition	Hypothesis	Expected sign
VOLAUDIT	Whether company would have a voluntary audit (1, 0)		
TURNOVER	Turnover in 2002 accounts (£k)	H1	+
CHECK	Audit provides a check on accounting records and systems (5 = Agree, 1 = Disagree)	H2	+
QUALITY	Audit improves the quality of the financial information (5 = Agree, 1 = Disagree)	H3	+
CREDIBILITY	Audit improves the credibility of the financial information (5 = Agree, 1 = Disagree)	H4	+
CREDIT SCORE	Audit has a positive effect on the credit rating score (5 = Agree, 1 = Disagree)	H5	+
FAMILY	Whether company is wholly family-owned (1, 0)	H6	-
EXOWNERS	Whether company has external shareholders (1, 0)	H7	+
BANK	Whether statutory accounts are given to the bank/lenders (1, 0)	H8	+
EDUCATION	Whether respondent has qualifications/training in business or management (1, 0)	H9	+

We are now ready to examine some of the descriptive statistics used to explore data in a univariate analysis. The methods we are going to use are simple statistical models, which will help us describe the data. Box 11.3 summarizes the statistics we are going to generate.

Box 11.3 Univariate analysis

Descriptive statistics

Frequency distribution
- Percentage frequency

Measures of central tendency
- Mean
- Median
- Mode

Measures of dispersion
- Range
- Standard deviation

Measures of normality
- Skewness
- Kurtosis

11.4 Frequency distributions

A **frequency** is the number of observations for a particular data value in a variable.

A **frequency distribution** is an array that summarizes the frequencies for all the data values in a particular variable.

A **percentage frequency** is a descriptive statistic that summarizes a frequency as a proportion of 100.

In statistics, the term **frequency** refers to the number of observations for a particular data value in a variable (the frequency of occurrence of a quantity in a ratio or interval variable and a category in an ordinal or nominal variable). A **frequency distribution** is an array that summarizes the frequencies for all the data values in a particular variable (Upton and Cook, 2006). For example, the data values in the survey for the variable TURNOVER were the figures reported in the companies' 2006 annual accounts. If no company had precisely the same figure for turnover as another, the number of observations for each data value would be 1. If the variable is measured on an ordinal scale (for example CHECK, which is coded 1–5) or a nominal scale (for example FAMILY, which is coded 1 or 0), the data values are the codes and the number of observations are the number of companies in each category.

A frequency distribution can be presented for one variable (univariate analysis) or two variables (bivariate analysis) in a table, chart or other type of diagram. Even if you only have a very small data set (say, 20 data values or less), an examination of how the values are distributed will aid your interpretation of the data.

11.4.1 Percentage frequencies

A **percentage frequency** is a familiar statistical model, which summarizes frequencies as a proportion of 100. It is calculated by dividing the frequency by the sum of the frequencies and then multiplying the answer by 100. This can be expressed as a formula:

$$\text{Percentage frequency} = \frac{f}{\Sigma f} \times 100$$

where

f = the frequency
Σ = the sum of

Example
The survey found that 633 companies out of 790 in the sample had a turnover of less than £1 million. Putting these figures into the formula:

$$\frac{633}{790} \times 100 = 80\%$$

The formula we have used is not difficult to understand, but if you are not a statistician, you may find the mathematical notation somewhat mysterious. However, it is merely a kind of shorthand that speeds up the process of writing the formulae and, once you know what the symbols represent, you can decipher the message. As we are going to show you how to use *SPSS* to generate the statistics you require, we will not examine the mathematical side.

11.4.2 Creating interval variables

In a large sample, you may find it useful to recode ratio variables into non-overlapping groups and create a new variable measured on an equal-interval scale. For example, the original variable TURNOVER was recoded into a different variable named TURNOVERCAT with five groups containing equal intervals of £1m. You need to take care that you can allocate each item of data to the appropriate group without ambiguity. Therefore, you should not use intervals of £0–£1m, £1m–£2m, £2m–£3m and so on, because a value of £1m could be placed in either the first or the second group and a value of £2m could be placed in either the second or the third group. The correct intervals are £0–£0.99m, £1m–£1.99m, £2m–£2.99m and so on. When deciding how many groups to create, you need to bear in mind that too few might obscure essential features and too many might emphasize minor or random features. A rule of thumb might be 5 to 10, depending on the range of values in the data.

Creating an interval variable allows the overall pattern in the frequencies and percentage frequencies to be discerned. However, much of the detail is lost in the process, so it is important to recode into a different variable (rather than the same variable) and keep the original precise information in case you need it for another purpose later on.

11.4.3 Generating frequency tables

Although a frequency table can be generated for a ratio variable, it is more usually associated with variables that contain groups or categories, such as interval, ordinal or nominal variables. To generate a frequency table in *SPSS*, start the program in the usual way and open the file named Data for 790 cos.sav.

- From the menu, select Analyze ⇒ Descriptive Statistics ⇒ Frequencies …
- From the list of variables on the left, select TURNOVERCAT and use the arrow button ➡ to move it into the Variable(s) box on the right (see Figure 11.5). If you also wanted to generate frequency tables for other variables, you would simply move them into the box on the right at this point.

The default is to display the frequency tables, so click OK to see the output (see Table 11.2).

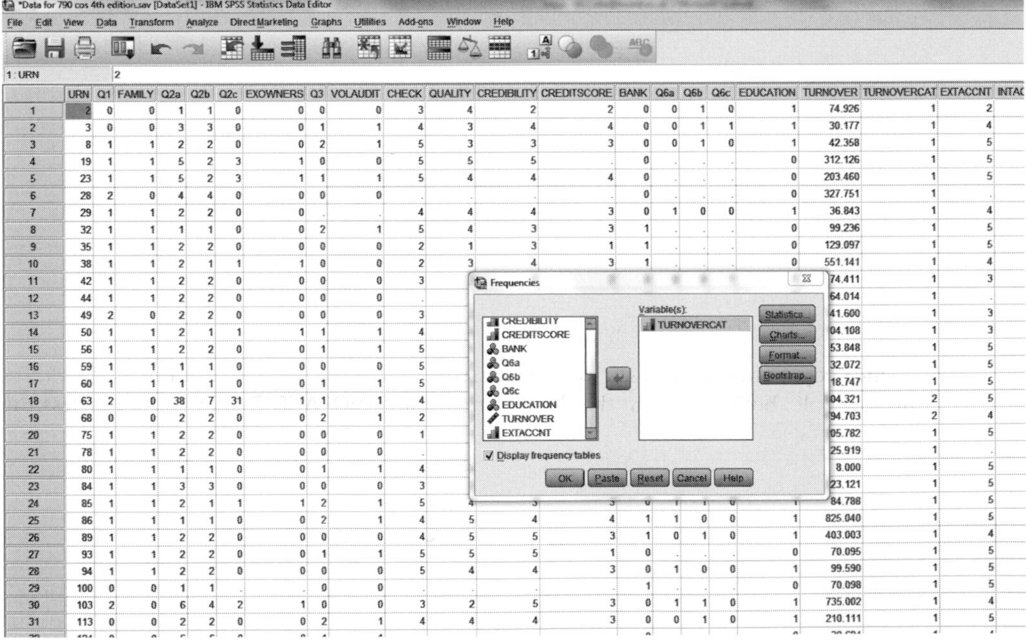

Figure 11.5 Generating a frequency table

Table 11.2 Frequency table for TURNOVERCAT

Statistics

TURNOVERCAT

N	Valid	790
	Missing	0

TURNOVERCAT

		Frequency	Percent	Valid Percent	Cumulative Percent
Valid	1 Under £1m	633	80.1	80.1	80.1
	2 £1m–£1.99m	55	7.0	7.0	87.1
	3 £2m–£2.99m	37	4.7	4.7	91.8
	4 £3m–£3.99m	40	5.1	5.1	96.8
	5 £4m–£4.9m	25	3.2	3.2	100.0
	Total	790	100.0	100.0	

To copy a table from the *SPSS* output file into a *Microsoft Word* document, left click with your mouse on the table to select it, and from the menu at the top of the screen, select Edit then Copy and you will then be able to paste the table into your document. You need to remember that every table should be accompanied by one or more paragraphs of explanation.

Table 11.2 shows the presentation of *univariate* data for a variable containing grouped data, but if you want to analyse data from two such variables, you need to generate a cross-tabulation. We will demonstrate this with the grouped data from the interval variable TURNOVERCAT and the categorical data from the dummy variable VOLAUDIT. You can generate a cross-tabulation for these two variables in *SPSS* using the following procedure:

- From the menu at the top, select Analyze ⇒ Descriptive Statistics... ⇒ Crosstabs and use the arrow button to move VOLAUDIT into Column(s) and TURNOVERCAT into Row(s).
- The default is to show the count of the observations, but it is often more useful to show the percentages. Be wary of showing too much data in a table (generally no more than 20 items of data) as this can detract from the main message. As we have put the dependent variable in the column(s), it makes sense to show the column percentages rather than the row percentages. To do this, select Cells and under Percentages select Column (see Figure 11.6).
- Then click Continue and OK to see the output (see Table 11.3).

Once copied into a *Microsoft Word* document, a table can be edited in the usual way. In this example, both groups in the dependent variable VOLAUDIT follow more or less the same size order. If your data do not conveniently coincide in this way, base the order on the group that contains the larger frequencies and let the other group follow that order.

11.4.4 Generating charts

Charts (and other graphical forms) can also be used to present frequency information. Some people prefer to read summarized information in a chart and detailed information in a table. In both cases, there must also be a written explanation. You need to consider the level at which the variable is measured when choosing the type of chart. If you have

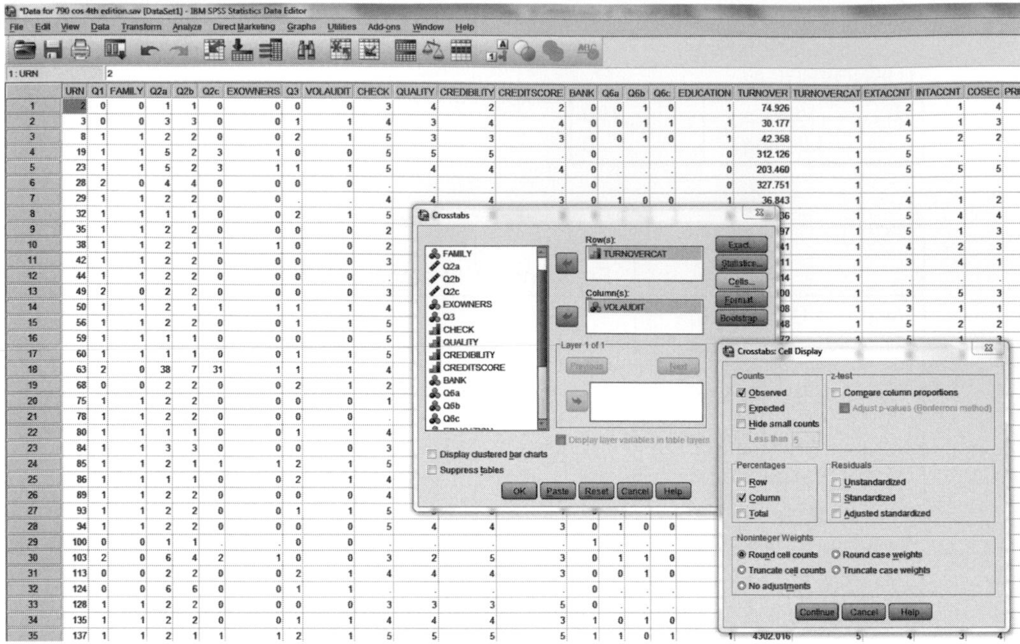

Figure 11.6 Generating a cross-tabulation

Table 11.3 Cross-tabulation for VOLAUDIT and TURNOVERCAT

Case Processing Summary

	Cases					
	Valid		Missing		Total	
	N	Percent	N	Percent	N	Percent
TURNOVERCAT * Volaudit	772	97.7%	18	2.3%	790	100.0%

TURNOVERCAT * VOLAUDIT Crosstabulation

			Volaudit		
			0 Otherwise	1 Yes	Total
Turnovercat	1 Under £1m	Count	406	214	620
		% within VOLAUDIT	92.7%	64.1%	80.3%
	2 £1m–£1.99m	Count	12	42	54
		% within VOLAUDIT	2.7%	12.6%	7.0%
	3 £2m–£2.99m	Count	10	26	36
		% within VOLAUDIT	2.3%	7.8%	4.7%
	4 £3m–£3.99m	Count	5	33	38
		% within VOLAUDIT	1.1%	9.9%	4.9%
	5 £4m–£4.9m	Count	5	19	24
		% within VOLAUDIT	1.1%	5.7%	3.1%
	Total	Count	438	334	772
		% within VOLAUDIT	100.0%	100.0%	100.0%

entered your data into a spreadsheet or into a specialist statistical program, you will find it easy to produce a variety of different charts. Table 11.4 shows how your choice is constrained by the measurement level of the research data.

Table 11.4 Charts for different types of data

Measurement level	Bar chart	Pie chart	Histogram
Nominal	✓	✓	
Ordinal	✓		
Interval			✓
Ratio			✓

The advantages of using a chart are:

- it is a good way to communicate general points
- it is attractive to look at
- it appeals to a more general audience
- it makes it easier to compare data sets
- relationships can be seen more clearly.

The disadvantages of using a chart are:

- it is not a good way to communicate specific details
- it can be misinterpreted
- the design may detract from the message
- designing a non-standard chart can be time-consuming
- it can be designed to be deliberately misleading.

You can create a chart in *SPSS* at the same time as generating a frequency table.

- From the menu, select Analyze ⇒ Descriptive Statistics... ⇒ Frequencies.
- From the list of variables on the left, move TURNOVERCAT into the Variable(s) box on the right and click Charts.
- Under Chart Type, select Bar charts, and under Chart Values, select Percentages and click Continue (see Figure 11.7).
- Click OK to see the output (see Figure 11.8).

Go through the same procedure again, to select a pie chart or a histogram (not surprisingly, *SPSS* does not anticipate that you might want all three, so you can only select one at a time).

In a bar chart, the frequency or percentage frequency for each ordinal or nominal category is displayed in a separate vertical (or horizontal) bar. The frequencies are indicated by the height (or length) of the bars, which permits a visual comparison. In a *component bar chart*, the bars are divided into segments. However, these are not recommended, as the segments lack a common axis or base line, which makes them difficult to interpret visually. The alternative is a *multiple bar chart* in which the segments are adjoined and each starts at the base line. This allows the reader to compare several component parts, but the comparison of the total is lost.

In a pie chart, the percentage frequency for each value or category is displayed as a segment of a circular diagram. Each segment represents an area that is proportional to the whole 'pie'. Figure 11.9 shows a pie chart representing the percentage frequencies for each category in TURNOVERCAT.

A histogram is a refinement of a bar chart, but the adjoining bars touch, indicating that the variable is measured on an interval or ratio scale. If you have data measured on an

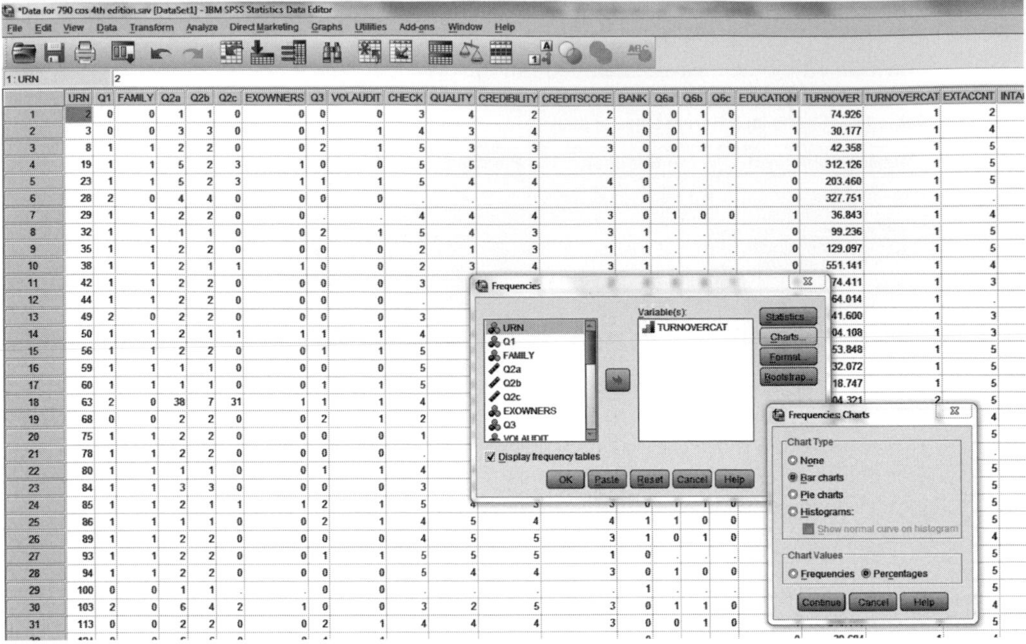

Figure 11.7 Generating a chart

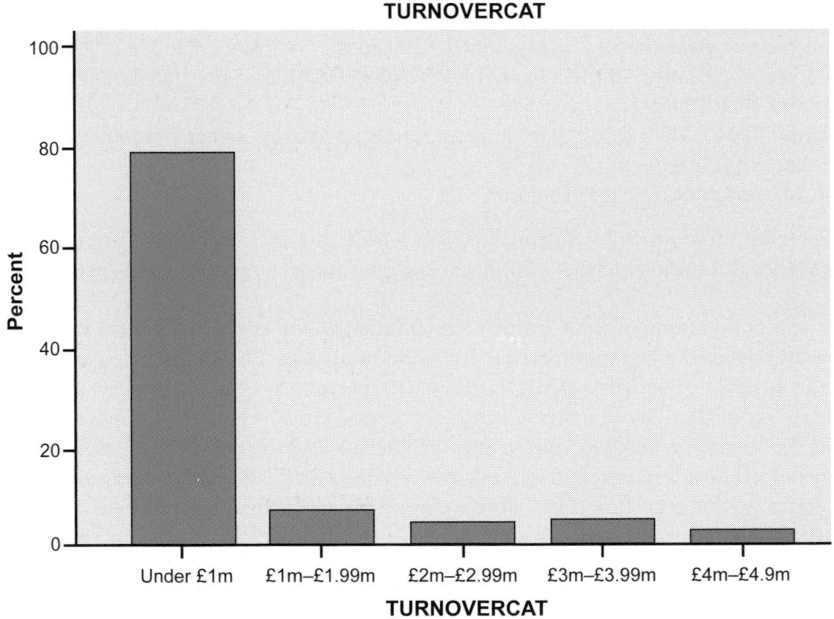

Figure 11.8 Bar chart for TURNOVERCAT

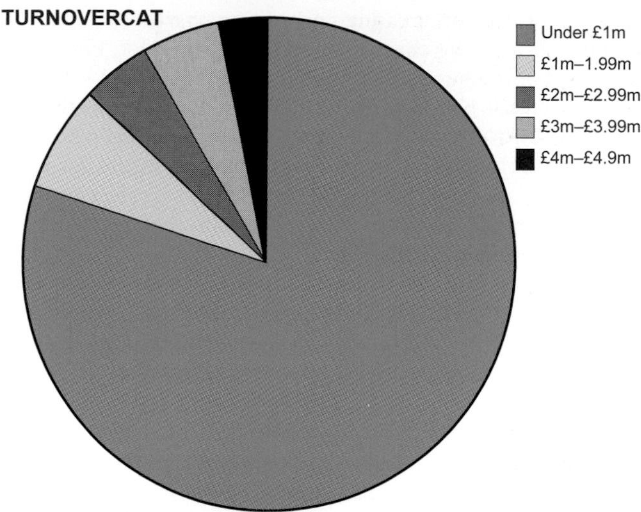

Figure 11.9 Pie chart for TURNOVERCAT

interval scale based on equal intervals, the width of the bars will be constant and the height of each bar will represent the frequency because Area = Width × Height. Thus, a histogram shows the approximate shape of the distribution. We will illustrate this with the original variable TURNOVER, which is measured on a ratio scale and the chart is shown in Figure 11.10.

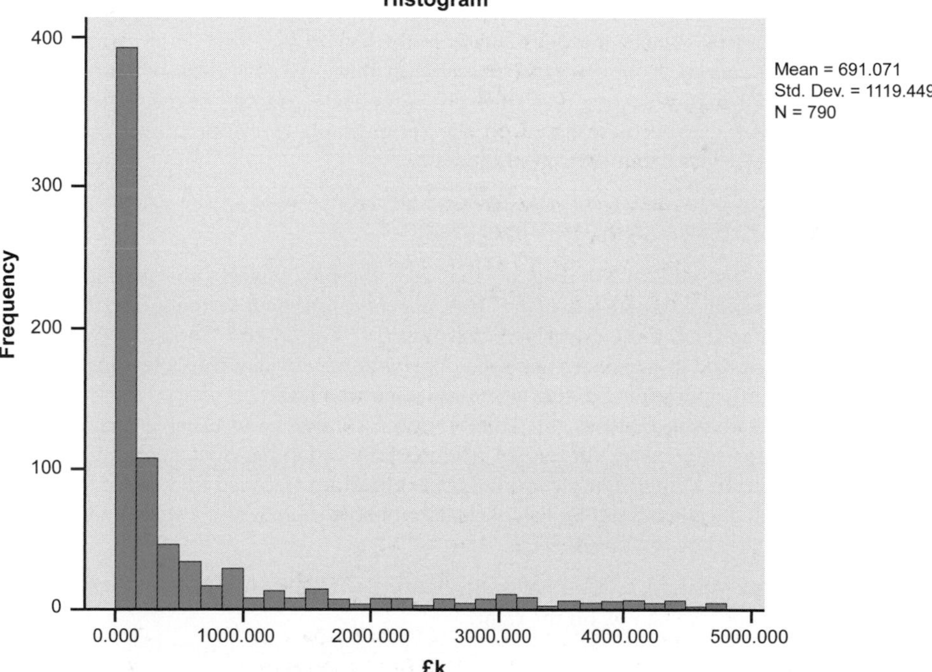

Figure 11.10 Histogram for TURNOVER

We suggest you run the tutorial on creating and editing charts. To amend the appearance of the chart, double click on the chart to open the Chart Editor. For example, in the bar chart and pie chart we have illustrated, it would be useful to add value labels to the segments, but specify 0 decimal places to reduce unwanted 'noise' in the communication. In the histogram for TURNOVER, you might want to use a scaling factor of 1,000, which would allow you to label the values in millions as shown in the bar and pie charts for TURNOVERCAT. For future reference, note that the histogram can also show the distribution curve, and the default is to show some descriptive statistics that summarize the data. We will examine these in the next section.

To copy a chart from the *SPSS* output file into a *Microsoft Word* document, left click with your mouse on the chart to select it, and from the menu at the top of the screen, select Edit then Copy and you will then be able to paste the table into your document. You need to remember that every chart should be accompanied by one or more paragraphs of explanation.

The Chart Editor allows you to generate a line graph to present continuous data (such as TURNOVER) across a number of categories. It is not appropriate to use a line graph to represent discrete data, such as number of employees. This is because you can represent turnover as a line by dividing it into fractional denominations (such as £1.01, £1.02, £1.03 and so on) but you cannot have 1.1, 1.2 or 1.3 employees. Line graphs are often used to present data collected at different points in time. For example, if you have turnover data for the past five years, you could use a line graph to illustrate any volatility, stability or trend over the period and compare companies with external shareholders with those that are owner-managed. The frequencies are always shown on the vertical axis (the Y axis) and data values for the categories on the horizontal axis (the X axis). In this example, TURNOVER would be shown on the Y axis (in £k or £m) and the years would be shown along the X axis. You might want to use EXOWNERS as the variable to distinguish the lines. If you did this, the two groups in EXOWNERS would be described as 'External owners' and 'Otherwise' in the legend.

You can see from this brief description that one advantage of line graphs over other charts is that, providing they share the same scale and unit of measurement, a number of variables can be represented on the same graph (a multiple line graph). This greatly facilitates visual comparison of the data.

11.4.5 Generating a stem-and-leaf plot

A stem-and-leaf plot is a diagram that uses the data values (observations) in a frequency distribution to create a display. Thus, it 'retains all the information in the data, while also giving an idea of the underlying distribution' (Upton and Cook, 2006, p. 409). The data are arranged in size order and each observation is divided into a leading digit to represent the stem, and trailing digits, which represent the leaf.

The diagram presents the data in a more compact and useable form, which highlights any gaps and *outliers*. An outlier is an extreme value that does not conform to the general pattern. In a small sample, outliers are important because they can distort the results of the statistical analysis. We will demonstrate how to generate a stem-and-leaf plot in *SPSS* using the data for TURNOVER.

- Select Analyze ⇒ Descriptive Statistics… ⇒ Explore and move TURNOVER into the Dependent List box on the right.
- From the buttons on the right-hand side, select Plots. Under Descriptive, the default is Stem-and-leaf, so click Continue (see Figure 11.11).
- Then click OK for the results (see Box 11.4).

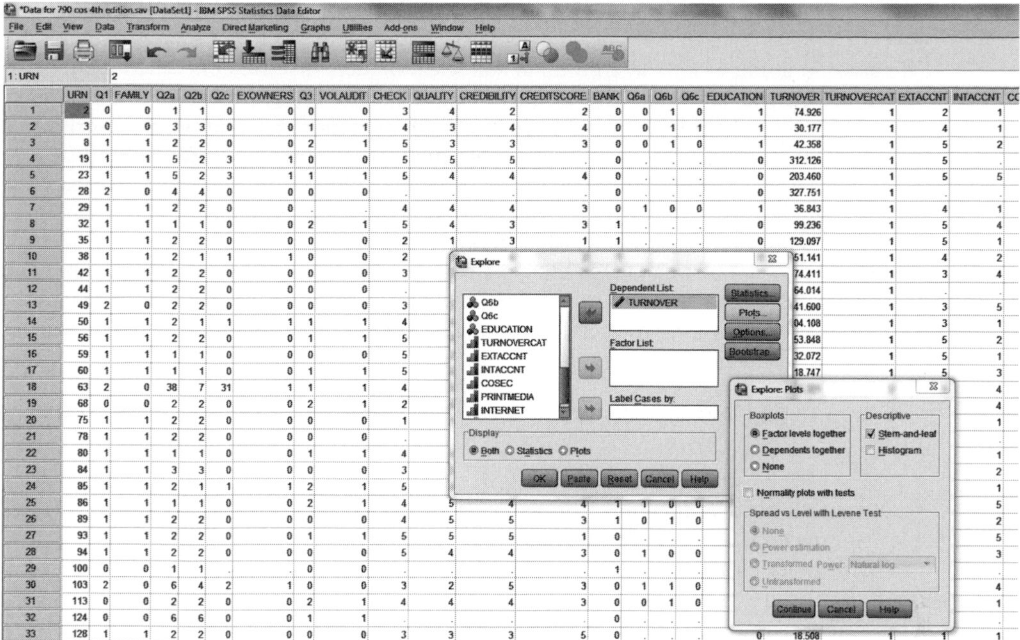

Figure 11.11 Generating a stem-and-leaf plot

Box 11.4 Stem-and-leaf plot for TURNOVER

```
£k Stem-and-Leaf Plot
 Frequency    Stem &  Leaf
   321.00       0 .  00000000000001111111111222222222222333333
4444444445555555566666667777777788888999999
   104.00       1 .  0001111122223334555678889
    65.00       2 .  001223344567899
    39.00       3 .  012345678&
    25.00       4 .  2578&&
    18.00       5 .  157&&
    18.00       6 .  02&&&
     6.00       7 .  &
    18.00       8 .  1245&
    19.00       9 .  1&&&&
     5.00      10 .  &
     5.00      11 .  &
     8.00      12 .  &&
     9.00      13 .  8&
     2.00      14 .  &
     6.00      15 .  &
    11.00      16 .  1&
     3.00      17 .  &
   108.00 Extremes    (>=1795)

 Stem width: 100.000
 Each leaf: 4 case(s)

 & denotes fractional leaves.
```

11.5 Measuring central tendency

We are now going to look at a group of statistical models that are concerned with measuring the central tendency of a frequency distribution. Measures of central tendency provide a convenient way of summarizing a large frequency distribution by describing it with a single statistic. The three measures are the mean, the median and the mode.

11.5.1 The mean

The **mean** is a measure of central tendency based on the arithmetic average of a set of data values.

The **mean** ($\bar{x}$) is the arithmetic average of a set of data in a sample and can only be calculated for ratio or interval variables. It is found by dividing the sum of the observations by the number of observations, as shown in the following formula:

$$\text{Mean} = \frac{\Sigma x}{n}$$

where

x = each observation
n = the total number of observations
Σ = the sum of

Example
A student's exam marks were as follows:

Module 1	*Module 2*	*Module 3*	*Module 4*	*Module 5*	*Module 6*
82%	78%	80%	64%	70%	64%

Inserting the data into the formula:

$$\frac{82 + 78 + 80 + 64 + 70 + 64}{6} = \frac{438}{6} = 73\%$$

The advantages of the mean are:

- it can be calculated exactly
- it takes account of all the data
- it can be used as the basis of other statistical models.

The disadvantages of the mean are:

- it is greatly affected by outliers (extreme values that are very high or very low)
- it is a hypothetical value and may not be one of the actual values
- it can give an impossible figure for discrete data (for example the average number of owners in the sample of small companies was 5.8)
- it cannot be calculated for ordinal or nominal data.

11.5.2 The median

The **median** is a measure of central tendency based on the mid-value of a set of data values arranged in size order.

The **median** (M) is the mid-value of a set of data that has been arranged in size order (in other words, it has been ranked). It can be calculated for variables measured on a ratio, interval or ordinal scale and is found by adding 1 to the number of observations and dividing by 2. The formula is:

$$\text{Median} = \frac{n + 1}{2}$$

where

n = number of observations

This is very straightforward if you have an even number of observations because the formula will take you directly to the observation at the mid-point. The following example shows what you need to do if you have an uneven number of observations.

Example

The student's exam marks in chronological order were:

Module 1	*Module 2*	*Module 3*	*Module 4*	*Module 5*	*Module 6*
82%	78%	80%	64%	70%	64%

The marks arranged in size order are:

64%	64%	70%	78%	80%	82%

Inserting the data into the formula:

$$\frac{6 + 1}{2} = 3.5$$

Therefore, the median is half-way between the third and the fourth of the ranked marks. A simple calculation will tell us the exact value:

$$\frac{70 + 78}{2} = 74\%$$

The advantages of the median are:

- it is not affected by outliers or open-ended values at the extremities
- it is not affected by unequal class intervals
- it can represent an actual value in the data.

The disadvantages of the median are:

- it cannot be measured precisely for distributions reflecting grouped data
- it cannot be used as the basis for other statistical models
- it may not be useful if the data set does not have normal distribution (we will be looking at this in section 11.7)
- it cannot be calculated for nominal data.

11.5.3 The mode

The **mode** is a measure of central tendency based on the most frequently occurring value in a set of data (there may be multiple modes).

The **mode** (m) is the most frequently occurring value in a data set and can be used for all variables, irrespective of the measurement scale.

Example

The student's exam marks were:

Module 1	*Module 2*	*Module 3*	*Module 4*	*Module 5*	*Module 6*
82%	78%	80%	64%	70%	64%

The mode is 64%.

The advantages of the mode are:

- it is not affected by outliers
- it is easy to identify in a small data set
- it can be calculated for any variable, irrespective of the measurement scale.

The disadvantages of the mode are:

- it is a dynamic measure that can change as other values are added
- it cannot be measured precisely for distributions reflecting grouped data
- there may be multiple modes
- it cannot be used as the basis for other statistical models.

One of the things you will have noticed from the analysis in this section is that the mean, the median and the mode each use a different definition of central tendency. Our analysis of the student's marks has produced a different result under each method. The reason for this will become apparent when we look at the importance of examining the spread of data values in section 11.6.

11.5.4 Generating measures of central tendency

With a large data set, you will need some help in calculating measures of central tendency, but *SPSS* allows you to do this at the same time as generating frequency distributions in tables and/or charts. The procedure is as follows:

- From the menu, select Analyze ⇒ Descriptive Statistics… ⇒ Frequencies.
- We will use the original ratio, so move TURNOVER into the Variable(s) box on the right. If you also wanted to generate descriptive statistics for other variables, you would simply move them into the box on the right at this point.
- Now click on Statistics and under Central Tendency, select Mean, Median and Mode and click Continue (see Figure 11.12).
- Then click OK to see the results table (see Table 11.5).

Table 11.5 Measures of central tendency for TURNOVER

TURNOVER

N	Valid	790
	Missing	0
Mean		691.07062
Median		158.06450
Mode		8.000

Interpreting the results, you can see that despite being called measures of central tendency, the 'centre' differs for each statistic. The reasons for this will become apparent in the next section. For the time being, we can simply say that the different results arise from the different definitions we used for each measure.

Before moving on to the next subject, we are going to demonstrate the importance of retaining the detailed data in the original variable TURNOVER by comparing the precise mean we have obtained for that variable with the mean we can calculate for the five classes of grouped data in TURNOVERCAT. To determine the mean for grouped data, we

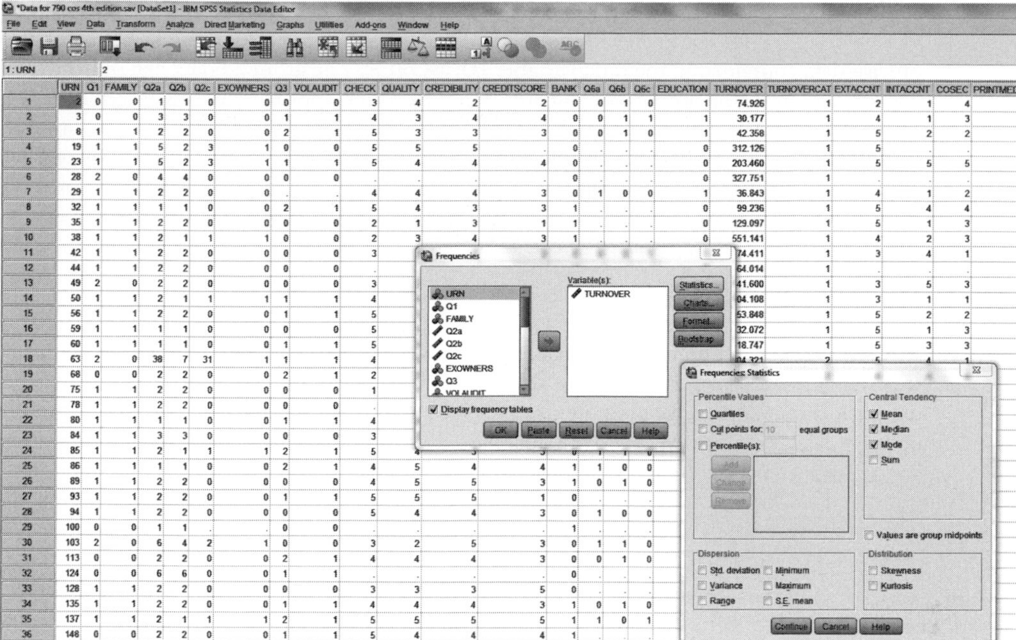

Figure 11.12 Generating measures of central tendency

need to take the mid-points of each class and multiply by the frequency, as shown in the following formula:

$$\text{Mean for grouped data} = \frac{\Sigma fx}{\Sigma f}$$

where

f = the frequency
x = each observation
Σ = the sum of

The calculations are as follows:

Turnover	*Frequency*	*Mid-point*	
	(f)	*(x)*	*(fx)*
Under £1m	633	0.5	316.5
£1m–£1.99m	55	1.5	82.5
£2m–£2.99m	37	2.5	92.5
£3m–£3.99m	40	3.5	140.0
£4m–£4.9m	25	4.5	112.5
Total	790		744.0

We can now substitute the figures we have calculated in the formula:

$$\frac{744}{790} = 0.94$$

The results shows that the mean for the grouped data in the interval variable TURNOVERCAT is £0.94m compared to the mean of £0.69m that we calculated earlier using the precise data contained in the ratio variable TURNOVER. The grouped data can only give an approximation of this important statistic. Moreover, this approximation is larger than the actual mean because it is based on the median in each category rather than every data value (observation). This helps demonstrate the superiority of ratio data over interval or ordinal data when it comes to measuring the mean, which lies at the heart of the most powerful statistical models used in inferential statistics. We will discuss this further in Chapter 12.

11.6 Measuring dispersion

Measures of central tendency are useful for providing statistics that summarize the location of the 'middle' of the data, but they do not tell us anything about the spread of the data values. Therefore, we are now going to look at measures of dispersion, which should only be calculated for variables measured on a ratio or interval scale. The two measures are the range and the standard deviation.

11.6.1 Range

The **range** is a measure of dispersion that represents the difference between the maximum value and the minimum value in a frequency distribution arranged in size order.

The **interquartile range** is a measure of dispersion that represents the difference between the upper quartile and the lower quartile (the middle 50%) of a frequency distribution arranged in size order.

The **range** is a simple measure of dispersion that describes the difference between the maximum value (the upper extreme or E_U) and the minimum value (the lower extreme or E_L) in a frequency distribution arranged in size order. You will remember from the previous section that the median is the mid-point, but in a large set of data (say, 30 observations or more) it can be useful to divide the frequency distribution into quartiles, each containing 25% of the data values. This allows us to measure the **interquartile range**, which is the difference between the upper quartile (Q_3) and the lower quartile (Q_1), and the spread of the middle 50% of the data values. When comparing two distributions, the interquartile range is often preferred to the range, because the latter is more easily affected by outliers (extreme values). The formulae are:

$$\text{Range} = E_U - E_L$$
$$\text{Interquartile range} = Q_3 - Q_1$$

Example

Inserting the data for Turnover (£k) into the formulae:

$$\text{Range} = 4{,}738.271 - 0.054 = 4{,}738.217$$
$$\text{Interquartile range} = 742.76625 - 52.74525 = 690.021$$

Unfortunately, the drawback of using the range is that it only takes account of two items of data and the drawback of the interquartile range is that it only takes account of half the values. What we really want is a measure of dispersion that will take account of all the values and we discuss such an alternative next.

11.6.2 Standard deviation

The **standard deviation** (sd) should only be calculated for ratio or interval variables, but it overcomes the deficiencies of the range and the interquartile range discussed in the

The **standard deviation** is the square root of the variance. A large standard deviation relative to the mean suggests the mean does not represent the data well.

The **error** is the difference between the mean and the data value (observation).

The **variance** is the mean of the squared errors.

previous section by using all the data. The standard deviation is related to the normal distribution, which we explain in the next section. The term 'standard deviation' was introduced by Karl Pearson in 1893 (Upton and Cook, 2006). It is based on the **error** and the **variance**, which are two statistical models used to measure how well the mean represents the data (Field, 2000).

In this context, the error is the difference between the mean and the data value (the observation). It is called an error because it measures the deviation of the observation from the mean (which is a hypothetical value that summarizes the data). We then add up the errors and make some adjustments. These are necessary because the difference between the mean and each value below the mean produces a negative figure while the difference between the mean and each value above the mean produces a positive figure. Unfortunately, when these are added together, the answer is zero. To resolve this problem, the errors are squared (in mathematics, squaring a positive or a negative number always produces a positive figure).

This allows us to calculate the variance, which is the mean of the squared errors. However, this is very difficult to interpret because it is measured in squared units (for example our turnover data would be in square £). To de-square the units, we calculate the square root of the variance. This gives us the standard deviation, which we can now define as the square root of the variance. A small standard deviation relative to the mean suggests the mean represents the data well; conversely, a large standard deviation relative to the mean, suggests the mean does not represent the data well because the data values are widely dispersed.

In case you only have a small data set and want to calculate the standard deviation unaided, the formula for individual data is:

$$\text{sd} = \sqrt{\frac{\Sigma(x - \bar{x})^2}{n}}$$

where

x = an observation
$\bar{x}$ = the mean
n = the total number of observations
√ = the square root
Σ = the sum of

The formula for grouped data is:

$$\text{sd} = \sqrt{\frac{\Sigma x^2 f}{\Sigma f} - \frac{(\Sigma xf)^2}{\Sigma f}}$$

where

x = the mid-point of each data class
f = the frequency of each class
√ = the square root
Σ = the sum of

The advantages of the standard deviation are:

- it uses every value
- it is in the same units as the original data
- it is easy to interpret.

The disadvantages are:

- the calculations are complex without the aid of suitable software
- it can only be used for variables measured on a ratio or interval scale.

The **standard error** is the standard deviation between the means of different samples. A large standard error relative to the overall sample mean suggests the sample might not be representative of the population.

The final term we are going to introduce is the **standard error** (se), which is calculated by 'taking the difference between each sample mean and the overall mean, squaring the differences, adding them up and dividing by the number of samples' (Field, 2000, p. 9). A small standard error relative to the overall sample mean suggests the sample is representative of the population, whereas a large standard error relative to the overall sample mean suggests the sample might not be representative of the population.

11.6.3 Generating measures of dispersion

By now you will have realized that *SPSS* allows you to generate frequency tables, measures of central tendency and measures of dispersion for one or more variables in a single set of instructions under the Analyze ⇒ Descriptive Statistics menu. We will now show you how to add the measures of dispersion we have been discussing:

- From the menu, select Analyze ⇒ Descriptive Statistics... ⇒ Frequencies and move TURNOVER into the Variable(s) box on the right. If you also wanted to generate frequency tables for other variables, you would simply move them into the box on the right at this point.
- Deselect the default to display frequency tables, as you already have them.
- Now click on Statistics and deselect any options under Central Tendency, as you have them already. Under Percentile Values, select Quartiles and under Dispersion click all the options and then click Continue (see Figure 11.13).
- Click OK to see the output (see Table 11.6).

Table 11.6 Measures of dispersion for TURNOVER

Statistics

TURNOVER

N	Valid	790
	Missing	0
Std. Error of Mean		39.828205
Std. Deviation		1119.448910
Variance		1253165.862
Range		4738.217
Minimum		.054
Maximum		4738.271
Percentiles	25	52.74525
	50	158.06450
	75	742.76625

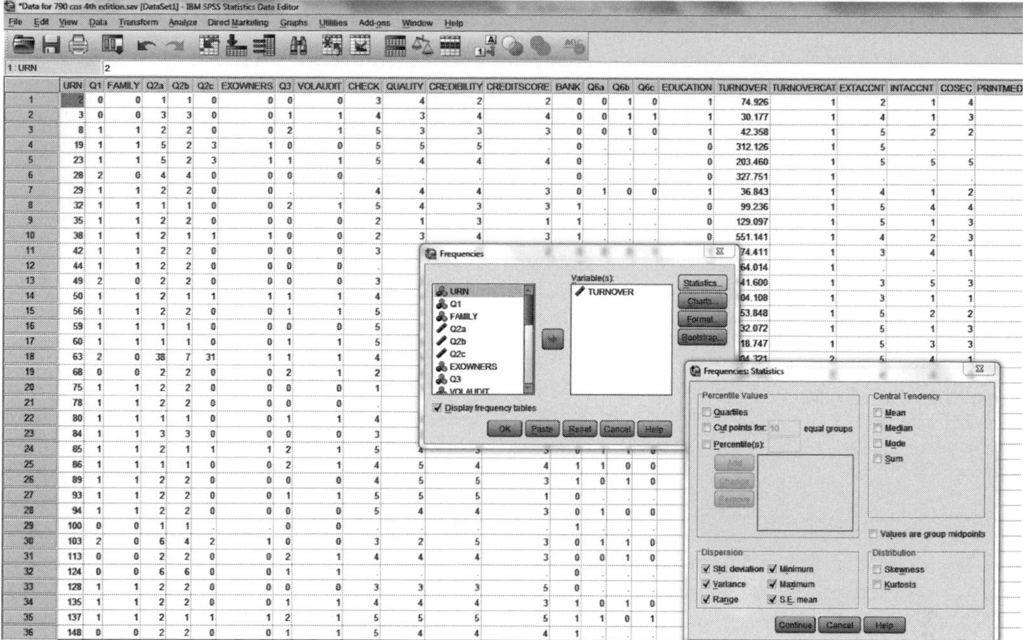

Figure 11.13 Generating measures of dispersion

11.7 Normal distribution

A **normal distribution** is a theoretical frequency distribution that is bell-shaped and symmetrical, with tails extending indefinitely either side of the centre. The mean, median and mode coincide at the centre.

We mentioned in the previous section that the standard deviation is related to the **normal distribution**. This term was introduced in the late 19th century by Sir Francis Galton, cousin of Charles Darwin who published *The Origin of Species* in 1859 (Upton and Cook, 2006), and refers to a theoretical frequency distribution that is bell-shaped and symmetrical, with tails extending indefinitely either side of the centre. In a normal distribution, the mean, the median and the mode coincide at the centre (see Figure 11.14). It is described as a theoretical frequency distribution because it is a mathematical model representing perfect symmetry, against which empirical data can be compared.

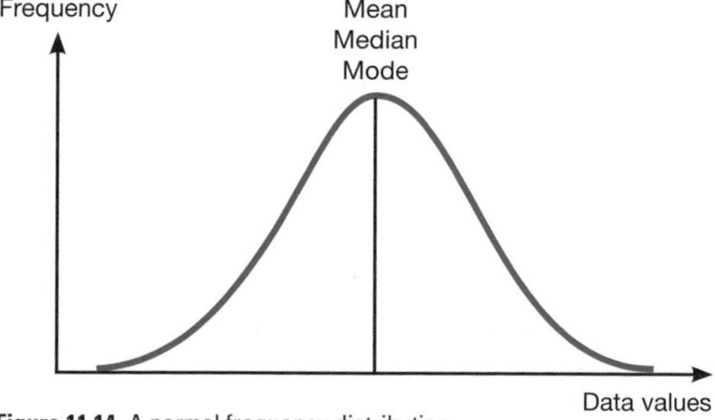

Figure 11.14 A normal frequency distribution

11.7.1 Skewness and kurtosis

When the frequency distribution does not have a symmetrical distribution, it is described as skewed. Thus, **skewness** is a measure of the extent to which a frequency distribution is asymmetric. In a skewed distribution, the mean, the median and the mode have different values. Indeed, we found that the mean turnover for the sample companies was £691,071, the median was £158,045 and the mode was £8,000. The skewness of a normal distribution is 0 (the distribution is symmetrical). When a distribution has a positive skewness value, the tail is on the right (the positive side of the centre) and most of the observations are at the lower end of the range (see Figure 11.15). When the distribution has a negative skewness value, the tail is on the left (the negative side of the centre) and most of the observations are at the upper end of the range (see Figure 11.16). A skewness value that is more than twice the standard error of the skewness suggests the distribution is not symmetrical.

Skewness is a measure of the extent to which a frequency distribution is asymmetric (a normal distribution has a skewness of 0).

Kurtosis is a measure of the extent to which a frequency distribution is flatter or more peaked than a normal distribution (a normal distribution has a kurtosis of 0).

A second important measure is **kurtosis**, which measures the extent to which a frequency distribution is flatter or more peaked than a normal distribution (Upton and Cook, 2006). The kurtosis value of a normal distribution is 0, which indicates the bell-shaped distribution with most of the observations clustered in the centre. A distribution with positive kurtosis is more peaked than a normal distribution because it has more observations in the centre and longer tails on either side. A distribution with negative kurtosis is flatter than a normal distribution because there are fewer observations in the centre and the tails on either side are shorter.

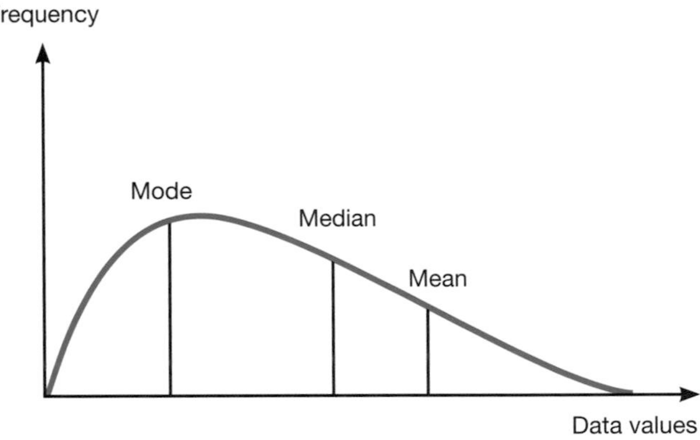

Figure 11.15 A positively skewed frequency distribution

Both the mean and the standard deviation are related to the normal distribution. While the mean represents the centre of the frequency distribution, the standard deviation measures the spread or dispersion of the data values around the mean. If the data set has a normal distribution, 68% of the data values will be within 1 standard deviation of the mean, 95% will fall within 2 standard deviations of the mean and 99.7% will fall within 3 standard deviations of the mean. This is illustrated in Figure 11.17.

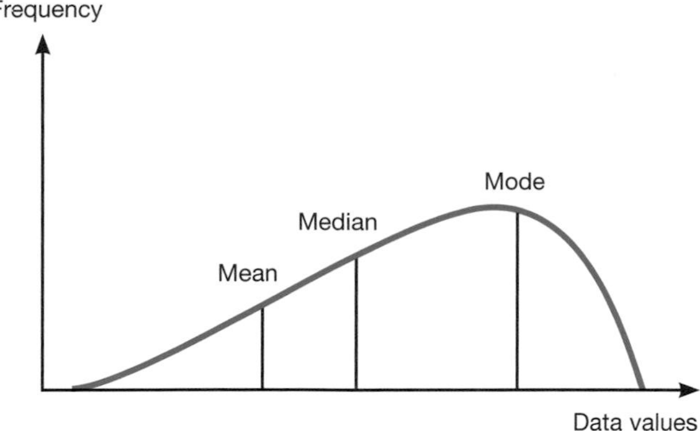

Figure 11.16 A negatively skewed frequency distribution

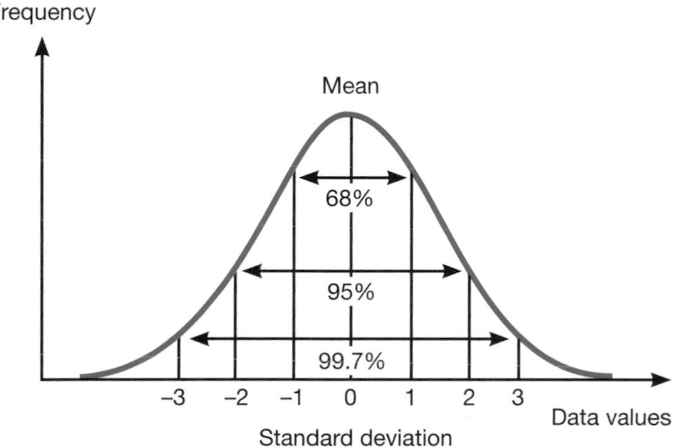

Figure 11.17 Proportion of a normal distribution under 1 standard deviation

11.7.2 Testing for normality

Although you can obtain measures of skewness and kurtosis under the Frequencies menu we have been using so far, if you want to run normality tests at the same time, you need to use the Explore menu. The procedure is as follows:

- Select Analyze ⇒ Descriptive Statistics... ⇒ Explore and move TURNOVER into the Variable(s) box on the right.
- The default is for both statistics and plots. Under Statistics, accept the default of Descriptives. However, under Plots, deselect the default Stem-and-leaf (you have this already), and select Normality plots with tests; then click Continue (see Figure 11.18).
- Click OK for the output (see Table 11.7).

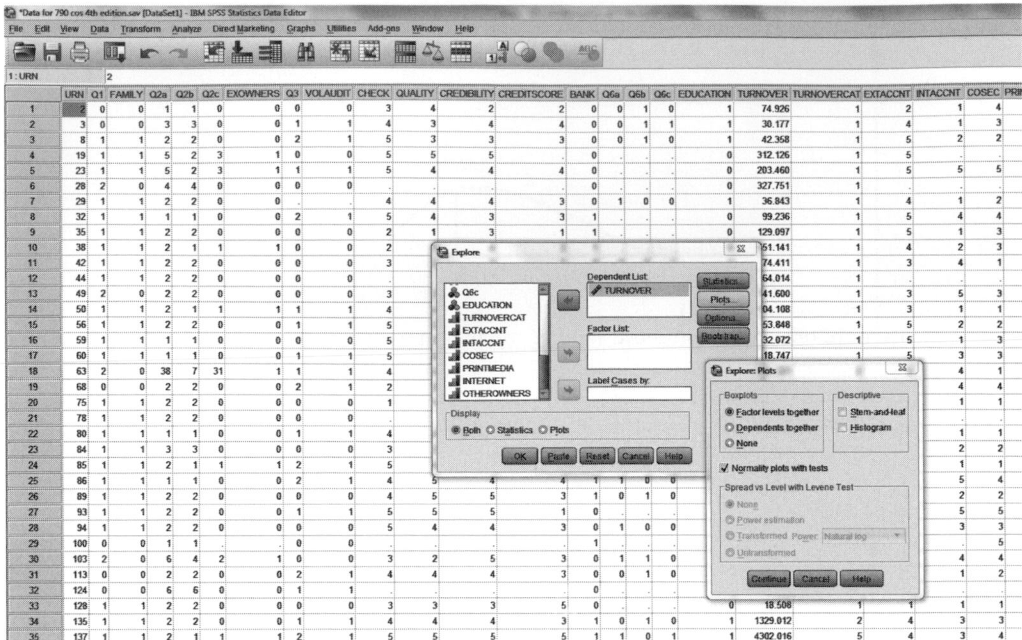

Figure 11.18 Generating descriptive statistics and testing for normality

Table 11.7 Descriptive statistics and normality tests for TURNOVER

Case Processing Summary

	Cases					
	Valid		Missing		Total	
	N	Percent	N	Percent	N	Percent
TURNOVER	790	100.0%	0	.0%	790	100.0%

Descriptives

			Statistic	Std. Error
TURNOVER	Mean		691.07062	39.828205
	95% Confidence Interval for Mean	Lower Bound	612.88884	
		Upper Bound	769.25240	
	5% Trimmed Mean		537.33076	
	Median		158.06450	
	Variance		1253165.862	
	Std. Deviation		1119.448910	
	Minimum		.054	
	Maximum		4738.271	
	Range		4738.217	
	Interquartile Range		690.021	
	Skewness		2.042	.087
	Kurtosis		3.170	.174

Tests of Normality

	Kolmogorov-Smirnov[a]			Shapiro-Wilk		
	Statistic	df	Sig.	Statistic	df	Sig.
TURNOVER	.276	790	.000	.643	790	.000

a. Lilliefors Significance Correction

The results confirm what we could see from the general shape of the data in the histogram and from the measures of central tendency: TURNOVER does not have a normal distribution. The positive value for skewness confirms the spread of the data is skewed with more observations on the right of the mean; the positive value for kurtosis indicates a more peaked distribution than expected in a normal distribution with a higher degree of clustering of observations around the mean and longer tail(s).

The normality tests compare the actual frequency distribution of the sample (the actual value) with a theoretical normal distribution (the expected value) with the same mean and standard deviation (Field, 2000). If the actual value is too far from the expected value, the test result is significant and this evidence leads us to reject the null hypothesis. Conversely, if the actual value is close to the expected value, the test result is not significant, and we do not have evidence to reject the null hypothesis. There are two cases when a test result leads to a correct result (Upton and Cook, 2006):

- H_0 is true and the test leads to acceptance of the null hypothesis
- H_1 is true and the test leads to the rejection of the null hypothesis.

However, there are also two cases when a test leads to an incorrect result (an error):

- H_0 is true, but the test leads to rejection of the null hypothesis (referred to as a **Type 1 error**).
- H_1 is true, but the test leads to the acceptance of the null hypothesis (referred to as a **Type II error**).

A **Type I** error occurs when H_0 is true, but the test leads to its rejection.

A **Type II** error occurs when H_1 is true, but the test leads to the acceptance of H_0.

The **significance level** is the level of confidence that the results of a statistical analysis are not due to chance. It is usually expressed as the probability that the results of the statistical analysis are due to chance (usually 5% or less).

Therefore, we need to specify the size of the critical region that determines whether the test result is significant by setting the **significance level**. If you are conducting research into issues relating to health or safety you would want this critical region to be less than 1%, but in most business and management research, a significance level of 0.05 is usually acceptable. This means that we would accept a 5% probability of a Type I or II error. This is reflected in *SPSS*, where the default significance level is 0.05. Therefore, you will interpret the result of a test as being significant if the significance statistic (Sig.) is ≤ 0.05. In some tests the significance statistic is referred to as a probability statistic (p) you will interpret the result of a test as being significant if $p \leq 0.05$.

Looking at the tests of normality in the second part of Table 11.7, you can see the results are significant (the value under Sig. is ≤ 0.05). This means we can reject the null hypothesis and we accept that the frequency distribution for TURNOVER differs significantly from a normal distribution. If a result showed $p > 0.05$, it would indicate that the size of the deviation from normality in the sample was not large enough to be significant. In this case, a significant result is not surprising, since small and medium-sized businesses account for 99.9% of all enterprises in the UK (BIS, 2012, p. 1), thus size is positively skewed in the population. When you have finished, save your files and exit from *SPSS*.

It may surprise you that the output files from *SPSS* often contain a large amount of information. This is because the program provides the entire analysis to allow you to make a full interpretation of the results. Your next task is to decide how to summarize all your results. You will have seen many examples of how researchers do this when reviewing previous studies for your literature review. Tables 11.8 and 11.9 show examples of tables that are suitable for summarizing descriptive statistics for continuous and categorical variables respectively.

Table 11.8 Descriptive statistics for continuous variable

Variable	N	Min	Max	Median	Mode	Mean	Std dev	Skewness		Kurtosis	
								Statistic	Std error	Statistic	Std error
TURNOVER	790	.054	4738.271	158.0645	8.000	691.07062	1119.44891	2.042	.087	3.170	.174

Table 11.9 Frequency distributions for categorical variables

Variable	N	Number coded 5	Number coded 4	Number coded 3	Number coded 2	Number coded 1	Number coded 0
CHECK	697	348	166	103	40	40	-
QUALITY	687	197	142	158	95	95	-
CREDIBILITY	688	300	182	126	40	40	-
CREDITSCORE	681	206	158	183	63	71	-
FAMILY	790	-	-	-	-	537	253
EXOWNERS	785	-	-	-	-	127	658
BANK	722	-	-	-	-	400	322
EDUCATION	790	-	-	-	-	553	237

11.8 Conclusions

In this chapter, we have demonstrated how to conduct a typical exploratory analysis of research data, how to generate tables, charts and other graphical forms, and how to summarize data using descriptive statistics. All students designing a study that includes the analysis of quantitative data need this knowledge to explore your data and decide how to summarize appropriate descriptive statistics. It does not matter whether you use *IBM® SPSS® Statistics software (SPSS)* or another software program to which you have access. If you have a relatively small data set, you could enter it into a *Microsoft Excel* spreadsheet, which also has facilities for generating statistics and charts. Although it is possible to calculate percentage frequencies, measures of central tendency and dispersion using a calculator, when time and accuracy are at a premium you will find it invaluable to learn how to use the statistical package at your disposal. These are transferable skills that will enhance your employability.

Table 11.10 summarizes the descriptive statistics we have examined in this chapter and helps you select those that are appropriate for the measurement level of your variables.

In addition to time constraints and your skills, your choice of statistics will depend on research questions, which may require the use of inferential statistics in addition to the descriptive statistics we have explained in this chapter. We discuss inferential statistics in the next chapter, but if these are not required for your study, you may find the checklist in Box 11.5 helps ensure the successful completion of your analysis.

Table 11.10 Choosing appropriate descriptive statistics

Exploratory analysis	Measurement level
Frequency distribution	
Percentage frequency	Ratio, interval, ordinal, nominal
Measures of central tendency	
Mean	Ratio, interval
Median	Ratio, interval, ordinal
Mode	Ratio, interval, ordinal, nominal
Measures of dispersion	
Range	Ratio, interval
Standard deviation	Ratio, interval
Measures of normality	
Skewness	Ratio, interval
Kurtosis	Ratio, interval

Box 11.5 Checklist for conducting quantitative data analysis

1 Are you confident that your research design was sound?
2 Have you been systematic and rigorous in the collection of your data?
3 Is your identification of variables adequate?
4 Are your measurements of the variables reliable?
5 Is the analysis suitable for the measurement scale (nominal, ordinal, interval or ratio)?

References

BIS (2012) *Statistical Release,* URN12/92, 17 October. [Online]. Available at: http://www.bis.gov.uk/analysis/statistics/business-population-estimates (Accessed 20 February 2013).

Collis, J. (2003) *Directors' Views on Exemption from Statutory Audit,* URN 03/1342, October, London: DTI. [Online]. Available at: http://www.berr.gov.uk/files/file25971.pdf (Accessed 20 February 2013).

Field, A. (2000) *Discovering Statistics Using SPSS for Windows.* London: SAGE.

Jensen, M. C. and Meckling, W. H. (1976) 'Theory of the firm: Managerial behavior, agency costs and the ownership structure', *Journal of Financial Economics,* 3, pp. 305–60.

Kervin, J. B. (1992) *Methods for Business Research.* New York: HarperCollins.

Lovie, P. (1986) 'Identifying Outliers', in Lovie, A. D. (ed.) *New Developments in Statistics for Psychology and the Social Sciences* 1. London: Methuen.

Moore, D., McCabe, G. P., Duckworth, W. M. and Alwan, L. C. (2009) *The Practice of Business Statistics,* 2nd edn. New York: W.H. Freeman and Company.

Upton, G. and Cook, I. (2006) *Oxford Dictionary of Statistics,* 2nd edn. Oxford: Oxford University Press.

Activities

This chapter is entirely activity-based. If you have access to *SPSS*, start at the beginning of the chapter and work your way through. If *SPSS* is not available, do the same activities using an alternative software package following the on-screen tutorials and help facilities.

Visit the companion website to try the progress test and for access to the data file referred to in this chapter at www.palgrave.com/business/collis/br4/

Have a look at the Troubleshooting chapter and sections 14.2, 14.5, 14.7, 14.10, 14.12, 14.13 in particular, which relate specifically to this chapter.

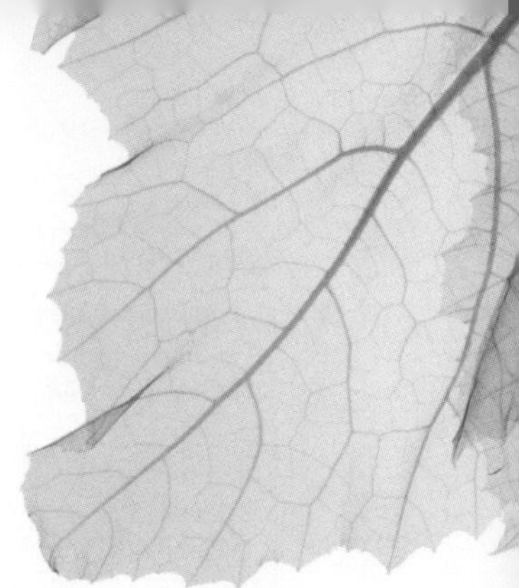

12

analysing data using inferential statistics

learning objectives

When you have studied this chapter, you should be able to:

- determine whether parametric or non-parametric methods are appropriate
- conduct tests of difference for independent or dependent samples
- conduct tests of association between variables
- conduct a factor analysis
- predict an outcome from one or more variables
- use time series analysis to examine trends.

12.1 Introduction

The descriptive statistics covered in the previous chapter lie at the heart of a univariate analysis of research data and allow you to examine frequency distributions and measure the central tendency and dispersion of the data. At the postgraduate or doctoral level, this will merely form the exploratory stage of your research and you will need to go on to conduct a further analysis based on inferential statistics.

We start this chapter by explaining the importance of planning your analysis. This involves examining your hypotheses and identifying the variables to be included in the analysis. You will also need to consider the underlying characteristics of your research data and decide whether parametric or non-parametric statistical tests are appropriate. We then go on to explain how to generate inferential statistics based on some of the main bivariate and multivariate methods of analysis. As in the last chapter, we will provide step-by-step instructions using *IBM® SPSS® Statistics software v20 (SPSS)* and use the data from Collis (2003) as our main example. For students conducting a longitudinal study, we devote a section to preparing longitudinal data for a time series analysis, which is used for forecasting trends.

Our intention is to provide a practical guide and provide sufficient theoretical content to help you gain a basic understanding of the most widely used methods. It is important to remember that we are only looking at a selection of the analytical techniques available and you may find it helpful to discuss other possibilities and further reading with your supervisor. You are strongly advised to do this at the proposal stage rather than waiting until you have collected your research data.

12.2 Planning the analysis

When planning your analysis, you will be guided by your hypotheses and the nature of your data. This will help you determine the appropriate tests and techniques to use. The starting point is to examine your hypotheses and identify the variables to be included in the analysis.

Vox pop What has been the highpoint of your research so far?

Adel, recently completed PhD in management accounting

I had had difficulty in deciding which statistical technique was appropriate because I had a large number of constructs, a complicated model and a small sample. The highpoint came when the results of my analysis came out and I started to see light at the end of the tunnel.

12.2.1 Hypotheses and variables in the analysis

You will remember from previous chapters that a hypothesis is a proposition that can be tested for association or causality against empirical evidence (data based on observation or experience). It is important to remember that the methods used by positivists conducting business research have their roots in the experimental designs used by the natural scientists. This is reflected in the language associated with some tests, when the dependent variable (DV) in the hypothesis is identified, whose values are influenced by one or more independent variables (IVs). In Chapter 10, we gave the example of a study where the intensity of the lighting (the IV) in an office was manipulated to observe the effect on the productivity levels (the DV). You might want to predict that there will be an effect in a specific direction, such as better lighting is associated with higher productivity levels. This is known as a *one-tailed hypothesis*. A *two-tailed hypothesis* is where you predict the IV has an effect on the DV, but you cannot predict the direction.

The analysis we are going to explain in this part of the chapter is based on the Collis Report (2003) and the data file is available at www.palgrave.com/business/collis/br4/. As you can see from Box 12.1, the nine hypotheses tested in that study were one-tailed because in each hypothesis the direction of the effect was predicted.

Box 12.1 Hypotheses to be tested

H1 Voluntary audit is positively associated with turnover.
H2 Voluntary audit is positively associated with agreement that the audit provides a check on accounting records and systems.
H3 Voluntary audit is positively associated with agreement that it improves the quality of the financial information.
H4 Voluntary audit is positively associated with agreement that it improves the credibility of the financial information.
H5 Voluntary audit is positively associated with agreement that it has a positive effect on the credit rating score.
H6 Voluntary audit is positively associated with the company being family-owned.
H7 Voluntary audit is positively associated with the company having shareholders without access to internal financial information.
H8 Voluntary audit is positively associated with demand from the bank and other lenders.
H9 Voluntary audit is positively associated with the directors having qualifications or training in business or management.

Table 12.1 summarizes the variables in the analysis, where VOLAUDIT is the DV (or outcome variable) and the other variables are the IVs (or predictor variables). The table also shows how the variables are coded, some of which you created in the last chapter.

Table 12.1 Variables in the analysis

Variable	Definition	Hypothesis	Expected sign
VOLAUDIT	Whether company would have a voluntary audit (1, 0)		
TURNOVER	Turnover in 2002 accounts (£k)	H1	+
CHECK	Audit provides a check on accounting records and systems (5 = Agree, 1 = Disagree)	H2	+
QUALITY	Audit improves the quality of the financial information (5 = Agree, 1 = Disagree)	H3	+
CREDIBILITY	Audit improves the credibility of the financial information (5 = Agree, 1 = Disagree)	H4	+
CREDITSCORE	Audit has a positive effect on the credit rating score (5 = Agree, 1 = Disagree)	H5	+
FAMILY	Whether company is wholly family-owned (1, 0)	H6	-
EXOWNERS	Whether company has external shareholders (1, 0)	H7	+
BANK	Whether statutory accounts are given to the bank/lenders (1, 0)	H8	+
EDUCATION	Whether respondent has qualifications/training in business or management(1, 0)	H9	+

12.2.2 Inferential statistics

Inferential statistics are a group of statistical methods and models used to draw conclusions about a population from quantitative data relating to a random sample.

The term **inferential statistics** stems from the fact that data are collected about a random sample with a view to making inferences about the population. You will remember that a population is a body of people or any collection of items under consideration, and a random sample is a representative subset of the population. Your reason for obtaining a random sample is to obtain estimates of theoretical population parameters. For example, you may want to use the sample mean ($\bar{x}$) and the sample standard deviation (s) to make inferences about the population mean (μ pronounced 'mu') and the population standard deviation (σ pronounced 'sigma'). Traditionally, sample statistics are represented by Roman letters and population parameters are represented by Greek letters.

Inferential statistics include *parametric* tests and *non-parametric* tests and you will need to decide whether parametric or non-parametric tests are appropriate for your data. Parametric tests make certain assumptions about the distributional characteristics of the population under investigation. To determine whether parametric tests are appropriate, you need to establish whether your research data meet the following four basic assumptions. Drawing on Field (2000), these can be summarized as follows:

- The variable is measured on a ratio or interval scale (therefore, you cannot use a parametric test for ordinal or nominal data).
- The data are from a population with a **normal distribution** (therefore, you cannot use a parametric test for ratio or interval data with a skewed distribution).
- There is homogeneity of variance, which means the variances are stable in a test across groups of subjects, or the variance of one variable is stable at all levels in a test against another variable.
- The data values in the variable are independent (in other words, they come from different cases or the behaviour of one subject does not influence the behaviour of another).

A **normal distribution** is a theoretical frequency distribution that is bell-shaped and symmetrical, with tails extending indefinitely either side of the centre. The mean, median and mode coincide at the centre.

A **Type 1 error** occurs when H_0 is true, but the test leads to its rejection.

A **Type II error** occurs when H_1 is true, but the test leads to the acceptance of H_0.

The reason why these assumptions are so important is that the calculations that underpin parametric tests are based on the mean of the data values. However, non-parametric tests do not rely on the data meeting these assumptions because the statistical software first arranges the frequencies in size order and then performs the calculations on the ranks rather than the data values. You need to bear in mind that since the ranks are proxies for the information contained in the original data, there is a greater chance the test will lead to the type of incorrect result known as a **Type II error**. This refers to the situation where H_1 is true, but the test leads to the acceptance of H_0 (see Chapter 11). Therefore, in a non-parametric test, you might not be able to detect a significant effect in the ranked data, but one exists in the original data (Field, 2000). This explains why non-parametric tests are less powerful and the results less reliable than for parametric tests.

If you look at the variables we are going to analyse in Table 12.1, you will see that TURNOVER is the only one that is measured on a ratio or interval scale. Therefore, the first assumption is met for this variable. However, the results of the normality tests we conducted as part of our exploratory analysis in Chapter 11 showed that TURNOVER does not have a normal distribution (it was positively skewed with the majority of companies having a turnover at the smaller end of the scale). Since all the other variables in the analysis are measured on an ordinal or nominal scale, it is clear that the next stage of the analysis must be based on non-parametric tests.

The tests you choose for your study will depend on your hypotheses and your research questions. A typical analysis might start with bivariate analysis to explore differences between two independent or related samples and to test for relationships between variables and measure the strength of those relationships. This might lead to multivariate analysis involving the analysis relating to three or more variables.

Table 12.2 summarizes the parametric and non-parametric methods we are going to examine. We will demonstrate the non-parametric methods using the data from the Collis Report (2003) first and then explain the equivalent parametric method. If you have longitudinal data, you will also need to refer to the final sections of the chapter where we discuss indexation methods and time series analysis.

Table 12.2 Bivariate and multivariate analysis

Purpose	For parametric data	For non-parametric data
Tests of difference for independent or dependent samples	*t*-test	Mann-Whitney test
Tests of association between two nominal variables	Not applicable	Chi-square test
Tests of association between two quantitative variables	Pearson's correlation	Spearman's correlation
Predicting an outcome from one or more variables	Linear regression	Logistic regression

12.3 Tests of difference

12.3.1 Mann-Whitney test

If you have non-parametric data for an IV measured on a quantitative scale (a non-normal ratio or interval scale, or an ordinal scale) and a DV containing two independent samples, you can use the Mann-Whitney test to establish whether there is a difference between the two samples. In the Collis Report, VOLAUDIT is the DV. This is a dummy variable relating to whether the company would have a voluntary audit, and is coded 1 = Yes, 0 = No. This gives us our two independent samples or groups of subjects. We are going to use the Mann-Whitney test for each of the following IVs: TURNOVER, which is measured on a non-parametric ratio scale; CHECK, QUALITY, CREDIBILITY and CREDITSCORE, which are measured on an ordinal scale where 1 = Disagree and 5 = Agree. The null hypothesis (H_0) is that there is no difference between the two groups.

Start *SPSS* in the usual way and open the file named Data for 790 cos.sav. We found that the new version of *SPSS* we are illustrating (version 20) does not accept independent variables if you have designated them as ordinal variables. Therefore, before you start the analysis, you will need switch the data editor to Variable View and categorize them as being measured on a scale.

Although we are going to run five tests, we can instruct *SPSS* to do this in one procedure as follows:

- From the menu, select Analyze ⇒ Nonparametric tests ⇒ Independent samples.
- The dialogue box opens by asking you about your objective. Accept the default, which is Automatically compare distributions across groups, as this leads to the Mann-Whitney test.
- Then click on the Fields tab at the top and move TURNOVER, CHECK, QUALITY, CREDIBILITY and CREDITSCORE to Test Fields box. The order does not matter, but our principle is to list them in the order of the hypotheses shown in Table 12.1 (which coincides with the level of measurement).
- Move VOLAUDIT to Grouping Variable (see Figure 12.1).
- Click ▶Run to see the output (see Table 12.3).

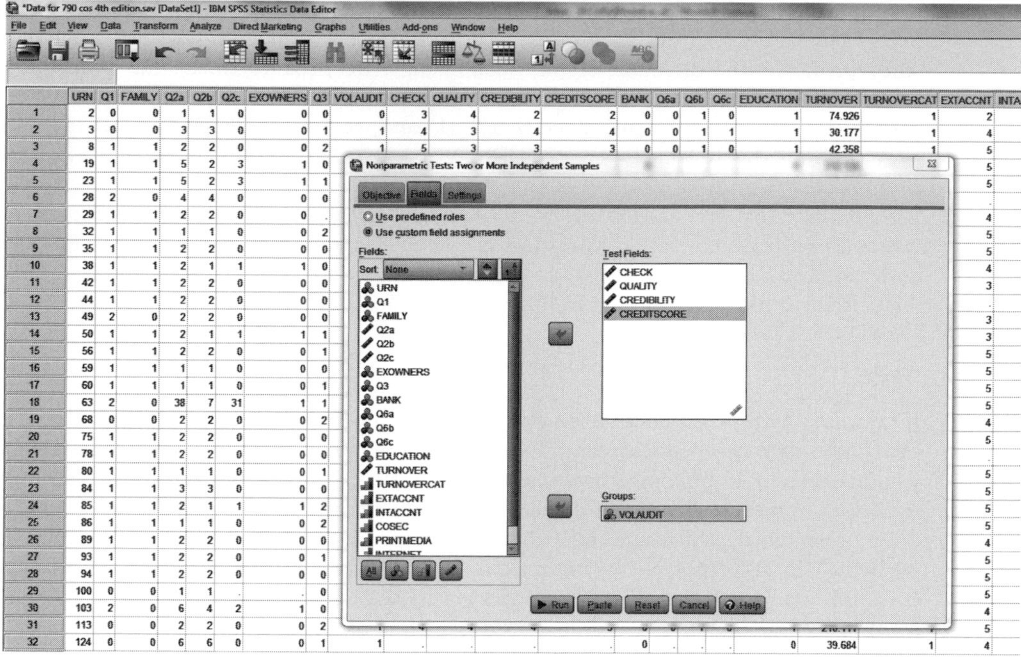

Figure 12.1 Running a Mann-Whitney test

Table 12.3 Mann-Whitney test for VOLAUDIT against TURNOVER, CHECK (Q4a), QUALITY (Q4b), CREDIBILITY (Q4c) and CREDITSCORE (Q4d)

Hypothesis Test Summary

	Null Hypothesis	Test	Sig.	Decision
1	The distribution of £k is the same across categories of Q3.	Independent-Samples Mann-Whitney U Test	.000	Reject the null hypothesis.
2	The distribution of Q4a is the same across categories of Q3.	Independent-Samples Mann-Whitney U Test	.000	Reject the null hypothesis.
3	The distribution of Q4b is the same across categories of Q3.	Independent-Samples Mann-Whitney U Test	.000	Reject the null hypothesis.
4	The distribution of Q4c is the same across categories of Q3.	Independent-Samples Mann-Whitney U Test	.000	Reject the null hypothesis.
5	The distribution of Q4c is the same across categories of Q3.	Independent-Samples Mann-Whitney U Test	.000	Reject the null hypothesis.

Asymptotic significances are displayed. The significance level is .05.

Although Table 12.3 does not show the test statistic (Mann-Whitney U), it shows the probability value (Sig.) for each of the five tests. Since our hypotheses were one-tailed (they predicted the direction of the relationship), we need to divide the probability values shown in the table for a two-tailed hypothesis by 2. The outcome is unchanged with a very high level of significance ($p \leq 0.01$) and we have evidence to reject the null hypothesis for this test in respect of TURNOVER, CHECK, QUALITY, CREDIBILITY and CREDITSCORE.

If you have two sets of scores from the same subjects, you would use the Wilcoxon W test and its associated z score instead of the Mann-Whitney test. For example, you may have conducted a longitudinal study where you have data from the same subjects that relate to the same variable collected on a previous occasion.

12.3.2 *t*-test

If you have parametric data for an IV measured on a ratio or interval scale and a DV containing two independent samples, you can use the *independent t*-test to establish whether there is a difference between the two samples or groups of subjects. The null hypothesis is that there is no difference between the two groups.

In a research design where independent samples are used, you might take groups to participate in difference phases of an experiment. Perhaps you are interested in the fuel consumption of vehicles where some drivers have been on a safe driving course and others have not. The first group is the experimental group and the second group is the control group. One problem with this is that because the two groups are independent, any difference could be due to other factors; for example, some drivers may be more experienced or more cautious than others. One way round this problem is to adopt a paired-samples design. In this case, you would match a driver in the experimental group with a driver in the control group, who has similar characteristics that might affect his or her driving performance (for example driving experience, accident rate and age). You will also need to use the *paired-sample t*-test for dependent samples if you have two sets of data for a single group of subjects.

The *t*-test was not used in the Collis Report, but if you want to find it on *SPSS*, the procedure is as follows:

- From the menu, select Analyze ⇒ Compare Means ⇒ Independent-Samples T Test... (or Paired-Samples T Test...).
- Move the appropriate variables into the Test variable(s) and Grouping variable boxes and then click the Define groups to identify the two groups.

The *SPSS* output for an independent *t*-test provides a table with descriptive statistics, which is followed by a second table, which requires a little explanation because you need to decide which of the two rows of results are relevant. You need to look first at the results of the Levene's Test for Equality of Variances. If the probability statistic (Sig.) is not significant ($p > 0.05$), you should refer to the *t*-test results in the row labelled Equal variances assumed. Conversely, if the probability statistic (Sig.) for the Levene's test is significant ($p \leq 0.05$), you should refer to the *t*-test results in the row labelled Equal variances not assumed (Field, 2000).

As discussed in the previous section, if you have predicted the direction of the relationship in your hypothesis, you will need to divide the probability value for the *t*-test by 2. If the result is significant ($p \leq 0.05$), you have evidence to reject the null hypothesis that there is no difference between the two groups.

12.3.3 Generalizability test

Now you know how to conduct a test of difference between two samples or two groups, we can explain how you can use it to test whether you can generalize results you have obtained from a sample to the population. In Chapter 10 we drew your attention to the problem of questionnaire non-response. This occurs when you conduct a questionnaire survey, but do not receive responses from all the members of your random sample. Therefore, you will be concerned that the data may not be representative of the population. Wallace and Mellor (1988) suggest three methods for testing for questionnaire non-response:

- Compare the characteristics of early respondents with those of late respondents, on the basis that late respondents are likely to be similar to non-respondents. One method of doing this is to send a follow-up request to non-respondents. If you intend to do this, you will need to keep a record of who replies and when. In a postal questionnaire survey, you are advised to send a fresh copy of the questionnaire (perhaps printed on different coloured paper or with an identifying symbol in addition to the unique reference number). You then use a Mann Whitney test or *t*-test as appropriate (see above) to compare the characteristics of those responding to the follow-up request (late respondents) with those of the early respondents. If there is no significant difference, you may conclude that your sample does not suffer from non-response bias.
- Compare the characteristics of your respondents with those of the population (assuming you know them) using one of the tests of difference mentioned above. If there is no significant difference, you may conclude that your sample does not suffer from non-response bias.
- Compare the characteristics of your respondents with those of the non-respondents in the sample (assuming you know them) using one of the tests of difference mentioned above. If there is no significant difference, you may conclude that your sample does not suffer from non-response bias.

12.4 Tests of association

12.4.1 Chi-square test

If you have non-parametric data for two variables measured on a nominal scale, you will remember from the previous chapter that you can use a cross-tabulation as part of your bivariate analysis. If the two variables each contain two categories, a cross-tabulation produces a 2 × 2 table containing 2 columns and 2 rows, with 4 cells altogether. We are going to take this a step further by conducting a chi-square (χ^2) test to find out whether there is a statistically significant association between the column and row categories. For a 2 × 2 table, the test is based on the assumption that the expected counts in each cell will be 5 or more (Moore *et al.*, 2009) and compares the observed frequencies (actual counts) with the expected frequencies (theoretical counts).

We are going to measure the association between the two groups in our DV (VOLAUDIT) and the dummy variables that represent the remaining IVs in the analysis: FAMILY, EXOWNERS, BANK and EDUCATION. The null hypothesis (H_0) we are testing is that there is no association between the two categories in each variable. Although we are going to run four tests, we can instruct *SPSS* to do this in one procedure as follows:

- From the menu at the top, select Analyze ⇒ Descriptive Statistics… ⇒ Crosstabs.
- Move FAMILY, EXOWNERS, BANK and EDUCATION into Row(s).

- Move VOLAUDIT into Column(s).
- Select Statistics and click Chi-square and Continue.
- Select Cells. Under Counts, you will see that Observed is the default, but also click Expected. Under Percentages, click Column and Continue (see Figure 12.2).
- Then click OK to see the output (see Table 12.4).

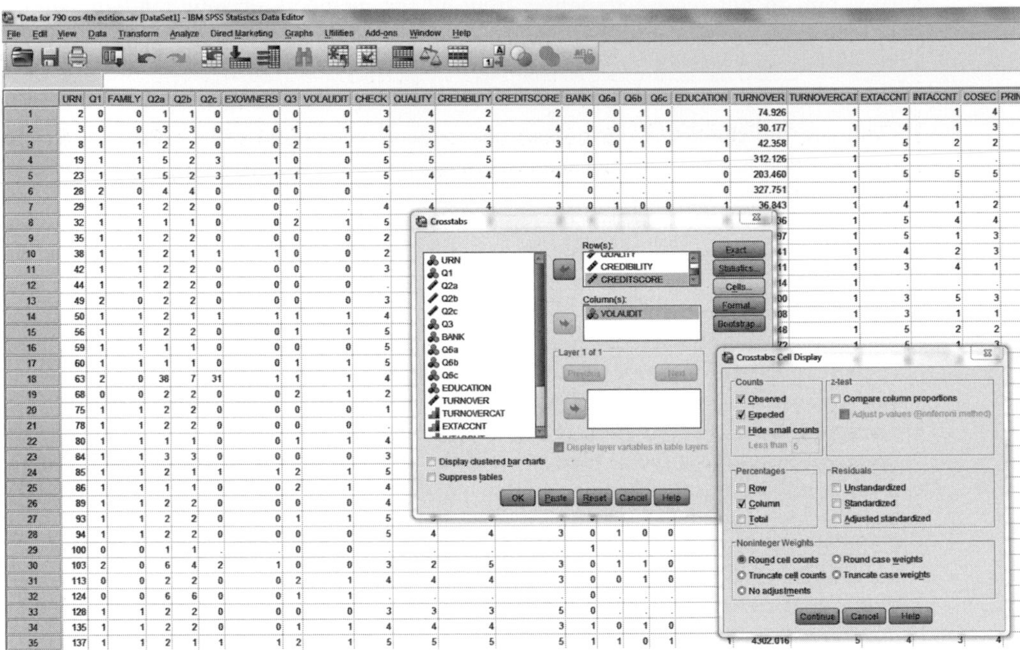

Figure 12.2 Running a chi-square test

Table 12.4 Chi-square tests for VOLAUDIT against FAMILY, EXOWNERS, BANK and EDUCATION

Case Processing Summary

	Cases					
	Valid		Missing		Total	
	N	Percent	N	Percent	N	Percent
Family * VOLAUDIT	767	97.1%	23	2.9%	790	100.0%
Exowners * VOLAUDIT	690	87.3%	100	12.7%	790	100.0%
Bank * VOLAUDIT	772	97.7%	18	2.3%	790	100.0%
Education * VOLAUDIT	772	97.7%	18	2.3%	790	100.0%

FAMILY * VOLAUDIT

Crosstab

			VOLAUDIT		
			0 Otherwise	1 Yes	Total
FAMILY	0 Otherwise	Count	102	144	246
		Expected Count	138.9	107.1	246.0
		% within VOLAUDIT	23.6%	43.1%	32.1%
	1 Wholly family-owned	Count	331	190	521
		Expected Count	294.1	226.9	521.0
		% within VOLAUDIT	76.4%	56.9%	67.9%
	Total	Count	433	334	767
		Expected Count	433.0	334.0	767.0
		% within VOLAUDIT	100.0%	100.0%	100.0%

Chi-Square Tests

	Value	Df	Asymp. Sig. (2-sided)	Exact Sig. (2-sided)	Exact Sig. (1-sided)
Pearson Chi-Square	33.103[a]	1	.000		
Continuity Correction[b]	32.212	1	.000		
Likelihood Ratio	33.031	1	.000		
Fisher's Exact Test				.000	.000
Linear-by-Linear Association	33.060	1	.000		
N of Valid Cases	767				

a. 0 cells (.0%) have expected count less than 5. The minimum expected count is 107.12

b. Computed only for a 2x2 table

EXOWNERS * VOLAUDIT

Crosstab

			VOLAUDIT		
			0 Otherwise	1 Yes	Total
EXOWNERS	0 Otherwise	Count	338	232	570
		Expected Count	318.0	252.0	570.0
		% within VOLAUDIT	87.8%	76.1%	82.6%
	1 External owners	Count	47	73	120
		Expected Count	67.0	53.0	120.0
		% within VOLAUDIT	12.2%	23.9%	17.4%
	Total	Count	385	305	690
		Expected Count	385.0	305.0	690.0
		% within VOLAUDIT	100.0%	100.0%	100.0%

Chi-Square Tests

	Value	Df	Asymp. Sig. (2-sided)	Exact Sig. (2-sided)	Exact Sig. (1-sided)
Pearson Chi-Square	16.289[a]	1	.000		
Continuity Correction[b]	15.483	1	.000		
Likelihood Ratio	16.210	1	.000		
Fisher's Exact Test				.000	.000
Linear-by-Linear Association	16.266	1	.000		
N of Valid Cases	690				

a. 0 cells (.0%) have expected count less than 5. The minimum expected count is 53.04
b. Computed only for a 2x2 table

BANK * VOLAUDIT

Crosstab

			VOLAUDIT		
			0 Otherwise	1 Yes	Total
BANK	0 Otherwise	Count	264	116	380
		Expected Count	215.6	164.4	380.0
		% within VOLAUDIT	60.3%	34.7%	49.2%
	1 Yes	Count	174	218	392
		Expected Count	222.4	169.6	392.0
		% within VOLAUDIT	39.7%	65.3%	50.8%
	Total	Count	438	334	772
		Expected Count	438.0	334.0	772.0
		% within VOLAUDIT	100.0%	100.0%	100.0%

Chi-Square Tests

	Value	Df	Asymp. Sig. (2-sided)	Exact Sig. (2-sided)	Exact Sig. (1-sided)
Pearson Chi-Square	49.468[a]	1	.000		
Continuity Correction[b]	48.452	1	.000		
Likelihood Ratio	50.092	1	.000		
Fisher's Exact Test				.000	.000
Linear-by-Linear Association	49.404	1	.000		
N of Valid Cases	772				

a. 0 cells (.0%) have expected count less than 5. The minimum expected count is 164.40
b. Computed only for a 2x2 table

EDUCATION * VOLAUDIT

Crosstab

			VOLAUDIT		
			0 Otherwise	1 Yes	Total
EDUCATION	0 Otherwise	Count	124	105	229
		Expected Count	129.9	99.1	229.0
		% within VOLAUDIT	28.3%	31.4%	29.7%
	1 Yes	Count	314	229	543
		Expected Count	308.1	234.9	543.0
		% within VOLAUDIT	71.7%	68.6%	70.3%
	Total	Count	438	334	772
		Expected Count	438.0	334.0	772.0
		% within VOLAUDIT	100.0%	100.0%	100.0%

Chi-Square Tests

	Value	Df	Asymp. Sig. (2-sided)	Exact Sig. (2-sided)	Exact Sig. (1-sided)
Pearson Chi-Square	.888[a]	1	.346		
Continuity Correction[b]	.744	1	.388		
Likelihood Ratio	.886	1	.347		
Fisher's Exact Test				.382	.194
Linear-by-Linear Association	.887	1	.346		
N of Valid Cases	772				

a. 0 cells (.0%) have expected count less than 5. The minimum expected count is 99.08

b. Computed only for a 2x2 table

Do not be alarmed by the quantity of tables produced! It is simply that after reporting on the number of cases in each test, *SPSS* generates a cross-tabulation and a table showing the results of the chi-square tests for each pair of variables tested. We will start by looking at the latter.

We are interested in the chi-square statistic in the first row, which bears the name of Karl Pearson, who proposed the chi-square test in 1900, following the publication of his work on correlation in 1895–8 (Upton and Cook, 2006; Moore *et al.*, 2009). Any deviation from the null hypothesis makes the chi-square value larger. We also need to look at the probability statistic for Pearson's chi-square, which is shown in the third column of the first row under Asymp. Sig. (2-sided). Since our hypotheses are all one-sided, we need to divide the probability statistic by 2. Apart from EDUCATION, the significance levels for the variables tested are very high ($p < 0.01$). However, we must check the notes beneath each table to confirm that none of the cells have an expected count of less than 5, which can be a problem with a small sample. However, the notes confirm that this assumption of the test is met. Therefore, we have evidence to reject the null hypothesis of no association in respect of FAMILY, EXOWNERS and BANK.

We need to look at the percentages in the cells of the cross-tabulations to interpret the association. These tell us that demand for voluntary audit is associated with companies that are not wholly family-owned, have external owners or give their accounts to the bank/lenders but not with the characteristics of the respondent capture by EDUCATION. This means we must accept the null hypothesis for H9.

12.5 Correlation

Correlation is a measure of the direction and strength of association between two quantitative variables. Correlation may be linear or non-linear, positive or negative.

Correlation is synonymous with its originator, Karl Pearson, who we mentioned in the previous section. Correlation offers additional information about an association between two quantitative variables (thus excluding those measured on a nominal scale) because it measures the direction and strength of any linear relationship between them. 'Most of the statistics used in the social sciences are based on linear models, which means that we try to fit straight-line models to the data collected' (Field, 2000, p. 11). In statistics, a *correlation coefficient* is 'a measure of the linear dependence of one numerical random variable on another' (Upton and Cook, 2006, p. 101). The two variables are not referred to as the DV and the IV because 'they are measured simultaneously and so no cause-and-effect relationship can be established' (Field, 2000, p. 78).

The correlation coefficient is measured within the range –1 to +1. The direction of the correlation is positive if both variables increase together, but it is negative if one variable increases as the other decreases. The strength of the correlation is measured by the size of the correlation coefficient:

1 represents a perfect positive linear association
0 represents no linear association
–1 represents a perfect negative linear association

Therefore, values in between can be graded roughly as:

0.90 to 0.99 (very high positive correlation)
0.70 to 0.89 (high positive correlation)
0.40 to 0.69 (medium positive correlation)
0 to 0.39 (low positive correlation)
0 to –0.39 (low negative correlation)
–0.40 to –0.69 (medium negative correlation)
–0.70 to –0.89 (high negative correlation)
–0.90 to –0.99 (very high negative correlation)

You need to take care when interpreting correlation coefficients, since correlation between two variables does not prove the existence of a causal link between them: two causally unrelated variables can be correlated because they both relate to a third variable. For example, the sales of ice cream and suntan lotion may be correlated because they both relate to higher temperatures.

12.5.1 Bivariate scatterplot

If you have parametric data, a preliminary step is to generate a display of the relationship between the two quantitative variables using a simple scatterplot. One variable is plotted against the other on a graph as a pattern of points, which indicates the direction and strength of any linear correlation. The more the points cluster around a straight line, the stronger the correlation.

- If the points tend to cluster around a line that runs from the lower left to the upper right of the graph, the correlation is *positive*, as shown in Figure 12.3. Positive correlation occurs when an increase in the value of one variable is associated with an increase in the value of the other. For example, an increase in the volume of orders from customers may be associated with increased calls to customers by the sales representatives.
- If points tend to cluster around a line that runs from the upper left to the lower right of the graph, the correlation is *negative*, as shown in Figure 12.4. Negative correlation occurs when an increase in the value of one variable is associated with a decrease in the value of the other. For example, higher interest rates for borrowing may be associated with lower house sales.
- If the points are scattered randomly throughout the graph, there is no correlation between the two variables as shown in Figure 12.5. Alternatively, the pattern may show non-linear correlation as illustrated in Figure 12.6.

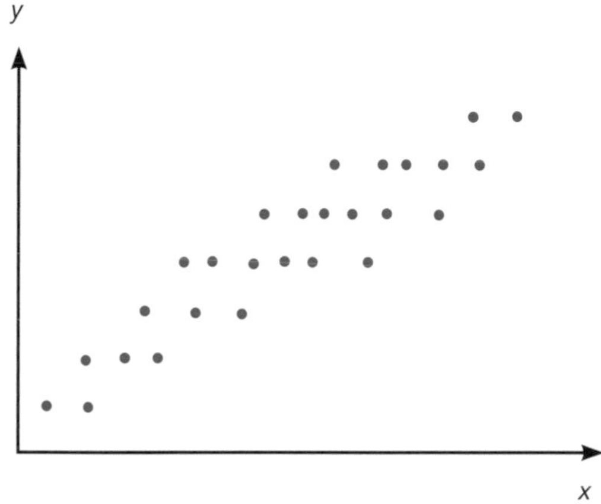

Figure 12.3 Scatterplot showing positive linear correlation

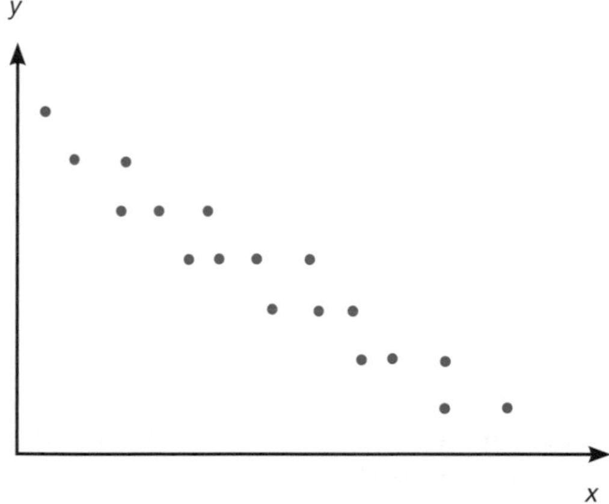

Figure 12.4 Scatterplot showing negative linear correlation

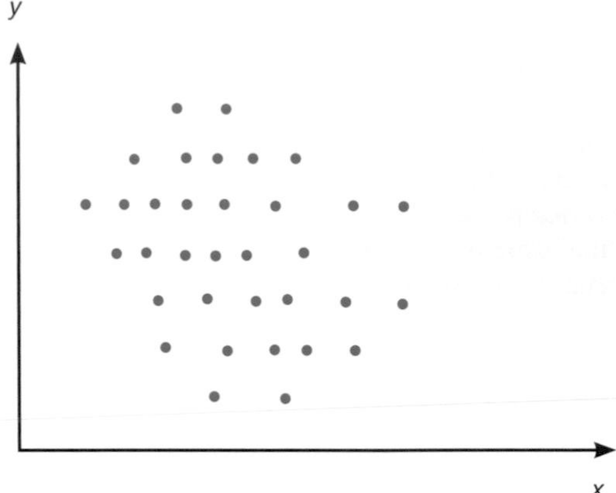

Figure 12.5 Scatterplot showing no correlation

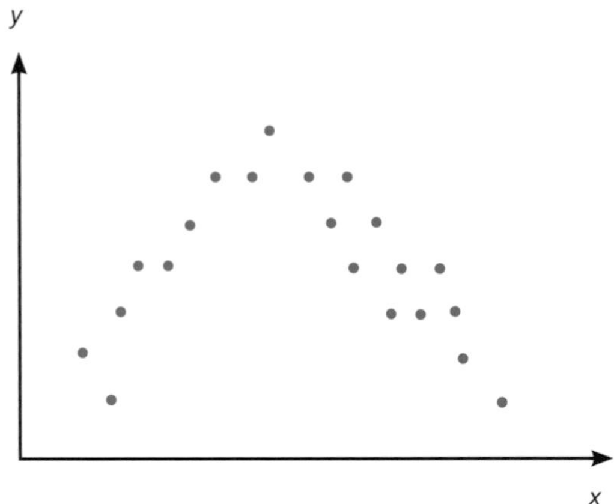

Figure 12.6 Scatterplot showing non-linear correlation

Using *SPSS*, the general procedure is as follows:

- From the menu at the top, select Graphs ⇒ Legacy Dialogs ⇒ Scatter/Dot.
- The default is a simple scatterplot, but you will see that you have other choices.
- Click on Define and move one variable into the Y Axis box and the other into the X Axis box.
- If you want different symbols or different coloured dots for different groups in the sample, move a third variable into the Set Markers by box. For example, if you used BANK, companies giving their accounts to the bank could be shown with a currency symbol and the default dot could be retained for the others.
- With a small data set, you can move a variable into the Label Cases by box to use the value labels to label the points on the plot. For example, if you used ID, the points would be labelled with the case numbers; alternatively, you could use the case numbers to label any outliers.

- Move one or more variables that contain groups into the Panel by boxes to generate a matrix of charts for each group. For example, if you used FAMILY, you could generate one chart for the companies that are wholly family-owned and another for the remainder.

12.5.2 Spearman's correlation

If you have non-parametric data for two variables measured on a ratio, interval or ordinal scale (including dichotomous variables which it can be argued are measured on a ratio scale), you can use a correlation coefficient called Spearman's rho (r_S) to measure the linear association between the variables. This overcomes the problem that the data are non-parametric by placing the data values in order of size and then examining differences in the rankings of one variable compared to the other.

We are going to use Spearman's rho to measure the correlation between CHECK, QUALITY, CREDIBILITY, CREDITSCORE and TURNOVER. The null hypothesis (H_0) we are testing is that there is no correlation between any two variables and we can instruct *SPSS* to do this in one procedure as follows:

- From the menu at the top, select Analyze ⇒ Correlate ⇒ Bivariate...
- Move TURNOVER, CHECK, QUALITY, CREDIBILITY and CREDITSCORE into Variables.
- Under Correlation Coefficients, deselect Pearson and then select Spearman.
- Under Test of Significance, click One-tailed and accept the default to Flag significant correlations.
- Under Options, you will see that the default for missing values is to Exclude cases pairwise, which we will accept, so you can now click Continue (see Figure 12.7).
- Then click OK to see the output (see Table 12.5).

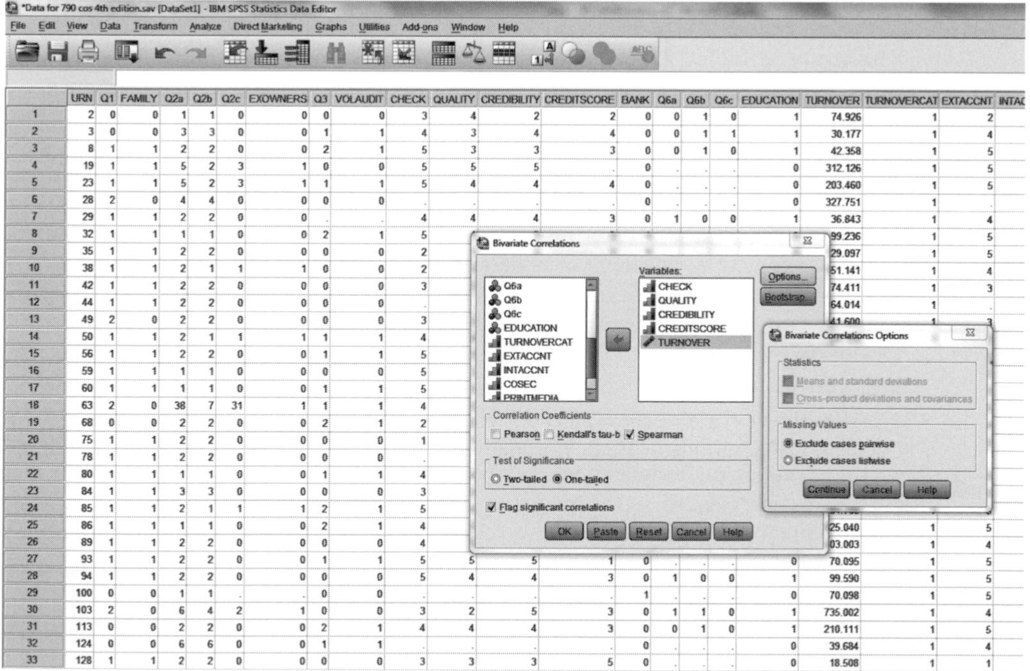

Figure 12.7 Running Spearman's correlation

Table 12.5 Spearman's rho for TURNOVER, CHECK, QUALITY, CREDIBILITY and CREDITSCORE

Correlations

			TURNOVER	CHECK	QUALITY	CREDIBILITY	CREDITSCORE
Spearman's rho	TURNOVER	Correlation Coefficient	1.000	.106**	.112**	.180**	.179**
		Sig. (1-tailed)	.	.003	.002	.000	.000
		N	790	697	687	688	681
	CHECK	Correlation Coefficient	.106**	1.000	.606**	.609**	.467**
		Sig. (1-tailed)	.003	.	.000	.000	.000
		N	697	697	681	682	674
	QUALITY	Correlation Coefficient	.112**	.606**	1.000	.651**	.529**
		Sig. (1-tailed)	.002	.000	.	.000	.000
		N	687	681	687	681	671
	CREDIBILITY	Correlation Coefficient	.180**	.609**	.651**	1.000	.532**
		Sig. (1-tailed)	.000	.000	.000	.	.000
		N	688	682	681	688	670
	CREDITSCORE	Correlation Coefficient	.179**	.467**	.529**	.532**	1.000
		Sig. (1-tailed)	.000	.000	.000	.000	.
		N	681	674	671	670	681

**. Correlation is significant at the 0.01 level (1-tailed)

The results in Table 12.5 are somewhat confusing because the statistics are shown for every possible pairing and this means some information is repeated. For convenience, we have added a shaded background to the duplicated information. We will now examine the results in the cells without shading. A correlation coefficient of 1 (shown as 1.000) indicates perfect positive correlation. You can see this in the results where a variable is paired with itself. In all the other bivariate tests, you can see that the probability statistic (Sig. 1-tailed) tells us that the results are significant at the 1% level ($p = \leq 0.01$). Therefore, we can conclude that there is evidence to reject the null hypothesis of no correlation, but you need to remember that this does not mean we have established causality because there may be several explanatory variables.

One of the reasons for conducting this analysis is to check for potential *multicollinearity*. This occurs when the correlation between independent (predictor) variables in a multiple regression model is very high (≥ 0.90), which can give rise to unreliable estimates of the standard errors (Kervin, 1992, p. 608). Multicollinearity can make it hard to identify the separate effects of the independent variables. Therefore, it is essential to establish that there is no major 'overlap' in the predictive power of the variables. Kervin (1992) advises that if two predictor variables are highly related, the one with less theoretical importance to the research should be excluded from the analysis.

If you look at the correlation coefficients in our results, none of them are higher than 0.7, which means that the strength of the correlation is not likely to be a problem at the next stage where we will be using multiple regression analysis.

12.5.3 Pearson's correlation

If you have parametric data for two continuous variables, you can use Pearson's product-moment correlation coefficient (r) to measure the linear association between the variables. You will remember that a continuous variable is a ratio or interval variable measured on a scale where the data can take any value within a given range (for example turnover or assets but not number of employees). The null hypothesis (H_0) is that there is no correlation between the two variables and the procedure in *SPSS* is as follows:

- From the menu at the top, select Analyze ⇒ Correlate ⇒ Bivariate...
- Move the appropriate variables into the Variables box.
- Under Correlation Coefficients, accept the default, which is Pearson.
- Under Test of Significance, select One-tailed if your hypotheses specify the direction of the correlation and accept the default to Flag significant correlations.
- Under Options, accept the default for missing values, which is to Exclude cases pairwise, so you can click Continue and OK.

12.5.4 Reliability tests

In Chapter 10 we mentioned that if you decide to use a rating scale to measure an abstract concept such as an ability or trait that is not directly observable (in other words, your explanatory variable is a hypothetical construct), you will want to be sure that the scale will measure the respondents' views reliably. The reliability of a measure refers to its consistency. The measure is reliable if you or someone else repeats the research and obtains the same results.

There are a number of ways of estimating the reliability of a scale measure. For example, the *external reliability* of a job satisfaction survey can be tested by asking the same group of people who completed the questionnaire to answer it again a few days later. The *test-retest reliability* requires two sets of responses for each person, which you compare by checking the correlation (see previous section). If the responses are reliable, there will be high positive correlation between the two sets (preferably ≥ 0.8). The drawback of the test-retest method is that it is often difficult to persuade respondents to answer questions a second time. Moreover, if they do agree to do this, they may think more deeply about the questions on the second occasion and give different answers.

Internal reliability is particularly important if you are using multiple-item scales. As the name suggests, the *split-half reliability* is tested by dividing the items in the scale into two equal groups (for example by placing odd numbered items in one group and even numbered items in another group). You then check the correlation coefficient of the two groups as above. This method offers the advantage that the questionnaire is only administered once.

Cronbach's alpha coefficient is one of the most widely used tests for checking the internal reliability of multiple-item scales. Each item is correlated with every other item that relates to the construct across the sample and the average inter-item correlation is taken as the index of reliability. Before you run the test, you need to reverse the rating scores relating to any negatively worded items. In the example shown in Box 12.2, the researcher is developing a multi-item scale to measure the concept of the professional organization as a major reference. The dimensions in items (a), (b), (d), (e) and (g) are worded positively, but the wording in items (c) and (f) are negatively worded to avoid response bias. This means that unlike the other items, the highest number in the rating scale for items (c) and (f) indicates the lowest level of reference to the professional organization. Therefore, you need to recode scores of 5, 4, 2 and 1 for items (c) and (d) as 1, 2, 4 and 5 respectively (see Chapter 11).

Box 12.2 Multi-item scale

1. Please indicate your level of agreement with the following statements regarding the professional body of which you are a member.
(Circle the number closest to your view)

	Agree				Disagree
(a) I attend the local meetings of my professional body	5	4	3	2	1
(b) I participate in professional development workshops for members	5	4	3	2	1
(c) I do not read the newsletters and reports sent by my professional body	5	4	3	2	1
(d) I do read about new issues on the website of my professional body	5	4	3	2	1
(e) I use the technical information on the website of my professional body	5	4	3	2	1
(f) I do not use the technical information on the websites of other professional bodies	5	4	3	2	1
(g) I contact my professional body if I need technical support	5	4	3	2	1

The procedure for calculating Cronbach's alpha coefficient in *SPSS* is as follows:

- From the menu at the top, select Analyze ⇒ Scale ⇒ Reliability Analysis...
- Move the items that make up the scale to the Items box.
- In the Model box accept the default, which is Alpha.
- Select Statistics and under Descriptives for select Item, Scale and Scale if item deleted. Under Inter-Item select Correlations.
- Click Continue and OK.

Look at the reliability statistics for the main result. If the scale is reliable, Cronbach's alpha should be ≥ 0.8. If the result is much lower than this, you may want to consider excluding any item with a low item-total correlation. If you look at the item-total statistics, you will see the alpha if the item is deleted. If your scale has fewer than ten items, this may also be a reason for a low alpha.

12.6 Factor analysis

Factor analysis is used to examine the correlation between pairs of variables measured on a rating scale (for example a Likert scale) and the analysis identifies sets of interrelated variables on the basis that each variable in the set could be measuring a different aspect of some underlying factor (Field, 2000). The resulting factor scores represent the relative importance of the variables to each factor. We will illustrate the technique using data from Collis (2003), although this analysis was not included in the Collis Report. One of the survey questions asked the directors to rate the importance of various sources of information for keeping up to date with matters relating to the statutory annual accounts and the audit using a rating scale of 1 to 5, where 5 = important; 3 = neutral and 1 = not important. Table 12.6 shows their responses.

Table 12.6 Sources for keeping up to date on statutory accounting and auditing

Source	Important				Not important	Total
	5	4	3	2	1	
External accountant	402	151	90	37	60	740
Internal accountant	132	98	125	75	225	655
Company secretary	88	94	164	104	225	675
Newspapers, journals and other publications	57	101	239	132	165	694
Internet	33	87	178	147	230	675
Other business owners	30	93	172	126	239	660

N = 790

Factor analysis encompasses a number of techniques We are going to use *principal components analysis,* which is widely applied in business research to reduce data to a smaller set of common composite variables (the components or factors). These composite variables can then be used to describe and explain patterns of relationship among the original variables. The variables in the analysis are those from Table 12.6, which are labelled EXTACCNT, INTACCNT, COSEC, MEDIA, INTERNET and OTHEROWNERS respectively. The procedure in *SPSS* is as follows:

- From the menu at the top, select Analyze ⇒ Dimension Reduction ⇒ Factor...
- Move the appropriate variables into the Variables box (see Figure 12.8).
- Select Descriptives... and accept the default of initial solution under Statistics; under Correlation Matrix select Coefficients, Significance levels and KMO and Bartlett's test of sphericity. The KMO (Kaiser-Meyer-Olkin) value gives you a measure of sampling adequacy and the Bartlett's test checks the assumption of sphericity (a form of compound symmetry). Click Continue.
- Now select Extraction... and accept the default, Principal Components, as the method and under Analyze accept the default of a Correlation matrix; under Display accept the default which is the Unrotated factor solution; under Extract accept the default of Eigenvalues greater than 1. Click Continue.
- Now select Rotation... and select Varimax, which maximizes the tendency of each variable to load highly on only one factor (select Direct Oblimin if you have theoretical reasons to presume that certain factors will interrelate). Under Display, accept the default which is for the Rotated solution.
- If you want to save the factor scores as variables (for example, if you plan to use them instead of the original variables in a regression analysis), now select Scores... and select the Anderson-Rubin method if you want to ensure that the factor scores are uncorrelated, and the Regression method if correlation between factor scores is acceptable.
- Finally, select Options... and under Missing Values select Exclude cases pairwise to exclude cases with missing data; under Coefficient Display Format select Sorted by size and Supress small coefficients, selecting Absolute values less than .40 as the appropriate level, and click Continue (see Figure 12.8).
- Then click OK to see the output (see Table 12.7).

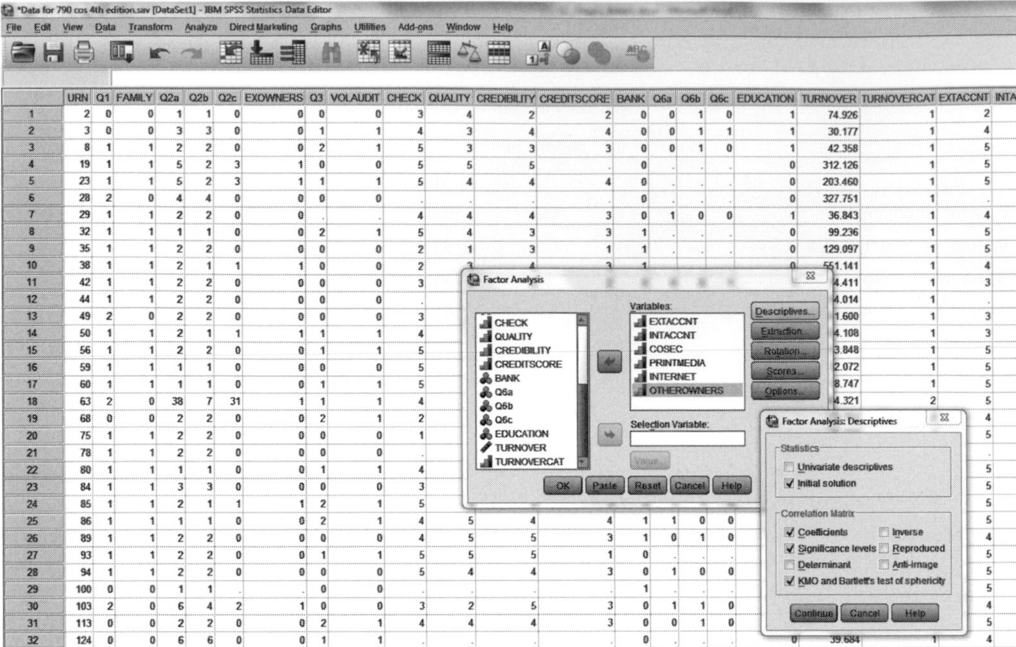

Figure 12.8 Running a factor analysis

Table 12.7 Results of the factor analysis

Correlation Matrix

		EXTACCNT	INTACCNT	COSEC	PRINTMEDIA	INTERNET	OTHEROWNERS
Correlation	EXTACCNT	1.000	-.042	.056	.009	-.015	.139
	INTACNT	-.042	1.000	.550	.264	.249	.240
	COSEC	.056	.550	1.000	.258	.247	.241
	PRINTMEDIA	.009	.264	.258	1.000	.573	.391
	INTERNET	-.015	.249	.247	.573	1.000	.473
	OTHEROWNERS	.139	.240	.241	.391	.473	1.000
Sig. (1-tailed)	EXTACCNT		.143	.073	.409	.351	.000
	INTACNT	.143		.000	.000	.000	.000
	COSEC	.073	.000		.000	.000	.000
	PRINTMEDIA	.409	.000	.000		.000	.000
	INTERNET	.351	.000	.000	.000		.000
	OTHEROWNERS	.000	.000	.000	.000	.000	

KMO and Bartlett's Test

Kaiser-Meyer-Olkin Measure of Sampling Adequacy		.680
Bartlett's Test of Sphericity	Approx. Chi-Square	747.866
	Df	15
	Sig.	.000

Communalities

	Initial	Extraction
EXTACCNT	1.000	.954
INTACCNT	1.000	.781
COSEC	1.000	.782
PRINTMEDIA	1.000	.677
INTERNET	1.000	.753
OTHEROWNERS	1.000	.608

Extraction Method: Principal Component Analysis

Total Variance Explained

Component	Initial Eigenvalues			Extraction Sums of Squared Loadings			Rotation Sums of Squared Loadings		
	Total	% of Variance	Cumulative %	Total	% of Variance	Cumulative %	Total	% of Variance	Cumulative %
1	2.405	40.077	40.077	2.405	40.077	40.077	1.951	32.510	32.510
2	1.122	18.692	58.769	1.122	18.692	58.769	1.561	26.008	58.518
3	1.029	17.147	75.916	1.029	17.147	75.916	1.044	17.398	75.916
4	.595	9.923	85.839						
5	.442	7.363	93.202						
6	.408	6.798	100.000						

Extraction Method: Principal Component Analysis

Component Matrix[a]

	Component		
	1	2	3
INTERNET	.756	.344	-.251
PRINTMEDIA	.737	.291	-.223
OTHEROWNERS	.685	.357	.104
COSEC	.639	-.558	.250
INTACCNT	.638	-.605	.092
EXTACCNT	.071	.338	.913

Extraction Method: Principal Component Analysis
a. 3 components extracted

Rotated Component Matrix[a]

	Component		
	1	2	3
INTERNET	.856	.120	-.078
PRINTMEDIA	.805	.156	-.070
OTHEROWNERS	.720	.152	.257
COSEC	.154	.867	.086
INTACCNT	.166	.865	-.078
EXTACCNT	.019	-.003	.976

Extraction Method: Principal Component Analysis
Rotation Method: Varimax with Kaiser Normalization
a. Rotation converged in 4 iterations

Component Transformation Matrix

Component	1	2	3
1	.806	.588	.058
2	.540	-.773	.334
3	-.242	.238	.941

Extraction Method: Principal Component Analysis
Rotation Method: Varimax with Kaiser Normalization

Component Transformation Matrix

Component	1	2	3
1	.806	.588	.058
2	.540	-.773	.334
3	-.242	.238	.941

Extraction Method: Principal Component Analysis
Rotation Method: Varimax with Kaiser Normalization

As you can see, the tables of results from *SPSS* are extensive. First of all we need to check the KMO (Kaiser-Meyer-Olkin) test in the second table. The value is 0.680, which indicates that the sample size is sufficient to give reliable results (it needs to be 0.6 or above). You can also see that the result of the Bartlett's test of sphericity is significant at the 1% level, which satisfies the assumption of sphericity. Now we can turn to the first table, which is the correlation matrix and you can see that it supports the components identified in the sixth table, which shows that rotated components analysis. If you look at the sixth table, you can see that the Varimax rotation converged in 4 iterations and 3 components were extracted, which together account for 75.916% of the variance (this last statistic comes from the fourth table). A useful way to summarize the key information is shown in Tables 12.8 and 12.9.

In Table 12.8 you can see that we have only presented the correlation coefficients and used asterisks to indicate the significance levels. In addition, all duplicated data in the matrix have been omitted to avoid distraction.

In Table 12.9 you can see that Component 1 is the most strongly correlated and accounts for 33% of the total variance in the original variables. It groups together three variables with loadings in excess of 0.7, which are highlighted in bold (INTERNET,

Table 12.8 Correlation matrix of sources for keeping up to date

	EXTACCNT	INTACCNT	COSEC	PRINTMEDIA	INTERNET	OTHEROWNERS
EXTACCNT	1.000					
INTACNT	–.042	1.000				
COSEC	.056	.550*	1.000			
PRINTMEDIA	.009	.264*	.258*	1.000		
INTERNET	–.015	.249*	.247*	.573*	1.000	
OTHEROWNERS	.139*	.240*	.241*	.391*	.473*	1.000

* Correlation is significant at the 0.01 level (2-tailed).

Table 12.9 Factor analysis of sources for keeping up to date

Variable	Component 1 *General sources* (32.5% of variance)	Component 2 *Internal professionals* (26.0% of variance)	Component 3 *External professional* (17.3% of variance)
INTERNET	**.856**	.120	–.078
PRINTMEDIA	**.805**	.156	–.070
OTHEROWNERS	**.720**	.152	.257
COSEC	.154	**.867**	.086
INTACCNT	.166	**.865**	–.078
EXTACCNT	.019	–.003	**.976**

PRINTMEDIA and OTHEROWNERS). This component has been labelled intuitively as 'general sources' to reflect the use of widely available information from websites, newspapers, journals and other publications, and other business owners. Component 2 accounts for 26% of the variance and groups two variables with loadings above 0.8 (COSEC and INTACCNT). This factor has been labelled 'internal professionals' to reflect the fact that the company secretary and internal accountant are professionals on the payroll who both have responsibilities that require them to keep up to date with changes in the accounting and auditing regulations. Component 3 accounts for 17% of the variance and contains one variable (EXTACCNT), which has a loading in excess of 0.9. This component has been labelled 'external professional' to reflect the role of the external accountant as a source of information on changes in the accounting and auditing regulations.

In an exploratory analysis, identifying and interpreting the factors may be the main purpose. However, you can also use the technique to reduce a large data set to a smaller set of factors, and then use the factor scores rather than the original data in a subsequent regression analysis. This has the added benefit of overcoming any problems with multicollinearity (see section 12.5.2).

12.7 Linear regression

Linear regression is a measure of the ability of an independent variable to predict an outcome in a dependent variable where there is a linear relationship between them.

We commented earlier that correlation offers additional information about an association between two variables because it measures the direction and strength of any linear relationship between them. **Linear regression** goes further by giving an indication of the ability of an independent variable to predict an outcome in a dependent variable where there is a linear relationship between them. The term *regression* was introduced in the late 19th century by Sir Francis Galton and refers to statistical models where 'the expected value of one variable Y is presumed to be dependent on one or more other variables (x_1, x_2, ...)' (Upton and Cook, 2006, p. 364). Linear regression is based on an algebraic equation that allows a straight line to be drawn on a graph from information about the slope (the gradient of the line in relation to the horizontal axis of the graph) and the intercept (the point at which the line crosses the vertical axis of a graph) (Field, 2000). The equation states the relationship between a dependent (outcome) variable Y and an independent (predictor) variable x (Upton and Cook, 2006, p. 243):

$$Y = \alpha + \beta x + \varepsilon$$

where

α (alpha) = the parameter corresponding to the intercept
β (beta) = the parameter corresponding to the slope
ε (epsilon) = a random error

In a linear regression model, an *error* (ε) is the difference between the observed (actual) values and the expected (theoretical) values in the model and therefore can be described as a *residual*. Drawing on Field (2000), the assumptions underpinning the linear equation can be summarized as follows:

- The DV (outcome variable) is a continuous quantitative variable (measured on a ratio or interval scale), but an independent (predictor) variable can be continuous or a dummy variable (categorical variables can be used if they are first recoded as dummy variables).
- There is some variation in the data values of IVs (predictor variables); in other words, none have a variance of 0.
- There is no perfect multicollinearity between the independent variables.
- None of the independent variables correlates with another variable that is not included in the analysis.
- The errors are uncorrelated and have a normal distribution with a mean of 0 and constant variance.
- The data values in the dependent variable are independent (in other words, they come from different cases).
- The relationship between the dependent variable and each independent variable is linear.

12.7.1 Simple or multiple linear regression

In a simple regression model, the outcome in the dependent variable is predicted by a single independent variable, while in a multiple regression model it is predicted by more than one independent variable. If your data meet the assumptions of the linear equation we have just described, you can use the following procedure in *SPSS*:

- From the menu at the top, select Analyze ⇒ Regression ⇒ Linear...
- Move your dependent (outcome) variable into Dependent and your independent (predictor) variable(s) into Independent.
- If you have theoretical reasons for choosing the predictor variables (in other words, your hypothesis is based on theory), accept the default method, Enter, which means the variables will be entered simultaneously as one block.
- Click on the Options button and under Statistics and Plots select any additional statistics you want to help you assess the fit of the model to the data and click Continue.
- Then click OK for the results.

It is useful at this point to summarize the results of the bivariate analysis of the data collected by Collis (2003) in which we have tested the variables that the theoretical framework suggested would influence the demand for the audit. This was represented by the dummy variable, VOLAUDIT. The bivariate analysis found a significant difference between the two groups in VOLAUDIT and TURNOVER, CHECK, QUALITY, CREDIBILITY and CREDITSCORE and significant association between VOLAUDIT when paired with FAMILY, EXOWNERS and BANK. The association with EDUCATION was not significant and we had no evidence to reject the null hypothesis for H9.

The next step is to run a multiple regression analysis with VOLAUDIT as the dependent (outcome) variable and the remaining eight variables as the independent (predictor) variables. However, if the dependent variable is a dummy variable, the relationship with an independent variable is non-linear, which means the assumptions of the linear equation are not met. To overcome this problem, the dependent variable can be transformed into a logit, which allows a non-linear relationship to be expressed in a linear form (Field, 2000). If the dependent variable is a dummy variable and one or more of the independent variables are continuous quantitative variables, a *logistic regression* model can be used. If none of your independent variables is a continuous quantitative variable, a *logit* model is appropriate (Upton and Cook, 2006).

Since our dependent variable (VOLAUDIT) is a dummy variable and one of our independent variables (TURNOVER) is a continuous quantitative variable, we should choose a logistic regression model.

12.7.2 Logistic regression

As explained above, logistic regression is a form of multiple regression that is used where the dependent variable is a dummy variable and one or more of the independent variables are continuous quantitative variables. Any other independent variables can be ordinal or dummy variables. Nominal variables can be used if they are first recoded as dummy variables, as described in Chapter 11. There is also an opportunity to do this automatically under the logistic regression options in *SPSS*. The procedure for logistic regression is as follows:

- From the menu at the top, select Analyze ⇒ Regression ⇒ Binary logistic...
- Move VOLAUDIT into Dependent (the term used by *SPSS* for the outcome variable).
- Move TURNOVER, CHECK, QUALITY, CREDIBILITY, CREDITSCORE, FAMILY, EXOWNERS and BANK into Covariates (the term used by *SPSS* for the independent or predictor variables). As we have mentioned before, the order does not matter, but it seems logical to list them in the order of the hypotheses shown in Table 12.1.
- We have theoretical reasons for choosing the independent variables, so accept the default method, Enter, which means they will be entered simultaneously as one block.
- If you have any nominal predictor variables that are not dummy variables, you can click on the Categorical button and move them into the Categorical Covariates box. You would highlight each variable in turn and under Change Contrast select First or Last to indicate which of these categories represents the characteristic is present and click Change. For example, if you did this for FAMILY, the variable would then be shown as FAMILY(Indicator(first)). Click Cancel to leave that dialogue box.
- Now click on the Options button and under Statistics and Plots select Hosmer-Lemeshow goodness-of-fit to help you assess the fit of the model to the data and click Continue (see Figure 12.9).
- Then click OK for the results (see Table 12.10).

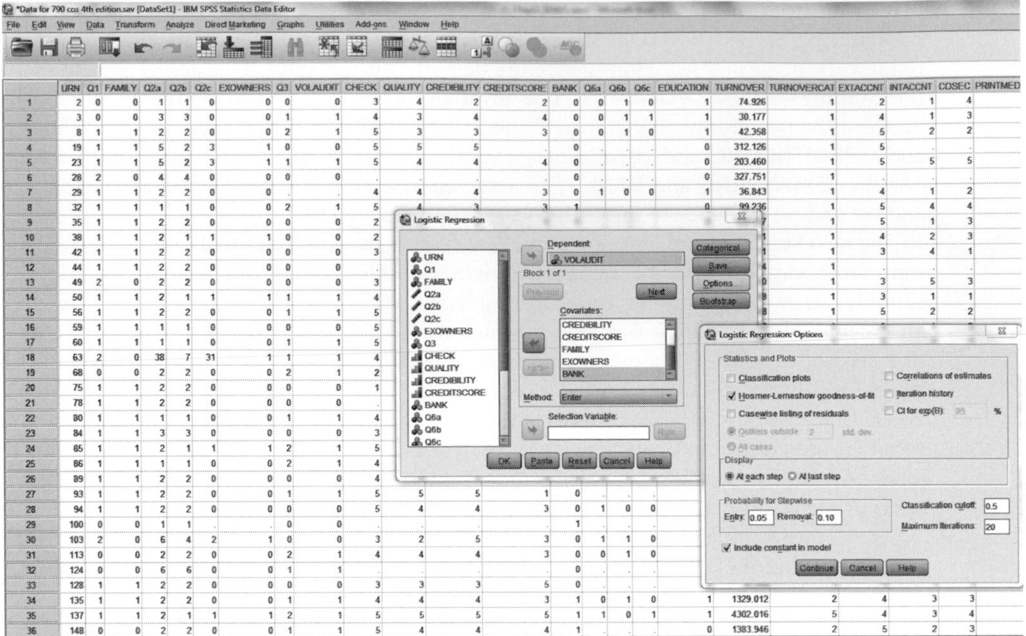

Figure 12.9 Running a logistic regression

Table 12.10 Logistic regression for VOLAUDIT

Case Processing Summary

Unweighted Cases[a]		N	Percent
Selected Cases	Included in Analysis	588	74.4
	Missing Cases	202	25.6
	Total	790	100.0
	Unselected Cases	0	.0
	Total	790	100.0

a. If weight is in effect, see classification table for the total number of cases

Dependent Variable Encoding

Original Value	Internal Value
0 No	0
1 Yes	1

Block 0: Beginning Block

Classification Table[a,b]

Observed			Predicted Q3 0 No	1 Yes	Percentage Correct
Step 0	Q3	0 No	306	0	100.0
		1 Yes	282	0	.0
		Overall Percentage			52.0

a. Constant is included in the model
b. The cut value is .500

Variables in the Equation

		B	S.E.	Wald	Df	Sig.	Exp(B)
Step 0	Constant	-.082	.083	.979	1	.322	.922

Variables not in the Equation

			Score	Df	Sig.
Step 0	Variables	TURNOVER	67.579	1	.000
		CHECK	58.876	1	.000
		QUALITY	82.641	1	.000
		CREDIBILITY	73.669	1	.000
		CREDITSCORE	65.224	1	.000
		FAMILY	25.419	1	.000
		EXOWNERS	14.612	1	.000
		BANK	39.666	1	.000
		Overall Statistics	173.140	8	.000

Block 1: Method = Enter

Omnibus Tests of Model Coefficients

		Chi-square	Df	Sig.
Step 1	Step	205.031	8	.000
	Block	205.031	8	.000
	Model	205.031	8	.000

Model Summary

Step	-2 Log likelihood	Cox & Snell R Square	Nagelkerke R Square
1	609.130[a]	.294	.393

a. Estimation terminated at iteration number 5 because parameter estimates changed by less than .001

Hosmer and Lemeshow Test

Step	Chi-square	Df	Sig.
1	8.306	8	.404

Contingency Table for Hosmer and Lemeshow Test

		VOLAUDIT = 0 No		VOLAUDIT = 1 Yes		
		Observed	Expected	Observed	Expected	Total
Step 1	1	55	55.356	4	3.644	59
	2	50	49.934	9	9.066	59
	3	43	45.181	16	13.819	59
	4	46	40.020	13	18.980	59
	5	31	33.309	28	25.691	59
	6	27	27.177	32	31.823	59
	7	21	23.189	38	35.811	59
	8	14	17.345	45	41.655	59
	9	16	10.681	43	48.319	59
	10	3	3.809	54	53.191	57

Classification Table[a]

			Predicted		
			Q3		
Observed			0 No	1 Yes	Percentage Correct
Step 1	Q3	0 No	225	81	73.5
		1 Yes	71	211	74.8
		Overall Percentage			74.1

a. The cut value is .500

Variables in the Equation

		B	S.E.	Wald	Df	Sig.	Exp(B)
Step 1[a]	TURNOVER	.001	.000	21.810	1	.000	1.001
	CHECK	.246	.124	3.932	1	.047	1.278
	QUALITY	.403	.104	15.086	1	.000	1.496
	CREDIBILITY	.124	.128	.939	1	.333	1.132
	CREDITSCORE	.256	.097	7.026	1	.008	1.292
	FAMILY	-.794	.214	13.767	1	.000	.452
	EXOWNERS	.644	.268	5.796	1	.016	1.905
	BANK	.448	.218	4.212	1	.040	1.565
	Constant	-4.116	.551	55.779	1	.000	.016

a. Variable(s) entered on step 1: TURNOVER, CHECK, QUALITY, CREDIBILITY, CREDITSCORE, FAMILY, EXOWNERS, BANK

This is another situation where there is a large volume of output to help you interpret the analysis. The first table to check is the Case Processing Summary at the beginning, which shows that 588 cases in the sample of 790 were included in the analysis. In multivariate analysis, a case is omitted if there is missing data for any one of the variables and this can be a problem with small samples. However, it is not a matter of concern here.

We can skip the tables in Block 0 where no variables have been entered in the model and concentrate on Block 1, starting with the Model Summary. In this table, the Nagelkerke R Square indicates that the model including our predictor variables explains .393 or 39% of the variance in the two groups in the outcome variable (whether the directors would have a voluntary audit). The hypothesis for the Hosmer and Lemeshow test is that the observed frequencies (actual counts) are not associated with the expected frequencies (theoretical counts). The probability statistic (Sig.) is .404, which is not significant. This means we can reject the null hypothesis and conclude that there is a good fit between the actual data and the model. The Hosmer and Lemeshow test is considered to be more robust than the traditional goodness-of-fit statistic used in logistic regression and is used for models with continuous covariates (as in this study) and studies where the sample size is small (which does not apply to this study).

The final table shows the results for the Variables in the Equation which we entered in one block:

- The probability statistics (Sig.) show that the results for all the predictor variables are significant ($p \leq 0.05$), apart from CREDIBILITY.
- The factor coefficient (B) for FAMILY indicates the expected negative relationship with VOLAUDIT (demand for voluntary audit comes from companies that are <u>not</u> wholly family-owned).
- The higher values of the Wald statistic and the lower values of the probability statistics for TURNOVER, QUALITY, CREDITSCORE, FAMILY and EXOWNERS indicate that these are the most influential predictors of voluntary audit.

We now have evidence to reject the null hypotheses for TURNOVER, CHECK, QUALITY, FAMILY, EXOWNERS and BANK (H1–H3 and H5–H8), but not for CREDIBILITY (H4). This concludes our interpretation of the statistics, but in a dissertation or thesis the analysis would lead on to a discussion of how these results confirm, contradict or contribute to the literature, as well as the limitations and theoretical and practical implications arising from the results. You will find further guidance in Chapter 13.

12.8 Time series analysis

Time series analysis is a statistical technique for forecasting future events from time series data.

A **time series** is a sequence of measurements of a variable taken at regular intervals over time.

A **trend** is a consistently upward or downward movement in time series data.

Seasonal variation is where a pattern in the movements of time series data repeats itself at regular intervals.

If you have collected longitudinal data for a random variable, you can use **time series analysis** to forecast future values. A **time series** is a sequence of measurements of a variable taken at regular intervals over time. The purpose of a time series analysis is to examine the **trend** and any **seasonal variation**. Both can be further analysed using linear regression (Moore *et al.*, 2009). However, before the analysis can commence, it is usually necessary to remove the effects of inflation or seasonal fluctuations. You can do this in *Microsoft Excel* or *IBM® SPSS® Statistics software (SPSS)*. By now you should be fairly confident with using *SPSS* so we will explain the methods in sufficient detail to allow you to calculate the statistics in *Microsoft Excel.*

12.8.1 Indexation

An **index number** is a statistical measure that shows the percentage change in a variable from a fixed point in the past.

If you have collected longitudinal data about a variable whose value changes over time, such as costs or prices, you may want to convert each value to an index number. An **index number** is a statistical measure that shows the percentage change in a variable, from some fixed point in the past. The base period of an index is the period against which all other periods are compared. A simple index shows each item in a series relative to some chosen base period value.

For a clearer indication of the pattern of movement of the value of such a variable over time, it is customary to choose an appropriate point in time as a base; for example a particular year for a variable that is observed annually. The base time-point should be chosen to reflect a time when values of the variable are relatively stable. The value of the variable at other points in time can then be expressed as a percentage of the value at the base time-point. The general formula is:

$$\text{Index number} = \frac{\text{Current value}}{\text{Value at base time-point}} \times 100$$

The resulting figure (known as the *relative*) is the simplest form of index number. The value of the index number at the base time-point is always 100. The following example shows how to construct a simple index.

Example

You have obtained the following historical data relating to the average price of a house in the UK over six years in the 1970s. You will use the first year in the series as the base year (thus, 1971 = 100) and then apply the following formula:

$$\text{Index} = \frac{\text{Current year price}}{\text{Base year price}} \times 100$$

This generates the index shown in the final column of Table 12.11.

Table 12.11 House price index 1971–6

Year	Price	Formula	Index (1971 = 100)
1971	£5,632	$\frac{£5,632}{£5,632} \times 100$	100.0
1972	£7,374	$\frac{£7,374}{£5,632} \times 100$	130.9
1973	£9,942	$\frac{£9,942}{£5,632} \times 100$	176.5
1974	£11,073	$\frac{£11,073}{£5,632} \times 100$	196.6
1975	£12,144	$\frac{£12,144}{£5,632} \times 100$	215.6
1976	£13,006	$\frac{£13,006}{£5,632} \times 100$	230.9

Index figures are very useful for transforming multiple sets of data so that they can be compared in a table or a graph. The following example illustrates how to do this.

Example

You want to analyse the following production data from a factory in your study.

Year	Production units (m)	Number of employees	Units per employee shift
2007	184	602	1.40
2008	180	571	1.45
2009	188	551	1.56
2010	188	524	1.65
2011	185	498	1.72
2012	179	466	1.80

You start by constructing a simple index for each variable, as previously demonstrated, where 2003 = 100. The results are shown in Table 12.12. When these are plotted on a multiple line graph (see Figure 12.10), you can see that the overall production has remained stable despite a steady reduction in the number of employees. This is because the number of units produced per employee shift has increased.

Table 12.12 Production indices 2003–8

Year	Production units index	Number of employees index	Units per employee shift index
2007	100.0	100.0	100.0
2008	97.8	94.9	103.6
2009	102.2	91.5	111.4
2010	102.2	87.0	117.9
2011	100.5	82.7	122.9
2012	97.3	77.4	128.6

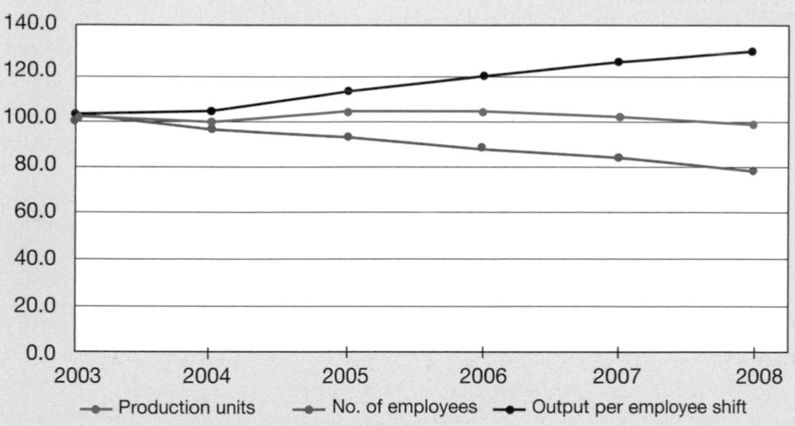

Figure 12.10 Production indices 2003–8

12.8.2 Deflating data

If you have collected financial data over a period when there has been inflation in the economy, this will obscure the underlying trend in the data. However, you can use indexation to deflate the data and thus remove the effect of inflation. The resulting data will then reflect the value of money as it was in the base year of the index you use. It is convenient to use an index such as the Retail Prices Index (RPI) as it is known in the UK or the Consumer Price Index (CPI) in the USA and some other countries. A price index is the weighted mean of the prices paid by consumers for a set of standard household goods and services. The following example illustrates how to deflate your research data using such a price index.

Example

You have obtained the following historical data relating to a company's profit over a five-year period in the 1980s and the RPI for each year. You find out that the base year for the RPI at that time was 1974 (thus, 1974 = 100). You then apply the following formula:

$$\text{Deflated profit} = \frac{\text{Base year RPI}}{\text{Current year RPI}} \times \text{Profit}$$

This generates the deflated profit figures shown in the last column of Table 12.13.

Table 12.13 Deflated profit 1982–6

Year	Profit	RPI (1974 = 100)	Formula	Deflated profit
1982	£12.0m	320.4	$\frac{100}{320.4} \times 12.0$	£3.7m
1983	£13.5m	335.1	$\frac{100}{335.1} \times 13.5$	£4.0m
1984	£15.1m	351.8	$\frac{100}{351.8} \times 15.1$	£4.2m
1985	£17.0m	373.2	$\frac{100}{373.2} \times 17.0$	£4.6m
1986	£19.0m	385.9	$\frac{100}{385.9} \times 19.0$	£4.9m

The deflated profit figures are now based on the value they would have had in 1974. They can also be plotted on a line graph, as shown in Figure 12.11, which illustrates the distorting effects of inflation very clearly. Far from the dramatic increase shown in the original data, the deflated profit figures show only a modest increase over the period, which puts a different complexion on the financial performance of the company and demonstrates the impact of inflation during the 1980s.

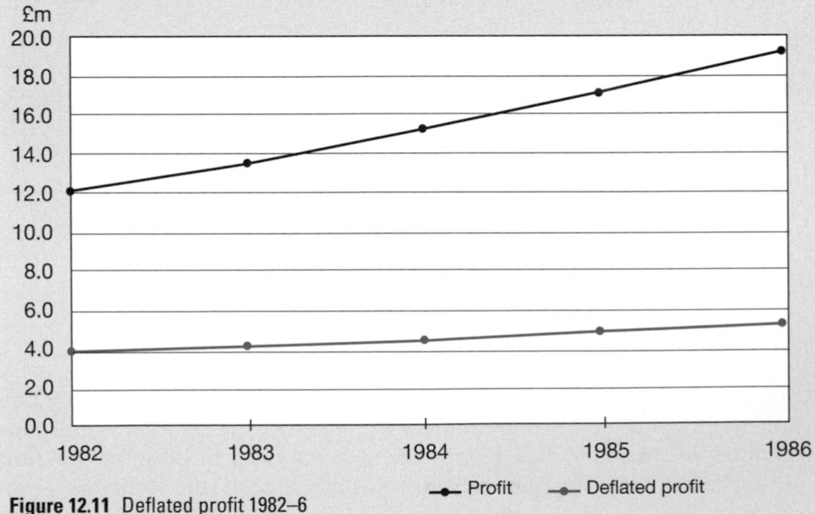

Figure 12.11 Deflated profit 1982–6

12.8.3 Weighted index numbers

A **weighted index number** is constructed by calculating a weighted average of a set of values. A weighted average is an average that can attach more importance to some values than others. For example, in a consumer price index, the prices are weighted to reflect the prices paid by consumers for different retail goods and services. Another example of a weighted index is the FTSE 100 Index, which represents the share prices of the largest 100 companies listed on the London Stock Exchange in any quarter and is calculated minute by minute. Unlike other indices, it has a base of 1,000 and this relates to prices on 3 January 1984 (Law, 2010).

A weighted index number is an index number constructed by calculating a weighted average of some set of values, where the weights show the relative importance of each item in the data set.

When calculating weighted index numbers, you should remember that the weights are held constant at their values for the base time-point. Since the weighting may change dramatically over a long period of time, it is only realistic to use weighted index numbers with fixed weights over short periods. An index can be calculated which is the average of a series of price relatives. To be realistic, it should take into account the amount of each commodity used and this is what a weighted index reflects. We will now explain two methods for calculating weight index numbers.

A *Laspeyres index* is a base period weighted index, where the weights relate to a chosen base period. The formula is:

$$\text{Laspeyres index} = \frac{\Sigma PcQb}{\Sigma PbQb} \times 100$$

where

Pc = Current price
Pb = Base price
Qb = Base quantity

The advantages of a Laspeyres index are:

- the index is easy to calculate for a series of years as it uses the same set of weights every time
- it allows a comparison of any one year with any other as all use the same weights
- it requires little data in terms of weights.

The disadvantages of a Laspeyres index are:

- the weights used will gradually become out of date and will no longer represent the contemporary situation
- it tends to overestimate price increase because it uses out-of-date weights.

A *Paasche index* is a current period weighted average where the weights are used to rebase to the current period. The formula is:

$$\frac{\Sigma PcQc}{\Sigma PbQc} \times 100$$

where

Pc = Current price
Pb = Base price
Qc = Current quantity

The advantage of a Paasche index is:

- the index always uses the current weights and thus reflects today's situation.

The disadvantages of a Paasche index are:

- the index involves more calculation for a series of years as the weights used are constantly changing
- it can only be compared against the base year as the weights for each year change
- it tends to underestimate price increases
- it requires new weights each period which can be both costly and time-consuming to collect.

12.8.4 Calculating the deseasonalized trend

We have already mentioned that the main use of time series analysis is to predict *trends*. A trend is a consistently upward or downward movement in the data values over the time period. A *seasonal variation* is where a pattern in the movements repeats itself at regular intervals. The two main statistical models for analysing time series data are the *additive model* and the *multiplicative model*. The formulae are as follows:

$$Y = T + S + C + I \text{ (additive model)}$$
$$Y = T \times S \times C \times I \text{ (multiplicative model)}$$

where

Y = the observation
T = trend
S = seasonal variation
C = cyclical component
I = irregular component

Although the additive model is simpler to analyse, the multiplicative model is generally considered to be more realistic. The adequacy of the multiplicative model may be tested by analysing the irregular component. If this is not random, the suitability of the model must be questioned. Any component may be absent from a particular time series (for example, annual data cannot include the seasonal variation component). We will use an example to explain this.

Example
Perhaps you have collected quarterly data relating to the number of ice creams sold (the sales volume) by a particular business over a five-year period.

- First calculate the 4 quarter moving total by adding the sales volume in groups of four.
- Then calculate the 8 quarter moving total by adding the 4 quarter moving totals in groups of two.
- Next, divide the 8 quarter moving totals by 8 to obtain the trend.
- Before you can eliminate any seasonal variations, you will need to calculate the de-trended series by dividing your original quarterly data (Y) by the trend (T).

These calculations are quickly computed on a *Microsoft Excel* work sheet and Table 12.14 illustrates this stage of the analysis. If you use a calculator, discrepancies may occur due to rounding.

If you have tried this for yourself on a spreadsheet, you can now plot the trend for ice-cream sales over the period on a graph and use the seasonal index to forecast the data for the next year in the series.

12.8.5 Evaluating the cyclical and irregular variation

In order to evaluate the cyclical variation (C) you need to obtain the de-trended, deseasonalized series:

$$\frac{Y}{T \times S} = C \times I$$

Next, smooth out the irregular component (I) by means of a moving average performed on the $\frac{Y}{T \times S}$ series.

Since the aim is to smooth and not to remove the cycle, a three-point moving average could be used. The irregular component (I) is obtained from:

$$\frac{Y}{T \times S \times C}$$

The irregular component should be random in nature; otherwise the adequacy of the proposed model must be questioned. Therefore, evaluation of the irregular component yields a measure of method suitability. For multiplicative models, the irregular component should be random about unity (± 1). If the irregular component is evaluated and shown to be random, it can be removed from the series, producing an error-free series:

$$\frac{Y}{I} = T \times S \times C$$

In order to be reasonably certain that components exist in a time series, there should be sufficient data to establish the reality of these components or complementary information to suggest their presence. In a short span of data, random phenomena can appear to be systematic and, conversely, systematic effects can be masked by random variation.

12.9 Conclusions

Apart from the important matter of whether your data meet the four basic assumptions that determine whether you can use parametric tests, you need to consider time constraints and your skills. The data used to illustrate the inferential statistics in this chapter relate to a study that was designed to address a set of hypotheses underpinned by theory. Although the research data were non-parametric, we have also explained the equivalent parametric models.

In the previous section we have showed how comparison of longitudinal data can be aided through indexation and time series analysis can be used to examine the trend and any seasonal variation. If the latter is present, the deseasonalized trend can be calculated and any cyclical and irregular variation evaluated. The trend and the seasonal variation can be analysed using linear regression.

Your choice of analysis will depend on whether your research data are parametric or non-parametric and whether you want to:

- summarize and/or display the data (descriptive statistics)

- test for significant differences between independent or related samples (inferential statistics)
- test for significant association between variables (inferential statistics)
- reduce data to composite variables (factor analysis)
- predict an outcome from one or more independent variables (inferential statistics)
- forecast trends from longitudinal data (time series analysis).

It is important to remember that you need to know how you are going to analyse your data before you collect them. We provided a checklist at the end of the previous chapter and Box 12.3 extends this by summarizing the main steps in analysing quantitative data.

Box 12.3 Main steps in analysing quantitative data

1. Quantify answers to open questions.
2. Identify each case and enter the data into your software program.
3. Name the variables and the coding labels, and identify the level of measurement.
4. If recoding is required, recode into a different variable, thus keeping the original intact.
5. For most business research, accept the *SPSS* default significance level of 0.05.
6. Decide whether your hypotheses are one-tailed or two-tailed.
7. Identify the dependent variable and the independent variable(s) (not applicable when testing for correlation).
8. Determine whether parametric or non-parametric tests are appropriate.
9. Decide whether you have independent or dependent samples.
10. Explore, describe and analyse the data using appropriate statistical methods to address your research questions.

References

Collis, J. (2003) *Directors' Views on Exemption from Statutory Audit*, URN 03/1342, October, London: DTI. [Online]. Available at: http://www.berr.gov.uk/files/file25971.pdf (Accessed 20 February 2013).

Field, A. (2000) *Discovering Statistics Using SPSS for Windows*. London: SAGE.

Kervin, J. B. (1992) *Methods for Business Research*. New York: HarperCollins.

Law, J. (ed.) (2010) *Dictionary of Accounting*, 4th edn. Oxford: Oxford University Press.

Moore, D., McCabe, G. P., Duckworth, W. M. and Alwan, L. C. (2009) *The Practice of Business Statistics*, 2nd edn. New York: W.H. Freeman and Company.

Upton, G. and Cook, I. (2006) *Oxford Dictionary of Statistics*, 2nd edn, Oxford: Oxford University Press.

Wallace, R. S. O. and Mellor, C. J. (1988) 'Non-response bias in mail accounting surveys: A pedagogical note', *The British Accounting Review*, 20, pp. 131–9.

Activities

This chapter is entirely activity-based. If you have access to *SPSS*, start at the beginning of the chapter and work your way through. If *SPSS* is not available, do the same activities using an alternative software package following the on-screen tutorials and help facilities.

Please visit the companion website for the progress test and to access the data file referred to in this chapter at www.palgrave.com/business/collis/br4/

Have a look at the **Troubleshooting** chapter and sections 14.2, 14.5, 14.7, 14.10, 14.12, 14.13 in particular, which relate specifically to this chapter.

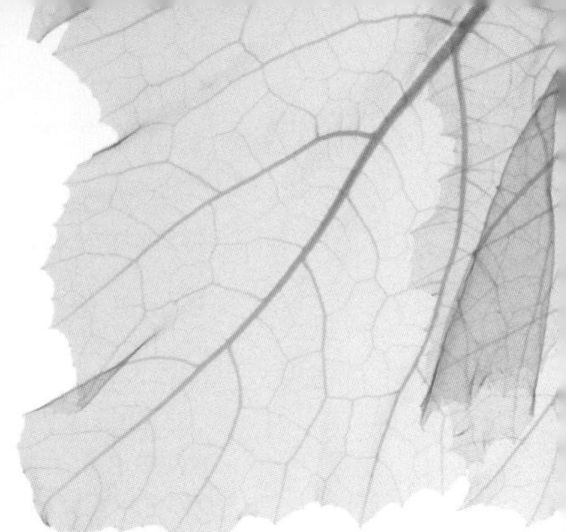

13

writing up the research

learning objectives

When you have studied this chapter, you should be able to:

- plan a strategy for writing up your research
- structure the chapters and content of your dissertation or thesis
- decide how to present qualitative and quantitative data
- understand the general standards for a dissertation or thesis
- develop a strategy for getting published.

13.1 Introduction

By the time you get to the final writing-up stage in your research, you should have collected and analysed a significant amount of literature and research data. Writing up your research can be a rewarding process if you have been writing draft material for your chapters as you conducted your study, discussing them with your supervisor(s) and making amendments. This chapter offers guidance on writing the first complete draft of your research report, which is the final stage in the research process.

At the undergraduate and taught Master's level you are likely to find that your time is fully taken up with your studies and doing your research, whereas MPhil students and doctoral students may have written and presented papers at conferences or had articles published. Once you have successfully completed your dissertation or thesis, all students should consider writing conference papers and articles. This will improve your academic reputation and enhance your employability. This chapter also gives guidance on getting published.

13.2 Planning

Writing up often presents the greatest challenge to research students, but it is made somewhat easier if you have been writing notes and rough drafts throughout the period of your research. If you are a doctoral student and you have put off writing until your final year, you are likely to encounter major difficulties or even failure. In our experience, time management is supremely important for students on an undergraduate or taught Master's programme as well, and putting off the writing-up stage until the last minute greatly reduces your chance of passing. Instead, you should start developing the sections in your proposal into the chapters of your dissertation or thesis as you proceed with your research.

13.2.1 Planning strategies

There are a number of strategies you can adopt when it comes to writing up your final research report. In a survey of 110 social science research students at British universities, Torrance, Thomas and Robinson (1992) found that 104 reported using the specified planning and writing strategies when producing their last substantial piece of academic text. These are shown in Table 13.1.

Table 13.1 Planning and writing strategies adopted by students

Strategy	% reporting
Brainstorming or writing down a checklist of ideas which might be included in the final document but which does not specify the order in which they might be presented	80
Taking verbatim notes from the relevant literature	78
Putting notes into some kind of order	63
Constructing a 'mind map' which gives a spatial representation of the links between particular ideas	54
Constructing a plan that details not only the content of the finished piece, but also the order in which it will be presented	84
Writing out full drafts in continuous prose but not necessarily in polished English	94
Revising full drafts	94

Source: Torrance, Thomas and Robinson (1992, p. 159). Reprinted by permission of the publisher (Taylor & Francis Ltd, http://www.tandf.co.uk/journals).

We can use advice from the general literature to expand these strategies into activities you can pursue. Most authors emphasize the importance of getting your thoughts written down in one way or another. Phillips and Pugh (2010) advocate using a brainstorming approach and putting down all the main points that come to mind. By generating all the main points in a random order, some students claim it frees the mind. Moreover, a point from the literature or methodology can generate points concerned with the research results and analysis.

As mentioned in Chapter 6, designing a map of the literature can be a useful preliminary step as it helps you summarize previous studies. You could use a mind map or a hierarchical diagram (see Chapter 2) that helps you organize the literature and shows where your study fits in. Not only can you use the diagram to guide the structure of your preliminary literature review, but you can use it on a slide if you are making a presentation at a research seminar or conference. This approach is not limited to your literature review and you can use diagrams to help you structure any of your chapters.

It is important to remember that you do not have to start the process of writing the chapters in your research report in any particular order. Some researchers prefer to write in the same order as the research report is structured. However, it is not advisable to finalize your introductory chapter, or even your title, until the end. Therefore, an appropriate chapter to work on at an early stage is your literature review, as in many cases it forms part of the research proposal. This would lead you on to your methodology chapter, which can be finalized once you have enough information to describe the more detailed aspects of the methods of data collection and analysis you have used. Doctoral students may have written conference papers or articles on parts of their research, which can be used to form the basis of different chapters in the final research report. It does not matter what strategy you adopt; the important thing is to start developing your draft chapters at an early stage in your research and getting timely feedback from your supervisor.

Some students put off writing up because they are still updating their literature or collecting more data because there has been a change. You must be strong willed and decide to impose a definite cut-off point on your research. Your dissertation or thesis will be an account of your research up to the chosen date and you need not worry about events after that time. Your supervisor(s) and examiners appreciate that you are not writing a newspaper which must contain the latest news!

13.2.2 Setting a timetable

While determining the structure of your thesis, it is also useful to draw up a timetable showing the critical dates when different sections will be completed. You will have a deadline for submission of your dissertation or thesis, and it is easy to think of this as coinciding with when you have finished writing up. However, finishing writing is not the final stage; you will also need time for editing, proofreading and binding the finished report.

It is difficult to estimate exactly how long the writing up and final tasks will take, as there are so many factors to be considered, but, even when you are an experienced researcher, it can take a good deal longer than you think. We recommend that you build in additional time for contingency factors, such as illness and domestic interruptions (both in your life and that of your supervisors), computer problems, lost documents and so on. In Table 13.2 we give an indicative breakdown of the main tasks and approximately how long they take for a full-time PhD candidate. This schedule assumes that some preliminary work has been done. By this we mean that the literature review and methodology chapters are in draft form, the analysis has been completed, some of the figures and/or tables have been prepared and a list of references has been kept. Even so, you can see that six months is given to the final writing-up stage for such a doctoral thesis of about 80,000 words.

Table 13.2 Indicative time for writing a PhD thesis

Chapter or task	Weeks
Introduction	2
Literature review	4
Methodology	2
Findings and discussion	8
Conclusions	2
Tables, figures, references, appendices and so on	1
Consultation with supervisor/others and revisions	4
Editing, proofreading and binding	3
Total	26

Editing is a process that involves re-reading and identifying errors and omissions in the content and structure of your work, and consequently amending it. There are no short cuts, but if your supervisor, colleagues and family will read and comment on your early drafts it will make your job easier. Before you start editing try to have a break of a week or two, so that you can return to it with a fresh eye and, possibly, a more open perspective. When you have finished editing your research report, you are ready to begin reading it for errors in spelling, grammar, chapter and section numbering, table and figure numbering, page numbering and so on.

13.2.3 Writing style

You should write your dissertation or thesis to inform and not to impress (Hakes, 2009). Your written communication skills are very important and it is essential that the meaning of each sentence and paragraph is clear, even if the content is technically or conceptually complex. Some students adopt a lengthy, complicated style of writing in the mistaken belief that it is more academic. Try to resist this temptation. Your dissertation or thesis is a unique piece of research (even if it is a replication study) and you want your supervisors and examiners to understand every aspect of it, so that you have the greatest chance of gaining high marks. Think about attracting and keeping the examiner's attention by using headings and subheadings, dividing the text up into digestible chunks, interspersing it with tables and diagrams if appropriate, and providing a clear layout with wide margins.

Chall (1958) identifies three key, interrelated elements of the readability of text which we advise you to take into account:

- interest (the ability to hold the reader's attention)
- legibility (the impact of factors such as typography and layout on the reader)
- ease of understanding (reading comprehension).

In Box 13.1 we offer some general guidance on the presentation of text. We recommend you use up-to-date reference sources, such as an authoritative dictionary, thesaurus and grammar guide. Use the *spelling* and *grammar checker* on your software, but be aware that it cannot take account of the sense in which the words are used or whether they represent an interesting or dull form of expression. However, the dictionary used by the spelling checker can be set to take account of cultural differences between English-speaking nations which give rise to differences in spelling. Before using an *abbreviation*, you should show the term in full the first time you use it, with the abbreviation in brackets next to it; subsequently you can simply use the abbreviation.

Box 13.1 Guide to the presentation of text

Writing style

- Text should be written as lucidly and clearly as possible.
- The language and style should be appropriate for your paradigm and your intended audience.
- Sentences should be kept short; preferably no longer than 20 words.
- A new paragraph should be started for each new idea.

Grammar and semantics

- The grammar, punctuation and spelling (especially of names) should be checked.
- Computerized spelling and grammar checkers should be used judiciously.
- Precise words, rather than general or abstract words, should be used.
- The meaning of words and phrases should be checked for correct usage.
- Jargon should be avoided and a glossary provided for any technical terms.
- The document should be carefully proofread for typographical mistakes, repetition, clichés, colloquialism, errors and omissions.

Although spelling, grammar and punctuation play an important role, writing is more than a matter of correct usage; it involves a careful choice of words to create a lucid, flowing style, which both attracts and maintains the interest of the reader. Therefore, it is important not to become pedantic over rules. This should allow a personal style of writing to develop. If you already have a good writing style, the above principles will be relatively easy to apply. Unfortunately, most of us are not so blessed, but we can, at least, aim to be competent.

One way to improve your style is to look at how the academic authors you admire express themselves. In addition, you should get others to comment on your work. Your supervisor can do this, but is more likely to be concerned with the way that you conducted the research and the results. Therefore, you may find it more useful if you can agree to exchange your written work with fellow students for comment. This kind of mutual support can be very encouraging and may also help you keep ahead of the various deadlines you set yourself.

13.2.4 Designing the report

In this section we consider the overall report design. When planning your research report, it is useful to bear in mind the concept of synergy: your dissertation or thesis should be greater than the sum of its parts. To achieve this, you must remember that the chapters which comprise your report do not exist in isolation from one another; they are interrelated and need to be integrated to form a cohesive whole. In Box 13.2 we offer a logical and structured approach to report design.

Box 13.2 Guide to report design

Structure

- The information should be presented in a logical sequence. Each section should have a logical progression and support a central message. Each item should lead to the next.

- A standard hierarchy of headings and subheadings should be adopted to structure the report.
- The chapters, main sections and subsections should be numbered sequentially. Thus Section 3.5.5 refers to the fifth subsection in section 5 of Chapter 3. Three is normally considered to be the maximum number of subdivisions. Therefore it is usual to divide the report into chapters which contain a number of main sections and, in turn, these are divided into subsections.
- It is not usual to number the paragraphs for in a dissertation or thesis. However, this may be required if you are designing a report for a non-academic sponsor, such as a government department or professional body. In such cases, you should seek guidance from your sponsor on the format and style.

Style and layout

- Throughout the document there should be consistency of style in terms of page size, layout, headings, fonts, colour, justification, and so on.
- A reasonable sized font (say 10 or 12 point) should be used to ensure legibility.
- The layout should aid the communication.
- Colour or space should be used to attract the reader's attention to key information.
- Do not distract the reader by using more than four or five colours (except for illustrations and photographs). Avoid the combination of red and green for adjacent data, which is a problem for people who are colour-deficient.

Presentational forms

- To maintain the interest of the reader, a variety of presentations should be used, as dictated by the type of data (for example interval or continuous) and the purpose (for example for comparison).
- Tables, graphs and other illustrations should relate to the text so that the information is supported by the different representations.
- Titles and headings used for tables, graphs and other illustrations should also be standardized and numbered sequentially. The first digit should refer to the chapter number and the second digit to the table/figure number. Thus, Table 3.5 refers to the fifth table in Chapter 3. It is helpful to the reader if the title is shown above the table or figure and the source of the data is shown below.

Even at the first draft stage, it is valuable to put the material in the format required by your institution. This will save you considerable time later on when you are trying to refine and improve the content of the document. You will need to ascertain from your university or college what the requirements are with regard to style, length and structure of your research report. You will be expected to submit your work in double spacing (or 1.5 lines), printed on only one side of the page. There are also likely to be requirements to meet regarding page numbering, font size and margin widths. For example, a left-hand margin of at least 1.25 inches leaves room for the document to be bound; a right-hand margin of 1 inch allows examiners to write comments. You must ensure that your document complies with your institution's regulations.

You will be restricted in the maximum length of your research report, and this is likely to be measured by the number of words it contains. Table 13.3 gives a general indication of the typical word count for a dissertation or thesis. The references and appendices are not usually included in the word count. You should bear in mind that supervisors and examiners are aware of students' ploys in placing information in an appendix rather than writing in a more succinct style to keep within the maximum length. At any level, a research report accompanied by a voluminous set of appendices is likely to give a poor impression.

Table 13.3 Typical length of a dissertation or thesis

Level	Research report	Word count
Undergraduate	Dissertation	10,000
Taught Master's	Dissertation	15,000
Master's by research	Thesis	40,000
Taught doctorate	Thesis	50,000
Doctorate by research	Thesis	80,000

13.3 Structure and content

13.3.1 Structure

The overall structure of your dissertation or thesis should be logical and clear to the reader, and you should bear this in mind when deciding on the wording of your headings for each section, table or figure. Table 13.4 shows a generic structure, with an indication of the approximate size of the chapters in relation to the whole report. It is important to note that this structure is only a guide; you will need to modify it to reflect your own research project after discussions with your supervisor. In practice, the size of each chapter will vary according to the nature of the research problem, the methodology adopted and the use of tables, charts and diagrams. In an undergraduate or taught Master's dissertation, there is often less scope for primary research and therefore the literature review will form a more substantial part of the report. On the other hand, at the doctoral level, particularly where the research is designed under an interpretivist paradigm, the methodology chapter plays a very significant role.

Table 13.4 Indicative structure of a research report

	% of report
1. Introduction – The research problem or issue and the purpose of the study – Background to the study and why it is important or of interest – Structure of the remainder of the report	10
2. Review of the literature – Evaluation of the existing body of knowledge on the topic – Theoretical framework (if applicable) – Where your research fits in and the research question(s) and propositions or hypotheses (if applicable)	30
3. Methodology – Identification of paradigm (doctoral students will need to discuss) – Justification for choice of methodology and methods – Limitations of the research design	20
4. Findings/results *(more than one chapter if appropriate)* – Presentation and discussion of the analysis of your research data/statistical tests and their results	30
5. Conclusions – Summary of what you found out in relation to each research question you investigated – Your contribution to knowledge – Limitations of your research and suggestions for future research – Implications of your findings (for practice, policy and so on)	10
	100
References *(do not number this section)* – A detailed, alphabetical (numerical, if appropriate) list of all the sources cited in the text	
Appendices *(if required)* – Detailed data referred to in the text, but not shown elsewhere	

It is useful if the chapter titles you use reflect the contents, but do not be over-imaginative; the examiner will have certain expectations about the content and the order in which it will appear. Therefore, it is best not to depart too far from a traditional structure, unless you have good reasons. There are no hard and fast rules about how individual chapters should be structured, but some form of numbering is common. You will have noted that in this chapter we have numbered the main sections 13.1, 13.2, 13.3 and so on. Where we have decided that there is a need for subsections they are numbered 13.2.1, 13.2.2, 13.2.3 and so on. Think carefully about the wording of the headings and subheadings you use, as these give important signals to the reader about content and sequence of different aspects of your discourse in your table of contents. You should consider carefully before dividing your subsections any further, as this may lead to a fragmented appearance.

The more logical you can make your structure, the easier it will be for you to write the report and for the examiner to read it. The ordering of the sections in the chapters is very much a matter of choice, influenced by the nature of the research and the arguments you are trying to make. Howard and Sharp (1994) suggest a number of different ways that the sections can be ordered:

- chronologically, where you describe events in the order in which they occurred. This is clearly most appropriate when you are trying to give a historical perspective or describe developments
- categorically, where you group the issues into various categories or groups, a good example of which is a geographical classification, although in business research you may choose to group matters by activity (for example production, administration, sales and so on)
- sequentially, where you describe the events in the sequence in which they occur. This is useful when explaining or analysing the events in a process, and is similar to chronological ordering but not so closely time related
- by perceived importance, where you present the information starting with the least important and move to the most important, or vice versa. The direction in which you move will depend on the nature of the argument you are making.

13.3.2 Preliminary pages

The preliminary pages precede the first chapter. The page numbers for these pages are normally small Roman numerals (i, ii, iii and so on). This allows the pages of the chapters to be numbered in Arabic numerals (1, 2, 3 and so on). The preliminary pages are typically as follows, but you should check the regulations at your institution:

- *Title page* (no page number) – Your research project will have been registered with a particular title, but you may wish to amend it to ensure that it clearly indicates the topic and focus of your study. Keep the title as short as possible and eliminate unnecessary words. Choose your words carefully and do not include general phrases such as 'A study of …' or 'An investigation into …' as they are superfluous. Sometimes a colon is used in the title, as in 'Demand for voluntary audit: The UK and Denmark compared'.
- *Copyright notice* (no page number) – Only include if appropriate.
- *Abstract* (start numbering the pages here) – If you are required to include an abstract, remember that it is not an introduction, but a brief summary of the purpose of the research, the methodology and the key findings.
- *Declaration* – Use the wording required by your institution, such as: 'I declare that all materials in this project report that are not my own work have been acknowledged and

I have kept all materials used in this research, including samples, research data, preliminary analysis, notes and drafts, and can produce them on request.'

- *Table of contents* – If you designate styles to your hierarchy of headings in your software, you can automatically generate this list of the chapters and sections within them, together with their associated page numbers.
- *List of tables* and *list of figures* – As appropriate.
- *List of abbreviations* – If required, you can list the acronyms in alphabetical order with the full term providing the explanation.
- The *acknowledgements* – If appropriate, these consist of one or two sentences thanking those who have helped you with your research; for example participants (while being careful to write in general terms to preserve their anonymity), your supervisor(s), colleagues and family.

Having described the preliminary pages, we are now ready to look at the chapters, which form the main body of the research report. You will need to divide each chapter into several numbered sections. All your chapters should have an introductory section and a concluding section, which allows you to provide links between the chapters, but it will not always be appropriate to head them 'Introduction' and 'Conclusions'. We will comment on this in the next section.

13.3.3 Introductory chapter

It may surprise you to know that once your supervisor(s) and examiner(s) have glanced at your contents page, the first two chapters they are likely to read are the first and the last. This is because your introduction and your conclusions chapters give overviews rather than the detailed information contained in the chapters sandwiched between them. Therefore, it is very important that you do not neglect these smaller chapters. Nevertheless, we suggest you do not finalize your introductory chapter until after you have completed your conclusions chapter to ensure they are complementary.

The introductory chapter will probably have four or five sections. As in all chapters, your first section will be an introduction to the chapter. This may cause you a problem if you've decided to call your first chapter '1. Introduction to the study'. A simple way round this is to call the chapter '1. Background to the study' or '1. Overview of ... [name of the research topic]', which will allow you to call your first section in the chapter '1.1 Introduction'.

The first few sentences of the introduction are crucial, as these will attract the reader's attention and set the tone for the entire document. Winkler and McCuen-Metherell (2012) offer three different strategies for beginning a research paper, which we believe can be used as a guide to the opening of the introduction in any research report:

- Use an appropriate quotation that is directly relevant to the research problem or issue and leads you on to develop an argument to support or refute the quotation.
- Pose a question that draws the reader into your discussion. This allows you to word the question to fit the arguments you wish to present.
- Use a carefully chosen illustration that is directly relevant to the research problem or issue that can capture the reader's interest immediately.

In the early sections you must explain the research problem or issue and the purpose of the study. You can then go on to provide the background to the study, which is a broad view of the topic that gradually narrows down to explain why your study is important or of interest. There is no need to go into great detail, as subsequent chapters will do this. Do not make the mistake of mentioning any of your findings or conclusions in this chapter.

Remember that you will need to review and amend any material you wrote for your proposal. The final part of your introduction will give a brief guide to the subsequent chapters of your research report. Therefore, this chapter does not need conclusions.

13.3.4 Literature review chapter(s)

In Chapter 5 we defined a literature search as a critical evaluation of the existing body of knowledge on a topic, which guides the research and demonstrates that relevant literature has been located and analysed. Thus, the main task is to evaluate the existing body of knowledge on the research problem or issue you have studied. If you are a positivist, you will draw out your theoretical framework and hypotheses. Your literature review will reflect the way in which you have analysed the literature. It will be a critical review that is structured thematically, rather than a descriptive list of publications you have read. The concluding sections will draw attention to the gaps and deficiencies in our knowledge, and identify which of these your study addresses. This will lead to a statement of your research questions and hypotheses (if applicable). Of course, your research questions must relate to the research problem you have identified in your introduction chapter.

By now you should be familiar with the methodologies and findings of the seminal studies in your topic area, and the names of the authors. These citations and others from the leading journals for your topic will play a key role in your literature review. If you have published an exploratory study or a paper on a related topic, or presented it at a conference, you should also cite that. This will demonstrate to your supervisors and examiners that your work has been exposed to a certain level of peer review.

On the subject of citations, we have a few tips to offer. If you are referring to an author whose work you think is important or whose argument you consider supports yours, you should start the sentence with his or her name. For example, 'Bloggs (2013) found evidence of a link with motivation that may explain …' On the other hand, if you want to place more emphasis on the idea than the author, cite the name within the sentence. For example, 'Although a link with motivation has been suggested as an explanation (Bloggs, 2013) …'. Remember that it is your research and you are setting out to be the authority in this specialized area, so do not be afraid to criticize their work, regardless of their status. However, it is essential that you justify your criticisms. If your supervisors or examiners have published on your topic, ensure that you fully understand their work and take note of any limitations they point out themselves in their papers. Cooper (1988, p. 107) provides a useful definition which covers all styles of literature review:

> First, a literature review uses as its database reports or primary or original scholarship, and does not report new primary scholarship itself. The primary reports used in the literature may be verbal, but in the vast majority of cases reports are written documents. The types of scholarship may be empirical, theoretical, critical/analytic, or methodological in nature. Second, a literature review seeks to describe, summarize, evaluate, clarify and/or integrate the content of primary reports.

While perusing the literature, you will read other authors' literature reviews. These should offer you an additional guide to what is required. The main point to remember is that your literature review should show a competent exploration of the background to the work and a comprehensive review of the relevant literature, including the most recent publications. It is a written discussion of the literature and forms a significant part of your dissertation or thesis.

If you are concerned that your literature review is too long, you may need to go through it summarizing where you have become too verbose. If you feel inclined to delete some of the less important items, pick out references to newspapers, commercial magazines and unpublished academic work, rather than articles in refereed academic journals. Only delete references to articles in the latter if they are not relevant. There is much more detailed guidance in Chapter 5, but we will conclude this section by looking at some of the common faults made by students when reviewing the literature

Box 13.3 Common faults when reviewing the literature

- Making assertions without stating where the evidence is
  - You must support all assertions with references to the literature, even if your claims are accepted wisdom; otherwise you will be guilty of plagiarism
- Failing to state the country, time, objectives, respondents, methodology of previous studies
- Listing the literature rather than providing a synthesis and a critical evaluation
- Poor structure, writing style, spelling and grammar
  - Use section headings within the chapter to signal themes and link ideas
  - Adopt a style that reflects your rhetorical assumptions
  - Avoid colloquial phrases in your own writing
  - Use the spelling and grammar checker
- Literature review fails to show relevance to the study
  - Identify the theoretical framework or context for your study
  - Conclude with the research question(s) addressed by your study

13.3.5 Methodology chapter

The methodology chapter is a critical part of the report in both a positivist and an interpretivist study, but will vary according to which paradigm you have adopted. From a general point of view, both approaches require a section which explains how the problem was investigated and why particular methods and techniques were used (Bell, 2010). Both will start with an introductory paragraph which briefly describes the main features of the methodology and the organization of the chapter. In a positivist study, this will be followed by a statement of the procedures adopted, description of the sampling methods, formulation of hypotheses and the statistical techniques of analysis employed. In an interpretivist study, the structure is more flexible and will be closely related to the methodology employed.

In a positivist study, the methodology section should describe the exact steps taken to address your hypotheses or research questions (Rudestam and Newton, 2007). If you are using well-known procedures and tests, there is no need to describe them in detail; you need only refer to them. You will also need to describe any little known techniques, or those you have devised or modified, in detail. In a positivist study, the methodology chapter can usually be divided into the main sections as shown in Box 13.4.

Box 13.4 Main sections in the methodology chapter of a positivist study

- Description of the sampling method, the sampling frame, size of the population, number of responses, and the response rate compared with previous studies.
- Explanation of the appropriateness of the methodology in the context of your paradigm.
- Description of the methods used to collect data for the literature review and the research data. Discussion of their strengths and weaknesses in the context of alternatives to justify your choice. If the research data were collected over a long period of time, include a timetable showing when specific activities took place and any critical events.

- Description of the methods used to analyse the literature and the research data. Discussion of their strengths and weaknesses in the context of alternatives to justify your choice.
- Description of the variables in the analysis, level of measurement, unit of measurement and codes used.
- Consideration of ethical issues and discussion of the limitations in the research design, making reference to generalizability, reliability and validity.

In an interpretivist study, the methodology chapter should stress the nature and rationale for the chosen methodology, before leading on to discuss the method(s) of data collection and analysis. You may consider that the philosophy and assumptions underpinning the methodology, and their appropriateness to the research problem, are so important that you devote a separate chapter to their discussion. Box 13.5 gives guidance on writing the methodology chapter(s) in an interpretivist study.

Box 13.5 Main sections in the methodology chapter of an interpretivist study

- Description of the sampling method, focusing on how cases were located and selected.
- Explanation of the appropriateness of the methodology in the context of your paradigm. As there are many variations within an interpretivist approach, quote a number of definitions of your methodology, explain the main features and refer to studies that have used it.
- Description of the methods used to collect data for the literature review and the research data. Discussion of their strengths and weaknesses in the context of alternatives to justify your choice. If the research data were collected over a long period of time, include a timetable showing when specific activities took place and any critical events.
- Description of the methods used to analyse the literature and the research data. Keep this general and do not start discussing your findings.
- Consideration of ethical issues and discussion of the limitations in the research design, making reference to generalizability, reliability and validity.

The philosophical assumptions of your paradigm must be woven into the way you write. Merriam (1988) identifies the following assumptions which provide a platform for interpretivists:

- You are concerned primarily with process, rather than outcomes or products.
- You are interested not in frequency, but in meaning; that is, how people make sense of their experiences and the world around them.
- You are the primary research instrument. It is by and through you that data are collected, analysed and interpreted.
- Your research is placed in a natural, rather than an artificial, setting. It is conducted in the field by you visiting the places where the activity takes place so that you can observe and record it.
- The research is descriptive and seeks to capture process, meaning and understanding.
- The process of research is mainly inductive because you are attempting to construct abstractions, concepts, hypotheses and theories from abstractions.

13.3.6 Findings/results chapter(s)

While positivists usually refer to their *results* because their analysis is based on statistical tests, interpretivists are more likely to use the term *findings*. More than one chapter may be necessary to present and discuss your analysis.

You should start by restating the purpose of the research and the research questions from your first chapter, since these should direct your analysis and discussions. You can then move on to a description of your sample or cases (positivists will provide descriptive statistics). This sets the scene for you to present the analysis of your research data, which you should structure in a logical order that allows the reader to relate your evidence to the research questions. Positivists will need to discuss their results in the context of their hypotheses and make reference to existing theory; interpretivists are more likely to be drawing out theory that emerges from the analysis.

Positivists will find it relatively easy to present the results of their analysis in tables and figures, whereas interpretivists will need to spend some time reflecting on diagrammatic forms to support their narrative findings. We will be looking at this more closely in section 13.4.

13.3.7 Conclusions chapter

It is very important that this final chapter in your dissertation or thesis complements your first chapter, because many examiners turn immediately to it after reading the introductory chapter. While your introductory chapter should start broadly and then became focused, your conclusions chapter should be the opposite.

Start by restating the purpose of the research and then summarize what you found out in relation to each research question. Do not introduce new information. This is a good time to check that you have used the same terms when describing the purpose of your research and your research questions throughout your dissertation or thesis.

You should then widen your discussion by explaining your contribution to knowledge, without being too ambitious in your claims. This will include making reference to the gaps and deficiencies in the literature that your study has addressed. Look at the aims of your research in the introductory chapter and ensure that your conclusions show that they have been achieved or explain why they have not. Of course, you must also summarize the limitations of your research, which you discussed in your methodology chapter, and this will lead you to make suggestions for future research. Do not be reluctant to be self-critical and demonstrate what you have learned from your experience.

Vox pop What has been the highpoint of your research so far?

Maysara, MBA student investigating healthcare systems management in occupied Palestinian territory

I feel that covering the gap in knowledge in an area where no research has ever been conducted was very significant. I hope it will open the doors for further studies and lead to better healthcare for the Palestinian people.

Ben, MBA student investigating the impact of the credit crunch on access to finance for SMEs

Although the government has introduced a number of incentives to help SMEs get access to finance, the findings from my interviews suggested that very few owner-managers knew about these schemes. This excited me as I hope to develop a consultancy helping businesses access this source of finance.

To end your dissertation or thesis on a strong, positive note, you might conclude by discussing the implication of your results/findings for practice, policy and so on. If you are an MBA or DBA student, you may be expected to make several practical recommendations based on your results/findings. Remember that the theme of the whole of this chapter is the conclusions that can be drawn from your study, so you will not head your final section of this chapter 'conclusions'. In the same way that you spent quite a bit of time choosing the opening of the introductory chapter, you should spend a long time on the last sentence. Aim for a convincing ending!

If your dissertation or thesis is going to be examined orally at a viva voce, this chapter often receives the greatest attention. Therefore, be careful not to make any sweeping statements or exaggerated claims. If you have found out something that is interesting and worthwhile, and we hope you have, discuss it fully and with enthusiasm. However, remember to acknowledge the contribution made by previous studies, which underpins your work.

If you are having difficulty in writing up your dissertation or thesis, or you are suffering from writer's block, have a look at Chapter 14 (sections 14.13–17).

13.3.8 Appendices

The place for information that is too detailed or not sufficiently relevant to be included in the main part of your dissertation or thesis is an appendix. Typically, the appendices (one for each group of items) will contain material such as background information on the industry or cases, regulations and published statistics.

Each appendix should be numbered sequentially and given a title. The numbering should relate to the order in which each appendix is first mentioned in your dissertation or thesis. If you have not mentioned an appendix in your report, perhaps the information in the appendix is superfluous and can be excluded. Most examiners are not impressed by large quantities of data in appendices and you should not make the appendices a dustbin for all those bits and pieces you could not fit into the main part of the document or a way of reducing your word count!

13.4 Presenting qualitative and quantitative data

The use of analytical software for analysing quantitative data and qualitative data greatly assists the generation of tables and figures, and the drawing facilities on *Microsoft Word* and other word processing programs help you develop your own diagrams using ready-made shapes, arrows, lines, flow chart symbols and callout balloons. We will start by looking at the presentation of qualitative data.

13.4.1 Qualitative data

Presenting qualitative data you have collected can pose a number of difficulties. The process involves taking field notes and other documentation and making an initial draft before writing a working, interpretative document which 'contains the writer's initial attempts to make sense of what has been learned' (Denzin, 1994, p. 501). This is a working document which you will need to reflect upon and discuss with your supervisor. You may make a number of drafts before you finalize the document that 'embodies the writer's self-understandings, which are now inscribed in the experiences of those studied' (Denzin, 1994, p. 502).

If your data are mainly qualitative, it is essential that you intersperse your text with quotations. This will give your text authenticity and vibrancy, and will enable the reader to share the world you are analysing. However, you must be careful that any illustrations or quotations you give are relevant and part of the fabric of the study. 'Provided they are supported by other forms of data and tie in clearly with other aspects of the analysis, using individual episodes can provide a powerful means of getting a hold on the problems of presenting complex qualitative data' (Allan, 1991, p. 187). You may wish to present short quotations embedded in the text, like the quotation from Allan in this paragraph. This method illustrates a point while maintaining the flow of the narrative. However, if you want to increase the importance of the quotation, you could present it as a separate indented paragraph like this:

> If your data are mainly qualitative, it is essential that you intersperse your text with quotations. This will give your text authenticity and vibrancy, and will enable the reader to share the world you are analysing. However, you must be careful that any illustrations or quotations you give are relevant and part of the fabric of the study as Allan (1991) points out: 'Provided they are supported by other forms of data and tie in clearly with other aspects of the analysis, using individual episodes can provide a powerful means of getting a hold on the problems of presenting complex qualitative data. (Allan, 1991, p. 187)

The data displays you used for analysing your research of the data can be used to great effect when presenting your qualitative data, although your main discussions will be in the text. You may also want to create your own diagrams. In an article reporting an ethnographic study conducted in a retail gift store, McGrath (1989) used data from participant observation, in-depth interviews and photographs to provide description and interpretative insights into the consumer gift selection and retailer socialization process.

13.4.2 Quantitative data

The general rule for writing numbers in the text is to use words for the numbers one to nine, and numerals for 10 onwards. For example, 'Only five of the respondents answered this question', as opposed to 'There were 52 respondents in this category'. There are many exceptions to this rule. For example, when numbers below 10 are grouped together for comparison with numbers 10 and above in the same paragraph, they should all appear as numerals. For example, 'Only 5 of the 52 respondents in this category answered this question'. Other exceptions are described by Rudestam and Newton (2007).

In the sections that follow, we have drawn together a number of principles to form guidelines for different forms of presentation. This is not intended to be a rigid set of rules and you may discover other principles.

Tables

The data in a table are tabulated or classified by arranging the data items in a framework of columns and rows. Research shows that some people prefer data presented in tabular form, but often need more time to get the main points from a table than they would need with a chart (Macdonald-Ross, 1977). However, tables offer the advantage of being compact and exact, and 'usually outperform graphics in reporting on small data sets of 20 numbers or less' (Tufte, 2001).

Iselin (1972) suggests that the way in which a table is constructed can aid the reader's comprehension. Construction signalling allows items that are grouped together to be identified, as well as differentiating names of items from names of groups. Iselin uses three different methods of construction signalling:

- lower and upper case letters
- the indentation of items under a group heading
- spacing between groups of items.

Although Iselin's experiments were confined to students and some of his findings require further research, he shows that effective construction signalling has a significant effect on the speed and accuracy of the extraction of information.

Drawing from the literature and our own experience, in Box 13.6 we offer guidance on the construction of tables in your research report.

Box 13.6 Guide to constructing tables

General advice

- Use a tabular presentation for an educated audience.
- Use columns rather than rows to compare figures. If comparison is the main purpose of the presentation, consider using a comparative bar chart.
- Restrict the size to no more than 20 numbers. This can be done by dividing a large table into two or more small tables. Consider a graph for large data sets.
- Minimize the number of words used, but spell words out rather than using abbreviations or codes.

Structure and layout

- Place the table number and title at the top to allow the reader to identify and understand the purpose of the presentation before proceeding to the body of the table.
- Use different fonts and styles to distinguish the table title, headings and subheadings.
- In pairs or sequences of tables, use identical labels for common headings and labels.
- Indent items under a group variable label.
- Set columns compactly so that the eye does not have to travel too far between labels and each column of figures.
- Add grid lines to facilitate the reading of columns and rows.

The quantitative data

- Round numbers to two significant digits, unless precision of data is important.
- Where possible, order columns/rows by size of numbers. Place any miscellaneous variable last, regardless of size.
- Provide column/row averages or totals where appropriate.
- Draw attention to key figures with colour, shading or bold typeface.

Charts and graphs

When using a graphical presentation for quantitative data, your aim is to present the information in a clear, concise, simple, effective, uncluttered and understandable manner. Research shows that some people prefer data presented in graphics, such as charts and graphs. Playfair, the 18th-century political economist, developed nearly all the basic graphical designs when looking for ways in which to communicate substantial amounts of quantitative data. He preferred graphics (pictures and charts) to tables because they show the shape of the data in a comparative perspective (Playfair, 1786). According to Tufte (2001), graphics are often the most effective way to describe, explore, and summarize a set of numbers, even if it is a very large set of numbers.

Graphics, especially when colour is used, can attract and hold the reader's attention and help identify trends in the data. Therefore, quantitative information displayed in a graph 'has the potential to be both read and understood. But effective communication does not follow automatically from graph use; the graph must comply with certain principles of graph design and construction' (Beattie and Jones, 1992, p. 30). Tufte (2001) suggests that both colour and monochrome presentations require careful handling to avoid detracting from the message or misleading the reader.

Although most commentators promote the graphical presentation of comparative data, there appears to be some conflict over acceptable levels of complexity. Ehrenberg (1975, 1976) advises that a graph should communicate a simple story, since many readers concentrate on the visual patterns, rather than reading the actual data. In Box 13.7 we offer general guidance on constructing charts and graphs.

Box 13.7 Guide to constructing charts and graphs

General advice

- Do not mix different types of data (for example percentage and absolute figures) on the same chart, but draw up separate charts.
- Items should only be compared on the same chart if they have the same basic data structure and a clear relationship.
- Label the axes.
- Label data elements directly and include the unit of measurement. If there is insufficient room to label the elements directly, provide a key.
- Minimize the number of words used but, if possible, spell words out, rather than using abbreviations or codes. The majority of ink used to produce the graph should present the quantitative data. Delete anything that does not present fresh information, since this represents a barrier to communication.

Structure and layout

- Place the chart number and title at the top to allow the reader to identify and understand the purpose of the presentation before proceeding to the body of the graph.
- Use different fonts and styles to distinguish the chart title, axes and data element labels.
- Select an unobtrusive background.

The quantitative data

- Select colours for the data elements with high contrast from adjacent items.
- Avoid the combination of red and green on adjacent elements, which is one of the most common problems for people who are colour-deficient.

Bar charts

Macdonald-Ross (1977) suggests that the elements of bars should be labelled directly; horizontal bars give room for labels and figures near the elements. However, for time sequences, he recommends vertical bar charts. Thibadoux, Cooper and Greenberg (1986) advise that bars should be of uniform width and evenly spaced; they are easier to read and interpret if a space of half the width of the bar is left as the distance between the bars. The scale should begin with zero and normally should remain unbroken. The number of intervals should assist with measuring distances and generally should be in round numbers, marked off with lines or ticks. They recommend that in general graphics which use horizontal and vertical scale, lines should be proportioned so that the horizontal scale is greater than the height. This view is shared by Tufte (2001) who proposes that if the nature of the data suggests the shape of the graphic, follow that suggestion; otherwise move towards a horizontal graphical presentation about 50% wider than tall.

With regard to shading, Thibadoux *et al.* (1986) suggest that black is appropriate if the bars are not extremely wide, when diagonal line shading or cross-hatching may be used. However, horizontal and vertical shadings should not be used in segmented bars because they may affect the perceived width and shape of the bar. With cross-hatching, care must also be taken not to create optical illusions. Box 13.8 shows additional principles that apply to bar charts.

Box 13.8 Additional principles for bar charts

General advice

- Use a bar chart for comparing data.
- In a bar chart, the bars represent different categories of data. The frequency should be shown by the length (horizontal bar chart) or height (vertical bar chart) of each bar. In a histogram, the frequency is indicated by the area of the bar.
- Use a vertical bar chart for time sequences with the scale on the left. The time elements should move from left to right on the horizontal axis.
- Use a multiple bar chart, rather than a segmented bar chart, since the former provides a common base for the segments.
- Use a histogram for continuous, ratio or interval data where the class widths are unequal.

The bars

- In a bar chart, the bars should be of uniform width and evenly spaced.
- The end of the bar should be straight, not rounded or any other shape.
- Horizontal bars give room for labels and figures near the elements. Values should only be given if the result is legible and does not look cluttered.
- When using three-dimensional bars, clearly label the dimension that indicates the measurement point.
- In multiple bar charts, do not use more than four elements.
- In histograms, the ordering of the bars should be sequential.
- If you are using pictograms, take care that the dimensions (length, area or volume) correctly reflect the changing value of the variable.
- Avoid pictograms with undefined measurement points, such as piles of coins.
- Black is appropriate if the bars are not extremely wide; alternatively use shades of grey.
- Horizontal, vertical and diagonal lines should be avoided, as they can create optical illusions.

The scale

- Commence the scale at zero.
- If a break in the scale is unavoidable, it must be clearly indicated.
- Proportion the horizontal scale so that it is about 50% greater than the vertical scale.

Pie charts

Pie charts are useful for presenting proportional data. The labels and figures should be placed nearby to facilitate comparison of the different segments. Thibadoux *et al.* (1986) suggest that the largest segment is placed at the central point of the upper right half of the circle, followed in a clockwise direction by the remaining segments in decreasing order, with any miscellaneous segment placed last. There is general agreement that a pie chart should contain no more than six categories and should not be used to compare different sets of data. Research by Flannery (1971) shows that if quantity is related to area, readers tend to underestimate differences. Box 13.9 shows the additional principles that apply to pie charts.

Box 13.9 Additional principles for pie charts

General advice

- Use a pie chart to present proportional data only.
- Use the angle at the centre to divide the circle into segments; the area of each segment should be proportional to the segment represented.
- Do not use pie charts to compare different sets of data; instead, consider a bar chart.

The segments

- Use no more than six segments.
- Place the largest segment at the central point of the upper right half of the circle, followed in a clockwise direction by the remaining segments in decreasing order.
- Place any miscellaneous variable last, regardless of size.
- Each segment should be labelled and its value given as a percentage of the whole.

Line graphs

In a line graph, the independent variable is shown on the horizontal axis and the dependent variable on the vertical axis. Although it is usual to place the scale figures on the left-hand side of the graph, in wide graphs it may be helpful if they appear on both sides. One advantage of line graphs over other forms is that a number of graphs can be superimposed on the same axes. This enables comparisons to be made very clearly. Thibadoux *et al.* (1986) recommend that if the curves are close together or cross, colour coding may be used to differentiate them or different patterns, such as solid, dash, dotted or dot-dash lines. However, Bergwerk (1970) found that experts on the communication of financial data preferred graphs showing only one or two elements. Box 13.10 shows the additional principles that apply to line graphs.

Box 13.10 Additional principles for line graphs

- The component categories should be represented by a series of points joined by a line.
- The axes must represent continuous scales with the independent variable shown on the horizontal axis and the dependent variable on the vertical axis.
- Place the scale figures for the vertical axis on the left. In a wide graph show the scale on both sides.
- Use no more than two elements.

As with tabular presentations, it is important to remember that however clearly presented your graphs and charts are, it is still necessary to offer some interpretation and, if possible, further analysis of the data. This should be given immediately after the graphical presentation.

13.5 General standards

13.5.1 Standards for a research report

When writing up your research you should bear in mind the standards your supervisors will be looking for. Table 13.5 summarizes the elements and associated criteria that are typically used to assess a dissertation or thesis.

Table 13.5 Elements and general criteria used to assess a dissertation or thesis

Element	Criteria
Objectives	Clarity Relevance Achieved
Research design	Appropriate Rationale Assessment: Reliable (replicable) Valid (accurate)
Literature review	Relevant Sources
Data collection and analysis	Primary/secondary Relevant to objectives Quality of analysis
Conclusions and implications	Persuasiveness/supported by evidence Any recommendations feasible/imaginative
Presentation	Style/use of language Clarity Use of tables/figures/summaries Word count
Internal consistency	Continuity Objectives/conclusions
Integration of academic knowledge	Originality/initiative 'A learning process'

The extent to which your dissertation or thesis must achieve these attributes depends on the level of your degree. Table 13.6 gives details of the assessment criteria for a research report at different levels. However, this is merely indicative and you will need to refer to the specific guidance you are given by your lecturers and follow the advice given by your supervisors. You can see that the criterion separating a doctoral thesis from the research report at other levels is originality and the contribution to knowledge. We advise doctoral students to discuss these important criteria with their supervisors.

Table 13.6 Indicative assessment criteria for a dissertation or thesis

Level	Description	Criteria
First degrees and some Master's degrees which require the completion of a project	Dissertation	1. A well-structured and convincing account of a study, the resolution of a problem, or the outcome of an experiment
Master's degree by study and dissertation	Dissertation	1. An ordered, critical and reasoned exposition of knowledge gained through the student's efforts. 2. Evidence of awareness of the literature
Master's degree by research	Thesis	1. Evidence of an original investigation or the testing of ideas 2. Competence in independent work or experimentation 3. An understanding of appropriate techniques 4. Ability to make critical use of published work and source materials 5. Appreciation of the relationship of the special theme to the wider field of knowledge 6. Worthy, in part, of publication
Doctoral degree	Thesis	1. to 6. as for Master's degree by research 7. Originality as shown by the topic researched or the methodology employed 8. Distinct contribution to knowledge

Source: Howard and Sharp (1994, p. 177). Reproduced with permission.

If you are worried about whether your work will be up to the standards required, have a look at Chapter 14 (section 14.16).

13.5.2 The viva voce

A viva voce is an oral examination that is always part of the assessment for doctoral students and is sometimes used for Master's and undergraduate students. The purpose is to give you an opportunity to defend your research in response to the examiners' questions. You will need to argue a coherent case. It is always a nerve-racking experience, but you can lessen the agony and improve your performance by practising answering questions. First, you find out how your viva voce will be conducted and the names of your examiners. At the undergraduate level, they are likely to be internal examiners (lecturers at your own institution), so you will know them. At higher levels, there may be one internal examiner and more than one external examiner. You may only know the latter by reputation. In all cases, it is useful if you reflect on their research interests and paradigms from their publications and from talking to your supervisors. This can help you avoid pitfalls or getting into heated discussions on topics where you know their opinions differ greatly from your own.

The atmosphere is likely to be fairly formal but cordial. Everyone (including you) will take a copy of your dissertation or thesis to the meeting for ease of reference. Many examinations start off with an open question inviting the student to explain the purpose of the research. It then moves on to the examiners asking questions and the student responding. These may be clarification questions or a question centred on some weakness the examiner considers is present. In either case, he or she is testing your knowledge. As the examination progresses, it is likely to become a discussion, with the student taking the lead in explaining the research. The examiners are not trying to trip you up, but they will want to explore any weaknesses in your dissertation or thesis. They will expect you to know your subject. This means you need to be very familiar with your research, even though it may have been several weeks or months since you submitted it to the examiners. Phillips and Pugh (2010) give detailed instructions on how to prepare for this by summarizing every page into a few words which capture the main idea and the page number. You can then use the summaries for revision before the examination and take them in with you so that you can refer the examiners to particular pages. Ask your supervisors if they can arrange a mock viva voce. If not, persuade colleagues, family and friends to help you. At the MPhil and PhD levels, it is imperative that you have practised presenting your research and this is why attending conferences, seminars and workshops is so valuable. These activities should have alerted you to potential weaknesses and the range of questions that might arise in your viva voce.

Be careful not to argue with the examiners, but where you have strong opinions and you can support them, do not hesitate to voice them strongly. Play to your strengths and not your weaknesses. Some of the questions put to you may appear to be on the edge of the scope of your study, so attempt to place them in a context where you are certain of the facts. You need to accept that there may be defects in your study and explain to the examiners how they arose and how you would set about remedying them. If you do not understand a question ask for clarification. This is far better than giving an inept response. Do not rush into giving replies. Many of the questions will be complex and you should take time to reflect on the question and your answer. Your responses should be balanced, with a review of the advantages and disadvantages, and conclude with your own opinions. The major advantage you have is that you conducted the research, not the external examiners. Therefore, you will certainly know more about the details than they do. Try to keep the discussions in this area and explain any interesting factors or aspects.

Even an amusing anecdote of an event while you were conducting the research would not go amiss, provided it is not too long.

Students and supervisors are sometimes permitted to use their laptops to refer to the research report. You need to check this in advance of your viva voce. If permission is granted, make sure that you and your supervisors have the version of your research report that you submitted to the examiners. You also need to be certain that you are fully conversant with its location on your laptop and the functions of your laptop. Examiners are likely to become irritated if they have to wait while the student searches through endless files for some interesting data 'that is on there somewhere'.

The outcome of a viva voce depends on the nature of the qualification. For an undergraduate or taught Master's degree, the research project is only one element that earns you credits towards your degree. With an MPhil and PhD, the degree rests solely on the thesis and viva voce and the following outcomes are possible:

- The award is made immediately after the viva voce and you have nothing else to do except receive the congratulations of your friends and family.
- The award is made, subject to minor amendments that must be completed within a specified period. These are usually modest changes and should cause you no problems. You will not be subjected to another viva voce and your internal examiner will be responsible for making certain that the final, bound thesis incorporates the amendments.
- The award is not made and you are asked to make substantial revisions. You have not failed and have the opportunity to resubmit and be re-examined. In this case the changes will be major and will take you a number of months to complete. However, you will have the benefit of having received guidance from the examiners on what is expected, and as long as you can meet these requirements you will receive the award.
- An outright fail with no possibility of being able to resubmit.
- In the case of a viva voce for a PhD, the examiners may decide that although the work is of some merit, it does not meet the standard required for a doctorate. If appropriate, they may recommend that an MPhil is awarded instead.

13.6 Conference papers and articles

Much of what we have suggested in this chapter also applies to writing for conferences and journals, but with some important differences. A research report as part of a programme of study is solely an academic document. You may decide to use your research to present papers at conferences or to write for journals and magazines. You will be communicating to different audiences in a different medium and in this section we will consider some of the issues.

13.6.1 Conference papers

Conferences can be divided into commercial and academic conferences. Commercial conferences are well advertised and the business people attending them often have to pay a sizeable fee. Usually there are a number of speakers who are regarded as experts in their field. If you are fortunate enough to be regarded as an expert, you can expect a substantial fee, but you must be articulate and know your subject well. The audience will not be interested in your research design, literature review or methodology, but in your research results and the implications for their businesses.

Academic conferences are less lavish affairs and can range from small regional conferences, with only a dozen participants, to large international conferences with an audience of thousands. Despite differences of size and location, both audiences will be interested in and critical of your research. The call for papers usually goes out several months before the conference and you are usually expected to submit a paper for consideration of approximately 5,000 words, together with an abstract. If the conference organizers consider it is worthy, they will allocate a certain length of time for you to present it. With some conferences this can be as short as 20 minutes; with others you may be allocated an hour. You should devise a presentation based on your paper, bearing in mind the time available and allowing time at the end for questions.

If you are looking for an academic career, you must present papers at academic conferences. You may find that this also leads to a publication, as some organizers publish a collection of selected papers presented at the conference. You will find out details of academic conferences from your supervisor(s), departmental notice boards and journals. The costs are usually fairly low, often involving little more than accommodation, meals, travel and hire of rooms. Once you have attended one or two conferences, you will find a network of other researchers.

Most conferences require you to submit an abstract some months before the conference with the full paper later on. Most conferences send the papers for review in order to ensure the quality of the research presented. A large conference may hold a doctoral colloquium where students can attend workshops and present their papers. Whether you are presenting at a conference or a doctoral colloquium, you will need to prepare a *Microsoft PowerPoint* presentation. The number of slides depends on how long the conference gives for each presentation. A typical allocation is 15–20 minutes for the presentation and 10 minutes for the discussion. You should allow approximately 2–3 minutes per slide. A typical presentation would cover:

- the purpose of the research and the context
- the conceptual framework or the theoretical framework and hypotheses
- the findings from the analysis or the results of the statistical tests
- the contribution and limitations of the study.

Your concluding remarks might focus on any areas where you would particularly like advice or your plans for further research. The conference organizers normally provide a chairperson who will introduce you and explain the protocols regarding the amount of time you have and when members of the audience can ask questions. Take notes of the questions and comments, as they provide valuable feedback that will help you develop your paper and build your confidence.

Vox pop What has been the highpoint of your research so far?

Hany, final year PhD student investigating the ERP impact on the internal audit function

Getting constructive feedback on my findings from academics and practitioners at conferences was an amazing experience!

13.6.2 Articles

Once you have presented your conference paper a number of times at high quality conferences, and developed it further each time based on the feedback you received, you will probably be thinking about using it as the basis for a publication. There are three main types of article that you might want to consider, each with its own style and word length. Table 13.7 gives details.

Table 13.7 Indicative lengths of articles

Type of article	Typical length
Newspapers and magazines	800–1,500 words
Professional journals	1,200–2,000 words
Academic journals	6,000–8,000 words

Popular publications include the local and national press, as well as commercially focused and other magazines. With these types of publication, it is likely that the editor will only commission an article if you have something to write from your research that is controversial and/or highly topical. Therefore, a study of the hardships suffered by textile workers in the 19th century is unlikely to be commissioned, but if you can use your research to illuminate and explain current events you may find an outlet for it. However, if your research is not topical but focuses on local industry or events, you may find that your local press is interested. Before you submit an article, read past copies of the publication so that you are familiar with the style and the topics they cover. At the local level you may not receive any payment, but at the national level you will normally receive a modest payment based on the length of the article.

The associations and societies of professional bodies, such as accountants, lawyers and engineers, produce their own professional journals, usually on a monthly basis. These concentrate on topical issues and other matters that are relevant to their members, including those that are of historical importance. You might find that your research contains something that will entice the editor to commission an article, but he or she may want you to put a certain slant on your story. You can expect payment, but again this is likely to be modest.

We will now consider academic journals. You need to discuss your publication with your supervisor and others working in your field. You may also consult journal rankings such as the *Association of Business Schools (ABS) Academic Quality Guide*, *Excellence in Research for Australia (ERA)* or *Maastricht Research Institute/School of Economics and Organizations (METEOR) Journal Classification*. If you are submitting an article to an academic journal, you will find details of how to do it on the journal's website. You will be required to submit the article without revealing the name(s) of the author(s). In some cases, you may have to pay a fee, which is not refundable even if the article is rejected. The editor decides whether the subject and general quality of the article is appropriate to the journal and, if so, will send it to members of the editorial board to be reviewed. In most cases, this is a 'double blind' review because the reviewer will not be told the name(s) of the author(s) or the other reviewer(s). The reviewers will make a recommendation to the editor that the article should be:

- published without any amendments
- resubmitted once the reviewers' comments have been addressed
- rejected.

Getting published in a prestigious journal is a considerable achievement because the competition is extremely high due to so many academics trying to get their work published in the best journals. The reward is that high quality publications greatly enhance your chances of getting an academic position and advancing your career. There is guidance in the literature to help you achieve success and we have distilled these recommendations into the following tips:

- Know what the journals publish – You need to do your market research and identify the journals that accept articles of the type you are trying to get published. Your own literature search should have identified those journals which may be interested in your offering. You will also find articles that have surveyed the types of articles published by specific journals (for example Beattie and Goodacre, 2004; Prather-Kinsey and Rueschoff, 2004) or identified topics that are hot in certain business disciplines (for example Piotrowski and Armstrong, 2005).
- Be realistic about your contribution – Your article must make a contribution to knowledge and the best way to do this is to demonstrate how it fits into the existing literature and the *impact* your contribution makes. Examples of impact include the results of your research being used by international or national policymakers, professional bodies, practitioners, industries or particular types of business; or the results might bring benefits to society or particular groups of individuals within society.
- Read the journal's guide to authors – Follow the instructions exactly. They vary from one journal to another. Go through copies of the journal for the past five years or so and identify articles in the same general area and make sure that you cite them in your article.
- Try not to become disillusioned by the reviewers' comments and recommendations, but discuss how to tackle them with your supervisor and/or other experienced researchers.

Box 13.11 shows an example of how the authors of an article responded to the comments made by the three anonymous academics who reviewed their article. You can see that both the reviewers and the authors have put a lot of thought into the process and you should not be surprised to find that it may take a number of iterations before you get the final decision on whether your article will be published or rejected.

Box 13.11 Responding to reviewers' comments

Comments	**Our response**
Reviewer 1	
Discuss the role of accountants as a more significant influence on filing decisions than respondents' limited awareness.	These issues are often closely related rather than distinct. Small company owners often rely on advice from accountants *because* they lack awareness of the consequences of filing decisions. The data from accountants suggest that for most, the default position with small company clients is to recommend filing abbreviated accounts. All or most small company clients reportedly file abbreviated accounts, suggesting a high level of accountant influence – or at least small company agreement with them (see pp. 11–12). But, in addition to advice from accountants, small company owners report a major benefit of filing abbreviated accounts, confidentiality. Such a benefit is perceived as tangible whereas the negative consequences of filing decisions are perceived as intangible or even nonexistent. Persuading small company owners that there *are* negative consequences of filing abbreviated accounts, even potentially (e.g. risk of limiting access to finance and markets), might require considerable effort. Small company owners might turn out to be right or wrong with regard to their beliefs about the consequences of their filing choices.

Comments	Our response
Reviewer 1	
P. 1 Define 'small company performance'.	Text amended on p. 2.
P. 2 Refer to UK government decision to adopt an extreme position with regard to small company exemptions.	Text amended on p. 4.
P. 2 Cite reference for 'cost of capital' claim.	The para on p. 2 only provides an overview of the paper. To add references seems unnecessary, but we are willing to be guided by the editor. The issue is discussed in more detail on pp. 6–7.
P. 3 Replace 'see the financial reports' with 'access'.	Text replaced.
Pp. 3–4 Refer to EC impact assessment.	Text amended on pp. 3–5 to clarify that the published Directive differs from the original draft, for which an impact assessment is available.
Pp. 6–9 Cite additional references to support the conceptual framework.	Text amended. The framework is based principally on previous work of one of the authors (unaccredited in the text as yet). Additional references have been added to support particular parts of the conceptual framework. No one, to our knowledge, theorizes regulation explicitly in the overall way presented here, particularly emphasizing the indirect influence of regulation and its partial visibility to the agents involved.
P. 9 Strengthen argument to support claim regarding 'strong qualitative component' and use of 12 interviews.	Text amended. While interviews were conducted with only 12 small company preparers, we also interviewed 20 accountants and 18 other stakeholders – as well as conducting a postal survey of small company preparers and two online surveys of accountants. Our arguments are built on the data from small companies *and* stakeholders. Most work in accounting/financial reporting is quantitative, so even a small qualitative study potentially offers insights into agents' motivations and the processes surrounding filing and use of accounts.
Table 1: Develop survey analysis; consider possibility of generalization.	We have not amended the text on this point. Our principal focus is on the qualitative data to elaborate processes specified in the conceptual framework. We prefer to keep it this way. We are interested in understanding filing choices and actors' motivations for the decisions they make. Developing the survey analysis would make it a quite different paper. We seek to generalize on the basis of the causal powers of regulation rather than on empirical associations between survey variables. We identify the contradictory influences set in motion by financial reporting regulation, contingent upon the exercise of agency by small companies and stakeholders. Our argument is intended to challenge studies of regulation that claim it is solely a burden/cost/ constraint on small businesses.

Comments	Our response
Reviewer 1	
P. 12 Clarify origin of claim regarding '... a further 15%'.	Text amended on p. 14.The source of this claim is highlighted at the start of the sentence. We have added 'of these accountants' for further clarification after the 15% claim.
The Directive on accounting regulation allows member states to opt for abbreviated accounts within certain guidelines; comment on the UK's extreme position adopted.	We have made this point clear now on p. 4.
P. 14 Elaborate explanation/ interpretation of the three quotations.	Text amended on p. 16. We have made the reasons clear for retaining all three quotations in the para preceding them, rather than adding supporting explanations for each. Each quotation makes a similar point, but in relation to three different types of stakeholder. Prior research has focused on competitors.
P. 14 Clarify perceptions referred to.	Text amended on p. 17, to clarify that we refer to data on the perceptions of clients of small companies.
Table 3: Clarify '% responding'.	Table 3 amended to show this refers to the small company survey. Table 2 amended similarly.
Reviewer 2	
Abstract: Claim about indirect effects of regulation unsupported.	Abstract revised.
P. 15 Qualify claims about (a) abbreviated accounts option being highly valued by small company directors; and (b) value of maintaining privacy.	Text amended on p. 17 to clarify that claims refer to the small company directors interviewed. We do, however, present our belief that such arguments are likely to be of wider import and are not peculiar to the 12 interviewed.
P. 16 Present evidence to support claim that firms struggle to access credit.	References added (BIS 2012c; Cowling *et al.*, 2012; BDRC 2013) on p. 19.
P. 16 Provide detail and argument to support the claim regarding the number of Companies House abbreviated accounts downloads.	Text amended on p. 18. Reviewer 2 correctly states that we base our estimate of 935,000 downloads on a straightforward extrapolation based on data for *all* Companies House accounts for a part-year. While we cannot provide a cast-iron defence of our approach, we do not know that any other approach would be superior. We have amended the text to make it clearer that this is an estimate which might be contested.
P. 16 Reconsider claim that Companies House abbreviated accounts downloads are underestimated.	Text amended on pp. 18–19 to remove the claim about 935,000 being an underestimate.
P. 17 Clarify that 'directors' means 'owners'.	Text added on p. 18, to show we refer to owners, rather than non-owning directors.

Comments	Our response
Reviewer 2	
P. 17 Evidence to support claims that (a) published accounts are a starting point and (b) influence the decision to continue.	Text added on p. 19. These claims have been made by us elsewhere. To avoid repeating what we have published elsewhere, and associated quotations, we cite the sources.
Pp. 19–20 Comment on possible partisanship of professional body quotation.	The source for the quotation was a trade association representing providers of various forms of credit and other forms of finance.
P. 25 Clarify who the small business agents are.	The term is defined on p. 9 – small company directors, managers and employees. It does not refer to external accountants.
Consider whether arguments about abbreviated accounts might also apply to unaudited accounts.	We are unable to comment further on this issue. We agree with the reviewer's suggestion that unaudited accounts might produce a similar response from stakeholders. A number of stakeholders made this point in passing as indicated in footnote 9. Many of those in 71% category (unaudited accounts) are likely to have filed abbreviated accounts too.
Reviewer 3	
Reorganize literature review and conceptual framework sections.	We prefer not to do this in order to keep the review of prior research, covering two distinct strands of literature, and our own analytical approach separate. Our framework (section 4) specifies how regulation produces business performance effects. It is not about information asymmetry/ agency per se, or even specifically about financial reporting regulation. The framework is intended to be applicable to all regulation. We have expanded this section to make its intended wider scope more prominent. The purpose of section 3 is, partly, to discuss the literature on information asymmetry, showing how financial reporting regulation influences this asymmetry, and the small company and stakeholder decisions that flow from this. Merging the two sections would, we feel, not only make the section twice as long and unwieldy, but also obscure these more wide-ranging elements of the conceptual framework.
Lack of systematic discussion of information/ agency-related theories, starting with Stiglitz and Weiss, related to the dynamic …	Our response to this issue overlaps with the one above. The paper is not fundamentally about information/ agency-related theories; we are unsure, therefore, what value this would add. The point we make about information asymmetry and its potential impact on the cost of capital is well rehearsed in the literature. We are happy to be guided by the editor on this issue.
No hypothesis is presented.	Text amended on p. 2. Research aims, incorporating hypotheses, are now set out more clearly.

Comments	Our response
Reviewer 3	
Current results are preliminary and offer limited support for the conclusions; rewrite the results sections to make it more focused; provide further evidence for the conclusions.	While no paper can claim to have the final word on anything, we believe that our conceptual framework and data provide strong support for the central conclusions, that: (1) regulation is a dynamic force generating contradictory influences on small firm behaviour and performance; (2) the contradictory consequences for small companies with regard to financial reporting regulation arise from the confidentiality/disclosure paradox; (3) that stakeholder risk assessments might be more sensitive to information disclosure during recessions than in more buoyant times; and (4) that regulation relaxing small company reporting obligations might inadvertently constrain small company performance by restricting access to finance and markets. We accept future research might say more on *how* these contradictory influences play out for particular small companies and stakeholders in particular circumstances – this depends on how small companies and stakeholders exercise their agency – but feel the conceptual model directs researchers to look for regulatory effects that narrower conceptions of regulation as solely constraining are unable to see.
Results cannot be traced to particular tables.	We rely predominantly on qualitative data presented as text, rather than quantitative data presented in tables. Our main data sources are the reported behaviours and motivations of small companies and stakeholders. We use quantitative data presented in tables sparingly.
No control group of non-users.	There is no specific control group of non-users of abbreviated accounts, but all stakeholders (banks, CRAs, insurers, clients, suppliers, etc.) reported use of both full and abbreviated statutory accounts. Stakeholders use whatever information they can lay their hands on.
Nothing is said about what happened, or should happen, in a non-recessionary environment.	Text amended. Our central arguments concerning the value of the conceptual framework are intended to apply in recession and non-recession environments, although – as we say above – how these dynamic forces play out in particular circumstances is likely to vary. We now make this point clearer in the conceptual framework and repeat it when presenting the empirical results. We stress that several stakeholders emphasized that comprehensive, timely information was particularly useful in a difficult economic climate in order to make business and credit decisions.

Comments	Our response
Reviewer 3	
Comment on sample selection issues or survivorship bias; comment on small company reports that few problems with access to credit.	Text amended on p. 12. We cannot be certain our small company samples are representative of the relevant population. But our argument about the impact of financial reporting regulation derives principally from primary data from stakeholders and secondary data sources on SME access to finance to make our argument – rather than the sample small companies themselves. Our point about limited small company awareness of the indirect influences of financial reporting regulation suggests we should not treat small company owners' views of the impact of regulation as synonymous with the entirety of regulatory effects. As with most research on small businesses, we are only talking about survivors. We are unable to say whether surviving small companies differ from non-survivors in their motivations for, and the consequences of, filing abbreviated accounts. The text has been amended to reflect this point.
No data descriptives on the sample firms.	The study does not rely primarily on quantitative data where it is conventional to provide descriptives. We provide employment size data for both the small company survey and interview samples.
Change title to reflect UK setting.	Title amended.
P. 1 Why a discussion of the different views regarding the regulation burden?	The brief discussion on p. 1 is intended to provide context for the paper – whether UK regulation is supportive of business, or a hindrance. Text shortened and moved slightly earlier.
P. 2 and other places 'UK Government' instead of 'government'.	This, we feel, is a matter of stylistic choice. We retain the original approach, but we are happy to switch on the editor's advice.
P. 5 Amend Bins et al., 1992.	Citation amended.
P. 7 Define 'stakeholders'.	Stakeholders are defined in terms of agents who interact with small companies whose actions affect them; and several are identified on p. 9.
P. 8, para 1 Sentences repeat.	These two sentences make related, though slightly different, points. We have moved the second sentence to the previous para where it is more relevant to the argument.
P. 9 Differentiate the survey and interview approaches.	Text amended p. 11, to reflect that the term 'survey data' refers to the postal and online survey material collected from small company respondents and stakeholders.
P. 10 How many of the 149 accounts preparers were also users?	Text amended, to provide details and to demonstrate the interview sample of 12 were a subsample of this larger group.
P. 12 Specify source for claim about survey data from accountants. Are the data presented in any tables?	New footnote added to clarify the base for the percentages presented in this sentence. The text refers to 'the survey data for accountants in practice' (n=255, Table 1). Of these 255, 240 reported small company clients. The claims about 71% and 15% refer to this subset of 240.

Comments	Our response
Reviewer 3	
Table 3. What is the 'any prompted sources' category?	Text amended, to clarify it refers to respondents reporting ANY of the sources in the Table.
P. 18, lines 42–49 Specify data for 'other things being equal' claim.	Text amended, to demonstrate that this was a widely held view among credit management professionals.
P. 20 Refer to demand-side limits on credit and sources.	Text amended; sources included.
P. 24 Provide summary table of results.	No text amendments made to p. 24, although we have extended the final para in the conceptual framework section to elaborate on the approach and links to the analysis. The results are presented in the form of our analysis of small company and especially stakeholder responses to questions about the pros and cons of filing and using abbreviated accounts. There were no specific questions about the invisibility of indirect regulatory influences.
P. 27, line 44 Provide supporting evidence for the claim that indirect regulatory influences impact small companies more than direct influences.	Text amended on p. 30 to remove claim.

Source: Reproduced with kind permission of the authors of the article.

For an inexperienced author there is considerable merit in writing the article jointly with someone with greater experience, such as your supervisor. If you are a PhD student, your supervisors will expect to co-author articles with you, even if at that stage they do little more than provide advice and editing. It is one of the ways in which you show appreciation for their contribution to the development of your research.

Ahlstrom (2010) gives detailed advice to potential contributors to the *Asia Pacific Journal of Management* in his role as editor, which can be summarized as follows:

- Ensure that your work is appropriate for the targeted journal.
- Follow the journal's guidelines regarding the formatting.
- There must be a clearly stated research question with a question mark.
- The contribution of the study must be identified.
- Do not claim that your study is exploratory research if there is an existing body of knowledge.
- Do not claim that you are filling a gap in the literature, if the gap is of no interest or little importance.

We suggest that if you ignore this advice, you risk a 'desk reject' by the editor, which means that it is not considered suitable for review. If your paper is considered of merit, it will be reviewed and in due course you may receive advice to 'revise and resubmit', which means that the editor is inviting you to revise the paper, taking the reviewers' comments into account. This does not mean it will be accepted and the process may be repeated several times before your article is finally accepted or rejected. As you can imagine, the process involves considerable work on your part (and also on the part of the reviewers), but if you address the criticisms of the referees successfully, there is a good chance that your article will be published. You may find that the referees' demands are so great that you have to alter your paper significantly to get it published.

There is considerable competition to get articles published in high quality journals and the extent of competition depends on the number of journals in your discipline, the number of issues they produce each year and the number of academics writing papers on the same topic and using the same research design. When targeting journals, you should be aware that despite the increasingly international nature of business, many journals are nationally oriented in the articles that they accept (Jones and Roberts, 2005). Despite the challenges, you must persist, if you are seeking an academic career.

13.6.3 Measures of quality

Unfortunately, it can be difficult to measure the quality of your publications, but this can be critical if you are applying for an academic position or wanting to move up the scale. There are three main methods of measurement:

- the number of publications you have, regardless of the reputation of the journal
- the quality of the journal in which you have published
- the impact of your publications, as measured by the number of citations they have received.

Volume is by far the easiest and, in the early stages of your career, your academic institution may only expect that you publish and, if possible, in a refereed journal. Credit is given for the number of articles published and you should ensure that you obtain the maximum output of articles from your research.

Quality of journals may be less easy to determine or, at least, to agree upon. Quality, in academic terms, does not mean the most read journals but those where it is most difficult to get an article accepted. There are several lists that have been compiled and there tends to be agreement as to which journals have particular merit. In addition, many universities and colleges will construct their own rankings, drawn from published sources but amended to fit their own particular needs.

The impact of your publications becomes more important as your career progresses. What you are hoping is that other researchers will refer to your work in their own articles. Citation counts also include self-citations, that is, where an author cites his or her own work. This would seem to be more common in some disciplines than in others (Hyland, 2003). Your research has therefore had an impact on what others are doing and thinking. There are several sources of information on citation impact, including the *Social Sciences Citation Index (SSCI)* and *Google Scholar.*

13.7 Conclusions

In this chapter we have looked at the planning and the practical side of writing, from designing the report to developing a suitable writing style and presenting the data. Writing up your research can be a highly rewarding process once you get started. The secret to completing on time is to write notes and draft sections of your dissertation or thesis from the outset, rather than leave it until the last minute. If, for one reason or another, you have not managed to start writing early enough, you will face major problems and we give advice in the next chapter on how these might be resolved.

If you are a serious researcher or wish to have an academic career, conferences and academic journals are highly important. We have offered advice on achieving publication in academic journals, but we will not pretend that it is easy. The best personal quality you can have is persistence – somewhere there is a journal that will publish your article even if it takes several revisions.

References

Ahlstrom, D. (2010) 'Publishing in the Asia Pacific Journal of Management', *Asia Pacific Journal of Management*, 27(1), pp. 1–8.

Allan, G. (1991) 'Qualitative Research', in Allan, G. and Skinner, C. *Handbook for Research Students in the Social Sciences.* London: The Falmer Press, pp. 177–89.

Beattie, V. and Goodacre, A. (2004) 'Publishing patterns within the UK accounting and finance academic community', *British Accounting Review*, 36(1), pp. 7–44.

Beattie, V. and Jones, M. (1992) 'Graphic accounts', *Certified Accountant*, November, pp. 30–5.

Bell, J. (2010) *Doing Your Research Project*, 3rd edn. New York: McGraw-Hill.

Bergwerk, R. J. (1970) 'Effective communication of financial data', *The Journal of Accountancy*, February, pp. 47–54.

Chall, J. S. (1958) *Readability – An Appraisal of Research and Application.* Columbus, OH: Ohio State University Press.

Cooper, H. M. (1988) 'The structure of knowledge synthesis', *Knowledge in Society*, 1, pp. 104–26.

Denzin, N. K. (1994) 'The Arts and Politics of Interpretation', in Denzin, N. K. and Lincoln, Y. S. (eds) *Handbook of Qualitative Research.* Thousand Oaks, CA: SAGE, pp. 500–15.

Ehrenberg, A. S. C. (1975) *Data Reduction.* New York, NY: Wiley.

Ehrenberg, A. S. C. (1976) 'Annual reports don't have to be obscure', *The Journal of Accountancy*, August, pp. 88–91.

Flannery, J. J. (1971) 'The relative effectiveness of some common graduated point symbols in the presentation of quantitative data', *Canadian Cartographer*, pp. 96–109.

Hakes, D. R. (2009) 'Confession of an economist: Writing to impress rather than to inform', *Econ Journal Watch*, 6(3), pp. 349–51.

Howard, K. and Sharp, J. A. (1994) *The Management of a Student Research Project.* Aldershot: Gower.

Hyland, K. (2003) 'Self-citation and self-reference: Credibility and promotion in academic publication', *Journal of the American Society for Information Science and Technology*, 54(3), pp. 251–9.

Iselin, E. R. (1972) 'Accounting and communication theory', *The Singapore Accountant*, 7, pp. 31–7.

Jones, M. J. and Roberts, R. A. (2005) 'International publishing patterns: An investigation of leading UK and US accounting and finance journals', *Journal of Business Finance and Accounting*, 32(5–6), pp. 1107–40.

Macdonald-Ross, M. (1977) 'How numbers are shown – A review of research on the presentation of quantitative data in texts', *AV Communication Review*, 25(4), pp. 359–409.

McGrath, M. A. (1989) 'An ethnography of a gift store: Trappings, wrappings, and rapture', *Journal of Retailing*, 65(4), pp. 421–49.

Merriam, S. B. (1988) *Case Study Research in Education: A Qualitative Approach.* San Francisco, CA: Jossey-Bass.

Phillips, E. M. and Pugh, D. S. (2010) *How to Get a Ph.D.* Buckingham: Open University Press.

Piotrowski, C. and Armstrong, T. R. (2005) 'Major research areas in organization development: An analysis of ABI/INFORM', *Organization Development Journal*, 23(4) pp. 86–92.

Playfair, W. (1786) *The Commercial and Political Atlas.* London.

Prather-Kinsey, J. and Rueschoff, N. (2004) 'An analysis of international accounting research in US and non-US based academic accounting journals', *Journal of International Accounting Research*, 3(1), pp. 63–82.

Rudestam, K. E. and Newton, R. R. (2007) *Surviving Your Dissertation*, 3rd edn. Thousand Oaks, CA: SAGE.

Thibadoux, G., Cooper, W. D. and Greenberg, I. S. (1986) 'Flowcharts and graphics: Part II', *CPA Journal*, March, pp. 17–23.

Torrance, M., Thomas, G. V. and Robinson, E. J. (1992) 'The writing experiences of social science research students', *Studies in Higher Education*, 17(2) pp. 155–67.

Tufte, E. R. (2001) *The Visual Display of Quantitative Information*, 2nd edn. Cheshire, CT: Graphic Press.

Winkler, A. C. and McCuen-Metherell, J. R. (2012) *Writing the Research Paper: A Handbook*, 8th edn. New York, NY: Cengage Learning.

Activities

Writing skills can be improved with practice and by attempting different styles of expression. It is best if you can wait a few weeks before comparing the writing exercises you do in this section

1 Take a piece text that you have written recently (about 500 words). Identify the key words you have used most frequently. Using a thesaurus or the tool in *Microsoft Word*, substitute synonyms as appropriate. Compare the two pieces of text and reflect on which is better and why.

2 Select a short section of text from a book (no more than one or two pages) and read it. Without referring to it again, write a letter to a friend explaining what the section is about. Put the original text and the letter aside for about two weeks and then try to reconstruct the text. Compare the two pieces identifying where there are significant differences in context and style.

3 Use a well-known proverb, phrase or verse and write a short narrative using the passive voice and the personal voice to reflect the two main paradigms. In addition, write it again in a colloquial style as if you were talking informally to a friend. This exercise will improve the flexibility of your style.

Example:
The mouse ran up the clock. The clock struck one, the mouse ran down.

Passive voice
It was observed that the mouse ascended the case of the grandfather clock in a rapid manner. When the chiming mechanism of the clock struck one o'clock, the rodent descended speedily. As this behaviour was only observed on one occasion, it is not possible to generalize from it. However, it is hypothesized that the rapid descent was associated with fright. This requires further investigation with a large sample of rodents in a controlled environment.

4 Conduct a literature search for articles that discuss the ranking of journals in your discipline. Compare the rankings across the articles and identify potential journals for articles you will write from your research.

5 Select four target journals as above and analyse the articles published over the past five years by methodology, topic, sample size, country and the affiliation of the author (university, college or other institution). Identify any pattern and determine how any article you might write fits into this pattern.

Visit the companion website to access a range of support materials at www.palgrave.com/business/collis/br4/

Have a look at the Troubleshooting chapter and sections 14.2, 14.9, 14.13, 14.14, 14.16, 14.17 in particular, which relate specifically to this chapter.

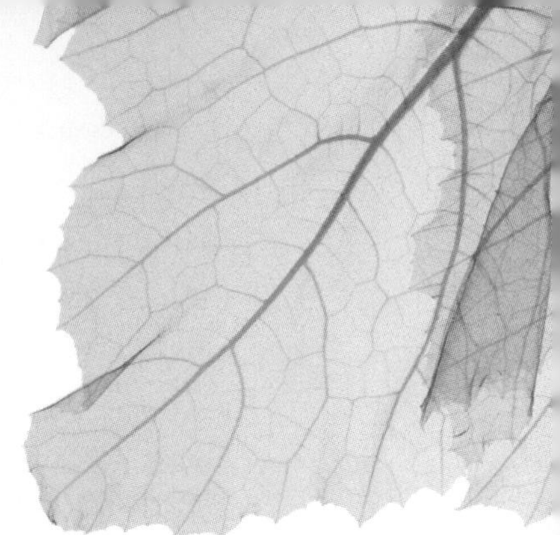

14

troubleshooting

14.1 Introduction

As we explained in Chapter 1, business research is not a simple linear process and even though you may have studied all the chapters in this book very carefully, you may encounter difficulties of one type or another. Regardless of how much support and guidance you receive from your supervisors, colleagues, friends and family, you are bound to make some mistakes, and this is true for researchers at all levels. In addition, things beyond your control may create problems. If the research you designed in your proposal does not come to fruition exactly as planned, you will need to explain what the problems were and, irrespective of whether you decide to take action to remedy the situation or decide to do nothing, you will need to justify your strategy by weighing up the alternatives.

In this chapter we examine typical challenges associated with the main stages of the research process. The solutions to these problems refer you to different chapters in the book where you will be able to obtain the appropriate guidance. You can also use the index and look up terms in the glossary. The problems we cover are:

- Getting started
- Managing the process
- Identifying a topic and/or a research problem or issue
- Making a preliminary plan of action
- Finding a theoretical framework
- Writing the proposal
- Deciding the methodology
- Searching and reviewing the literature
- Collecting research data
- Organizing qualitative research data
- Analysing the research data
- Structuring the dissertation or thesis
- Writing the dissertation or thesis
- Dealing with writer's block
- Achieving the standards
- Eleventh-hour strategies for writing up.

14.2 Getting started

Problem
You are unable to start because you are totally confused over what research is all about and what you are expected to do.

Before you can start your research, you will find it useful to gain an understanding of what business research entails by implementing the following plan of action:

1 Start with the basics and read about the nature and purpose of research, focusing on the definitions of research and the different types of research (see Chapter 1).
2 The next steps are to:
   - Identify a research topic (see Chapter 2)
   - Identify a research problem or issue to investigate (see Chapter 5)
   - Design the project (see Chapters 3, 4 and 6)
   - Collect the data (see Chapters 7 and/or 9 and/or 10)

– Analyse the data (see Chapters 8 and/or 11 and/or 12)
– Write up the research (see Chapter 13).

14.3 Managing the process

Problem
You are ready to get started, but you are worried about how you will manage your research project.

To manage your research efficiently and in the time available, you should try the following:

1 Find out when you will have to submit your dissertation or thesis.
2 Read about the research process, set yourself a timetable for each stage (some will overlap) and agree it with your supervisor (see Chapter 1).
3 To ensure that your time is spent efficiently, you must use your knowledge, skills and personal qualities to manage the process of the research (see Chapter 2).

14.4 Identifying a topic and/or a research problem or issue

Problem
You are unable to find a suitable topic and/or research problem or issue to investigate.

If you are unable to identify a suitable topic and/or a research problem or issue to investigate (or you have to abandon your choice because it was not feasible), you should take the following steps:

1 Try techniques such as brainstorming, analogy, mind mapping, morphological analysis and relevance trees to generate a research topic that is relevant to your degree (see Chapter 2).
2 Consider issues such as your skills, potential costs, access to data and ethics (see Chapter 2).
3 Arrange to meet your supervisor to discuss your ideas (see Chapter 1).
4 Once you have identified a research topic, conduct a literature search to identify gaps and deficiencies that suggest a specific research problem or issue to investigate (see Chapter 5).

14.5 Making a preliminary plan of action

Problem
You know the research topic you want to investigate but you do not know how to plan the first stages of the research.

The research proposal is going to be your detailed research plan, but you have to carry out some preliminary investigations before you can write it. Your preliminary plan of action should be as follows:

1 Carry out a literature search using keywords related to your research topic to find the most important academic articles and other publications on this topic (see Chapter 5).
2 Identify a research problem or issue to investigate and conduct a focused search to find the key articles and other publications (see Chapter 5).
3 Write a preliminary review of this literature for your research proposal that leads the reader to the research question(s) your study will address (see Chapter 5).
4 Make a decision on the appropriate method(s) for collecting the data (see Chapters 7 and/or 9 and/or 10) and analysing them (see Chapters 8 and/or 11 and/or 12). Describe and justify your choices in the methodology section of your proposal (see Chapter 6).

14.6 Finding a theoretical framework

Problem
You cannot write a research proposal because you have difficulty in finding a theoretical framework.

If a theoretical framework is appropriate under your research paradigm, you should take the following steps:

1 Ensure that you have clearly specified the purpose of the research (see Chapter 6) and that you have conducted a literature search (see Chapter 5).
2 You should then be able to identify the theories and models used by other researchers studying the same or similar issues, and develop a theoretical framework (see Chapter 6).
3 You can then define the unit of analysis and construct the hypotheses you will test, which are the propositions you will investigate to answer your research questions (see Chapter 6).

14.7 Writing the proposal

Problem
You are uncertain about how to write a research proposal that will be acceptable to your supervisor(s).

If you are worried about how to write your research proposal, you should implement the following plan:

1 Start by looking at the indicative structure of a research proposal and read about what is usually contained in each section (see Chapter 6).
2 Your preliminary review of the literature forms a major part of your research proposal. It focuses on the most influential articles and other publications in the literature and should lead the reader to the research question(s) your study will address (see Chapter 5).
3 You must mention how you will solve any problems relating to covering costs, gaining access to data and issues concerning ethics (see Chapter 2).

4 Identify a research problem or issue to investigate and conduct a focused search to find the key articles and other publications (see Chapter 5).
5 Write a preliminary review of this literature (see Chapter 5) for your research proposal that leads to your research question(s).
6 Make a decision on the appropriate method(s) for collecting the data (see Chapters 7 and/or 9 and/or 10) and analysing them (see Chapters 8 and/or 11 and/or 12). In the methodology section of your proposal, describe and justify your methodology and methods, commenting on ethical issues and the limitations of your research design.
7 Conclude with remarks about the expected outcomes of the study (related to the purpose) and include a timetable for completing the various stages of the research (see Chapter 6).

14.8 Deciding the methodology

Problem
You are unable to decide which methodology to use.

Deciding which methodology to use is made easier when you realize that your choice is limited by a number of factors. Your action plan should be as follows:

1 Start by considering the constraints placed by the research problem or issue your study will address (see Chapter 6) and your research paradigm (see Chapter 3).
2 Identify which methodologies are usually associated with your research paradigm (see Chapter 4).
3 Consider whether triangulation is appropriate and/or feasible (see Chapter 4).

14.9 Searching and reviewing the literature

Problem
You are unable to find articles and other publications on your research topic or you are unable to write the literature review.

Planning is the key to an efficient and successful literature search and a critical review of the relevant literature. We advise you adopt the following strategy:

1 Before you begin your search, you need to define your terms and determine the scope of your research (see Chapter 5).
2 Then you should start a systematic search (see Chapter 5).
3 You must be certain to record the references (see Chapter 5) and avoid plagiarism when writing your literature review (see Chapters 5 and 13).
4 You should take an analytical approach to reviewing the literature rather than writing a descriptive list of items you have read (see Chapter 5). By pointing out the gaps and deficiencies in the literature, you will be able to lead the reader to the research question(s) your study will address.

14.10 Collecting research data

Problem
You are unable to decide how to collect your research data.

Deciding which data collection method to use is made easier when you realize that your choice is limited:

1. Start by considering the nature of the research problem or issue your study will address (see Chapter 5) and any access to data that will be needed.
2. Then consider your research paradigm (see Chapter 3) and your methodology (see Chapter 4).
3. This should enable you to select appropriate methods for collecting the data (see Chapters 7 and/or 9 and/or 10). You must make this choice in the context of the methods you plan to use to analyse the data (see Chapters 8 and/or 11 and/or 12).

14.11 Organizing qualitative research data

Problem
You plan to collect qualitative research data, but you do not know when to start the analysis.

In an interpretivist study, it is difficult *not* to start the process of analysing qualitative data during the collection stage. Therefore, this is not usually a problem once you get started. Your plan of action should be as follows:

1. As you collect the research data, you need to be clear about your choice of methodology (see Chapter 4) and issues relating to reliability and validity (see Chapters 3, 8 and 9).
2. You need to ensure that your methods for capturing primary data (using equipment such as a camera, video or audio recorder) are supported by notes taken at the time (see Chapters 7 and 9).
3. If you are collecting secondary research data, you need to ensure that you have followed a systematic method (see Chapter 8).
4. While you are collecting the qualitative data, use methods for reducing the amount of material data by restructuring or detextualizing the data (see Chapter 8).

14.12 Analysing the research data

Problem
You are unable to decide how to analyse the data you have collected.

Deciding which method of data analysis to use is made easier when you realize that your choice is limited:

1. The first step is to consider whether you have designed your study under a positivist or an interpretivist paradigm (see Chapters 3 and 4).

2 If you are a positivist, you want your research data to be in numerical form so that you can use statistical methods of analysis (see Chapters 11 and 12). You may first need to quantify any qualitative data (see Chapter 10).
3 All positivists will conduct an exploratory analysis of their data using descriptive statistics (see Chapter 11). However, some undergraduates and all postgraduate and doctoral students will need to go on to use inferential statistics (see Chapter 12).
4 Depending on their philosophical assumptions, interpretivists who have collected qualitative data can use either quantifying methods or non-quantifying methods for analysing their research data (see Chapter 8).

14.13 Structuring the dissertation or thesis

Problem
You are uncertain about how to structure your dissertation or thesis.

If you are uncertain about how to structure your dissertation or thesis, the following plan of action should help:

1 Adopt or adapt the indicative structure of main chapters in a research report (see Chapter 13).
2 Read about what needs to be included in each chapter and add names for the main sections within each chapter (see Chapter 13). Remember that each chapter will need to have some kind of introduction and a conclusion section that will help provide links between chapters.
3 Based on the indicative proportion of the whole report that each chapter represents, allocate an approximate number of words to each of your chapters (see Chapter 13).
4 The last step is to decide what form any tabular or diagrammatic summaries of your results/findings will take (see Chapters 10–13).

14.14 Writing the dissertation or thesis

Problem
You are worried about writing up the research.

If you have followed the guidance in this book, you will have decided on the main structure of your dissertation or thesis at an early stage and will have used the sections in your proposal as the basis of some of the chapters. You will have added further draft material as you embarked on different stages in the research. You should now adopt the following plan of action:

1 You will need to draw up a plan and give some thought to the overall design of the report (see Chapter 13).
2 You will then be in a position to finalize your literature review, methodology and analysis. Once you have drafted your conclusions chapter, develop the introductory section you wrote for your proposal as the first chapter in your dissertation. Then check all chapters to ensure that you use the same terms and wording every time you mention the purpose of the research and the research questions.

3 As you write, add the bibliographic references for all the sources you cite. It is essential to follow the referencing system recommended on your course and avoid plagiarism (see Chapters 5 and 13).
4 If you have run out of time, use our eleventh-hour strategies at the end of this chapter.

14.15 Dealing with writer's block

Problem
You are part way through writing up your research, but suffering from writer's block.

Make sure you are having regular, balanced meals and drinking enough liquid to stop you becoming dehydrated. All this helps your brain process information efficiently. Take a short break (a 20-minute walk is ideal) to give your mind a rest and relieve the aches and pains of spending hours at the computer. Even though you may be feeling weary, do something aerobic during the break as it will increase your sense of wellbeing in general and improve your circulation. In addition, try the following tips:

1 Stop trying to write the particular section that is proving to be problematic and turn to a different part of your report.
2 Alternatively, start a totally different task, such as checking your references, preparing tables and diagrams, running the spelling and grammar check or improving your writing by looking up synonyms.
3 Try to find a way round the impasse you are experiencing with the problematic section by generating a mind map or other diagram to help structure your thoughts. Alternatively, reflect on what you have written in that section so far and draw up a list of its strengths and weaknesses. You can also do this by making an audio recording of your thoughts and reviewing them.
4 Have a brainstorming session with your supervisor or a fellow student.
5 Sometimes a good moan to a sympathetic member of the family or a friend is enough to clear the tension and clarify your thoughts.

14.16 Achieving the standards

Problem
You are worried about whether your work will be up to the standards required.

Apart from the advice that you should always do your best, the following suggestions should help:

1 The most important source of guidance on standards is the handbook or other source of information provided by your institution.
2 You can discuss these criteria with your supervisor (see Chapter 1), who provides feedback in the form of comments on your proposal and draft chapters (see Chapters 6 and 13).
3 There are a number of general characteristics of a good research project (see Chapter 1) and indicative assessment criteria that will give you an idea of what is expected at different degree levels (see Chapter 13).

14.17 Eleventh-hour strategies for writing up

If you have left all or most of the writing up until the eleventh hour, you will be feeling very worried indeed. The submission date is looming and you have little to show for the work you have done. If this applies to you, we suggest the following strategy:

1 Decide on a structure of chapters and main sections within each chapter, but do not take too long over it; no more than half a day, even for a doctoral thesis. Use the sample structures given in Chapter 13 and put in as many of the subsections as you can. Work out the approximate word count you are aiming for with each chapter.
2 On your computer, open a document for each chapter and name it. Set up the page layout to the required size, margins, pagination, font, line spacing and so on. Type in the number and name of the chapter and the number and heading for each main section within the chapter.
3 Now aim for volume. Do not worry unduly about grammar, punctuation or references. You must get as many words down as possible in each of the chapters. Leave the introductory chapter and concentrate on those sections you know well. You should find that the act of writing one part will spark off other aspects which you want to include. This will entail switching from chapter to chapter. In your hurry, you may put things in the wrong places, but that does not matter.
4 When you have written approximately two-thirds of your target word count, stop and print each chapter. This will use up a lot of paper, but you are in a crisis situation and cost must come second to speed now. Put your printout in a ring binder file, using dividers to separate the chapters.
5 Read all the chapters, marking any changes on the hard copy in a bright colour as you go, adding text wherever possible as well as references and quotations from other authors. Now make these corrections and additions to the computer files and open a new file for the references/bibliography. You should find that you are now within 10% to 15% of your target number of words.
6 Print two copies and persuade a friend or member of the family to read through one and mark down any comments. We imagine that you have missed the deadline to submit draft material to your supervisor and you have been told that you must simply hand in your work by the due date for submission.
7 Meanwhile, collect all your articles and other literature together and skim through them looking for quotations, illustrations or other items you can fit into your thesis. As you have just read it, it should be easy to spot relevant items. Write each item on a separate piece of paper and insert them into your ring binder containing your copy of your latest printout.
8 When you receive your friend's comments, systematically work through your own and your friend's suggestions on your computer files, one chapter at a time, in order. Make sure you have cited your sources and included all the details in your list of references. Use the spelling and grammar check. As you finish each chapter print it off and read it.
9 Make any final changes and draw up the preliminary pages. Print the required number of copies for binding.
10 Buy a drink for all those who have helped you, but make sure that you are never tempted to procrastinate again!

Visit the companion website to access a range of support materials at www.palgrave.com/business/collis/br4/

glossary

Please visit the companion website for this book **www.palgrave.com/business/collis/br4/** for an online searchable version of this glossary.

Abstract A brief summary of the purpose of the research, the methodology and the key findings.

Action research A methodology used in applied research to find an effective way of bringing about a conscious change in a partly controlled environment.

Analogy A means of designing a study in one subject by importing ideas and procedures from another area where there are similarities.

Analytical research A study where the aim is to understand phenomena by discovering and measuring causal relations among them.

Anonymity Assurance given to participants and organizations that they will not be named in the research.

Applied research Describes a study that is designed to apply its findings to solving a specific, existing problem.

Archival study An empirical study using publicly available data.

Axiological assumption A philosophical assumption about the role of values.

Bar chart A graphical presentation of a frequency distribution of an ordinal or nominal variable in which the data are represented by a series of separate vertical or horizontal bars. The frequencies are indicated by the height (or length) of the bars.

Basic (or pure) research Describes a study that is designed to make a contribution to general knowledge and theoretical understanding, rather than solve a specific problem.

Bibliography A list of publications relating to a topic.

Bivariate analysis Analysis of data relating to two variables.

Brainstorming A technique that can be used to generate research topics by listing spontaneous ideas with one or more interested people.

Case study A methodology that is used to explore a single phenomenon (the case) in a natural setting using a variety of methods to obtain in-depth knowledge.

Categorical variable A nominal variable measured using numerical codes to identify categories.

Chi-squared (χ^2) test A non-parametric test of association for two variables measured on a nominal scale.

Citation An acknowledgement in the text of the original source from which information was obtained.

Closed question A question that requires a 'yes' or 'no' answer or a very brief factual answer, or requires the respondent to choose from a list of predetermined answers.

Coding frame A list of coding units against which the analysed material is classified.

Coding unit A particular word, character, item, theme or concept identified in the data and allocated a specific code.

Cognitive mapping A method based on personal construct theory that structures a participants' perceptions in the form of a diagram.

Confidence interval A parametric technique for estimating a range of values of a sample statistic that is likely to contain an unknown population parameter at a given level of probability; the wider the confidence interval, the higher the confidence level.

Confidentiality The assurance given to participants and organizations that the information provided will not be traceable to the individual or organization providing it.

Confounding variable A variable that obscures the effects of another.

Content analysis A method by which selected items of qualitative data are systematically converted to numerical data for analysis.

Continuous variable A ratio or interval variable measured on a scale where the data can take any value within a given range, such as time or length.

Correlation A measure of the direction and strength of association between two quantitative variables. Correlation may be linear or non-linear, positive or negative.

Critical incident technique A method for collecting data about a defined activity or event based on the participant's recollections of key facts.

Cross-sectional study A methodology designed to investigate variables or a group of subjects in different contexts over the same period of time.

Cross-tabulation A bivariate analysis of frequency distributions (usually relating to ordinal or nominal variables) in the form of a table.

Data (singular datum) Known facts or things used as a basis for inference or reckoning.

Data display A summary of data in diagrammatic form that allows the user to draw valid conclusions.

Data integrity Characteristics of the research that affect error and bias in the results.

Data reduction A stage in the data analysis process that involves selecting, discarding, simplifying, summarizing and reorganizing qualitative research data

Deductive research A study in which a conceptual and theoretical structure is developed which is then tested by empirical observation; thus particular instances are deduced from general inferences.

Delimitation Establishes the scope of the research.

Dependent variable A variable whose values are influenced by one or more independent variables.

Descriptive research A study where the aim is to describe the characteristics of phenomena.

Descriptive statistics A group of statistical methods used to summarize, describe or display quantitative data.

Diary A method of collecting data where selected participants are asked to record relevant information in diary forms or booklets over a specified period of time.

Dichotomous variable A variable that has only two possible categories, such as gender.

Discourse A lengthy treatment of a theme that involves a formal discussion of a topic.

Discourse analysis Refers to a number of approaches to analysing the use of language in a social-psychological context.

Discrete variable A ratio or interval variable measured on a scale that can take only one of a range of distinct values, such as number of employees.

Dissertation A detailed discourse that is written as part of an academic degree.

Dummy variable A dichotomous quantitative variable coded 1 if the characteristic is present and 0 if the characteristic is absent.

Empirical evidence Data based on observation or experience.

Epistemological assumption A philosophical assumption about what constitutes valid knowledge in the context of the relationship of the researcher to that being researched.

Error The difference between the mean and the data value (observation).

Ethnography A methodology in which the researcher uses socially acquired and shared knowledge to understand the observed patterns of human activity.

Evaluation The ability to make qualitative or quantitative judgements; to set out a reasoned argument through a series of steps, usually of gradually increasing difficulty; to criticize constructively.

Experimental study A methodology used to investigate the relationship between two variables, where the independent variable is deliberately manipulated to observe the effect on the dependent variable.

Exploratory research A study where the aim is to investigate phenomena where there is little or no information, with a view to finding patterns or developing propositions, rather than testing them. The focus is on gaining insights prior to a more rigorous investigation.

Extraneous variable Any variable other than the independent variable which might have an effect on the dependent variable.

Feminist study A methodology used to investigate and seek understanding of phenomena from a feminist perspective.

Field experiment An experimental study conducted in a natural location.

Focus group A method for collecting data whereby selected participants discuss their reactions and feelings about a product, service, situation or concept, under the guidance of a group leader.

Frequency The number of observations for a particular data value in a variable.

Frequency distribution An array that summarizes the frequencies for all the data values in a particular variable.

Generalizability The extent to which the research findings (often based on a sample) can be extended to other cases (often a population) or to other settings.

Grounded theory Grounded theory is a framework in which there is joint collection, coding and analysis of data using a systematic set of procedures to develop an inductively derived theory.

Harvard system of referencing A system where citations are shown as author and date (and page number if quoting) in the text and the references are listed in alphabetical order by author at the end of the document.

Hermeneutics A methodology that focuses on the interpretation and understanding of text in the context of the underlying historical and social forces.

Histogram A refinement of a bar chart where adjoining bars touch, indicating continuous interval or ratio data. Frequency is represented by area, with the width of each bar indicating the class interval and the height indicating the frequency of the class.

Hypothesis (plural hypotheses) A proposition that can be tested for association or causality against empirical evidence.

Hypothetical construct An explanatory variable that is based on a scale that measures opinion or other abstract ideas that are not directly observable.

Independent variable A variable that influences the values of a dependent variable.

Index number A statistical measure that shows the percentage change in a variable from a fixed point in the past.

Inductive research A study in which theory is developed from the observation of empirical reality; thus general inferences are induced from particular instances.

Inferential statistics A group of statistical methods and models used to draw conclusions about a population from quantitative data relating to a random sample.

Information The knowledge created by organizing data into a useful form.

Interpretivism A paradigm that emerged in response to criticisms of positivism. It rests on the assumption that social reality is in our minds, and is subjective and multiple. Therefore, social reality is affected by the act of investigating it. The research involves an inductive process with a view to providing interpretive understanding of social phenomena within a particular context.

Interquartile range A measure of dispersion that represents the difference between the upper quartile and the lower quartile (the middle 50%) of a frequency distribution arranged in size order.

Interval variable A variable measured on a mathematical scale with equal intervals and an arbitrary zero point.

Interview A method for collecting primary data in which a sample of interviewees are asked questions to find out what they think, do or feel.

Keywords Words used by software to search databases or by search engines to search websites on the Internet for items containing those words.

Kurtosis A measure of the extent to which a frequency distribution is flatter or more peaked than a normal distribution (a normal distribution has a kurtosis of 0)

Laboratory experiment An experimental study conducted in an artificial setting.

Limitation A weaknesses or deficiency in the research.

Line graph A graphical presentation of a frequency distribution in which the data are represented by a series of points joined by a line; only suitable for continuous data.

Linear regression A measure of the ability of an independent variable to predict an outcome in a dependent variable where there is a linear relationship between them.

Literature All sources of published data on a particular topic.

Literature review A critical evaluation of the existing body of knowledge on a topic, which guides the research and demonstrates that the relevant literature has been located and analysed.

Literature search A systematic process with a view to identifying the existing body of knowledge on a particular topic.

Location The setting in which the research is conducted.

Logistic regression A form of multiple regression that is used where the dependent variable is a dummy variable and one or more of the independent variables are continuous quantitative variables. Any other independent variables can be ordinal or dummy variables.

Longitudinal study A methodology used to investigate variables or group of subjects over a long period of time.

Mann-Whitney test A non-parametric test of difference for two independent or dependent samples for ratio, interval or ordinal variables.

Mean A measure of central tendency based on the arithmetic average of a set of data values.

Median A measure of central tendency based on the mid-value of a set of data arranged in size order.

Method A technique for collecting and/or analysing data.

Methodological assumption A philosophical assumption about the process of research.

Methodological rigour Refers to the appropriateness and intellectual soundness of the research design and the systematic application of the research methods.

Methodology An approach to the process of the research encompassing a body of methods.

Mind map An informal diagram of a person's idea of the key elements of a subject that shows connections and relationships.

Mode A measure of central tendency based on the most frequently occurring value in a set of data (there may be multiple modes).

Morphological analysis A technique for generating research topics whereby the subject is analysed into its key attributes and a 'mix and match' approach is adopted.

Multivariate analysis Analysis of data relating to three or more variables.

Nominal variable A variable measured using numerical codes to identify named categories.

Non-participant observation A method of observation in which the observer is not involved in the activities taking place and the phenomena studied.

Normal distribution A theoretical frequency distribution that is bell-shaped and symmetrical with tails extending indefinitely either side of the centre. The mean, median and mode coincide at the centre.

Observation A method for collecting data used in the laboratory or in a natural setting to observe and record people's actions and behaviour

Ontological assumption A philosophical assumption about the nature of reality.

Open question A question that cannot be answered with a simple 'yes' or 'no' or a very brief factual answer, but requires a longer, developed answer.

Ordinal variable A variable measured using numerical codes to identify order or rank.

Paradigm A framework that guides how research should be conducted based on people's philosophies and their assumptions about the world and the nature of knowledge.

Parameter A number that describes a population.

Participant observation A method of observation in which the observer is involved in the activities taking place and the phenomena studied.

Participative inquiry A methodology that involves the participants as fully as possible in the study, which is conducted in their own group or organization.

Pearson's correlation coefficient A parametric test that measures linear association between two continuous variables measured on a ratio or interval scale.

Percentage frequency A descriptive statistic that summarizes a frequency as a proportion of 100.

Personal construct A set of concepts or general notions and ideas a person has in his or her mind about certain things.

Phenomenon (plural phenomena) An observed or apparent object, fact or occurrence, especially one where the cause is uncertain.

Pie chart A circular diagram showing the percentage frequency distribution of a nominal variable in which the data are represented by a series of segments. Each segment represents an area that is proportional to the whole 'pie'.

Plagiarism The act of taking someone's words, ideas or other information and passing them off as your own because you fail to acknowledge the original source.

Population A precisely defined body of people or objects under consideration for statistical purposes.

Positivism A paradigm that originated in the natural sciences. It rests on the assumption that social reality is singular and objective, and is not affected by the act of investigating it. The research involves a deductive process with a view to providing explanatory theories to understand social phenomena.

Pragmatism Contends that the research question should determine the research philosophy and that methods from more than one paradigm can be used in the same study.

Predictive research A study where the aim is to generalize from an analysis of phenomena by making predictions based on hypothesized general relationships.

Primary data Data generated from an original source, such as your own experiments, surveys, interviews or focus groups.

Protocol analysis A method for collecting data used to identify a practitioner's mental processes in solving a problem in a particular situation, including the logic and methods used.

Purpose statement A statement that describes the overall purpose of the research study.

Qualitative data Data in a nominal (named) form.

Quantifying methods Methods used to analyse qualitative data by converting it into quantitative data.

Quantitative data Data in a numerical form.

Quantitative variable A ratio, interval or dummy variable.

Questionnaire A method for collecting primary data in which a sample of respondents are asked a list of carefully structured questions chosen after considerable testing, with a view to eliciting reliable responses.

Random sample An unbiased subset of a population that is representative of the population because every member had an equal chance of being selected.

Range A measure of dispersion that represents the difference between the maximum value and the minimum value in a frequency distribution arranged in size order.

Ranked data Quantitative data arranged in size order so that statistical tests can be performed on the ranks.

Rating scale A hypothetical construct for obtaining ordinal data, such as the Likert scale.

Ratio variable A variable measured on a mathematical scale with equal intervals and a fixed zero point.

References A list containing bibliographic details of the sources cited in the text.

Relevance tree A diagram that can be used as a device for generating research topics and develops clusters of related ideas from a fairly broad starting concept.

Reliability The accuracy and precision of the measurement and absence of differences in the results if the research were repeated.

Repertory grid technique A method based on personal construct theory that generates a mathematical representation of a participant's perceptions and constructs.

Replication Repeating a research study to test the reliability of the results.

Research A systematic and methodical process of inquiry and investigation with a view to increasing knowledge.

Research design The detailed plan for conducting a research study.

Research instrument A means of collecting data, such as a questionnaire, that has been used in a number of studies and can be adopted by any researcher.

Research problem The specific problem or issue that is the focus of the research.

Research proposal A document that sets out the research design for a proposed study.

Research question The specific question the research is designed to investigate and attempt to answer.

Research topic The general area of research interest.

Results currency The generalizability of the research results.

Rhetorical assumption A philosophical assumption about the language of research.

Sample A subset of a population.

Sampling frame A record of the population from which a sample can be drawn.

Scatter plot A diagram for presenting data where one variable is plotted against another on a graph as a pattern of points, which indicates the direction and strength of any linear correlation. The more the points cluster around a straight line, the stronger the correlation.

Seasonal variation Where a pattern in the movements of time series data repeats itself at regular intervals.

Secondary data Data collected from an existing source, such as publications, databases and internal records.

Significance level The level of confidence that the results of a statistical analysis are not due to chance. It is usually expressed as the probability that the results of the statistical analysis are due to chance (usually 5% or less).

Skewness A measure of the extent to which a frequency distribution is asymmetric (a normal distribution has a skewness of 0).

Spearman's correlation coefficient A non-parametric test that measures linear association between two variables measured on a ratio, interval or ordinal scale.

Standard deviation A measure of dispersion that is the square root of the variance. A large standard deviation relative to the mean suggests the mean does not represent the data well.

Standard error The standard deviation between the means of different samples. A large standard error relative to the overall sample mean suggests the sample might not be representative of the population.

Statistic A number that describes a sample.

Statistics A body of methods and theory that is applied to quantitative data.

Stem-and-leaf plot A diagram that uses the data values in a frequency distribution to create a display. The data values are arranged in size order and each is divided into the leading digit (the stem) and trailing digits (the leaves).

Stratified sample A random sample chosen by selecting an appropriate proportion from each strata of the population.

Supervisor The person responsible for overseeing and guiding a student's research.

Survey A methodology designed to collect primary or secondary data from a sample, with a view to generalizing the results to a population.

Synthesis The ability to build up information from other information

Systematic sample A random sample chosen dividing the population by the required sample size (n) and selecting every nth subject.

Tally A simple stroke used to count the frequency of occurrence of a value or category in a variable.

Theoretical framework A collection of theories and models from the literature which underpins a positivist study. Theory can be generated from some interpretivist studies.

Theoretical saturation When the inclusion of new data does not add to your knowledge of the phenomenon under study.

Theory A set of interrelated variables, definitions and propositions that specifies relationships among the variables.

Thesis A detailed discourse that is written as part of an academic degree.

Time series A sequence of measurements of a variable taken at regular intervals over time.

Time series analysis A statistical technique for forecasting future events from time series data.

Trend A consistently upward or downward movement in a time series data.

Triangulation The use of multiple sources of data, different research methods and/or more than one researcher to investigate the same phenomenon in a study.

***t*-test** A parametric test of difference for two independent or dependent samples for ratio or interval variables.

Type I error An error that occurs when H_0 is true, but the test leads to its rejection.

Type II error An error that occurs when H_1 is true, but the test leads to the acceptance of H_0.

Unit of analysis The phenomenon under study, about which data are collected and analysed.

Univariate analysis Analysis of data relating to one variable.

Validity The extent to which a test measures what the researcher wants it to measure and the results reflect the phenomena under study.

Vancouver system A system of referencing where citations are shown as an in-text number each time the source is cited and the references are listed in numerical order at the end of the document.

Variable A characteristic of a phenomenon that can be observed or measured.

Variance The mean of the squared errors.

Viva voce A defence of a dissertation or thesis by oral examination.

Weighted index number An index number constructed by calculating a weighted average of some set of values, where the weights show the relative importance of each item in the data set.

appendix: random number tables

03 47 43 73 86	36 96 47 36 61	46 98 63 71 62	33 26 16 80 45	60 11 14 10 95
97 74 24 67 62	42 81 14 57 20	42 53 32 37 32	27 07 36 07 51	24 51 79 89 73
16 76 62 27 66	56 50 26 17 07	32 90 79 78 53	13 55 38 58 59	88 97 54 14 10
12 56 85 99 26	96 96 68 27 31	05 03 72 93 15	57 12 10 14 21	88 26 49 81 76
55 59 56 35 64	38 54 82 46 22	31 62 43 09 90	06 18 44 32 53	23 83 01 30 30
16 22 77 94 39	49 54 43 54 82	17 37 93 23 78	87 35 20 96 43	84 26 34 91 64
84 42 17 53 31	57 24 55 06 88	77 04 74 47 67	21 76 33 50 25	83 92 12 06 76
63 01 63 78 59	16 95 55 67 19	98 10 50 71 75	12 86 73 58 07	44 39 52 38 79
33 21 12 34 29	78 64 56 07 82	52 42 07 44 38	15 51 00 13 42	99 66 02 79 54
57 60 86 32 44	09 47 27 96 54	49 17 46 09 62	90 52 84 77 27	08 02 73 43 28
18 18 07 92 46	44 17 16 58 09	79 83 86 16 62	06 76 50 03 10	55 23 64 05 05
26 62 38 97 75	84 16 07 44 99	83 11 46 32 24	20 14 85 88 45	10 93 72 88 71
23 42 40 64 74	82 97 77 77 81	07 45 32 14 08	32 98 94 07 72	93 85 79 10 75
52 36 28 19 95	50 92 26 11 97	00 56 76 31 38	80 22 02 53 53	86 60 42 04 53
37 85 94 35 12	83 39 50 08 30	42 34 07 96 88	54 42 06 87 98	35 85 29 48 38
70 29 17 12 13	40 33 20 38 26	13 89 51 03 74	17 76 37 13 04	07 74 21 19 30
56 62 18 37 35	96 83 50 87 75	97 12 25 93 47	70 33 24 03 54	97 77 46 44 80
99 49 57 22 77	88 42 95 45 72	16 64 36 16 00	04 43 18 66 79	94 77 24 21 90
16 08 15 04 72	33 27 14 34 90	45 59 34 68 49	12 72 07 34 45	99 27 72 95 14
31 16 93 32 43	50 27 89 87 19	20 15 37 00 49	52 85 66 60 44	38 68 88 11 80
68 34 30 13 70	55 74 30 77 40	44 22 78 84 26	04 33 46 09 52	68 07 97 06 57
74 57 25 65 76	59 29 97 68 60	71 91 38 67 54	13 58 18 24 76	15 54 55 95 52
27 42 37 86 53	48 55 90 65 72	96 57 69 36 10	96 46 92 42 45	97 60 49 04 91
00 39 68 29 61	66 37 32 20 30	77 84 57 03 29	10 45 65 04 26	11 04 96 67 24
29 94 98 94 24	68 49 69 10 82	53 75 91 93 30	34 25 20 57 27	40 48 73 51 92
16 90 82 66 59	83 62 64 11 12	67 19 00 71 74	60 47 21 29 68	02 02 37 03 31
11 27 94 75 06	06 09 19 74 66	02 94 37 34 02	76 70 90 30 86	38 45 94 30 38
35 24 10 16 20	33 32 51 26 38	79 78 45 04 91	16 92 53 56 16	02 75 50 95 98
38 23 16 86 38	42 38 97 01 50	87 75 66 81 41	40 01 74 91 62	48 51 84 08 32
31 96 25 91 47	96 44 33 49 13	34 86 82 53 91	00 52 43 48 85	27 55 26 89 62
66 67 40 67 14	64 05 71 95 86	11 05 65 09 68	76 83 20 37 90	57 16 00 11 66
14 90 84 45 11	75 73 88 05 90	52 27 41 14 86	22 98 12 22 08	07 52 74 95 80
68 05 51 18 00	33 96 02 75 19	07 60 62 93 55	59 33 82 43 90	49 37 38 44 59
20 46 78 73 90	97 51 40 14 02	04 02 33 31 08	39 54 16 49 36	47 95 93 13 30
64 19 58 97 79	15 06 15 93 20	01 90 10 75 06	40 78 78 89 62	02 67 74 17 33
05 26 93 70 60	22 35 85 15 13	92 03 51 59 77	59 56 78 06 83	52 91 05 70 74
07 97 10 88 23	09 98 42 99 64	61 71 62 99 15	06 51 29 16 93	58 05 77 09 51
68 71 86 85 85	54 87 66 47 54	73 32 08 11 12	44 95 92 63 16	29 56 24 29 48
26 99 61 65 53	58 37 78 80 70	42 10 50 67 42	32 17 55 85 74	94 44 67 16 94
14 65 52 68 75	87 59 36 22 41	26 78 63 06 55	13 08 27 01 50	15 29 39 39 43

Abridged from R. A. Fisher and F. Yate (1953) *Statistical Tables for Biological, Agricultural and Medical Research*, Edinburgh: Oliver and Boyd by permission of the authors and publishers (Longman Group UK Ltd).

subject index